HUNGOCHANI

Hungochani

The History of a Dissident
Sexuality in Southern Africa

MARC EPPRECHT

McGill-Queen's University Press
Montreal & Kingston · London · Ithaca

© McGill-Queen's University Press 2004
ISBN 0-7735-2750-8 (cloth)
ISBN 0-7735-2751-6 (paper)

Legal deposit fourth quarter 2004
Bibliothèque nationale du Québec

Printed in Canada on acid-free paper that is 100% ancient forest
free (100% post-consumer recycled), processed chlorine free.

This book has been published with the help of a grant from
the Canadian Federation for the Humanities and Social Sciences,
through the Aid to Scholarly Publications Programme, using funds
provided by the Social Sciences and Humanities Research Council
of Canada.

McGill-Queen's University Press acknowledges the support of the
Canada Council for the Arts for our publishing program. We also
acknowledge the financial support of the Government of Canada
through the Book Publishing Industry Development Program (BPIDP)
for our publishing activities.

National Library of Canada Cataloguing in Publication

Epprecht, Marc, 1957–
    Hungochani: the history of a dissident sexuality in southern Africa/
Marc Epprecht.

    Includes bibliographical references and index.
    ISBN 0-7735-2750-8 (bnd)
    ISBN 0-7735-2751-6 (pbk)

    1. Homosexuality – Africa, Southern. 2. Homosexuality, Male –
Africa, Southern – History. 1. Title.

HQ76.3.A356E66 2004   306.76'62'0968   C2004-901948-1

Typeset in Sabon 10/13
by Caractéra inc., Quebec City

Contents

Preface

Research for this book began in 1996 when I was employed as a lecturer at the University of Zimbabwe. My original goal was a simple one – to test the homophobic and xenophobic claims of certain Zimbabwean leaders against the empirical evidence. I hoped to gain new perspectives on myself as a scholar, hoping to see better and so expunge heterosexism in another research project that was then coming to a close. Over the years, I also increasingly grew to admire the courage and *joie de vivre* of the many gay rights and feminist activists in the region with whom I came in contact. I thus sought to make the research useful to their struggles and to strengthen their ability to enrich Zimbabwean civil society.

Developments have since added urgency to that motivation. Indeed, the health and political situation in southern Africa has worsened considerably. The epidemiological terms of the deterioration alone bear reiterating here, as they do in each and every forum possible, so calamitous are they. As the Worldwatch Institute summarized it, referring *only* to the HIV/AIDS pandemic and not the related famine, other health crises, and political violence: "In Zimbabwe, without AIDS, life expectancy in 2010 would be 70 years, but with AIDS, it is expected to fall below 35 years. Botswana's life expectancy is projected to fall from 66 years to 33 years by 2010. For South Africa, it will fall from 68 years to 48 years. And for Zambia, from 60 to 30 years. These life expectancies are more akin to those of the Middle Ages than of the modern age" (Brown 2000).

The HIV/AIDS pandemic has exacerbated what sociologist Allison Goebel has termed the "gender wars" in the region – domestic violence, child abuse, witchcraft, and more. It has increasingly drawn the urgent attention of activists, health practitioners, and scholars across the disciplines. The president of South Africa, Thabo Mbeki, further underscored the urgency when in 1999 he appeared to condone the suppression of evidence and of fearless discussion of sexuality. Mbeki's government aligned itself (briefly) against the overwhelming weight of scientific research by seeming to deny that HIV causes AIDS. He suggested as well that those who advocate explicit and honest sexual education might be pursuing a racist agenda against black males. Partly on this basis, and appealing to African nationalist claims about the need for African independence from Western domination, the government of South Africa prevented the importation of cheap anti-retroviral drugs and refused to take advantage of unprecedented price and patent concessions by Western drug manufacturers. This was a shocking development to those of us who worked and lived in the region and have seen colleagues, friends, students, and loved ones die of the disease – the large majority of the population, in other words.

Such is the context that shaped the course of the research and the way I have written this book. Many individuals also directly contributed to the development of the ideas within it. Above all I need to express my deepest gratitude to the members and ex-members of Gays and Lesbians of Zimbabwe (GALZ), who welcomed me as an ally. Keith Goddard, first, graciously accepted a stranger's congratulations when he was so obviously exhausted from the book fair imbroglio that introduced homosexuality into Zimbabwean political discourse back in 1995. Since then Keith has been unfailingly generous in sharing his time, energy, and wonderful critical powers.

The members of the "Gay Oral History Project" who conducted interviews were Rodgers Bande, Romeo Tshuma, Polyana Magwiro, Wallace Zimunya, Tina Machida, Douglas Zinguwo, and Lionel Dube. Susie Bruce and Bev Clark gave time and thought to helping me. We all owe a debt to those informants who shared their knowledge and insights while requesting anonymity.

Outside of GALZ but still in Zimbabwe, Nyaradzo Dzobo did stellar interviews in the rural areas. Students of my 1997 History of Southern Africa class at the University of Zimbabwe also contributed short interviews that enriched our understanding of the migrant life: Cuthbert Karise, Joshua Chakawa, Tongai Mazorodze, Samboko Manfred, Pemberayi Zambezi, Last Hobwani, Dee Jamela, Norman Makuyana, Silvernos Chipodzo, Hazvinei Chitsike, and Ephraim Chisalo. Tapiwa Zimunya, Debra Lovinsky, and Koni Benson helped with archival material.

Some of my travel and local knowledge was made possible by the generous hospitality of Kings Phiri, Nick Southey, Shirley Brooks, John

Gay, Judith Gay, Gerard Mathot, Graeme Reid, Chris and Vin Hamblin, Charles Shayanewako, Nyaradzo Dzobo, Mary Turner, and Dag Henrichson.

Funding over the years has been provided by the University of Zimbabwe, the South-South Exchange Programme for Research in the History of Development, Gays and Lesbians of Zimbabwe, and the Social Sciences and Humanities Research Council of Canada. I would like as well to thank the organizers of the Colloquium on Masculinities, University of Natal, July 1997; the organizers of the Future of the Queer Past conference at the University of Chicago, September 2000; Local 3908 of the Canadian Union of Public Employees; the Canadian Association of African Studies; Queen's University; and the Social Science Research Council (of the United States), for help in getting to various important conferences.

I would also like to thank (in more or less chronological order) Wolfram Hartmann, David Beach, Patricia McFadden, Susan Heald, Nick Southey, Jock McCulloch, Zackie Achmat, Stephen O. Murray, Robert Morrell, Kendall, Tim Burke, Gerhard Mathot, Amy Kaler, Oliver Phillips, Deborah Amory, Neville Hoad, Graeme Reid, Chris Dunton, Karen Dubinsky, Alan Jeeves, Dunbar Moodie, Mark Carlton, Glen Elder, Doug Saunders, Belinda Bozzoli, David Coplan, Jeanne Penvenne, Jeremy Martens, Guy Thompson, Antony Manion, Gerald Mazarire, and Peter Garlake for adding their critical comments and specialist tidbits of knowledge. Others who added their two cents worth at various conferences, archives, saloons, or around a braai in the backyard of 2 Rollo Drive are too numerous to do justice to except by saying I thank you all for your support. Meanwhile, Allison Goebel was there for it all, and particularly to remind me to cut my sentences in half and to remove over-zealous adjectives from my first few drafts. Maureen Garvie provided astute input at the copy editing stage.

Bits and pieces of this book have been published in other fora, in some cases "prematurely," meaning that my ideas have since matured and I may no longer agree with the way I expressed myself in the heat of the first moment of discovery. Where readers notice a nuance in meaning between here and there, the present interpretation supercedes anything that came before. I should like to thank the editors and anonymous readers who helped me with those earlier versions, as well as the publishers of the following journals for permission to reproduce revised versions of my articles: *Canadian Journal of Development Studies, International Journal of African Historical Studies, History in Africa, Journal of Southern African Studies, Culture, Health and Sexuality,* and *Journal of Men's Studies.*

Throughout the book I have used place names as they occurred at the time, for example, Salisbury during the colonial period and Harare after independence. This is not to imply nostalgia for colonialism but rather reflects a historian's harmless obsession with anachronism. I also identify people using the terms that were common parlance at the time, for example, Matabele prior to 1980 and Ndebele thereafter. Labels such as "European," "white," "black," "coloured," and so on are similarly employed without in any way intending to suggest a racial or ethnic essence. The same precaution applies to "gays," "queers," "queens," "straights," and so on, who may or may not be quite what the labels proclaim but who exist in the discourse of the communities I intend to respect. (GALZ members, for example, have repeatedly resisted the label "transgendered" in favour of "queens.")

The word "dissident" that I have highlighted in the title is a possible exception to this rule. Many of the more politically conservative gays and lesbians in the region would rather avoid the term and would emphasize instead their politeness and respectability. This is particularly true in Zimbabwe where the government in the mid-1980s used the word "dissident" as a euphemism for anti-government insurgents and their civilian sympathizers in Matabeleland province. Those dissidents were ruthlessly repressed. Gays and lesbians in Zimbabwe today do not as a group remotely face such a level of repression, nor have they ever advocated anti-state violence. Nonetheless, I do believe that the word "dissident" and the analogy to the state's behaviour in Matabeleland are warranted and usefully provocative. The mere existence of out gays and lesbians (regardless of their actual politics) evokes a similar irrationally violent emotion in many people. In the contemporary Zimbabwean context, moreover, to insist upon personal dignity, democratic citizenship, sexual honesty, and sexual responsibility is profoundly unsettling to political elites. Dissident (i.e., "disagreeing, esp. contentiously") is thus empirically accurate in describing the ideals to which GALZ and other gay rights associations in the region aspire. With apologies to my more respectable friends, therefore, *viva la dissidence!*

Glossary of Terms and Acronyms Used in the Text

ACDP   African Christian Democratic Party

ANC   African National Congress

bukhonxana   Shangaan or Tsonga for male-male thigh sex

chidhoma/zvidhoma   A *tokoloshi* in Shona tradition

chikwambo   See *tokoloshi*

chibado, chibanda, chibudo   A powerful diviner/medicine man reputed to gain his powers by ritual sodomy among the Ovimbundu of southern Angola

chitsina   "Bad luck" in not being able to marry in Shona tradition

divisi   A charm that works through illicit sexual acts like incest or male-male sex

GALASA   Gay and Lesbian Archives of South Africa

GALZ   Gays and Lesbians of Zimbabwe

gangisa   Tsonga or Shangaan for non-penetrative thigh sex

GASA   Gay Association of South Africa

Gayle   White South African gay argot

GLOW   Gay and Lesbian Organization of Witswatersrand

hlobonga   Zulu for non-penetrative thigh sex

HUMCC   Hope and Unity Metropolitan Community Church

hungochani   A Shona neologism meaning "homosexuality" in the sense of an innate orientation

iqenge   Zulu for male-gendered homosexual men

inkotshane (pl. *izinkotshane*)   A colonial-era spelling of *ngotshana* or *ngochani*

isikhesana   Zulu for female-gendered men or homosexual wives

Isingqumo   An African gay argot

jigijigi, jiga jiga, jigger   Euphemism for "fuck" used throughout the British empire in Africa

KAB   Kap Argeif Bereplek (Cape archives)

kupindira   "Raising seed" (also *kusikira rudizi*) in Shona

kupinga nyika   "To protect the land" by ritual incest in Manyika (eastern Shona) tradition

kusenga   Manual stretching of the labia majora (Shona)

LGBT   Lesbian, gay, bisexual and transgendered

LEGABIBO   Lesbians, Gays, and Bisexuals of Botswana

lobola   Brideprice

mabhoyi   Shona-ization of "boys," somewhat mocking of colonial discourse

matenyera   Shona for street or latrine cleaner, a man who does thigh sex with another man

matanyula, matanyola   Zulu and Sotho for "male prostitution"

maotoane   Sesotho for male thigh sex

mbonga   A female "guardian" whose celibacy protects the chief and his people in Shona tradition

moffie   Originally a derogatory term for homosexual, typically conflated with cross-dressers, queens, or passive sodomists

mukadzirume   "Woman-man" in Shona, a woman who lives as a male-gendered person

mupfuhwira   "Husband-taming herbs" or love potions in Shona

muremukadzi   "Man-woman" in Shona, a man who lives as a female-gendered person

muti   Shona for medicine, magic

NAB   Natal Argeif Bereplek (Natal archives)

n'anga, ngaka   Doctor or diviner in Shona and Sesotho, respectively

NCGLE   National Coalition of Gay and Lesbian Equality

ngozi   An avenging spirit

ngochani, ngotshana, nkotshane   Various local renditions of "sodomy," or "homosexual"

sahwira   An intimate male friend in Shona

sangoma   Doctor or diviner in Zulu and Ndebele

SAPA-AFP   South African Press Association – Agence France Press

setsualle   An intimate relationship, potentially of either sex, in Sesotho

shave   "Stranger spirit" in Shona, often attacking neglected wives

skesana   Passive or effeminate sexual partner, possibly derived from *inkotshane*

TAB   Transvaal Argeif Bereplek (Transvaal archives)

TAC   Treatment Action Campaign

tokoloshi Malevolent, impish spirit who often brings dreams of sexual transgression

UDF United Democratic Front

ukumetsha Xhosa for non-penetrative thigh sex

umteto ka Sokisi "Sokisi's rules" or the etiquette governing male-male mine marriage or prison relationships

ZANU Zimbabwe African National Union

ZAPU Zimbabwe African People's Union

ZNA Zimbabwe National Archives

The earliest known image from Africa south of the Sahara that depicts young men apparently engaged in anal or thigh sex dating from an estimated two thousand years ago. Like many Bushmen cave paintings, its exact location in the Harare area is kept secret in order to protect it from vandalism. Photo courtesy of Peter Garlake

An *umfaan* at a beryl mine, Bikita, 1951.
Photo courtesy of National Archives
of Zimbabwe

Globe and Phoenix mine compound near Gwelo (Gweru). Note different styles
of accommodation, from hostel in the rear to impromptu huts in the foreground. Photo
courtesy of National Archives of Zimbabwe

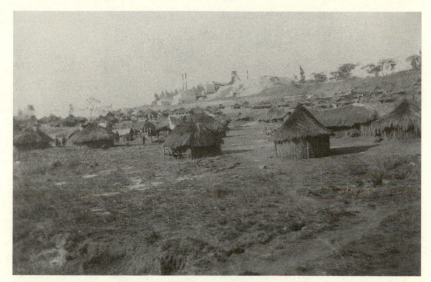

Selukwe mine compound, open to the veldt. Photo courtesy of National Archives of Zimbabwe

Women at the Giant Mine compound, circa 1930. Photo courtesy of National Archives of Zimbabwe

For all its horrors, World War II, for white gays and lesbians, was also a time of fun, discovery, and coming out. These photos are from the collection of Renée Liddicoat, whose doctoral dissertation on homosexuality helped to temper the wilder homophobic

sentiments being expressed by South African politicians and police in the 1960s.
Photo courtesy of Gay and Lesbian Archives of South Africa

Jacaranda Queen contestants, Harare, October 2003. Photos courtesy of GALZ

Renée Liddicoat, circa 1942. Photo courtesy of Gay and Lesbian Archives of South Africa

The "banned stand," back in business, Zimbabwe International Book Fair, August 2003. Left to right, Keith Goddard, Lewis Kunzi, Dumisani Dube. Photo courtesy of GALZ

Centre: Peter Joanetti; right, Martha Tholanah, program manager for Health at GALZ, at Access to Treatment meeting, August 2003. Photo courtesy of GALZ

GALZ staff, 2003. Left to right, Sarah Zhaneti, Dumisani Dube, Chesterfield Samba, Fadzai Muparutsa, Samuel Matsikure, Keith Goddard, Brian Patrick. Photo courtesy of GALZ

Colonial Southern Africa.

HUNGOCHANI

Introduction

Hungochani means "homosexuality" in chiShona, the main indigenous language of Zimbabwe. The same term is spelled *ubunkotshani* or *iNkotshani* ("a homosexual") in siNdebele, the second indigenous language. Both words appear to have been coined in the mid-1990s by gay rights activists through the simple addition of the prefix *hu-* and *ubu-/i-* to an older, highly derogatory term. The prefix points to a state of being or an intrinsic nature, rather than an opportunistic life-style choice. It thus opens the door to be inclusive of lesbians, bisexuals, and transgendered persons as well as self-identified gays or other men who have sex with men.

Although the word is not used by gay rights activists elsewhere in the region, obviously related terms are understood in major African languages far beyond Zimbabwe, and with roots far back in time. Cage (2003), for example, suggests that the derogatory term for passive homosexual (*skesana*) that is widely used throughout the region derives from the same root. In Zulu, the main African language of South Africa, the word *nkoshana* is defined as "copulation between male persons; sodomy" (Dent and Nyembezi 1969, 434). Tsonga informants from southern Mozambique and lowveld Transvaal define *tintoncana* or *bukhonxana* as "boy wives" or "mine marriages" (Sibuyi 1993, Harries 1990a, 1990b, 1994). A Sesotho-ized version of the word (*boukonchana*) appears in Henri Junod's novel *Zidji* (1911, 260) and again in Hamel's dictionary, compiled in the 1950s (1965, 258). The same word crops up even further afield as common parlance a century ago among men from present-day southern Malawi, Zambia, and central Mozambique. "An 'ingotshana,'" according to an Ndebele police constable in 1907, "is a small boy who is used by the Zambesi boys on the mine as a wife."[1]

All of this suggests a pan-regional, proto-queer identity firmly rooted in history that is politically appealing to Zimbabwean gays and lesbians and their sympathizers. They take the evident African-ness of the word to validate the integrity of black Africans who come out as homosexual. To gay rights activists in Zimbabwe, the word is thus a small assertion of why they deserve the same rights and dignities that are ostensibly guaranteed to all citizens. As such, it is a powerful statement of dissent from the prevailing heteronormative culture.[2] Similar claims have also been made upon the word *matanyera* or *matanyola*, "an old, proper Tswana word" (HRW 2003, 137) that in fact derives from Malawian migrant workers in Zimbabwe in the early twentieth century.

Notwithstanding these recent and well-intentioned appropriations, the older meaning of both *ngochani* and *matanyera* continues to evoke shame, anger, and denial for most Zimbabweans. In 1995, in one especially high-profile case, a Zimbabwean police inspector by the name of Jefta Dube shot and killed a fellow officer after the man had called him *ngochani mukadzi*, or "homosexual wife." Dube did not deny that he had indeed been the passive recipient of the sexual attentions of his employer (the former president of the country, Canaan Banana). But the judge still felt that to name this relationship in public constituted an insult so horrible that it diminished Dube's responsibility for the murder.[3] Shona-speaking Zimbabweans will also frequently point out that *ngochani* does not sound Shona but rather has a foreign ring about it (hence, implicitly negating gays' claims to Zimbabwean citizenship and rights). One Zimbabwean *n'anga* (traditional healer) even claimed that white settlers had invented the word in order to bring shame upon Africans (that is, by falsely making a "white man's disease" sound as if it were indigenous).[4]

Such attitudes have been amplified in recent years at the highest level of the state. President Robert Mugabe set the tone with a speech in 1995 which infamously described gays and lesbians "as worse than pigs and dogs." By 1999 they had become "gangsters." Homosexuality was "an abomination, a rottenness of culture," he declared the following year, which Britain's "gay government" was attempting to impose upon Africans.[5] Zimbabwean patriots were urged to defend the nation against this new form of Western imperialism, a theme earnestly taken up in the state-controlled media and by leaders elsewhere in Africa. The king of Swaziland, the presidents of Namibia, Kenya, Zambia, and Uganda, and leading church officials from around the continent have all publicly attacked homosexuals or equated them with external threats. Yoweri Museveni of

Uganda in 1999 defended himself for doing so with the claim that "Homosexuals are the ones provoking us." In September 2000 Namibia's minister of Home Affairs went so far as to urge new police recruits to "arrest on sight gays and lesbians and eliminate them from the face of Namibia." Homosexuality, declared President Sam Nujoma, was one of the two top enemies of the national government.[6]

This kind of rhetoric has contributed to a climate where individual gays and lesbians have been subject to blackmail, job discrimination, police harassment, family ostracism, and even mob violence. For many gays and lesbians in Zimbabwe, it has inflamed pre-existing feelings of homophobic self-hatred and closetedness that the word *hungochani* was intended to assuage. The results have sometimes been tragic, and have drawn widespread international condemnation. Human Rights Watch and the International Gay and Lesbian Human Rights Commission have recently catalogued a litany of homophobic abuse with poignant testimony from the victims (HRW 2003). State-sanctioned homophobia in Zimbabwe has even been successfully invoked as grounds for claiming political refugee status in the West.

Yet if human rights activists find offensive the assertion that same-sex sexual relations are "un-African" and that gays and lesbians are therefore deserving of abuse and repression, the claim is even more remarkable given the history and ongoing problem of racialism toward black Africans. In the colonial era, racialism was predicated on the belief that Africans were essentially different from (and inferior to) the so-called civilized branches of humanity; they possessed no history, or they were uniformly childlike and incapable of sophisticated thoughts and emotions. The outstanding achievement of Africanist research since the 1940s has been to demonstrate the falseness of this belief and to amass evidence that shows how history, culture, and humanity in Africa are assuredly as complex and diverse as in other regions of the world. The very idea of Africa as a single entity is Eurocentric. How disconcerting for Africanists, then, that certain African leaders and Africanist intellectuals now seek to confine African people once again to a narrow and fundamentally dehumanizing stereotype. Ironic and sad also is how the rants of some self-identified African progressives feed into lingering Western stereotypes of Africa as a Dark (or seriously clouded) Continent. There *are* white racists in the southern African and Western press who are only too happy to exploit these stereotypes. But comments by men like Namibia's minister of Home Affairs (for instance) often seem to make those racists' ability to sneer all too easy: "Gay and lesbian rights can never qualify as fundamental rights," the Honourable Jerry Ekandjo explained to the international press, "because if a male dog knows its right partner as a female dog, how can a human being fail to notice the difference?"[7]

This book takes bigots like Ekandjo strenuously to task. But it is also aimed at those in the West who rush to judge and patronize Africans on this topic. Indeed, blanket denunciations of state-sanctioned homophobia obscure some sophisticated cultural mechanisms that mitigate the impact of homophobic rhetoric, as well as some remarkable successes in achieving gay rights. For example, as early as 1991 Lesotho was one of only two African nations to support the principle of expanding gay rights internationally in order to enrich democracy in the region.[8] Then, following the attainment of black majority rule in South Africa in 1994, the gay rights movement scored victories that now make that country one of the most liberal, if not radical, in the world. Freedom from discrimination based on sexual orientation has been explicitly enshrined in the national constitution and consummated in successful court challenges to discriminatory laws and practices. High state officials, including the first black president, Nelson Mandela, have met with gay rights activists and publicly endorsed their cause. This is clearly not out of shallow "political correctness" or to kowtow to Western pressure, as has sometimes been whispered by enemies of gay rights in the region. On the contrary, the highest court in the land has shown a profound appreciation of the interconnectedness of discriminatory attitudes and of the interrelationship between oppressive gender ideology, racism, and economic underdevelopment. As Judge L. Ackerman remarked upon overturning the old colonial-era law against sodomy, homophobia "gives rise to a wide variety of other discriminations, which collectively unfairly prevent a fair distribution of social goods and services."[9] Many socialist movements in the West have shown far less radical insight on the subject.

Also noteworthy is the fact that even the most rhetorically homophobic regimes in the region have implicitly accepted the need to promote research about homosexuality and to entrench gay rights. An addendum to the Declaration on Gender and Development signed by all eleven heads of state or government of the Southern African Development Community in September 1998 called for, among other things, joint action "promoting the eradication of elements in traditional norms and religious beliefs, practices and stereotypes which legitimise and exacerbate the persistence and tolerance of violence against women and children," "introducing and promoting gender sensitisation and training of all service providers engaged in the administration of justice," and "undertaking and sharing research of the gathering of statistics and other information on the causes, prevalence and consequences of violence against women and children."[10] Since lesbians are women, and since questions around sexual orientation and homophobic violence among males typically begin in childhood, this declaration is surely gay friendly.

Indeed, gay rights organizations have been allowed to develop, if not to flourish, in many southern African countries in recent years – LEGABIBO in Botswana, GALESWA in Swaziland, Sister Namibia and the Rainbow Project in Namibia among them. Gays and Lesbians of Zimbabwe (GALZ) now openly provides counselling, legal, and other support services to men and women struggling with issues of sexuality, and promotes a politics in Zimbabwe that would embrace sexual orientation as a human right in the model pioneered by South Africa. The membership and executive of GALZ are now both overwhelmingly black Africans. GALZ even enjoys congenial relations with the local police, who regularly drop by the GALZ centre to type up their reports and who provide security for the annual Jacaranda contest, a popular drag queen beauty contest held at a public venue.

The crass prejudice of some southern African politicians is meanwhile hardly unique in the world today. The most outspoken homophobes in the region often use biblical, public health, or "family values" arguments that appear to be borrowed wholesale from social conservatives in the West, while the repressive laws are a direct legacy of colonial rule. Even the claim that same-sex sexual behaviour is un-African appears to have originated in the West rather than Africa itself. This point will be taken up in a subsequent chapter, but it deserves emphasis. As Rudi Bleys (1995), Stephen Murray and Will Roscoe (1997, 1998), and Neville Hoad (2000) have all cogently argued, from as early as the late eighteenth century, European men of a certain class expressed a desire (in Sir Edward Gibbon's words) to "believe, and hope" that Africans were "exempt from this moral pestilence" of sodomy (Gibbon [1781] 1925, 506). This hope was then put to polemical use in making the case for the "natural" right to rule of heterosexually virile, bourgeois, white men, both within Europe and beyond.

Sir Richard Burton provided one of the most definitive expressions of this logic when he divided the world into "Sotadic" and "non-Sotadic" zones based on whether homosexual behaviour was supposedly indigenous to the region or not. This eminent Englishman, known for his deeply racist opinions about black Africans and writing on the eve of British imperial expansion on the continent, located black Africa together with northern Europe in the non-Sotadic zone (Burton 1885, 246). Why this huge claim, which flew in the face of accounts and fiction emerging from Portuguese and French sources? By placing black Africans in a geographically vulnerable position *vis-à-vis* Sotadic zone Arabs and Portuguese, Burton's division of the world added one more justification to the mounting clamour for British and German imperial expansion.

Subsequently a few European anthropologists, travellers, and "sexologists" alluded discreetly to exceptions to Burton's rule.[11] For the most part, however, early European accounts of African societies did not substantively challenge the claim that same-sex sexual relations were muted or rare in "traditional" settings. The diversity of men and women who made or implied this claim, often with little or no direct research on the topic, is remarkable. Caldwell et al., for example, present a magisterial overview of the anthropology up to the late 1980s to conclude that there is a "distinct African sexuality," without referring to, let alone investigating, same-sex activities or even masturbation (Caldwell, Caldwell, and Quiggin 1989). That even self-consciously gay authors have contributed to the stereotype of a homo-free Africa is also of interest. Michael Davison (1988, 187) noted that in a year of living among the Zulu in the 1920s, "I never saw a sign of any kind of homosexual behaviour or understanding." A salacious anthro-pornography, which incidentally contains significant contradictory evidence, explains this invisibility in blunt terms: "The abnormal in sexual life is despised in Africa" (Bryk 1964, 230).

In the case of Zimbabwe, a respected and prolific anthropologist of the Shona, Michael Gelfand, was unusually explicit in making this point (1979, 1985). The manner he did so hints again at a European need to believe in exclusive heterosexuality among black Africans, a belief that could then be used for polemical purposes. After a cursory enquiry, Gelfand concluded: "The traditional Shona seems to have none of the problems associated with homosexuality. Obviously they must have a valuable method of bringing up children, especially with regard to normal sex relations, thus avoiding this anomaly so frequent in Western society – yet another feature of their rich society" (1985, 138).

Such assertions of the infrequency or non-existence of homosexuality in African society laid the ground for explaining homosexual behaviours in non-traditional settings primarily by reference to external influences. Arabs and Portuguese, above all, were held to blame according to the dominant prejudice of the colonial era.[12] Freudian psychologists B.J.F. Laubscher (1937) and John Ritchie (1943), using more sophisticated language, posited a combination of Portuguese influence, the demographic imbalance in certain modern institutions like the mine hostels and prisons, excessive breast-feeding for boys, and "the psychosis of defeat." The psychologist Frantz Fanon also argued in the 1950s that colonialism was to blame by systematically humiliating African men in a sexual way (Fanon 1967, 156). This theme is recurrent in French- and English-language fiction from Africa, where African homosexuals have tended to be portrayed as tortured, neurotic, and often of mixed race or culture.[13]

Less didactically, the same theme has been developed by the historian Charles van Onselen. In his pioneering study of migrant labour in colonial Zimbabwe, van Onselen argued that the mining companies tacitly tolerated if not actively abetted prostitution, bestiality, and homosexuality among African men as partial compensation for their prolonged, enforced separated from wives and children (van Onselen 1976, 175–6 and footnote 91, 307). "Sex in the service of industry," as he phrased it, helped to secure a relatively docile labour force with minimal expenditure on wages, social services, and urban infrastructure – distracted and presumably demoralized by sexually sordid affairs, the men were disabled from organizing effective resistance against the appalling working and living conditions. Van Onselen subsequently elaborated on this analysis in his social histories of the Witwatersrand, where he also noted "a startling decree" issued by the leader of a prominent criminal gang (van Onselen 1984, 15). Nongoloza, alias Jan Note, had purportedly ordered his men to have sex with each other or with boy servants rather than with women sometime in the mid-1890s. The intention in so doing was to protect urban gang members from sexually transmitted diseases. Racial capitalism, rather than the possibility of sensual, sexual preference of some men for other males, was therefore to blame.[14]

But all of this begs several questions. For example, how can a man be forced or commanded to be the active partner in a sexual relationship with another male? Did having sex with a female donkey or a dog really have the same cultural significance as having sex with another male human? If men's physical "need" for orgasm is so strong that it forces them to have sex with animals and other men or boys when women are not present, how do we explain the existence of males who took the passive role in these relationships or who remained celibate? Why was masturbation so unspeakable? How can peoples otherwise so culturally and ethnically diverse as Africans be unified by one all-embracing explanation of such a complex, protean, and difficult-to-know thing as sexuality? Can mass change in human sexual behaviour convincingly be attributed to a single exemplary individual like Nongoloza or isolated cases of cultural Others (like whites)? Did the experience of being a mine or prison "wife" affect the men's attitudes toward women? And would there be an analogous history of female sexuality related to male migrancy?

Scholars of Zimbabwe have not aggressively pursued evidence to address such questions. On the contrary, they have commonly simply avoided the issue or disregarded the evidence before their eyes. The latter is strikingly evident in several studies of gender and sexuality. Terence Ranger (1994), for example, wrote a paper on "Criminal Court Data for Gender Relations in Colonial Matabeleland" after systematically going through the court dockets for Gwanda, Zimbabwe. He carefully analyzed the cases of heterosexual rape and assaults he found there but equally carefully avoided any comment upon several highly suggestive cases of male-male sexual assault. Diana Jeater, to give another example (1993), has written a compelling study of marriage and "perversion" in colonial Gweru that manages scarcely a couple of paragraphs on male-male sex. McCulloch's monograph on "sexual crime in Southern Rhodesia, 1902–1935" (2002) also makes not a single reference to literally hundreds of male-male indecent assaults and sodomy cases that appear in his primary source.

Scholars who have suggested alternative interpretations of same-sex sexuality in black Africa have meanwhile been denounced in strong terms. Ifi Amadiume's attack upon African-American lesbians who speculated about the possibility of lesbian sex in woman-woman marriages is a well-known example (1987, 7). Oppong and Kaliperi also dismiss bisexuality among Africans as a "myth" posited by white academics "without a shred of evidence" (1996, 100). My own early ruminations on the topic earned crude mockery from Ian Phimister, an established scholar of Zimbabwean labour history (1997). Phimister's screed gives some credence to Zackie Achmat's critique of South African labour history (1993), in which, *inter alia*, Achmat accuses van Onselen of editing Nongoloza's testimony to remove a sentence that contradicts the they-were-forced-to-do-it thesis. It appears that the will to be blind to same-sex sexuality or sensual preference among black Africans can extend as far as scholars not only ignoring but actually suppressing or trying to squelch discussion of pertinent evidence.

Clearly, something more profound is going on with the stereotype of a heterosexually pure Africa than opportunistic homophobia on the part of African patriarchs like Robert Mugabe and Sam Nujoma. Unspoken, unexamined assumptions about race, masculinity, power, national identity, class – as well as the meaning of "sex" itself – would also appear to be at play at the level of Africanist scholarship. Unravelling the history of both same-sex sexuality and the homosexuality-is-un-African stereotype might offer a way to examine those assumptions. Such a history could potentially shed new light on a range of gendered relationships and dis-courses, including those submerged in academic language that poses as scientific or gender blind. Such a history has begun to be made possible by the activism, theorization, and research of black African scholars, from whom the present study takes much of its inspiration and significant direction.

Before tackling these broad research questions, however, let me briefly review the theoretical underpinnings and working assumptions of the study. I begin from a point now agreed upon by most researchers in the field of sexuality. The homosexuality/heterosexuality dichotomy is a false one. The two orientations occur only as theoretical extremes on a contin-uum of behaviours and feelings that are determined by a wide range of influences. These include genetic predisposition, culture, family socializa-tion, geographic space, physical proximity, gender imbalance, life cycle, age, consumption of alcohol or other disinhibiting drugs, and innumerable idiosyncratic factors. The small percentage of the population found at either extreme in terms of their innate sense of sexual preference is probably constant across the world and throughout history. The percentage of people who act in accordance with more ambiguous feelings in their choice of sexual partners, however, varies enormously over time and across cultures.

Sexuality, in other words, is not merely a natural or instinctive phenom-enon. Rather, it is a key component of gender relations. Gender relations, in turn, are key to understanding the ways that race, class, and other social relations have developed. Understanding sexuality thus offers one way to understand the system of racial capitalism that has been so profoundly carved upon southern African cultures and landscapes. Racial capitalism not only corrupts scholarship on and about Africa but also arguably, under the guise of globalization, now threatens the survival of the planet that all people share.[15]

What this means is that understanding sexuality and gender relations in Africa is not merely of interest for its own sake or because it has been identified as a key developmental priority by African governments and intellectuals themselves. Understanding the construction and contestation of African sexualities is also demonstrably germane to those in the West who seek to develop strategies to humanize capitalism in a global sense. Such is the explicit objective of an important new collection on the theme of "queer globalizations" (Arnaldo-Cruz and Manalansan 2002). The authors, drawing upon several radical traditions within the humanities and social sciences, argue that a greater appreciation of local subaltern cultures and histories of dissident or illicit sexualities can reveal oppressive discourses hidden within the dominant culture or "common sense." This applies even to those oppressive discourses like heterosexism or eurocentrism that are subtly replicated within self-consciously liberatory politics such as Marxism, feminism, Third World theory, and queer theory.[16]

If we concede the theoretical importance of this line of research, the question nonetheless remains: how feasible in practice is research into the history of sexuality in southern Africa? After all, human sexuality is fundamentally mysterious – to ourselves, let alone to third parties. Even the most rigorously scientific studies in the West have often been deeply flawed in their attempts to demystify it. The obstacles to knowing about sexuality are especially formidable in a context like colonial Africa where conventional historical sources are either altogether silent about sex or are thickly encrusted with prejudice. How can one even find credible evidence when the conspiracy of silence around same-sex sexuality extends from gays' and lesbians' secret, protean argot to the destruction of key documents that allude to same-sex desire?[17] As noted above, moreover, the prejudices of colonial-era sources linger in some of the most recent scholarly enquiry. How can one sort out truths from claims (often never made explicit) that are imbued with androcentric, phallocentric, eurocentric, and heterosexist assumptions or silences? How can one calculate the effect of one's own sexuality and other aspects of subjectivity as a researcher upon the interpretation of such evidence? How can one produce an account of contests over sexuality that is more than simple counter-assertion or wishful thinking against an oppressive status quo, that adheres to standards of professional integrity, and that can stand the test of the critical, indeed sometimes viscerally hostile opinion that discussions of dissident sexualities can evoke?

Queer theory directly addresses itself to these questions, and to the tasks of locating and deciphering often-cryptic sources around sexuality issues. Michel Foucault pioneered the method through his analysis of changing discourses around sodomy and homosexuality in nineteenth-century Europe, but queer theory has since been elaborated with considerable sophistication and care. For example, the better to discern and interpret moralism, laziness, silences, blind spots, or outright hostility toward same-sex sexuality in the textual evidence, queer theorists have proposed a "critical linguistics," "homotextuality," or "double reading" of the text. Anthropologists Stephen O. Murray and Will Roscoe (1998, 16–18) lucidly explain such double reading as the disentanglement of facts (what happened as understood by the historical actors involved) from tropes (how and why the facts are described, represented, or "spun"). As well, we need to consider carefully the provenance of those facts and tropes, including how and why the documentary record was produced, the particular way it was preserved, and how and why certain memories were valorized over others. This enjoins that we ask about and account for differences between what the eye of the beholder actually beheld and what the beholder thought or wished to believe she/he saw. We need, in other words, to constantly contextualize and historicize as precisely as we can what words like "sex," "man," "woman," and even "is" or "has" meant to the people who used them. Subtle power dynamics can be revealed at work in the assumptions about the meaning of words and silences around sexuality and gender.[18]

Queer historians since the late 1970s have shown that these goals can be achieved. Building upon the insights of Foucault, they began systematically examining the ways that specific gay and lesbian subcultures developed in different North American and European cities and countries at different historical moments.[19] Of particular interest to many of these authors was how people who transgressed heteronormative culture interpreted and performed stereotypes of femininity and masculinity, and how their often subtle plays upon heteronormative gender roles in turn pulled the dominant culture and politics in new directions. They looked as well for evidence of how fear and ignorance about sexuality in general and homosexuality in particular shaped institutions and cultures, or how the discursive creation of sexual Others served particular class interests or the forging of national identities. These lines of enquiry clearly promise rich rewards when applied to colonial or former colonial societies, where racial and sexual tensions have been especially fraught. Indeed, scholars have recently begun to pose critical queer questions of Latin American, Asian, and African historiography, and to call for sensitive but bold research into the empirical evidence upon non-Western sexualities – plural.[20] Also of importance to the present study is the proliferation of research that employs queer and feminist methods to deconstruct or historicize cultures of masculinity. Men's behaviour that was hitherto assumed to be more or less natural or unproblematic is revealed in this scholarship to have been often hotly contested and contingent.[21]

The first books specifically dedicated to the exploration of gay and lesbian experiences in Africa appeared in South Africa (notably, Isaacs and McKendrick 1992; Krouse and Berman 1993; Gevisser and Cameron 1994). Since then dissertations, memoirs, articles, and films have appeared from around the continent to attest to and in several cases unabashedly to celebrate indigenous African homosexualities.[22] As will be discussed in depth, these studies show that black Africans expressed a wide variety of same-sex sexually intimate relationships in pre-modern settings and were active agents in developing new forms of same-sex conduct in modern milieux. Murray and Roscoe's eclectic collection (1998) in particular puts paid to the notion that Africans needed Europeans or Arabs to teach them about same-sex sexual behaviour.

Much of this "celebratory" or corrective material focuses on relatively recent history or contemporary out gay life in which white South Africans have played a disproportionately visible role. This research is a remarkable achievement, and I will be referring often to it to support my own arguments. But it also exposes a critical weakness in the practice of queer theory in southern Africa, a weakness that has also been noted (and denounced) in Western feminist scholarship in Africa. That weakness is the unconscious privileging of whites or Western categories and concepts such as gender, individual identity, or scientific rationality. Nigerian scholar Oyèrónké Oyéwùmí calls this privileging "Westocentrism," an epistemic system that effectively denies the complexity and subtlety of African perspectives and agency (1997). Oyéwùmí overstates her case, and indeed, one South African wag has made the issue a joke rather than an intellectual crime by calling Western scholars' over-eager search for trans-cultural, trans-historical gays in the ethnographic haystack "Anthrohomo-apology."[23] But queer scholars themselves have fretted about "ethnocentrism and gay imperialism" that can result from the uncritical or incautious application of an activism/scholarship whose terms of reference and strategies come out of the specific history of struggle in the modern West (Wieringa and Blackwood's terms 1999, 3). Such misreadings or false claims upon African evidence may be relatively harmless in most cases, but the potential is clearly there that they could be damaging to the political needs of local gays and lesbians, could impugn African dignity, or could endanger efforts by African gays and lesbians to carve out or preserve an indigenous identity.

A number of examples caution us to the difficulty of avoiding that trap. *The Man Who Drove Mandela,* first, is an outstanding documentary film that aligns itself squarely with the anti-racist politics of South Africa's African National Congress (Schiller 1998). It seeks in part to explain how the ANC came to possess the enlightened attitude towards sexual orientation that it demonstrated when it arrived in power. An unspoken but obvious subtext, however, is that it took a heroic white man to break down African prejudice and ignorance on this topic. This ignores important evidence from the time that shows black men who preferred sex with men forthrightly challenging the homophobia of their leaders (Dlamini 1984,

132). To give another example, the hyperbolic denunciations of homophobia among African leaders that are a staple to queer scholarship (and I include some of my own earlier interventions in this criticism) may also fuel an arrogance or conceit about Western progressiveness on the issue versus African backwardness.

Similarly, the fact that within the region the term "queer" has been embraced mainly by South Africans potentially exacerbates a long-standing issue of South African exceptionalism and parochialism *vis-à-vis* the other countries of southern Africa. Yes, by all means we can celebrate the achievements of self-identified queers in South Africa, but when this blinds us to quieter, non-queer identified efforts elsewhere, it is not only unfair but could be seen as racist. In the triumphalism over the South African constitution, for instance, people commonly forget that the first African countries explicitly to support the principle of gay rights were Lesotho and Ethiopia. Their support for the original application of the International Lesbian and Gay Association to the United Nations is all the more remarkable since it came at a time (1991) when leading figures in the South African liberation movements were still denouncing homosexuality as a Western frivolity or perversion. Even the meticulously careful collection by Arnaldo-Cruz and Manalansan unintentionally feeds into Westocentrism in this way. Its sole chapter dealing with Africa focuses on white and coloured men in Cape Town (Leap 2002).

Jarrod Hayes provides finesse upon "queer" which is helpful in separating the Westocentric connotations of the word from the theoretical insights that it offers. In his study of homosexual themes in Maghrebian literature of the colonial period he explains, "in spite of the potential applicability of the term 'queer' to the Maghreb, I shall use it here less as an adjective to describe sexual acts [or, presumably, a sexuality-based identity] than as *a verb to signify a critical practice in which nonnormative sexualities infiltrate dominant discourses to loosen their political stronghold*" (2000, 7, my emphasis). In other words, "queer" to Hayes signifies an approach to research that explicitly recognizes, values, and promotes the diversity of human sexualities. This approach does not seek to prove the existence of an invented gay archetype scattered throughout the historical record or to impose radical Western standards of sexual liberation wherever it goes. It begins instead with the assumption that both feelings and expressions of sexuality are socially constructed to a significant (possibly predominant but ultimately unknowable) extent in relation to other contests around the social distribution of material resources. It carefully differentiates a continuum from unacted-upon fantasy to discrete same-sex sexual acts to isolated behaviour to more frequent conduct up to presumably permanent or innate orientation. It carefully differentiates as well between active forms of homophobia and passive acceptance of received heterosexist assumptions and ignorance.

Queer theory problematizes genitocentric conceptions of sex and asks us to consider the body's sensuality more holistically. It considers the role of dissident sexualities in defining heterosexual norms. As well as identifying and historicizing the hitherto almost unimaginable diversity of combinations of biological sex, social gender, and sexual orientation (male lesbians, gay transwomen, intersexed, and so on), queer theory draws subtle but important distinctions between normative attitudes towards this diversity. For the purposes of this study, recent theorization of "transphobia" (fear or anger of public transgression of gender norms, rather than fear or revulsion against private homosexual conduct) allows us to appreciate better what the blunt accusation of homophobia often obscures. Transphobia also helps us to understand the otherwise sometimes puzzling hostility to transgender politics from gay-positive or feminist activists and scholars, who prefer clear battle lines drawn on unambiguous identities (Monro 2002).

Hayes demonstrates in his study that queer research can – indeed must – go off from the beaten (urban, white) track to counter the "Westocentric" tendencies of the existing literature and sources. Glen Elder has also used queer theory to illuminate the lives of an extremely marginal group in South Africa, African women who pioneered the transformation of male-only hostels to family accommodation on the fringes of industrial Johannesburg (Elder 2003). Elder makes the further point that words must be held accountable to their full meaning, and that new words may be necessary to make the heterosexism of existing vocabulary transparent. He employs the term "heteropatriarchy," for example, rather than "patriarchy."

In seeking to do all this, queer theory foregrounds issues of class, race, and ethnicity in the construction of sexualities (and vice versa). As Rudi Bleys (1995, 10) has succinctly expressed it, "each of these discourses' discriminatory weight sprang from their links with each other" rather than from their independent (il)logic. Queer theory, in other words, does not simply add gays to the soup of history and stir. It questions how contests over sexuality are forged right into the pot itself. In the tradition of earlier radical approaches to history like Marxism and feminism, it aims as well to suggest creative ways of breaking the pot.

Several historical studies from southern Africa chart a path towards that goal that the present study aims to push further. Diana Jeater's *Marriage, Perversion and Power* only briefly touches upon homosexuality (1993,

194–5), but it offers a compelling Foucauldian analysis of contestations over heterosexuality and masculinity in early colonial Zimbabwe that invites us to ask more. Jeater argues that African (and to a lesser extent European) men's sexual unruliness in the foundational period of colonial rule threatened key material interests in the new colony. Policy-making around sexuality issues consequently assumed considerable importance to the process of state formation. Jeater focuses on a particular conflict of opinion among Europeans about the nature of African sexual Otherness in order to explore that process. Were Africans immoral by ancient custom, or were they perverse by modern choice?

In retrospect such a debate seems absurd. At the time, however, profound financial and policy implications hinged upon its outcome. In the first instance, Europeans needed to be reassured about the superiority of their own sexual and marital ideals. Without such constant reassurance, the ethics of empire were more than a little troubling to a Christian or liberal conscience. The otherization of African sexuality played a key role in achieving this reassurance and in defining a hegemonic European masculinity and femininity suited to imperial rule, viz., We (civilized, controlled, monogamous, discreet, companionate) are not like Them (lusty, savage, violent, polygynous, thoughtless) and therefore are more qualified to rule (and be rewarded handsomely for the effort) than They are. Yet that construct begged the question of what "caused" the Otherness in the first place. If it were the result of Africans' ancient immoral customs and peasant way of life, as missionaries and liberals tended to argue, then encouraging Africans to adopt bourgeois English standards of education, work, family structure, and consumption patterns in an industrializing context would cause such immorality to wither away. This position not only obliged government to spend money on African improvement but it also suggested an eventual end to the many privileges that white settlers had carved out for themselves by conquest. If, however, Africans were perverse out of their own free will, then precisely the opposite could be argued. Westernization or "detribalization" would only undermine customary restraints upon African perversity and open the door to ever-more-troublesome sexual behaviour. Rather than providing Africans with schools and well-paying jobs, the perversity view advocated enhancing the power of the state in order to police African sexual relations. This too would be expensive but much less so and without the unfortunate implications for white privilege of the immoral school of thought.

According to Jeater, different material interests of different groups of Europeans and Africans influenced their views on such matters and ultimately decided the course of the debate. The powerful mine-owners tended to come down on the side that Africans were perverse or sexually self-indulgent by choice rather than immoral by custom. In this view, "detribalized" or "demoralized" Africans were refusing to honour marriage bonds, engaging in prostitution and spreading debilitating diseases, and rebelling against their fathers and chiefs out of selfish, libidinous desire. In so doing, they upset both the smooth flow of cheap male labour to the mines and farms and efficient native administration in the rural areas. Perversity, as such, added significant costs to the production process. Particularly worrisome were "alien natives" – migrants far from home who seduced local women and distressed the local patriarchy. The need to appease those African men, whose cooperation was essential to keeping the system functioning, ultimately resulted in the Native Adultery Punishment Ordinance of 1916, one of several state interventions to regulate African sexuality. This made it a criminal offence for Africans to commit adultery.

Debates and struggles over appropriate state policies to control African sexuality took place as the hegemonic African patriarchy itself began to fracture. It did so partially as a result of growing female assertiveness and a culture of individualism and self-gratification made possible by the suffusion of cash throughout society. For women in town, for example, adultery was one of a small number of ways that they could negotiate for accommodation and food. For male migrants, the relative sexual freedom of town was one of the few perks they could enjoy in a labour market characterized by violence and harshly exploitative working conditions. As well, the relentless European propaganda about Africans' perversity began to be absorbed and internalized by African youth. Forms of sexual violence and exploitation that had hitherto been rare or unheard of were, in Jeater's term, "discoursed" into existence along with new, overt expressions of misogyny, with harsh, long-term consequences for African women.

Homophobia was strongly implicit or latent in this process of the "creation of [heterosexual] perversion." Other social historians from Zimbabwe suggest how an explicitly misogynist masculinity was also an implicitly homophobic one. Tim Burke's study (1996) of the fetishization of the body and its odours, and of the modern commodity market's ability to conjure new desires (and fears), is particularly suggestive. Amy Kaler's work (2003) alerts us to the possibility a homophobic subtext developing within the radically pro-natalist gender ideology that many black Zimbabweans embraced in response to white settler birth control policies and pronouncements. Oliver Phillips explores this theme through his examination of Zimbabwean jurisprudence on a variety of sexual crimes. He illustrates the continuities from Rhodesian to contemporary Zimbabwean discourses around heterosexual rape and homosexual indecent assault in the press and in the courts and shows how these have "been used to shore up a national identity appropriate to the maintenance of a hegemonic masculinity" (1997a, 485–6). Important questions still hang, however. Critically, how, when, and why did this cultural transference of white settler homophobia to black African masculinity take place?

From south of the Limpopo, a number of studies have made same-sex sexuality among Africans a central research concern. Dunbar Moodie (1988, 1994) used Foucault to frame questions about male-male relationships among migrant mine workers in South Africa. Moodie (and subsequently Patrick Harries, 1990a, 1990b, 1994) drew largely upon a 1907 report on an enquiry into so-called unnatural vice among African workers, a 1916 polemic by the Swiss missionary Henri Junod, and oral informants recalling the 1930s to '70s. Moodie and Harries not only established that male-male sexuality at the mines was indeed commonplace. They also sought to explain the puzzle of why mature men from a culture in which heterosexual reproduction was central to gender identity would seek out sexual relationships with boys or other men in such apparently large numbers as they did. Moodie and Harries posit that the decision to take a boy "wife" at the mines was basically rational or functional to traditional mores. The men sought to protect their virility, and rural-based definitions of masculinity, by engaging in sex that was free from the dangers of venereal disease, from responsibility to scarce, demanding women and children in town, and from the dangers of death or mutilation at the hands of rival men for those women in the townships. Taking boys as "wives" in the compounds would enable the "husbands" to graduate from the mines with relatively good health and savings, thence to establish themselves back home as husbands and fathers in customary terms. Male-male thigh sex, in other words, was one of many strategies to resist proletarianization and to protect masculine ideals in a context that otherwise so profoundly undermined them.

For boys, the decision to become "wives" was also at bottom both rational and consistent with customary expectations of masculinity. Drawn into a terrifying industrial maw, boys and young men would have adhered to the gerontocratic ethic of their society and done as they were told by their elders. They would also have been attracted by the security an older, experienced patron could offer. The gifts no doubt helped mitigate any surprise or shock at the proposals, as did the knowledge that with age, experience, and income, they could graduate from the wife role to become husbands themselves. This argument fits well with the view prevalent today that hostel-dwellers are a bastion of reactionary neo-traditionalism. It also helps to explain the purported demise of the mine marriage system in the 1970s. As the female urban population approached parity with the male, as homophobic African nationalist discourses became more insistent, and as the men themselves lost any realistic hope of establishing themselves as patriarchs back in the rural areas, there was no longer any functional purpose for non-homosexual men to engage in homosexual relationships.

Moodie and Harries have drawn their share of critics (notably Achmat 1993), but they have indisputably laid the groundwork for a growing body of scholarship upon the history of masculinity in Africa. I will be considering this scholarship closely in subsequent chapters. At this point, however, let me call attention to recent theorization of female sexuality and feminine identity in southern Africa that also informs the present research. K. Limakatso Kendall (1999) in particular has made an important contribution by showing how, apparently contrary to the strongly heteronormative ideals of Sesotho culture, "many" African women in Lesotho enjoy sensual touching, kissing, and sex-play with each other. Moreover, they do not see this kind of intimacy as a Western influence but on the contrary as something embedded in Sesotho tradition. That they do not engage in lesbian-like play openly or even have a specific word to describe homoerotic relationships can be explained in part by the women's structural vulnerability in an intensely patriarchal society. Why risk inciting men's humiliation, wrath, divorce, shame, and impoverishment by flaunting a sexual and emotional life that is utterly independent of men? The ability to conduct such discreet lesbian-like relationships, however, may be decreasing. Kendall warns that Westernization (including growing familiarity with explicit terms that name and derogate same-sex behaviour) is eroding the social space that allowed female-female sexual intimacy in Sesotho culture.

Kendall's research makes a case for rethinking the ways that we conceptualize "having sex" or what it means to be "queer." She argues convincingly that the dominant discourse around sex is overly focused on male orgasm and, in the case of queer theory, on visible non-conformity and the performance of queerness. Such discourse is technically inaccurate in describing what Basotho (and perhaps other African) women in the region do. Scholars should therefore seek to move beyond that discourse and to challenge their own Western-specific, possibly homophobic assumptions about sexuality. A small number of African feminists have begun to argue precisely this as part of the project of questioning romanticized and restrictive matrifocal constructions of African women's sexuality (see, for example, Zinanga 1996 or Beyala 1996). Although the main sources on the history of same-sex sexuality in southern Africa are overwhelmingly androcentric and hence severely limit our ability to push such questioning back in time, that goal can still be borne in mind in interrogating the historical evidence.

Hungochani: The History of a Dissident Sexuality in Southern Africa engages the above debates along the following structure. The first chapter examines sexuality and gender relations in the "traditional" or pre-modern societies of Zimbabwe. It contextualizes the Zimbabwean experiences with that of neighbouring peoples as discussed in the ethnography of the region. The focus is on how sexual expressions that deviated from the fecund heterosexual ideal were variously contained, explained, honoured, or "invisibilized" by pre-modern cultures.

Chapter 2 examines male-male sexualities as they began to appear in the colonies that eventually constituted South Africa. It looks in particular at the emergence of "mine marriage" in the Johannesburg area (1880s-1910s). A focus upon the 1907 enquiry into "Unnatural Vice" among Africans at the mines calls into question subsequent historiography about mine culture.

The third chapter looks at an urban space that is often erroneously conflated with the mines in discussions of situational homosexuality: prisons. Prison sex did indeed have many similarities with mine marriages. Significant differences, however, included the fact that by the 1950s at least, there were considerable numbers of women and girls in southern African prisons or reformatories as well as men and boys. The relationships formed under such oppressive conditions shed light on the relationship between sexuality and violence and on the construction, contestation, and meaning of changing gender identities for both women and men.

Chapter 4 continues the latter theme by examining emerging sexualities in early colonial Zimbabwe as revealed primarily by forensic evidence from the period 1891–1935. It assesses whether male-male sexual relationships in those years can be best understood in terms of situation (men-only hostels, poverty, and so on) or whether they represented a more fundamental renegotiation of masculinity. It specifically assesses the thesis that Zimbabwean Africans were "forced to do it" or corrupted by foreign men, whether Europeans, "MaBlantyres," "Zambezis," or Shangaans.

Chapter 5 considers the major non-African roots of the kinds of homophobia that contemporary African leaders now cite as "African tradition." Missionary, medical, and legal arguments among white elites in

Rhodesia, South Africa, and the wider international community are examined in light of their sometimes bewilderingly contradictory claims and tendencies. Particular attention is focused on the 1960s-1980s when homosexuality and tolerance of homosexuality were politicized among whites as signs of weakness or vulnerability to "communism" and African nationalist struggles.

Chapter 6 considers the ways that these European fears and obsessions percolated into and were transformed by "respectable" African opinion. This chapter also looks at the role of African nationalist struggles in narrowing the social spaces and the social fictions available for making same-sex sexualities possible within an overwhelmingly heteronormative environment.

Chapter 7 tests both the contagion theory of homosexuality that underpinned much of the early homophobia, and the present claim that "African values" could act as a prophylaxis against supposedly corrupt Western gender roles. The focus is on another colony in the region, Basutoland (modern Lesotho), which was a principal supplier of male labourers to South African industry. Those men came to possess one of the strongest reputations for heterosexual virility and machismo in the region. This chapter considers what changes to Basotho masculinity and femininity were experienced in response to colonial rule and the migrant labour system, with a focus on the ways that same-sex sexual conduct "spread" among men at the mines and the women who remained behind.

The final chapter discusses the emergence of the contemporary, politicized out identity or modern gay rights movement since the 1980s. The power of that identity to destabilize invented nationalist fictions about African masculinity may help us to understand the rise of political homophobia in recent years. It may help to explain otherwise perplexing aspects of contemporary African nationalist leadership, such as the government of South Africa's tardiness and confusion in responding to the HIV/AIDS pandemic, or the government of Zimbabwe's apparent willingness to allow widespread sexual torture and starvation of its own citizens. I conclude by arguing that, indeed, there are links between national identities, state priorities, cultures of masculinities, and sexual otherization that we ignore at peril to our understanding of some of the wider developmental impasses or injustices that the region currently experiences.

Two substantive appendices follow the last chapter. In the first I discuss specific sources, obstacles to knowing, and methodologies for knowing that I encountered or adopted in the course of the research. I add this in the hope that future researchers will gain ideas and be inspired to pursue the gaps that I have left and the questions that I raise. The so-called greatest taboo is not insurmountable. On the contrary, Africans in my experience were often willing and even keen to explore issues around sexuality with me as a researcher, however un-traditional those issues may have seemed and however much they flew in the face of the opinions of political elites. Appendix 2 provides a glimpse of that willingness with sample interviews from the Gay Oral History Project.

The bibliography is intended to bring together the wide range of scholarship, literature, videos, and other resources that attests to African openness to frank reassessments of the evidence on same-sex desire. May it assist future researchers to keep their queer idealism and politics firmly grounded in the historical and cultural context of the region.

The book in short seeks to queer (to query, to problematize, to destabilize) homophobic and heterosexist as well as just plain sexist and racist discourses around identity and politics in southern Africa. It aims in particular to clarify the record about historical and actually existing homosexualities. What kinds of same-sex sexual behaviours existed in southern Africa before colonial rule, and how did traditional societies regard or cope with them? Where did the antecedents of the term *hungochani* come from and how precisely have their meanings changed over time? What are the origins of today's homophobia and the myth of the Really Heterosexual African? What relationship exists between the history of class formation and conflict on the one hand and changing ideals, norms, practices, and dissidences around sexuality on the other? What conditions and struggles have made it possible for hitherto repressed or submerged homosexualities to come out as the gay activism of today? Are there knowable continuities between urban, modern, out sexualities and rural, pre-modern, closeted sexualities? Was there a relationship between colonial borders (including colonial constructions of ethnicities) and sexualities? Why have historians not pursued these questions with rigour before now? And what can this history of a particular non-Western place tell us about the nature of sexuality worldwide in a field of enquiry that remains so heavily dominated by Western evidence, tropes, and assumptions?

I

"Traditions"

The original inhabitants of Zimbabwe were Bushmen similar to those found elsewhere throughout southern and eastern Africa and known in modern times among Shona-speakers as Basili or *zvidhoma*. A rich legacy of paintings upon the walls of caves they sometimes occupied attests to their ancient way of life and spiritual beliefs. Archaeology and ethnologies of their modern-day descendents also suggest strong continuities with the past and allow us to surmise something of their sexuality.

The ancient *zvidoma* were gatherers and hunters who used Stone Age tools and weapons. They lived in small, nomadic, self-sufficient groups that met from time to time to arrange exogenous marriages. They comprised a classless, communitarian society where property, little as it was, was shared by all. Decision-making was likewise by group consensus, "group" including females. Indeed, while there was a clear sexual division of labour that tended to tie women closer to the hearth than men, and while men's activities and interests overwhelmingly predominate in the cave paintings, gender relations among the ancient *zvidoma* were probably as close to egalitarian as ever recorded in Africa. Bushmen throughout southern Africa traditionally married monogamously, for example, but women could divorce fairly easily and retained considerable rights to sexual autonomy (Schapera 1963; Lee 1979; Shostak 1981). Where the ancient paintings depict scenes of daily life, a healthy respect for women's role in giving and maintaining life is a strong and recurrent theme. Women's genitals are depicted as the source of vital, mystical energy at least on par with men's (Garlake 1995).

Zimbabwe's ancient *zvidoma* probably never numbered more than a few thousand at any time, scattered over an area of wilderness roughly equivalent to the size of Germany or California. This was (and remains) an area of prolific natural abundance and variety. The ancient *zvidoma* would thus have mostly had a rich, varied, and healthy diet. Yet without the safety net of an agricultural surplus, the fluctuations in weather and animal migration to which the region is subject could quickly bring the small groups of nomads to the point of starvation. Few as they were, therefore, and in common with other Stone Age societies worldwide, the ancient *zvidoma* likely felt the pressure of "overpopulation" to the extent that they consciously sought to limit their numbers. David Beach has speculated that they avoided the danger of too many mouths to feed during the hungry times by practising (undefined) "sexual restraint and even infanticide" (Beach 1980, 5). One rock painting, however, dating from at least two thousand years ago, shows male *zvidoma* who may have been rather more imaginative and playful in reconciling their desires for sexual intimacy and their need for population control. The painting depicts what appears to be three males engaged in anal or intercrural intercourse, plus two male couples, one embracing face to face while in the other one partner guides an enormous erect penis toward his behind (Garlake 1995, 28).

That only one such homoerotic scene has been found from among thousands of paintings at sites around Zimbabwe cannot be interpreted as an indication that same-sex relations were rare or disapproved. On the whole, Bushmen artists were not concerned with the mundane, and images of non-hunting, non-religious activities (including heterosexual sex) are almost as rare as this one.[1] Anthropologists of the Bushmen and related Khoi in recent times, by contrast, do confirm that same-sex sexual practices not only existed in pre-modern milieux but were common enough to be socially acceptable. The German anthropologist Kurt Falk explicitly researched the question during his ten years in some of the most remote regions of Namibia and Angola. He found there a variety of same-sex sexual relations and vocabularies, including women's use of an artificial penis with a female partner. Interestingly, "married Bushmen women are said to be very devoted to it" (that is, tribadism) as were "newly married wives" among the Khoi. Men masturbated each other and had anal intercourse with, in Falk's view, a casual *faute de mieux* attitude (Falk 1998: 190, 191, 194).

It would be mistaken, of course, to assume an unchanging Bushman culture stretching back thousands of years, or to attribute a straightforward, rational birth control function to such same-sex relationships. We are probably on at least as safe ground to consider those possibilities, however, as to speculate about sexual restraint and infanticide. That mutual same-sex activities were so apparently widespread and non-threatening to society in Falk and Schapera's day would also have been consistent with women's relative power to refuse unwanted sexual advances by men.

The Bantu-speaking migrants who began to arrive in the region about two thousand years ago established an economy that supported very different notions of gender, sexuality, and class.[2] These migrants brought with them iron tools, pottery, livestock, and knowledge of agriculture that could sustain a larger population. It could provide surpluses that both protected against periodic drought and allowed elders to survive long past their productive years. This relative wealth attracted poorer, more vulnerable groups to Iron Age communities as wives, servants, and clients, and over time Zimbabwe's autochthonous peoples were mostly assimilated. Productivity, however, was limited. For example, Iron Age peoples possessed the hoe but not the plough; they possessed the axe but not the saw. Clearing and preparing land for cultivation thus remained an exceedingly labour intensive activity. Similarly, at a time when wild predatory animals abounded, keeping herds of domestic animals demanded a high level of attention to protect them. Labour shortages at key points in the production cycle could thus endanger the survival of a family. This danger then constituted a powerful incentive to maximize family size, construct gender relations that emphasized fertility, and conflate sexuality with procreation.

The religious beliefs of the newcomers exalted the link between sex and reproduction. The ancestors of the Shona, who mostly migrated from the south beginning around 1,000 years ago, held this view in common with Bantu-speaking societies throughout the region.[3] They believed in a hierarchy of spirits from god-like territorial to familial ancestors. The latter were revered as elders who could be consulted and appeased for their power to influence rains, improve soil fertility, resolve family disputes, and intervene in just about any aspect of community life. To have many children was thus not merely to acquire a source of labour to support one through to old age. It was also to acquire descendants who would look to you as an ancestral spirit with a role in community decision-making that could linger for many generations after death. The most powerful spirits (*mhondoro*) were in fact precisely those ancestors who had been most politically successful in life, that is, who had established a prolific lineage. Conversely, failure to procreate precluded persons from receiving full burial rites, consigning their spirits to shameful obscurity.

The centrality of fertility to ancient Shona religion has led some scholars to see sexual imagery as pervading or even dominating ancient public spaces and rituals, notably in vaginal and phallic-shaped structures, carvings, and divination tools.[4] Such claims are likely excessive. Evidence from modern

Zimbabwe, however, does suggest that the cultural construction of a spiritual meaning to sex has deep roots. For example, among the Karanga (one of the largest ethnic components within the Shona and the architects of Zimbabwe's first and most enduring states), the anthropologist Herbert Aschwanden found the beliefs that a man's semen "makes him immortal," that "the act of procreation is a sacred event" and that the male orgasm was comparable to God descending to the people (Aschwanden 1989, 38). The Shona tradition of praise poetry also valorizes sexual intercourse resulting in male orgasm and female pregnancy. In all three types of praise poem that were performed at public ceremonies, sexual accomplishment in that sense is central (Fortune and Hodza 1974). Shona aphorisms idealize this purposefulness as well. Hence, "a man can find a meal very tasty, but if he vomits afterwards, then it has not done him any good" – that is, orgasm without impregnation is useless (Aschwanden 1982, 207).

Shona traditions do acknowledge slightly variant sexualities within the dominant narrative of fertility. These were attributed to men of different totems that cut across ethnic lines: Ngara men were reputed for their sexual prowess and virility, for example, Mhofu for their secretiveness, and Shiri for coarseness.[5] Variations in normative female sexuality were also acknowledged. The key factors in this were age and successful pregnancies. The more children a woman had, the greater the prestige she enjoyed in the community. Women who reached menopause with many successful pregnancies were accorded almost as much respect and influence in the community as senior, demonstrably virile men. Conversely, a married woman who could not get pregnant or successfully carry a pregnancy to term was an object of scorn and pity, not least of all to herself.

Over time men's and women's differential fertility contributed to the development of a pronounced class hierarchy and the rise of sophisticated state structures. These then added a further, political imperative to sexual reproduction. The control of female sexuality through the institution of *roora/lobola* ("brideprice") was central to this process. *Lobola* seems originally to have been a token gift of cattle from the family of the groom to the family of the bride (that is, the exact opposite of a dowry). *Lobola* acknowledged that the young woman's labour and offspring were lost to her natal family upon marriage and went instead to contribute to the wellbeing and prosperity of her in-laws. Symbolic as its origins may have been, the exchange nonetheless imposed a logic of progressive accumulation. Cattle received for *lobola* provided a direct source of wealth for the bride's family (meat, milk, draught power). *Lobola*-received could also quickly be recycled as *lobola*-given to secure proper wives for sons, to expand a polygynous household with new wives, and to strike strategic alliances with other men by offering them the means to negotiate marriages beyond their own families' ability. Wives so secured produced children who accrued to the man's lineage and whose labour enriched the man further. *Lobola* even protected the husband and his family against inheritance disputes that potentially arose from a wife's infidelity. Any children so conceived belonged to the husband, with all the benefits including *lobola*-received for daughters. A polygynist could also deploy the labour and sexuality of wives, concubines, pawns, slaves, and daughters in order to attract male clients. The labour of male clients could in turn be directed to new forms of wealth creation – notably, raiding or enforcing tribute payments from neighbours, mining, smelting, and trading gold.

From around 1000 C.E., some families began to be distinctly successful in parlaying daughters into cattle into wives into power. By 1200, a class structure had more or less consolidated. Karanga elites controlled huge herds of cattle with which they secured the loyalty of their subjects by paying *lobola*, by loaning the cattle out, and by conspicuously rewarding followers with feasts and ceremonies that secured the good will of the ancestors. They began to have monumental houses of stone, or *madzimbabwe*, built for themselves and family. By the time the Portuguese arrived in Zimbabwe in the early sixteenth century, the most important Shona rulers were said to have hundreds or even thousands of wives of varying status and to exercise political authority from the Indian Ocean in the east almost to the Kalahari in the west.[6]

In the context of state formation on this scale, senior men, female elders, and brothers had strong incentives to maintain careful vigilance over younger people's heterosexual contacts. The mother of a girl who was certifiably a virgin upon marriage benefited directly with a bonus to the *lobola* payment known as the *mombe ye amai*. The chances of making an upwardly mobile marriage and particularly of becoming the senior or favoured wife in a large polygynous household were also hugely increased by a girl's virginity. Her virginity thus became a prized asset politically as well as economically and socially. By contrast, the families of girls who could not be attested to be virgins forfeited both the bonus payment and the potential of social advance. A girl who got pregnant before marriage also showed a potentially dangerous streak of disrespect for her elders that brought shame upon the family. Her behaviour invited the family of the groom to negotiate a lower *lobola*. The potentially frustrating consequences for her brothers (who then had to wait longer until their parents had the means to acquire wives for them) increased the pressure on girls to remain chaste.

Blackwood and Wierenga have claimed that some Shona girls in this state of enforced chastity satisfied their supposed need for sexual gratification with each other while doing their chores away from the watchful eyes of the village (1999, 29, note 3). This seems unlikely, at least in the modern sense of lesbian love that it implies. In the first place, girls were normally married soon after or even before puberty. (Indeed, female children could be pledged by their families even before they were born, leaving limited scope for imaginative sexual play.) Secondly, judging from the evidence of early European missionaries and the colonial court records, corporal punishments against girls who transgressed traditional expectations around sexuality could be exceedingly harsh. Thirdly, and probably most decisively, is how powerfully the norms of society colonized children's sexual consciousness. Indeed, children were exposed from a very early age to discreet daily example and instruction about proper sexual demeanour. Girls also learned their sexual vocation directly by instruction from aunts (*vatete*) or other elder women.[7] The principal and unwavering injunctions for a girl centred on serving her future husband and his family. In addition to preserving virginity until marriage, the girls were enjoined to remain faithful and fecund thereafter. Outside of periods of menstruation and parturition, a wife was to be constantly and unhesitatingly sexually available for her husband (and through him, her extended family). A young girl was taught that she could look forward to a rest from such availability at menopause, especially if by her hard work and fertility she enabled her husband to pay *lobola* for a second, younger wife who could pick up the sexual slack.

Yet along with submission to male power over their sexuality, girls were also taught that the role of wife brought with it a strong entitlement to sexual satisfaction derived from regular sexual intercourse.[8] From the woman's point of view, semen on a regular basis was needed to help keep her healthy, biologically as well as spiritually. Intercourse in the early months of pregnancy was also needed to nourish the growing foetus. Young women thus learned ways to stimulate men's sexual performance without threatening men's self-assurance. Praise poems known as *madanha emugudza* ("endearments under the blankets") focused on the virility of the husband and his ancestors with, hopefully, erotically stimulating effect (Fortune and Hodza 1974, 71). Should the flesh still prove weak, however, the wife could yet ensure that her husband did his duty with requisite regularity by the use of "love potions" or "husband-taming herbs" (*mupfuhwira*). The herbs remain much feared by Shona men to this day for their power to keep men from getting an erection with any woman other than their lawfully wedded wives, with whom the penis engorges prodigiously (Goebel 2003).

All-important in a good wife's demeanour was achieving her right to sexual satisfaction without showing undue (implicitly uncontrollable) enjoyment. For a woman to initiate sex or to become moist in anticipation of the act could threaten the sanctity of the male role. Hence a woman properly became moist only after male ejaculation, as is implicit in the aphorism *mvumira mutondo*, "to answer the mutondo tree" (Aschwanden 1989, 100). A good wife could avoid trouble by using herbal astringents to prevent unseemly vaginal moistness (Runganga et al. 1992; Ray et al. 1996). Female sexuality also included knowledge of methods to balance the expectations of the husband and his family with personal health. The discreet use of charms and herbs, for example, could prevent or abort (rare) unwanted pregnancies (Kaler 2003; see also Bradford 1991 on South Africa).

This focus on male ejaculation into the vagina eroticized the female body in a way that disconcerted European observers. Almost complete nudity and much touching were simply not regarded as sexual. *Kusenga*, for example, was the practice of unmarried girls to manually stretch their *labia majora* through a daily exercise. A girl might spend hours at *kusenga* even with a little help from a close friend without for a moment doubting that the activity was not completely in the interest of pleasing the future husband. A brother-in-law could meanwhile fondle the breasts and even buttocks of his unmarried sisters-in-law without raising eyebrows. But should a man touch a woman's heel (which was tucked under a woman's genitals when she sat respectably), it was to make a bold sexual advance. Boys, it should be added, like girls, could hold hands and drape themselves around each other physically, indeed, could sleep together in intimate embrace, without construing the closeness as sexual.

Boys in this society also learned their sexual vocation from a very early age in largely homosocial environments.[9] As long as they kept quiet, they were allowed to sit in and listen to the men's *dare* (court). There, sexual and other political matters came up for freewheeling discussion and debate. Direct instruction from uncles and older peers also conveyed not just the notion that sex was normal and natural but also the seriousness of a man's responsibility in sex. This included an appreciation of the importance of keeping women satisfied, an awareness of the moral, health, and political consequences of failure to perform genitally, and knowledge of the use of male aphrodisiacs to avert such failure. A boy learned that sex was not something frivolous or of individual preference but that his performance would ultimately stand before the court of family, community, and ancestral opinion. The pressure could be onerous. Men at the head of polygynous households, for example, were morally obliged to be scrupulously fair in attending to the separate needs of each wife on a nightly, rotating basis. Woe to him if a wife let a sexual grievance against him be known outside the household. Even for the monogynous majority, fear of being shamed by a wife for neglect fuelled a sense of phallic dutifulness and performance that profoundly conditioned masculine sexuality. To phrase that in another way, phallocentrism was central to masculine sexual pleasure, but this was not simply a patriarchal conceit or indulgence. Rather, it was to a significant extent a reflection of female phallocentric expectations internalized though boys' socialization.

Homosexual experimentation among adolescents took place as a normal part of this learning process. Boys did the herding. Out in the bush, sexual play with each other was "actually expected" as "experimental" at the age of puberty.[10] Interest in male-to-male sex play was expected to wither away as a boy matured, coached on if necessary by the mockery of peers and perhaps a discreet talking-to by elders.

A further key to understanding masculine sexuality in pre-modern society is that the transition from boyhood to manhood was not necessarily either quick or self-evident with physical maturity. Young men normally had to wait for a marriage with a suitable bride to be arranged by his parents. A very strong incest taboo (extending to totem, not just near family) complicated the search for a bride. Even when the prospective groom took the initiative in choosing a partner, the marriage required negotiation over *lobola* and the production of at least the first instalments before the youngsters could cohabit. In times of hardship, or if a family had no daughters to bring in *lobola*, the prospective groom could have a long wait for this to happen. Moreover, the fact that wealthy men and chiefs had the ability to marry many wives contributed to a structural shortage of suitable brides for poorer men.

Young men in the frustrating position of waiting until their parents could afford to pay *lobola* were ill-advised to seek heterosexual gratification outside the properly sanctioned process. A son who showed disrespect in this way not only brought shame upon his father; his family was also required to pay compensation for the damages to the family of the girl. A young man who impregnated a girl prior to betrothal also potentially endangered his family's interests if that girl were of a poor or socially marginal family.

The Shona, meanwhile, did not practise the non-penetrative sex play between adolescent boys and girls that was found in many other southern African societies (known as *hlobonga* in Zulu, for example, or *ukumetsha* in Xhosa). During the period of waiting between physical maturity (as males) and social maturity (as married men), therefore, young males were coached in and expected to exercise self-restraint. Beach has estimated that in the nineteenth century as much as a third of the physically adult male population may have been celibate in this way.[11] Far from being regarded as unmanly, young men's sexual self-restraint was honoured as contributing to the greater social good. The same applied to non-polygynous husbands (the majority). Wives had the right to insist upon post-partum abstinence for as long as the new infant was suckling (two to three years). At the very least, post-partum abstinence extended until the midwife was paid for her services (four to five months after birth). During that time the husband was expected to exercise self-control or to "go hunting" – that is, to masturbate out in the woods (Aschwanden 1989, 97, 99). As in the case of youthful homosexual experimentation, such behaviour was of no concern to the community provided it remained discreet, but was the subject of mild mockery if it became known.

Conformity to heteronormative sexuality was overdetermined by lifelong socialization and by the intricate web of moral and material obligations that made nonconformity difficult to conceive as an option, let alone to enact. Who in their right minds would choose poverty, intense family pressure, and possible violence, shame, and lack of spiritual meaning by not marrying and producing children? Who in their right senses could believe that they could transgress norms without the wider community getting to know about it, particularly since the community was well known to be watched by the unseen eyes of the ancestors?

Nonetheless, situations inevitably arose in which individuals did transgress norms and by so doing potentially endangered the standing and security of their families or even the stability of the wider community. In such cases, elders would confer punishments designed to contain the danger. These punishments were assessed in consultation with *n'angas* (diviners) according to the level of the potential threat. If the sexual transgression did not cross rank, age, and totem (incest) lines, for example, the punishment could be as little as the payment of compensation of a few beasts to the family of the "victim." A typical case would be a neglected wife who committed adultery with a non-kinsman. Save for a thrashing to maintain the social appearance of her husband's power over her sexuality, she would likely be forgiven fairly quickly, especially if a child resulted that enriched the household.[12]

On the other hand, if sensitive social lines were crossed in an illicit sex act, the punishment increased accordingly. Incest was a particularly strong taboo, evoking punishments ranging from exile to death. In the nineteenth century men who dared interfere with one of the Ndebele rulers' wives also faced a death sentence – a level of punishment that was reported widely throughout other states in pre-modern Africa and that may have been present in the early Shona states as well.

In addition to the specific nature of the infraction and the status of the parties involved, cause was important to consider when assessing punishments. Some sexual infractions were judged to arise in a straightforward way when men's natural lustiness or women's legitimate need for sexual intercourse was frustrated. Payment of compensation and public shaming of the guilty parties were considered sufficient in such cases. Other transgressions, however, defied this easy explanation and could only be understood as the result of intervention by one of the many different types of unseen powers that the Shona recognized. The most feared of these was witchcraft (*muroyi*, pure evil). An act such as bestiality would typically be explained in these terms. The perpetrator in such cases had to be expunged from the community by exile or even death.

Another type of spirit that was greatly feared and that could manifest itself in dangerous sexual behaviour was the avenging spirit known as the *ngozi*. Unlike the pure evil of *muroyi*, its evil stemmed from the legitimate grievance of a deceased person against a past injustice – an innocent victim of war or murder, for example, but also commonly a wife who had been neglected or ill-treated in life. *Ngozi* were especially prone to incite outrageous sexual behaviour. Girls who flaunted sexual brazenness by kissing in public or seducing men indiscriminately could do so with impunity if the cause were determined to be possession by a spirit of this nature. The only solution was to appease the *ngozi* by offering the afflicted family compensation, typically a virgin daughter of the family that had caused the offence that provoked the *ngozi* in the first place. That girl would normally become a servant or slave in the family with the *ngozi*, but in extreme cases she could be ritually executed.[13]

A third example of a spirit that affected women's sexuality was the *chidhoma*, the Shona equivalent of the *tokoloshi* known throughout South Africa. A *chidhoma* was a well-hung imp that, among other mischief, sometimes crept into married women's huts at night to stimulate them sexually. Nocturnal visits by a *chidhoma* could explain both a woman's otherwise unseemly sexual arousal or her lack of interest in her husband's attentions. Rather than punishing the woman for these inappropriate behaviours (and so inflaming the *chidhoma's* capricious anger), a "cure" would be affected by the husband making sacrifices or other prescribed gestures of appeasement.

According to *n'angas* interviewed in the course of this research, same-sex sexual infractions traditionally had several possible causes and consequently were regarded with ambivalence. For example, what we today would now term homosexual orientation or transgender identity was not necessarily an offence at all but a respected attribute if caused by certain types of spirit possession and manifested in certain ways. This would have included rare cases of physiological hermaphrodism as well as possession by benign spirits of the opposite sex. Such explanations of cause removed blame from an individual, and same-sex couples so possessed could live together as husband and wife without attracting opprobrium. A male who took the role of wife, doing all the public duties and chores that a female wife would do, was known as *murumekadzi* (literally, "man-woman"). A woman who took the role of a man in an analogous relationship with another woman was *mukadzirume* ("woman-man"). In both cases what happened between the couple inside their hut was not the subject of close investigation.[14] Similarly, a man who never married or who appeared well-adjusted to a life of celibacy was thought to have *chitsina*, an otherwise inexplicable streak of bad luck. The concept of *chitsina* obviated close enquiry into actual sexual behaviour or inclinations (Davies 1931).

Lack of blame or even concern about such explicable deviance from the sexual norm is widely attested by oral informants and in the ethnography of the Shona and other Africans who came to settle in Zimbabwe from elsewhere in the region. A hint of it comes through in the testimony of Slopo Mazinge to the High Court in 1927. Mazinge was a Xhosa immigrant from the eastern Cape who had settled in a *kraal* near Gwelo (Gweru) – *kraal* being shorthand for a rural homestead and suggestive that he had married a local woman. It was trouble with their adult son, Nomxadana, alias Maggie, that brought Mazinge before the Rhodesian courts. Nomxadana had been discovered posing as a female nurse and wearing female clothes including underwear and high heels.

When questioned in an accusatory tone by the prosecutor about his son's behaviour as a boy growing up in the village, Mr Mazinge defended himself to the court: "I have never noticed anything peculiar about Accd [accused, sic] I have always thought him sound in his mind ... At the kraal Accd used always to dress in female clothes. He has always worked as a nurse. He associated mostly with girls at the kraal. My son has been wearing dresses ever since he was a baby. He has never discarded them although I have often given him males' clothes but he has refused to wear them. I have never thought him mentally affected."[15]

Even in cases involving otherwise normal males beyond the years of acceptable experimentation, same-sex sexual acts were not necessarily taken as serious breaches of morality. Such an act might be a mere "accident" stemming from physical proximity. After all, bachelors normally slept together, typically in the nude and huddled together for warmth in ways that sometimes unavoidably stimulated genital arousal. "Accidents" were also prone to happen after having imbibed too much beer. Punishment in such cases would be an essentially token compensation payable to the family of the "victim." The *only* discussion of sodomy and indecent assault on a male in Shona legal traditions, by Native Commissioner F.W.T. Posselt in 1935, puts it this way. First, the two offences "are not clearly distinguished. Where several males sleep together and the offender pleads that the act was done in his sleep, he will be excused from criminal liability; cognizance will, therefore, in practice, only be taken where direct force has been applied. The penalty consisted of damages of several head of cattle, payable to the victim's family" (Posselt 1935, 59).

Headman Mbata, testifying on "native custom" in a 1921 case from Mazoe district, more or less confirms this, setting the compensation for a deliberate attempt at sodomy or indecent assault at one beast only. "If however it was done while sleeping we would still require reparation but only a small amount."[16] As comparison, and indicative of the relative harmlessness of the crime, the compensation imposed for female adultery or breach of promise was set at ten to twelve beasts.

Also noteworthy, according to Posselt, is that violent male-male assault intrinsically differed from heterosexual rape in that females were not expected to resist. Lack of resistance or even active consent by the girl or woman did not in any way mitigate the rapist's crime – which, after all, was not an offence against the individual female but against her family, especially her father. By contrast, a male who did not demonstrably resist had no grounds to lodge a complaint.

Cases of flagrant and persistent homosexual behaviour were naturally regarded with much greater concern. If the community suspected witchcraft to be at play, it could in fact demand exile or death. Some contemporary Zimbabweans claim that execution with torture was the norm on account of the great danger posed. As one traditional herbalist told Rudo Chigweshe, a researcher at the University of Zimbabwe, "The traditional society believes that homosexuality pollutes the country. A lot of misfortunes, for example, droughts, hunger and diseases we are having in Zimbabwe are being caused by this evil thing."[17] It seems, however, that ambiguity about cause acted as a powerful restraint against capital punishment, even in clear cases of homosexual rape. What if the unrepentant, incurable, violent man in such a case were accused of witchcraft when in fact he was really possessed by a transient "stranger spirit" (*shave*)? If executed rather than appeased by the proper rituals, that man could return as an *ngozi* to wreak even greater havoc. Elders thus sometimes went to great lengths to avoid finding the "proof" needed to justify an execution:

In my home village there were several men staying in homosexual relationships and the community never talked about it. They were regarded as unstable or bewitched or witches themselves. People were afraid that maybe they would be violent because of the assumed instability or that they [the accusers] might in turn be bewitched. So basically the homosexuals were left alone. But sometimes the accusations would be a mobilized issue so the chief would have to call a *dare* where they would be tried ... For them to be killed it would take the village elders a long time going to several traditional healers to find out the truth. Sometimes the healers would refuse to find out because they would not want to be the cause of someone's death.[18]

It needs to be stressed that all of the above took place within a tradition of great public discretion about sexual matters. Shona praise poems performed at public ceremonies did allude to sexual prowess in often ribald ways. However, these were invariably couched in terms of fertility and virility that strengthened confidence in normative sexuality. Public talk that undermined that confidence or called institutions and social hierarchies into question was strictly taboo. Whatever debates and discussions took place in homosocial environments like the men's *dare*, therefore, they could not be repeated in mixed company. Even in the company of each other, men were loathe to broach the topic of male-male behaviour. In the words of one straight informant (after several beers had loosened his tongue): "Yes, traditionally it [homosexual orientation] was there, but it was never talked about. Never! As a child you would be told to stay away from the hut of a man who was known by the elders to be that way. But you were never told why. Only after you were grown and you gave those same elders much beer, perhaps, they might be coaxed to say something. But it took a lot of beer."[19]

This culture of discretion around sexual matters meant that acts that were forbidden in theory could be tolerated in practice as long as the community was not compelled to pay explicit attention. Important traditions developed that enabled communities to avert their collective eyes. Such wilful blindness was not necessarily as difficult to achieve as we might assume in the close-knit peasant villages of yore. The custom of *kupindira* or *kusikira rudizi* ("the raising of seed"), for example, allowed families to avoid the shame of a man's inability (or lack of interest) to impregnate his wife. By this custom either the man himself, his parents, or his in-laws secretly invited a trusted male relative to fulfil the task, typically a brother.[20] The child so conceived would bear a family resemblance, so no one would know that the husband had failed in his fundamental duty as a man. He himself might not know it if the arrangement were made at the behest of a frustrated wife. In this way the public mask of an apparently fertile marriage enabled a man to be heterosexually impotent without losing social standing and the all-important descendants.

Similarly, the institution of an intimate male friend (*sahwira*) provided a respectable public mask behind which non-normative behaviour could take place. The men bonded in this lifelong relationship could share the most intimate sexual and social discussions, including those about their wives' sexual performance and physical appearance. Indeed, they could temporarily exchange wives as a gesture of friendship. Also, while *sahwira* in no way connoted homoerotic attraction, its very respectability meant that young men so inclined or curious could "play" with each other without bringing social opprobrium upon themselves. For that reason the word *sahwira* has been co-opted by contemporary gays and lesbians.[21]

The power of customary etiquette to avert collective eyes from discreet sexual transgressions could be quite compelling. One case that came before the colonial courts in 1923 starkly illustrates this. The men involved were a middle-aged BaSili (Bushman) named Mashumba and a youth named Njebe who lived in a village in far western Zimbabwe. They were brought before the village headman, Maboma, upon Mashumba's complaint that the youth Njebe had beaten him. In their evidence to Maboma about the assault, Mashumba and Njebe both made the untroubled admission that they had been having mutual penetrative sex together in the open veldt three times a week for the previous three years. However, Njebe explained that as he matured he had begun to worry if he were not in danger of becoming pregnant. The lovers separated amicably on these grounds but later quarrelled when Mashumba proposed having another go. According to Njebe: "I struck accd [sic] because he said, 'Come on, let us mount one another as before.'"[22]

I will return to this case in the next chapter to consider what it tells us about same-sex sexual love. For now, however, the salient point is that the headman of a rural village evinced astonishment at the information he was being given. In all those years Maboma had never noticed or heard anything "abnormal" about a pair of male lovers whose affair took place in and around the village of which he was head. The case would have remained invisible to historians had Njebe not taken the unusual step of confessing his quarrel to an African police constable, who then brought the case to the local European magistrate for resolution.

Traditional culture, in short, was de facto more tolerant of sexual diversity than modern literalists recognize. The danger of some sexual transgressions was contained in the sense that the community tacitly agreed not to see them. This phenomenon was apparently common throughout the region and was expressed, perhaps with hyperbole, by Kurt Falk in his reflections upon the Herero of Namibia (1998, 192): "The act is allowed but speaking about it is forbidden." Gays and lesbians in Zimbabwe today also acknowledge that tradition in the form of powerfully wilful blindness works in their favour. One of my researchers, an out lesbian in a small agricultural village, put it this way: "They [neighbours] don't want to know that I am lesbian, though I bring my girlfriends here. They prefer to think that I'm just a very moral girl when they see I don't hang around with boys. I don't see how you can really be blind to two people who are lovers, but they are."[23]

Pre-modern Shona states at different times were powerful enough to keep their neighbours at bay, inflicting defeats upon the Portuguese as late as the early nineteenth century. Their power rested in part upon dramatic demonstrations of their material wealth (the *madzimbabwe*) and by their ability to muster military force. In addition, high state officials were shrouded by a calculated mystery that distinguished them from commoners and enhanced their political authority. From the early sixteenth to the nineteenth century, the king or *Mutapa* of the main Shona state remained hidden from public view behind walls and screens. His words were communicated to the people by a class of praise singers and spirit mediums, couched in terms that equated the wisdom and health of the *Mutapa* with the prosperity of the people as a whole. He was "divine" in the sense that he was the political interpreter of the will of the ancestral spirits. Through his mediums he could ensure that those spirits brought rain and fertility. Or, should his people be recalcitrant to his rule, he could have the spirits deny rain and fertility. As the physical embodiment of the spiritual health of his people, the *Mutapa* could not die by natural or accidental causes. Rather, when the time approached, he was supposed to perish in a ritual suicide (assisted if necessary) that ensured that the ancestral spirits passed without disturbance to his successor.

Ritual incest also irrevocably placed the *Mutapa* outside the realm of . normal humanity. The *Mutapa* married his full sister to break one of society's biggest taboos. The intent was not to produce offspring; there were many other wives for that purpose. On the contrary, offspring were purposefully averted by *coitus interruptus*. The role of this incestuous marriage was rather symbolically to "fortify installation" against rival claimants to the status of *Mutapa*.[24] In the case of the Manyika in eastern Zimbabwe, the king for the same reason was reputed to have sex with his own daughter on the back of a tethered crocodile, a symbol of the inscrutable power of the kingship.[25] Such unions were known as *kupinga nyika* ("to protect the land/nation"). *Kupinga nyika*, practised correctly, enhanced the mystery and hence the power of the institutions of governance.

Celibacy as well could be a public demonstration of difference that commanded respect by so dramatically breaking both the rules of normative society and the dictates of economic common sense. Parents would be the first to notice if a child were developing in this abnormal way – an effeminate boy, for example, or a girl who preferred to play with boys rather than girls. Efforts would be taken to "cure" the problem, first by shaming and perhaps by a beating or two, later by consultation with *n'angas* and appropriate sacrifices. If, after all this, the child still did not change, it could be interpreted to mean that he or she was possessed by a spirit of the opposite sex. A child in such a case would likely be apprenticed to learn the arts of divination. As time went on, the female spirit who occupied a male body would manifest itself in increasingly feminine characteristics in the man and even, as Gelfand noted in one case, insist that the man wear women's clothing (1964, 84–5). Some informants attest that the more flamboyant the effemininity, the more efficacious the *n'anga*.[26]

A male ancestor or water sprite (*njuzu*) whose spirit occupied a female body, meanwhile, could hardly be expected to tolerate that body having sex with a man. Aschwanden (1989, 161–4) describes such a case of a woman, Angela, being inhabited by an *njuzu* whose increasingly violent possessions made it impossible for her to have sex with her husband and eventually even to have fantasies about sex with men. Women in such cases would be assumed to be celibate, although they could be married to a succession of young girls who served them, in public, as a regular wife would a husband. These female wives as they reached puberty would be replaced and married off to men in the proper fashion. The celibacy or virginity of the woman so possessed could become a valued spiritual asset to a community, as one informant explained:

There are no lesbians in our culture, but we have special women who will be given powers by strong *n'angas* to act as *mbonga* [guardians] for the chief. The woman will not marry for the rest of her life [but instead] will be pledged to a spirit that acts as guardian for the chief. For the spirit to guard the chief properly, it needs a wife, because it is obvious that a strong bodyguard must be a man. The *mbonga* is given the woman as his wife. She will be used as his wife without her knowledge when she is asleep. In return she is given all the favours of the chief. The *mbonga* will be treated as if she is someone else's real wife because if any man tries to court her, the spirit will cause bad luck for him. That is why she will never ever have sex with a man.[27]

Mbonga were often the actual sisters or aunts of the ruler. Kings depended upon them for advice as well as *muti* (medicine) to such an extent that "in war the *mbonga* was supreme" (Shire 1994, 154). Women who fulfilled this role are revered in praise poems as being among the most important founding ancestors of the clan or nation (Fortune and Hodza 1974, 70).

No historical case illustrates this role more famously than that of Nyemba, also known with the masculine honorific as VaNyemba. VaNyemba lived in the eastern part of Zimbabwe in the early to mid eighteenth century. According to senior male informants interviewed in the late 1970s, she was variously an actual lesbian, had both female and male sex organs, and was "normal" except that she kept real bullets in her vagina.[28] Accounts recorded by colonial officials remember her simply as a beautiful maiden, while among the Chihota people she is revered as both *mamuna* (literally, "man or husband") and *mbonga*.[29] Her *muti* was defiled with political consequences that are still celebrated to this day.

The tradition goes as follows. VaNyemba was accompanying her brothers on an elephant-hunting expedition, providing by her abstinence from sex the *muti* necessary to protect them from danger. At one point the brothers entrusted her to the care of a local headman while they tracked the elephants. That headman broke the trust by raping her. Shamed, and fearful that her brothers' lives were now in danger, VaNyemba killed herself. So heinous was the headman's crime that an army was raised against him and he fled in ignominy. VaNyemba's elder brother, Chihota, established his family as a new and powerful dynasty in the area.

Ritual incest and celibacy may not have been the only forms of calculated "sexual inversion" for political purposes. In other parts of southern Africa (best attested in Angola and Namibia) there existed a caste of male diviners known by variations of *chibudi, chibanda, quimbanda, gangas,* or *kibambaa.* Described as "passive sodomites" by early European explorers and traders, they were reputedly possessed by especially powerful female spirits. They were said to have dressed as women except with a loincloth open at the back to invite anal penetration. They would entice men into sex, charging a fee for the service. The active partner either gained by contact with the spirit (good crops or hunting, health, protection from evil spirits, and so on) or realized his own homosexual preference: "When an Ukuanyama man falls a prey to this practice he discards his weapons, his bow, his arrows and his assegai (the distinguishing marks of manhood) and plays the *ekola*. He is no longer regarded as a man, but as one whom God has intended to be a man, but who is after all only 'half man, half woman.'"[30]

Travel accounts from as early as the sixteenth century remark that *chibados* "married" each other and were esteemed in their societies as "powerful wizards."[31] To the consternation of the Portuguese, they even turned up in the holds of slave ships bound for the Americas where they inflamed a disturbed spirit (of resistance?) among the other captives (Sweet 1996). Transvested African slaves were also among those interrogated and executed for the "nefarious sin" of sodomy during the Inquisition in both the Americas and in Spain itself (Burshatin 1999). The prominent male homosexuality and transvestism among the priests of the *caboclo* or *candomblé* possession cults of northeastern Brazil are likely traceable to this Angolan heritage (see Landes 1940, also discussed by Strongman 2002 and Murray 2000).

Whatever their actual sexuality, symbolic sexual inversion or difference among certain elite women and men was clearly functional to the process of forging and maintaining relatively centralized state structures in the context of "medieval" southern Africa – sparsely populated, pre-literate, and horseless. Indeed, transvestism and symbolic sexual inversion were fairly common features of African societies throughout much of Africa south of the Sahara at the time of the European expansion.[32] The evidence that a caste equivalent to the *chibados* existed in medieval Zimbabwe is slight but suggestive. The main war chiefs to the *Mutapa* in the sixteenth and seventeenth century, for example, were known as *Sono*, meaning "women," and described by Beach as "swaggering dandies" (Beach 1980: 106). Below them "was a special group described as 'women' to the Portuguese, almost certainly honoured *karanga* [literally, 'wives,' but figuratively 'advisors'] of the *Mutapa*."[33]

Ritual gender inversion also appears in societies that were dominated by Karanga who migrated southwards in the sixteenth to eighteenth centuries. Among the Venda, notably, the women in charge of initiation schools were called "masters" (*nematei*), while the senior men who instructed boys were known as "mistresses" (*nyamungozwa*, Huffman 1996: 86). Among the Lovedu, another Karanga offshoot from roughly 1600, the inversion involved women rather than men. The authority of the Lovedu "rain queen" (in fact, a king in status) was believed to be dependent upon her virginity and her marriage to girls (Krige 1974).[34]

The swaggering dandies, praise singers, and musicians described by the early Portuguese explorers lived in a period when the power of the Monomutapa state was at its height. With the coming of the Portuguese, however, the power of the *Mutapa* and his court began to wane. In 1629 the Portuguese succeeded in imposing a Catholic convert as the *Mutapa*, to the disgust and rebelliousness of many of his subjects. As the power of the state subsequently devolved to local, often very small and ephemeral polities, the Shona not only stopped building great ceremonial structures but warrior castes of male "women" and "wives" similarly lost much of their political function. By the early nineteenth century, they had become a largely forgotten memory.

Oral testimony nonetheless suggests that ritual male-male sexual acts continued to be practised by ambitious individuals long after the disappearance of Zimbabwe's large medieval states.[35] This form of *muti* had its own term: *divisi rakaipa* (bad). By most accounts, bad *divisi* among the Shona involved incest with a female relative for the purpose of curing an otherwise incurable disease or persistent misfortune. As one Shona scholar expressed it, "for medicinal purposes a brother and sister may mate" (Hatendi 1973, 136). Male-male *divisi rakaipa* was even more powerful and could be used to cure impotence, improve soil fertility, or advance political ambitions. Male-male sexual acts for the sake of *divisi rakaipa* were deemed to be so powerful and extreme, however, that they approached the quality of witchcraft and could be punished by death. Fear of the act's power would tend to keep victims and their families silent, which may partially explain early anthropologists' failure to report its practice.

Around 1000 C.E. the ancestors of the Shona came into contact with peoples who had significantly different ideas about sexuality. It was then that Muslims first arrived at the Mozambique coast and began trading with the interior. These traders were mostly Arabs, but over the centuries they also included Persians, Indians, and mixed-race Swahili. All of them, it seems fair to say, had an ancient familiarity with diverse types of same-sex sexual behaviours, including notions of homosexual sex for purely sensuous enjoyment. X*anith* or *mashoga* (Swahili words with an Arabic root) and *mabasha* (from Persian), for example, are well documented in the Swahili cities along the Indian Ocean (Amory 1998, Porter 1995). It seems likely that Shona men who travelled to coastal trading centres such as Kilwa and Sofala would have learned about such behaviours and perhaps, far from home, sampled them. There is no evidence to suggest that they then carried the new ideas about sexuality home to Zimbabwe. Indeed, even that minority of Shona-speakers who converted to Islam and adopted other aspects of Arab/Swahili dress and culture (known as the Varemba) did not appear to proselytize Arab/Swahili notions about gender or sexuality. The first Portuguese description of the vestigial Muslim communities among the Shona (1810) actually indicates the opposite. With the exception of practising male circumcision and endogamy, the sexual mores and marital customs of the Varemba were virtually indistinguishable from those of the general society (Mandivenda 1989: 98).

Similarly, we know that the Portuguese who arrived in Zimbabwe in the early 1500s came from a society where homoerotic behaviour was relatively tolerated. King Affonso VI (1656–83) was himself a "notorious homosexual" (Mott 1988, 92). Careful scrutiny of the records of the court of Inquisition and other Portuguese documents may one day turn up evidence to support twentieth century speculation that the Portuguese were to blame for introducing their homosexual peccadilloes to unwary Africans. For now, however, neither oral tradition nor published accounts suggest anything of the sort. On the contrary, the Portuguese were renowned for their lusty behaviour with African women and for the tendency for each generation of Portuguese to become progressively more African in appearance and behaviour. By the end of the nineteenth century, many so-called Portuguese in the Zambezi valley not only had African physical features but also had assimilated to heteronormative African culture, including taking up polygyny and *lobola*.[36] The British traveller J.T. Bent described his scandal at the life-style of officials just over the frontier of Mashonaland, where "dusky beauties" supposedly lived in fear of the Portuguese men's sexual appetite (1892, 340).

The Portuguese presence in Zimbabwe was in any case minimal after successful military campaigns to expel them in the late 1600s. Two later groups of invaders to the plateau had a more enduring impact upon Shona mores around sex and gender still vividly and sometimes angrily recalled in oral history. These were the Ngoni (latterly, the Gaza Ngoni, Shangane, or Shangaans) and the Ndebele (or Matabele). Both groups were offshoots of the Nguni-speaking peoples of what is now KwaZulu-Natal and Swaziland during the *mfecane* (early 1810–20s). This period of transformation of small agricultural communities into highly militarized and expansive kingdoms has been termed both a revolution and a gradual process rooted in climatic and food production changes in the late eighteenth century. An agreed-upon key element in the transformation was the assertion by the emergent states of direct control over individuals' sexuality. The great Zulu ruler Shaka famously abolished the traditional months-long circumcision schools supervised by local elders and herbalists. In their place, he had young men form into regiments for year-round military training. The latter purportedly included fostering a culture of exaggerated contempt for women and femininity in order to prepare the men to endure campaign hardships and to conduct war mercilessly against (feminized) male enemies and female non-combatants alike. Warriors were subsequently not allowed to marry or even *hlobonga* with girls until they had completed their service satisfactorily – an incentive to bravery.[37]

The first Ndebele king, Mzilikazi, led his people away from the Zulu state in 1822 to settle eventually in southwestern Zimbabwe in 1840. The Ndebele incorporated peoples and customs as they migrated to become a distinctive culture from the Zulu. Mzilikazi is said to have maintained most aspects of Zulu military organization, however, and even to have extended Shaka's incentives to bravery by maintaining control over his warriors after they married. Instead of punishing alleged cowards by executing them (as had been the case under the Shaka), for example, Mzilikazi simply banished the men from their wives. The missionary Robert Moffat actually visited an Ndebele town populated by women and children only, separated by eight miles from the men's village. All contact between the communities was forbidden on pain of death until the men redeemed themselves in battle against the Zulu.[38]

Cobbing (1974) has estimated that the Ndebele state's assertion of control over young men's sexuality deferred their marriage for an average of five to ten years. Moreover, marriage when it eventually happened was arranged to reify a strict caste system – elites (amaZansi) could not marry outside their caste. Children born outside ethnic and caste parameters were killed, enslaved, or ostracized. Large-scale polygyny as practised by the Ndebele rulers meanwhile imposed a de facto celibacy on hundreds of amaZansi women, many of whom languished in remote military camps awaiting infrequent conjugal visits. Sometimes, it seems, such women paid with their lives for being tempted by lingering notions of female sexual rights: "She pleaded guilty [to adultery], adding that she had no idea that she, a woman, was intended to live with the mere name of wife or concubine, that she had acted according to her own impulse as a woman, and did not see wherein she had erred; that she knew she would be killed and that she preferred death rather than live with the mere name of wife" (Wallis 1945, 2: 84).

The Ngoni meanwhile settled in the southeast. They came to be known after their leader, SoShangane, whose violence was even more feared among the Shona than Mzilikazi's. A marital alliance with the Ndebele kept the two migrant kingdoms from each others' throats, but under the leadership of Gungunyana in the 1880s, the Ngoni withdrew southwards into Mozambique. The Ngoni-ized Shona-speakers who remained behind from this retreat, the MaNdau, are still colloquially known as Shangaans.

Like the Shona kingdoms they superseded, the Ndebele and Ngoni invaders drew upon ritual as well as brute military demonstrations of their power. Indeed, the Ndebele brought with them from Zulu culture a strong association between sexual inversion and spiritual, political authority (Ngubane 1977, 142; Bozongwane 1983, 35). The most effective Ndebele healers and diviners (*izisangoma* and *izisanuse*) were men with the most exaggerated effemininity (or masculinity in women). Shaka himself was said to have had this trait (purportedly even feigning menstrual cramps), while the Ndebele elevated the sexually abstinent *mbonga* (guardian) role. Lozikeyi was such a guardian, and reputedly the most powerful of the wives of Mzilikazi's successor, Lobengula. Since Lobengula was not allowed to have sexual intercourse with her, Lozikeyi was married to her uncle's daughter who then bore children from Lobengula on Lozikeyi's behalf (Mahamba 1996, 19).

Abstention from sexual intercourse immediately prior to battle was an injunction for both Ndebele and Ngoni warriors as a means to heighten their preparedness for combat. In both militaristic states, battle preparations could also reputedly entail sex with males, from the warriors going into battle right up to the highest level of command. What kind of sex has never been specified but presumably it followed the model of *divisi rakaipa*, that is, the warrior (the man in need of protection) taking his satisfaction on a passive vessel.[39]

To the extent that they were in fact practised, such same-sex acts would not have particularly affected the birth rate. But the many political restrictions on marriage and sex clearly did, resulting in a dearth of children, which was immediately evident to the first missionary visitors to the Ndebele. Those missionaries interpreted (and rued) the low birth rate as symptomatic of sexual "immorality." In this case they probably meant adulterous thigh sex and the use of abortificients to terminate illicit pregnancies.[40] The dearth of children also gave rise to the immorality of kidnapping, one of the most burdensome aspects of Ndebele rule over the Shona, indeed one cited by Shona men as a grievance that sours ethnic relations in Zimbabwe to this very day. Whether by kidnapping, by regular tribute demands, or by proper *lobola* payments, the Ndebele became large-scale net importers of young Shona women who were assimilated into the invading kingdom. During the decades of Ndebele dominance, the shortage of marriageable females among the Shona – a pre-existing problem, as we have seen – was significantly exacerbated.

Shona men did not take these exactions passively. Some joined the Ndebele and Ngoni states, albeit as low-caste clients or as slaves. Others, however, maintained a steady resistance. Over the decades their ability to defend themselves against the invaders and even to turn the military tide became more and more effective. This resurgence of Shona power and self-confidence was made possible in part by the influx of guns from South Africa and Mozambique. It also reflected the gradual transformation of the invaders from a sternly disciplined warrior elite into partially Shona-ized, settled agriculturalists. While still identifying as brave and dogmatically patriarchal as compared to the Shona, Ndebele men grew lax in some of their practices. The strict regimental system of the early period of Ndebele rule, for example, gave way to mixed-gender communities in which the young men and their parents exercised much greater freedom to choose marriage partners than before. The Ndebele also abandoned their male initiation ceremony over the course of the nineteenth century, in line with the practice of their Shona subjects. Cobbing and Mahamba have argued that ideals of abstinence for warriors had also become considerably muted in practice, with premarital heterosexual liaisons even across caste lines becoming increasingly common during Lobengula's reign (Cobbing 1974, 613; Mahamba 1996, 11).

The shift in the balance of power between the Shona and their invaders may also have stemmed in part from cultural exchange in the other direction, that is, the Shona emulating those aspects of Ndebele and Ngoni life that were perceived to have given the invaders their military prowess and economic wealth. By the 1880s, Shona warriors were making bold and successful cattle raids almost into the heart of Ndebele territory. Where did they get the courage? According to one Karanga informant, the answer is well known among the elders even down to the present generation: "I know the *ngochani* was traditionally done by chiefs and the leaders of soldiers here in Zimbabwe. The chiefs here were given strong medicines by the Ndebele and Zulu [Ngoni] *n'angas* ... I also know that even the Ndebele and Shona, when they were fighting, the soldiers they were made to have sex with other men for the whole group to be powerful. You see the Ndebele and Zulus were practising it since long back. But due to friendship, we Shona people have learned about that medicine from them and we are also doing it."[41]

The whites who colonized Mashonaland (1890) and Matabeleland (1893) were attuned neither to the subtleties of Shona/Ndebele relations nor to the role of sexuality in Shona and Ndebele cosmology. One missionary account, however, lends credence to the view expressed above that cultural exchange between two groups may have led to an increase in male-male *divisi rakaipa* among the Shona. Jesuit Father F.J. Richartz in 1896 described "sodomy" (and bestiality) as "simply common" in the Zezuru villages around Salisbury (Harare).[42] This he disgustedly attributed to their perversity in general. In fact, however, unbeknownst to Richartz, the Zezuru at that very moment were preparing to join other Ndebele and Shona groups in a desperate but relatively well-coordinated uprising against colonial rule. Could it be that such "sodomy" as the good father heard rumour of was an element in the rebels' preparations to drive him and his kind out of the country once and for all?

Sexuality in pre-modern Zimbabwe clearly did not conform to the idealized heterosexuality that contemporary African leaders prefer to claim as African tradition. Certainly the ancestors of the Shona and Ndebele of today placed great emphasis on sex as a means to reproduction, but they also did not associate it with either romantic notions of individual love or personal gratification. On the contrary, sex done properly with procreation in mind connected the individual to the family, to ancestors, and ultimately to God. Sex done properly had direct material benefits to the individual, the extended family, and the state. It was a means to good standing in the community and was understood as essential to good health. So strong were the injunctions to do sex properly that breaking them acquired special symbolic power. Depending on how the ostensible cause or intent were diagnosed, the transgression of sexual norms could generate powerful *muti* for good or evil.

The hegemony of heteronormative culture in pre-modern Zimbabwe was sustained in part by sometimes dire punishments for flagrant sexual transgression. But that hegemony was also preserved by allowing sexual transgressions to take place as long as they were explained in non-threatening terms – or better yet, not named at all. The ideal of heterosexual marriage resulting in numerous offspring for all adults was thus belied by enforced celibacy for large numbers of young men, by de facto celibacy (or adultery) for neglected wives of large-scale polygynists, and by a culture of discretion or respect for privacy that effectively enabled tolerance for a diversity of sexual behaviours or natures behind closed doors. Tellingly, even inmates in that most modern of institutions – prison – commonly justified their same-sex behaviour to researchers in Zimbabwe by appealing to "tradition" (Antonio 1997, 306).

Pre-modern sexualities were not immutable, however, and within the limitations of the sources one can discern changes in both normative and transgressive sexuality over time in relation to changes in the political economy. The transition from the gathering and hunting economy of the ancient Bushmen to the increasingly productive cattle-based economy of Bantu-speakers, for example, brought about increasing control by men over female sexuality through *lobola* and other institutions. This in turn gave rise to a class hierarchy and to state structures that imposed differential access to sexual outlet. These state and class structures were themselves buttressed by ritual sexual inversion, notably incest but also, at the time of greatest centralized power in the sixteenth and early seventeenth centuries, by a caste of at least discursively feminized male leaders and powerful heterosexually celibate women. With the decline of centralized power and of a semi-professional military among the Shona, the male ritual inversions (though not the female) were largely attenuated or abandoned altogether. The Ndebele and Ngoni invasions from the late 1830s, however, appear either to have revived or introduced new male-male sexual practices for specifically military and political purposes.

In short, sexuality in Zimbabwe on the eve of European conquest was both more diverse than has hitherto been recognized and in a state of flux. As we shall see, a striking irony in light of contemporary African accusations of Western sexual decadence is how scandalized many of the first Europeans in the region were by African willingness to bend supposed natural laws of sexuality.

2

Cities

The first European attempt to colonize Zimbabwe came from the east in the sixteenth century. This ultimately resulted in little more than a few isolated trading posts and itinerant Portuguese and mixed-race *sertanjeros* (backwoodsmen). The second and enduring attempt came from the south via the Cape Colony beginning in 1890. This was done through a complex mix of violence, chicanery, and high idealism, the legacy of which remains very much alive today. A rich historiography shows how colonial rule imposed internal borders, reified ethnic divisions, destabilized gender relations, denigrated indigenous culture, elevated colonial and Christian ethics, and introduced new ethnic minorities to the country. It set in motion the economic dynamics and environmental change that tended relatively to impoverish African communities while enriching white settlers. It also initiated the development of a "middle class" of educated Africans who adhered to Western ideologies of progress, development, and nationalism. That nationalism, when frustrated by settler intransigence and racism, eventually inspired war against the white settler regime. It culminated in 1980 with the achievement of political independence. Yet more than two decades after that achievement, Zimbabwean leaders are still urging citizens to decolonize. From land invasions to the empowerment of indigenous black entrepreneurs to a return to idealized African family values, nationalist politicians enjoin Zimbabweans to undo tenacious structures and cultural attitudes that were implanted in the colonial era.

Changes to the ways people felt, thought, talked about, and acted sexually were part and parcel of the colonial experience. They were recognized as such at the time. Changes in sexual propriety were in fact the topic of often heated debates and hyperbolic assertion. The journalist Lawrence Vambe, to give but one example, entitled a chapter in his book on the rise of African nationalism in the 1940s and '50s as, simply, "Sex, the Possible Main Root of the Racial Problem" (Vambe 1976, 107). Historians of Zimbabwe have also given considerable attention to exploring links between sexuality and the way that the colonial political economy and modern consumer society developed. As noted in the introductory chapter, Charles van Onselen's analysis of "sex in the service of industry" charted a course that now includes Diana Jeater on the "creation of perversion," Tim Burke on the "fetishization" of hygiene, and Jock McCulloch on the role of "Black Peril" discourses in the entrenchment of white male supremacy.

These studies help to explain the ambivalent decolonization process as it relates to sexual mores. But none of these historians has adequately treated the topic of same-sex sexual relations among Africans. In part this may be explained by their desire to respect presumed African sensitivities around a taboo behaviour, or by the assumption that homosexual relations were so rare that they paled in significance beside other issues. From the evidence in the previous chapter, however, we can see that this disregard is unwarranted. The ways that pre-modern Zimbabwean cultures expressed and explained non-normative sexuality held quite important ramifications for gender and class relations.

Moreover, queer historians from elsewhere (notably Foucault, whom many of the historians of Zimbabwe referred to above also cite) have shown that discourses around homosexuality were integral rather than peripheral to the construction of hegemonic masculinity in the modern era. A real man, this argument runs, could only be known by starkly defining what he was not. Any study of gender relations that neglects to consider how men have defined themselves as not-feminine or not-homosexual would therefore seem to be missing a crucial piece of the puzzle. This is particularly striking when significant numbers of presumably heterosexual men were in fact having sex with males, as van Onselen showed nearly a quarter of a century ago was the case in colonial Zimbabwe. The surprising thing is that it took President Robert Mugabe's crude denunciations of gays and lesbians to alert us to the need to search for the missing or neglected evidence.

The following three chapters will approach these questions. Understanding who did what sexually to whom, and how, when, where, and why they did it could help us understand the development of the hegemonic masculinity of the present. Understanding hegemonic masculinity may in turn help us to understand the gender dynamics that impede (for example) the effectiveness of anti-HIV and other sexual and social health campaigns or the development of "good governance" in contemporary Zimbabwe and elsewhere in the region. Before getting to the evidence of same-sex sexuality in early to mid-colonial Zimbabwe, however, we need to place the Zimbabwean experience in the context of its (dysfunctional) mother colonies. I begin this task by examining the earliest known incidences of *"venus monstrosa"* or "unnatural vice" as they were recorded by European colonists at the Cape and in the other territories that subsequently became South Africa – Natal, the Orange Free State, and Transvaal. The changes (and continuities) in sexual practices and discourses in early South Africa helped set the stage for subsequent transformations throughout the region.

The Dutch who established the first European colony at the Cape came from a society with the highest level of urbanization, the most vibrant international links, and the most developed humanistic legal traditions in Europe. Yet the Netherlands in the seventeenth and eighteenth centuries also experienced long periods of political domination by immoderate Calvinist factions who sought to impose their dour philosophy on the nation. Calvinism in its extreme form was intolerant of any sensuous pleasure, while sex that deviated from the prescribed norm was viewed as especially reprehensible. Thus, *venus monstrosa* (literally, "monstrous lust") was potentially a capital offence. *Venus monstrosa* included a wide range of sexual practices, from self-masturbation to heterosexual intercourse between a Christian and a Jew (Phillips 1999, 180). Male-male sodomy was at the high end of culpability. According to Jan Oosterhoff, cases that actually came to trial were rare but were "generally" punished by death (1988). Even rarer, but by their mere existence indicative of an unusual determination to discern and to punish all forms of same-sex sexuality, were the prosecutions of lesbian affairs that took place in the Netherlands in the eighteenth century (van der Meer 1997, Phillips 1999).

Both the apparent infrequency of these crimes and the severity of the punishment may have stemmed in part from a desire to distinguish a national Dutch identity from that of the former hated suzerains, the Spanish (whose Catholic faith was more amenable to self-confession and forgiveness for sins of this nature). Theo van der Meer has noted that when a network of Dutch men who had sex with men was revealed in 1730, the common outraged contention was that it had been introduced to Holland by their old depraved Catholic foes. A virtual witch-hunt then ensued that culminated in nearly eighty death sentences (1997, 1). A similar association in early seventeenth century England was made in the form of anonymous accusations of sodomy against King James I, part of a wider attack upon his purportedly over-tolerant attitude toward Catholics and the Spanish (Shepherd 1996, 110). An irony in this "sodomy is un-Protestant" construct is that the Spanish themselves otherized their colonial subjects in much the same way. As Richard Trexler has shown (1995), Spanish accounts from the period characterized native Americans as *passivos* worthy of contempt (and conquest), while sodomy among Spaniards was viewed as an infection derived from the Moors.

In the isolated outpost of Kaapstadt (Cape Town), male-male sexuality seems to have assumed a somewhat higher profile than back home. Kaapstadt had been established in 1652 as a refreshment stop for ships making the arduous journey between Europe and the Far East. Unlike the Portuguese, who refreshed themselves on their journeys to the East among the large, heterosexually hospitable societies of West Africa, Dutch sailors came to a port with a scanty local population. Employees of the Dutch East Indies Company, meanwhile, rarely brought their wives and were prohibited by law from taking concubines locally. The number of female slaves available to cater to the men's sexual needs was also sharply limited. Over the first century of Dutch rule, males outnumbered females among slave shipments by as much as eight to one (Shell 1994, 17), while as late as 1770 there were 360 males to every 100 female slaves throughout the colony (Elphick and Shell 1979, 200). This imbalance "forced" men to turn to each other and to animals for sexual release, according to Ross (1979, 432). Oosterhoff (1988) reports that one to five cases of sodomy were tried at the Cape per year over the course of the eighteenth century, an amount equal to as much as 10 per cent of all criminal cases in any given year.

Shortage of females cannot by itself explain why male-male sexuality was more visible and presumably more common at the Cape than at home. An additional factor may be that same-sex practices were not uncommon and particularly prohibited among the local Khoi peoples, as ethnographies and travellers later recorded.[1] As well, most of the imported slaves came from Madagascar, the Indian subcontinent, and southeast Asia, ancient civilizations where same-sex sexuality was well known and even at times extolled in the literature. As many as 750 were housed together in a teeming slave lodge near the port. Ross reports a married slave couple living there in 1725, as well as other isolated cases of heterosexual monogamy. For the majority of the men so confined, however, as well as the sailors coming ashore after months at sea and faced with a relative dearth of female prostitutes, heterosexual contact was simply not an option. They thus looked for sexual release in disapproved ways to an extent that kept company officials relatively busy.

The Kaapstadt sodomy trials included bestiality and cases where confessions had been extracted through torture. Punishments included imprisonment on desolate Robben Island, likely contributing to what Ross describes as "a definite homosexual culture" in the penal colony (1979, 431). The determination to expunge the community of the guilty also went to the extent of destroying valuable property. On 13 May 1728, for instance, two unnamed slaves were condemned to death for sodomy.[2] Sexual relations across racial and class lines were also prosecuted, including the case in 1735 of Dutch sailor Rijkaart Jacobse and the "Hottentot" Claas Blank (Reid 2002, Newton-King 2002), and in 1751 an un-named couple noted by Ross (1979, 431, footnote 48). In another case from 1753, three men of different races were found guilty of consensual anal sex, bound together, and thrown to their deaths in the harbour (Oosterhoff 1988, 231).

When the British took over the Cape Colony for good in 1806 they maintained the local jurisprudence, which they referred to as Roman-Dutch law, but interpreted it according to British precedents. By precedent and in principle, British magistrates shared the Dutch revulsion against sodomy, which they similarly ascribed to despised Latin, Catholic, and oriental cultures. In practice, however, the harsh Dutch regime was quickly tempered. Both the frequency of trials and the severity of punishments diminished. Indeed, by the 1830s, years sometimes went by without a single such case. The cruelty of drowning for male-male sexual crimes was replaced by hanging as the form of capital punishment.

Several factors may explain the diminishing visibility and seriousness of male-male sexual crime under British rule. First is the fact that in 1808 the British stopped slave imports. The rapid creolization of the slave population, together with the deliberate efforts to colonize the territory with English settlers, put to an end the enormous gender imbalance of the Dutch period. This meant that heterosex at the port became more cheaply and conveniently accessible. That element of the itinerant population that was not particularly discriminating about sexual partners was able to find satisfaction in more conventional brothels than had been the case under the Dutch regime. A growing population also created an urban milieu in which it was easier for men who preferred sex with males to evade the gaze of the law.

The decline in cases of male-male sexual crime may also reflect a pragmatic approach to administration by the British. It was politically imprudent to make unnecessary impositions upon a potentially rebellious population of Dutch (or Boer) property-owners in a context of severe labour shortages. Jailing, whipping, or executing the Boers' valuable property would hardly have endeared them to British rule. This factor is certainly suggested by the tendency towards lighter sentences meted out as punishment for male-male sexual assault. Only two death sentences appear ever to have been carried out for such crimes under British rule at the Cape. These were Fortuin, a slave in Graaff-Reinet in 1830, and Adam January, a "Bastard Hottentot" (that is, mixed-race Khoi) in Swellendam in 1852.[3] A third death sentence was carried out upon one Hogoza in the nearby colony of Natal in 1868, the last known execution for sodomy in the region. This, however, was clearly anomalous, and may reflect the fact that the accused had aggravated the charges against him by attempting to bribe the police.[4] Convictions by this time more typically resulted in sentences of three to ten years in prison.

The need for caution in administering capital punishment for sodomy was finally made explicit in 1871, on the eve of the Cape Colony's attainment of responsible government and about a decade after the repeal of the death penalty for sodomy in Britain. The governor himself intervened effectively to preclude future executions for this crime under British rule at the Cape. The case involved a European teacher named Albertus Frederick la Brookes who had been found guilty of brutally assaulting several of his pupils and sentenced to death by the circuit court of Clanwilliam. Reviewing the case, Sir Henry Barkly reduced that sentence to life in prison in solitary confinement with hard labour and fifty lashes. He explained his "leniency" to the Colonial Office on the grounds that "the feeling of society is everywhere opposed to Death Punishment save in so far as it may be deemed essential for the protection of human life," the "ancient severity [of Roman-Dutch law] having fallen into desuetude" in consequence. Barkly even expressed fleeting regret over the Adam January case, the last execution to have been carried out in the Cape Colony nearly two decades previously. The poor "Bastard" had been hanged, in Barkly's opinion, more "from inadvertence on the part of the Government than from proved necessity or deliberate design."[5]

The frontier of white settlement and colonial jurisprudence expanded continuously throughout the nineteenth century, as well as attracting refugees or migrants from Bantu-speaking societies of "the interior." These societies shared much in common with the Shona and Ndebele discussed in the previous chapter. The first European observers noted that they had strong imperatives for heterosexual reproduction and that they made close associations between fertility/virility and good health and spirituality.[6] Europeans also took note of the range and relative ease of Bantu-speakers' heterosexual arrangements and rituals. Presumably consequent upon all of the above, same-sex practices were seen to be rare. It was generally assumed, for example, that male-male sexual conduct among the Xhosa was "unnecessary" because of the ease with which men and youths could gratify their lusts by sex with females. This easy gratification included non-penetrative thigh-sex with girls known as *ukumetsha (hlobonga* among the Zulu, and *gangisa* among the Tsonga), and seemingly wide-spread and relatively consequence-free adultery. It was also generally assumed by early European commentators that African women and girls were virtual chattels to be disposed of at the will of their male owners. Enquiries about female-female sexuality/sensuality were thus not pursued, even when certain common practices such as woman-woman marriage, the lengthening of labia majora, and girls' initiation schools were potentially lesbian-like.

As in pre-modern Zimbabwe, there are hints that more was going on behind closed doors and behind carefully constructed social fictions than crude enquiries about "unnatural crime" would admit. It was sometimes whispered about the great Zulu leader, Shaka, for example, that he ordered his warriors not only to abstain from sex with females but to gird them-selves for battle by sex with their boy servants (as Bullock alludes, 1950, 254–5). Recent anthropologies from South Africa have also shown how same-sex acts and behaviours could take place without necessarily being regarded as criminal, unnatural, or even sexual. Indeed, discreet same-sex relations were allowed for, respected, and possibly even expected in certain specific circumstances. Njinge and Alberton (2002), notably, confirm what Ngubane (1977) and Bozongwana (1983) have described about the power of gender inversion among Zulu traditional healers (*sangomas*). Customary attitudes towards gender inversion and around the interrelatedness of orgasm, blood, and health did not simply vanish as Bantu-speakers were incorporated in the expanding colonial culture. On the contrary, notions about the medicinal value of male-male sex acts come through in one of the first cases of sodomy involving Bantu-speaking Africans to be heard by an urban magistrate in the region. In this case from Durban in 1880, a Zulu youth named Umkongwana alleged that fellow servant Jim alias Uhliza had penetrated him anally while he was sleeping. Uhliza did not deny his actions when confronted. He allegedly defended his behaviour with the claim that "I am trying to take the salt out of you," a selfless act reflecting the traditional belief that the penis sucks in whatever it encounters from its surroundings during ejaculation.[7]

Male-male sex for *muti* (medicine) was unlikely to have been a common practice and was certainly not seen or commented upon by missionaries as a concern. However, the missionaries did early on perceive a grave danger in a sexual culture that was governed primarily by obligations and appearances to the external community rather than to an internalized god-voice – by shame, in other words, rather than by guilt. No matter how sternly, patriarchally heteronormative that culture might be, it would be vulnerable when the source of shaming was removed.

Doubts about the stability of heterosexual norms among Bantu-speaking Africans in fact began to surface almost as soon as the frontiers of settlement, of Christianity, and of cash as a medium of exchange washed over them. As early as the 1850s, notably, Resident Magistrate William Girdwood denounced the way that Fingoes (Mfengu) were being settled in European-style villages. The new geography, he argued, when combined with education and Christian ideas was engendering new, unspecified, but eminently undesirable sexual practices. As he warned in a highly suggestive turn of phrase, Africans' physical proximity to each other in the modern-style villages turned the villages into "*unnatural* [my emphasis] religious hotbeds liable to be choked with the rank growth of vice."[8]

Girdwood may have been referring to heterosexual affairs outside of marriage. The fact is, however, that charges of male-male sexual assaults by Bantu-speakers upon their countrymen began to crop up in British courts as early as 1860: that is, soon after Africans began to take up employment in the growing white cities and farms but well before the development of the closed compound system. Udelela in Natal was the first identifiably Bantu-speaking African to be charged and convicted of attempted sodomy.[9] Probably Zulu, Udelela was sentenced in Pietermaritzburg to fifty lashes followed by eighteen months of imprisonment with hard labour. A handful of other Zulu, "Basutos," and "Itonga" men and boys over the next few years then joined the multinational trickle of accused and accusers appearing before the magistrates of the Cape and Natal.

By 1886 the instability of African sexuality in the new urban environment was sufficient for Durban's superintendent of police, W. Fraser, to issue a confidential warning to the colonial government. Although Fraser was responding to concerns about Black Peril type assaults on white women, he also explained that "nine-tenths of the female Natives of this City are prostitutes, either secret or declared, and the greater number of them more or less diseased; alien Natives residing here, and those youths who from time to time seek service amongst us, fully aware of the danger they run in consorting with such women, *avoid them to a great extent, and seek other means of gratifying their passions.*" He went on to explain how, "where there exists no direct outlet for certain passions, hideous crimes and unnatural offences constantly crop up."[10] "Reliable," a correspondent to the *Natal Advertiser,* was the first to publicly name those offences by alleging a black male assault upon a white male boy.[11]

A small number of these early criminal cases involved drunken, racist, and abusive European men who used their power to coerce African males to submit to a sex act.[12] Overall, however, there is no evidence to show a pattern of white tutelage, nor a direct corrupting influence from Cape Town and Durban, nor that the males involved were simply passing through an adolescent phase. On the contrary, the ages of the men or boys so charged ranged widely. Hogoza was a mere seventeen or eighteen years old when he was executed for sodomy in 1868, but Jim Zulu was forty when he indecently assaulted John Booi (1892).[13] Ndukwana kaMbengwana was no less than fifty-seven years old at the time he was propositioned in the streets of Ladysmith by a group of British soldiers in 1900 (Webb and Wright 1986, 341). Ndukwana seems to have been scandalized by this proposition, which he recalled to the missionary Alfred Bryant with some bitterness decades after the fact. His testimony is at least suggestive, however, that British soldiers had had previous successes in offering cash for sex to mature African men. (See also Qalizwe in Webb and Wright 2001, 247).

The first hint that something more profound was taking place than these isolated incidents might suggest, and that a new type of male-male sexual relationship was beginning to emerge among black Africans in the burgeoning industrial centres, comes from the year 1885. Zulu independence had just been crushed, large swathes of land had been alienated to white farmers, and a vicious civil war had catastrophically undermined the traditional subsistence and tributary economy. Dispossessed Zulu men were increasingly joining the thousands of Shangaans who already tramped through northern Natal on their way to and from the diamond mines at Kimberly. Kimberly, a patch of hardscrabble farms in 1869, was by this time a bustling city with a sex ratio that made Cape Town under the Dutch look balanced in comparison. By 1878 there were approximately 25,000 African men working there, mostly housed in barracks on the property of the different mining companies. In 1885 the first of these compounds was closed off by fencing, ostensibly to prevent diamond smuggling but also to prevent the men from getting into trouble or getting drunk and sick from the canteens that had sprung up around the town. De Beers's West End compound alone enclosed over three thousand men within four acres (Harries 1994, 67). Ad hoc huts and small barracks were replaced by huge hostels divided into rooms where, typically, between eight and sixteen men shared bunks together.

Ladysmith was a transportation hub en route to the mines. In September 1885, five Zulu men employed by the railway at Ladysmith lodged accusations of indecent assault against their overseer, an Austrian named

Gerhard Maria Hager.[14] The complainants ranged in age from twenty to twenty-five years. They testified that they had acceded to Hager's propositions to have sex in spite of the shame and fear that it provoked in them. They had then initially kept quiet about it because, in the words of twenty-year-old Tabalana, Hager was "one of our masters" and they feared his power. Hager denied everything and successfully argued that he was the victim of an extortion attempt. That may or may not be true. Of interest here, however, is the whiff of uncertainty about Tabalana's testimony that the court translator inserted in the transcript of the trial. Very unusually, the original Zulu word – *nkotsana* – was included in parentheses following "masters," as if the translator were not fully confident about what he had just heard. Indeed, "masters" for this type of relationship should have been *amankosi* or, allowing for an unusual stretch in meaning, *amankhosana* (singular, *inkosana*). The "t" sound makes a big difference and is unlikely to have been a careless error. So why did the translator seem confused? Was Tabalana employing a new slang word unfamiliar to him? Given that a respectable court translator is unlikely to have been *au courant* about sexual innovations and argot among youth, it may well be that Tabalana actually let slip to an uncomprehending court that he was one of the accused's "boy wives." Tabalana's own admission of being seduced (with gin and talk of sex with girls) rather than raped further hints at this possibility.

Did the *nkotshana* relationship originate in Kimberly, the progenitor of the closed compound system, thence to spread along the main transport routes and other industrial centres? The criminal court records from Kimberly unfortunately do not shed light on the question.[15] Certainly, however, the city in later years was well known as a place where "sodomy is prevalent," a fact also alluded to by the Sesotho vernacular for the city ("Sotoma").[16] Given how almost the exact conditions that prevailed at Kimberly were later identified as "causing" *nkotshana* in Johannesburg (male-only hostels and a heavy presence of Shangaan migrants), it would be surprising if the practice, if not the word to describe it, cannot ultimately be traced back to Kimberly. This would be a significant finding, for if so, it would underscore a point made earlier and which will resurface abundantly in later evidence. It was not difficult for African men to move from a strongly heteronormative culture to one in which those norms were violated on a regular basis. Rather than a decade or two of resistance to the homosexual temptations implicit in the male-only compounds, it may have been only a matter of months.

The most unequivocal statement that significant numbers of African men began having sex with African males through their own initiative comes in Nongoloza Mathebula's testimonial to the director of Prisons in 1912.

Nongoloza, alias Jan Note, was reflecting back on his years as leader of the criminal gang, the Ninevites or 28s. This gang became infamous in the late 1890s for both their vicious criminality and their active, predatory preference for sex with males, a reputation that it keeps to this day. The director of Prisons maintained in his commentary on the interview that the Ninevites had acquired this preference from Mozambican labourers at the mines. However, Nongoloza's actual testimony makes no such claim. Quite to the contrary, he explicitly denied that male-male sexual preference was a strictly mine compound or prison phenomenon: "As to the practice of hlabonga which you complain of as existing among the Ninevites in gaol, in that the soldiers subject the piccanins to immoral practices, *that has always existed*. Even when we were free on the hills south of Johannesburg some of us had women and others had young men for sexual purposes."[17] Unlike his interlocutor (and indeed, later historians), Nongoloza did not attempt to explain this behaviour or attribute to it any particular function. It just was.

It was, however, becoming known to the mine owners, government officials, and missionaries from as early as 1892 – that is, barely six years after the discovery of gold and the commencement of large-scale industrial activity on the Witwatersrand. One Chopi ex-miner testified in 1907 that it "prevailed" when he first arrived at Glencairn and Crown Reef mines around that time, while a European compound manager recalled that *nkotshane* was already "common" in 1896.[18] Testimony by African witnesses about an attempt to repress it by the Shangaan king Gungunyana (exiled 1895) also suggests that it was well known from this early period. As the official enquiry into the matter explained, "The common legend throughout the mines is that a Shangaan named 'Sokisi' had, while in prison [circa 1892–95], practiced unnatural vice, and that he introduced the custom of keeping 'izinkotshane' at the Brakpan mines, from whence it spread" (Leary/Taberer 1907, 2).

No conclusive documentary record of Sokisi has yet been found.[19] We may, however, safely put to rest the suggestion by Krouse and Berman (1993, 64) that "Sokisi" was a metaphorical reference to the knee socks that mine workers wore (and, thence, to the life they lived). We may similarly put to rest van Onselen's speculation that he was the Ninevite leader George Schoko (1982, 179, 181), with whom Nongoloza was allied in the early 1910s. "Diamond" testified at the same enquiry that Sokisi was already dead by that time, and indeed, all of the witnesses in 1907 who spoke about him used a vaguely distant past tense. Sokisi is remembered as well in oral evidence taken from as far afield as central Zimbabwe, a century after his exploits:

Yes, I heard and I know about *ngochani*. The word comes from Shangaan people and their king [*Ishe*], Socks. The word means sex between man and man, that is, just joining. The men who do this are men who are afraid of STDs, which was common at that time in South Africa. The disease was serious – it made the penis rot and the only cure was to cut the penis off. *Ishe* Socks who was in South Africa is the one who found homosexuals as the best solution because the disease was coming from prostitutes. Those women were fewer than men, that's why they had the disease. They were the only suppliers of sex at our Stilfontein [?] and Brivol [sic] gold mines. I was there and I can say even us people from Rhodesia, we were doing *ngochani*.[20]

Sokisi may have been a real historical person, but his name nonetheless came to acquire a metaphoric quality in the expression *umteto ka Sokisi*, meaning "the rules of mine marriage" (Moodie 1994, 128). According to witnesses from the 1907 enquiry right up to informants in the 1980s, *umteto ka Sokisi* specified a very precise etiquette, the violation of which was harshly punishable. Notably, it prohibited anal penetration and con-fined the sex between males to the model of *hlobonga*, the between-the-thighs sex widely practised in the region (with parental approval) between adolescent girls and boys. The junior partner, *inkotshane*, also known as *nsati* ("wife") or *umfaan* ("young boy"), was not allowed to reciprocate. In addition to providing an outlet for the senior partner (*nuna* or "hus-band"), the *inkotshane* performed many of the other tasks typically performed by women in Shangaan (and other Bantu-speaking) society, including cooking, fetching water and firewood, and sending messages: "In return for these services, the 'inkotshane' is well fed and paid, presents and luxuries are lavished upon him, and he appears generally not to object to his lot" (Leary/Taberer 1907, 2). Later accounts, particularly Junod (1962), Sibuyi (1993), and Niehaus (2002), describe the *inkotshane* as adopting feminine attire, wearing false breasts fashioned from coconuts, putting on scent, keeping their faces well-shaven, and even sipping wine or other sweet liquors (as opposed to the "husband's" manly swilling of beer). Sokisi himself was reputed to have taken many *izinkotshane*, whom he main-tained in the style of a harem.

The Anglo-Boer War of 1899 interrupted this aspect of the emergent migrant culture by bringing mine production to a standstill. When peace was restored, however, many of the Mozambicans came back to work in apparent anticipation of Sokisi's rules. They brought with them young boys in such numbers and of such youthfulness that official eyebrows on both sides of the border began to rise in concern. When rumours drifted back to

Portuguese authorities that the *umfaans* were performing more than the usual services, concern turned to outrage. In July 1902 the governor-general of Mozambique made a formal representation to the secretary for Native Affairs for South Africa, Sir Godfrey Lagden, about the suspected sexual exploitation of African boys by men at the mines.[21] Lagden acted promptly by ordering his district inspectors to make discreet, informal enquiries about it.

The reports that came back were of divided opinion. At one extreme was the inspector for Boksburg, Charles Pieterson. Shocked when he learned of the existence of *nkotshane* in his district, Pieterson raised the alarm. "I deem it my duty," he wrote, "to draw your attention to the fact, that the crime of sodomy has in the past been extensively practiced by natives in the Compounds. Although it is but seldom that a culprit is brought to justice – owing to the extreme difficulty in obtaining evidence sufficient to convict – cases have occasionally been brought before the Courts. I would beg to suggest that the umfaans in every Compound be segregated from the adults, and that it be a punishable Offence on the part of a Compound Overseer should he allow any umfaan to sleep in an adults [sic] room or vice versa."[22]

The chief inspector of the Native Affairs Department, a Mr Pritchard, at first conceded there was a problem, but he urged Lagden to exercise caution: "This is a point with which I think it inadvisable for us to interfere. It is a common practice among natives and would be impossible in my opinion for an Inspector to cope with."[23] Pritchard subsequently retreated from his use of the word "common," suggesting that those who had described the practice this way were exaggerating. This view may also have been whispered in Lagden's ear by influential mine owners. Indeed, as Pieterson later testified, the Chamber of Mines directly contradicted his 1902 report in an effort to suppress further enquiry (Leary/Taberer 1907, 29 January 15). The Portuguese concerns were duly fobbed off.

The main reasons for this reluctance to pursue enquiry, and the willingness to risk relations with a neighbouring colonial power by ignoring its official representations, are not difficult to discern. British plans for the rapid reconstruction of the postwar economy were threatened by a critical shortage of industrial labour, in particular at the gold mines. African men were simply not pitching up to sell their muscle power in the numbers that were needed to make the mines productive and profitable again; the wages being offered were too low and the work too dangerous to be attractive. Moreover, white workers had tightened their pre-war stranglehold on the best-paid jobs and the definition of "skill" which effectively blocked

African advancement. Many of the Africans who had returned for work in 1901–02 thus deserted when they saw how conditions had worsened. From the point of view of the government and the mine owners, adding to Africans' reluctance to remain at the mines by making intrusive enquiries into their sexual behaviour hardly seemed worth the risk. Hence, it was not just the Portuguese that were fobbed off. The top Johannesburg detective also raised the issue in his submission to the 1904–05 South Africa Native Affairs Commission. He not only maintained that "unnatural offences are very prevalent in the mines among the Natives" but also described a dramatic suicide that stemmed from a broken homosexual affair.[24] No further investigation resulted.

Yet soon after the incipient scandals of 1902–05 had been hushed up, new and potentially more damaging allegations surfaced. These were sparked by another controversial policy, the importation of indentured labourers from China. Between 1904 and 1906, the Chamber of Mines contracted over sixty thousand of these men. Their labour proved crucial to getting the mines back into full operation and to undermining the dangerous bargaining power of both white and African workers. Indeed, by 1905–06 the average monthly wages for Africans had been pushed down to 80 per cent of what they had been in 1890.[25] White workers also suffered cuts. Even worse, however, they feared that the Chinese would eventually be used to break the white monopoly on the better-paying jobs. Opposition to the Chinese was consequently intense. White workers staged several violent strikes and lobbied to win political support from white small-scale traders and farmers. Much of this anti-Chinese campaign was overtly racist and emphasized the moral shortcomings that the "coolies" were purportedly bringing to the country (such as addiction to gambling). When this failed to dissuade the Chamber of Mines, the smear tactics and fear-mongering became more extreme. In 1905 the rumour was spread that there were "catamites" (or passive sodomists) among the Chinese labourers. One missionary actually maintained that the Chinese men's hostels were full of professional homosexual prostitutes, that they serviced clients in the open field, even in view of passing European women, and that they were teaching "unnatural vice" to the African workers.[26]

"Chinese slavery" in South Africa was already a controversial political issue back in Britain, and these inflammatory accusations soon resounded in Westminster. A formal commission of enquiry was hastily launched. One suspects that this was more to appease the critics and contain the damage than to find evidence that might substantiate the allegations and force government to change its policy. The Bucknill enquiry nonetheless did identify a small number of said catamites, who were duly deported with attendant publicity. But it also concluded that these were isolated cases and that the vast majority of Chinese men were in fact probably more "moral" than the white workers in that they did not spend their hard-earned wages on drink or prostitutes. Calls to repatriate the Chinese en masse on moral grounds were thus stilled. Conveniently, the governor-general was even able to use the same stone to kill a third bird. He took advantage of Bucknill's enquiry to cast aspersions on the Portuguese, perhaps to pre-empt further meddling from them about labour conditions: "So far as the vice prevails at all among the Kaffirs, its prevalence is due to the fact that some of the Portuguese have the Eastern, rather than the Western view of this matter. There is no evidence whatever that they [African workers] have been contaminated by the Chinese."[27]

This might have been the end of the story but for a missionary who worked among African men in the mine compounds of the Johannesburg area. The Reverend Albert Baker had followed the outcry against the Chinese and in all good conscience rebelled against the Bucknill enquiry's understatement of male-male sexual conduct among African workers. "Unnatural vice" among Africans, he claimed in a letter to the governor-general, was in fact much more widespread than it had ever been among the Chinese. Moreover, unlike the few so-called catamites who were paid or given favours for their services, Baker alleged that homosexual relations among Africans often involved coercion, child abuse, corruption of authority, and violence extending right up to murder. The worst offenders were the compound police to whose abuses the mine owners allegedly turned a blind eye. Baker named names and demanded an immediate investigation to root out the evil.[28]

Baker, it should be added, was not insensitive to the labour shortage issue, and for that reason he claimed in his letter to have repressed his own private indignation about the men's behaviour for several years. Now that the secret was out, however, and that the word "sodomy" had been pronounced in no less a place than British Parliament, he felt obliged to speak. The government had little choice but to respond to such serious charges, which it did expeditiously. It did so, as well, with apparently less cynicism than had been the case with the Chinese enquiry. Two eminently respected officials were appointed – J. Glenn Leary, a magistrate, and Henry M. Taberer, a fluent Xhosa-speaker then with the Native Affairs Department. Their mandate was to determine the extent of the problem and to propose solutions that would satisfy the Rev. Baker and other missionaries – without, of course, impugning the proud reputation of British imperialism or endangering the profitable extraction of gold. So instructed, Leary and Taberer toured the major mining compounds on the Rand. Over the space of nine days in January 1907, they gathered testimony from fifty-four African and European witnesses, including workers, "picannins," "boss boys," managers, mine inspectors, medical doctors, and missionaries. The questions they asked, and the answers they received, were remarkably explicit about sexual activity and motives for why the men were doing as they did.

Leary and Taberer submitted to government the following month an eight-page summary of the evidence that they had gathered. It dismissed two of the Rev. Baker's key allegations, namely that the men in these relationships were formally married with traditional bridewealth or *lobola* and that violence was endemic to homosexual relationships on the mines. The report's main conclusion, however, was that Baker's claims "were to a large extent justified." Although Leary and Taberer maintained that the practice of keeping *izinkotshane* was mostly confined to the "East Coast boys" (primarily the Shangaans), these men constituted around two-thirds of the total African work force at the time.

The extent of the practice could thus hardly be clearer, but it is worth going straight to the testimony of the witnesses themselves to get a fuller appreciation. The men volunteered such words as "common," "a good deal," "many," "universal," "widespread," "practically all," "often," "very greatly," "everyone," and "pretty general" to describe it. One (European) witness described how, out of eleven new recruits at his mine, eight were taken as *izinkotshane* by the next day (R.O. Tillard, 24 January, 8). Another witness, Benjamin, an African guard, offered: "The custom is very prevalent on the mines. The natives would not stay here so much if it were not for this thing ... If this practice did not prevail the tribes would all go home ... *There is no grown-up man who has not got his 'inkotshane'*" (29 January, 3, my emphasis).

In light of such evidence, the government could clearly no longer pretend that large-scale migrant labour and the mine hostel environment had not facilitated the emergence of a kind of behaviour among African workers that brought disrepute to British policy. The sole consolation, such as it was, was that "actual sodomy" (meaning anal penetration) was "very rare and is generally looked upon with disgust" (Leary/Taberer, 3). The government would nevertheless need to be seen to be taking action to clean up, as one author later phrased it, "the slimy depths where man craves man" (Lewis [1933] 1984, 111).

As discussed in the introductory chapter, Dunbar Moodie and Patrick Harries have attempted to explain why the Shangaans in particular invented and popularized *nkotshane*, why it was carefully constrained by rules, and how the practice affected African working-class culture both at the mines and back home. Conceding a possible leadership role by Sokisi, they emphasized Leary and Taberer's more fundamental explanation. Mozambican men outnumbered Mozambican women in the Johannesburg area in 1896 by an estimated thirty thousand to ninety, a greater disparity than any of the other main groups of African workers.[29] Leary and Taberer speculated in passing that men of any nationality, even "civilized" Europeans, might be induced to homosexual acts by such an imbalance between the sexes.

Harries (1994) offers an additional insight that is supported to some extent by the testimony other Africans gave to Leary and Taberer about Shangaan women, as well as by Henri Junod's 1916 ethnography. Shangaan society customarily accorded women a relatively large degree of sexual and social autonomy: "They are a sort of loose people," one Zulu man explained to the commissioners, "far different from the Zulu" (23 January, 3). Shangaan men who migrated thus could not expect their betrothed or their wives to remain faithful if the men did not continually earn that faithfulness with regular remittances and other gifts. For a man to squander his mine earnings or his health in the brothels of Johannesburg was to risk returning home a laughable cuckold facing an impoverished, childless, landless future. Shangaan men sought to protect their rural-based sense of masculinity from such a fate by engaging in safe sex with boys, an interpretation also supported by Moodie. Rather than any sensual desire for the boys as physical males, such arousal as took place by the husband did so because the boys enacted an idealized gender role, the stereotype of a submissive wife. The potentially radical act of mutual anal penetration (or, presumably, other forms of mutual stimulation) was banned because it endangered this fundamentally conservative, if not reactionary, culture of masculinity.

Achmat (1993) and Spurlin (2001) have criticized Moodie and Harries as overly functionalist, naïve in accepting affirmations about the non-existence of anal penetration, and disregardful of the possibility of same-sex desire among African men, a desire that they imply is an antecedent to contemporary radical queer identity. To be fair, however, Harries and Moodie do acknowledge this possibility, and indeed Moodie has been criticized for almost romanticizing the positive elements of male-male love at the mines and downplaying the violence (see Breckenridge 1990). Again to be fair, those African men who have spoken nostalgically of *izinkotshane* have tended to emphasize the gift-giving, the cuddling, or the loyalty between the partners rather than any particular attraction to male physiques or an eroticized transgression of taboos.[30] African men themselves also fairly consistently prefer the functionalist interpretation to justify their behaviour. As Chopi miner Bob Zandamela explained to Leary and Taberer, for example, "I think they prefer young men. I think the reason is that they are afraid of getting disease."[31] The fact that there were dramatically lower rates of venereal disease among Shangaans compared to those Africans who went to female prostitutes seemed to vindicate that view.

Achmat and Spurlin thus overstate their critique of Moodie's work in particular. Nonetheless, the actual testimony given to Leary and Taberer (as opposed to their summary report) does support their broad intention of querying the conventional rationalizations of male-male sexual relations among Africans at the mines (and in prisons, which Achmat implicitly presents as analogous). Significant conflicting evidence to the dominant view can in fact be found in the testimony given to Leary and Taberer. This evidence was dismissed or denied in the final report and has similarly been disregarded in subsequent official and missionary characterizations of *nkotshane*. But it calls into question the neat analysis of *nkotshane* as a strictly rule-bound, essentially conservative, and Shangaan-specific phenomenon.

For the remainder of this chapter I would like to draw on the voices of the men themselves to highlight some of those contradictions, and hence to gain a more nuanced understanding of the meanings of male-male sexual relations for the millions of African men and boys who passed through the mine compounds between the 1890s and the 1970s.

First of all, we need to be clear that Leary and Taberer were not neutral in their enquiries. The major voice throughout the gathering of testimony (and presumably in shaping the final report) was clearly that of Taberer, an ambitious man who at the time was seeking to establish his career at the head of the emerging labour recruitment bureaucracy. We can safely assume that a report that was over-critical of the mine companies or over-sympathetic to African workers would have compromised those ambitions. For Taberer, blame had to be apportioned very carefully on such a sensitive topic – meaning, in a manner that did not challenge the dominant discourse around race and colonial rule. The period immediately after the Anglo-Boer war was particularly fraught in that respect. Powerful British interests favoured a quick rapprochement with the defeated Boers. This implied the betrayal of those Africans who had supported the war against the Boers, who hoped that Britain would honour its promises of a racially just political dispensation. Africans in town, meanwhile, implied a physical proximity with the growing population of urban white women. This gave rise to an anxiety, almost verging on hysteria, about sexual intimacy between the two groups. Several Black Peril panics gripped Transvaal, Natal, and Southern Rhodesia in the years from 1902 to 1916, resulting in executions of African men.[32] In this context, Taberer's careerism alone would have tended to confirm prior assumptions and prejudices stemming from the dominant discourse.

That discourse flowed from a long tradition that exoticized, otherized, or pathologized African sexuality. In the seventeenth and eighteenth century, the travel stories, novels, and ethnographies on the topic that circulated in Europe were often simply and unabashedly salacious (Castilhon 1990 [1769], Bleys 1995). "Researches" in the mid-nineteenth century were couched in more scientific-sounding language, but the construction of an essential difference between Africans as primitive and whites as civilized continued. Similarly, prejudice against same-sex sexuality survived the transition from pre-industrial moral discourses to the scientific language of Taberer's day.

The result is evident from the way Leary and Taberer prompted or even necessitated answers from witnesses to their commission that confirmed the sensual, sexual otherness of both Africans and homosexuality. The façade of objective sociological enquiry is immediately belied by the way that the commissioners made known their repugnance for the "obnoxious and loathsome custom" that they were charged to investigate. We can only surmise what disapproving looks and tone of voice are hidden from the transcription. The constant probing for "remedies" or "cures" and the use of descriptive words like "offenders," "this thing," or "the other thing" left little doubt that they regarded same-sex sexuality as a disgusting, pathological condition.

We can see quite clearly from the leading questions, moreover, that the two men preferred their witnesses not to challenge pre-existing theories of contagion and racial hierarchy. One particularly strong prejudice was that African men themselves were too primitive or too lacking in the level of imagination assumed to be necessary for non-procreative sex. Homosexuality, after all, when not construed as a disease, was a "refinement of immorality" (as Henri Junod subsequently phrased it). Since Africans were judged to be unrefined by definition, they must therefore have learned the practice from elsewhere. That the witnesses did not always cooperate fully in confirming this prejudice is suggestive of the commissioners' eagerness in that respect:

(Mr Taberer) I have heard that the Portuguese soldiers practice this with your people? – [Phillip Nyampule] I have heard so. I have not seen it to my knowledge. [18 January, 12]

(Mr Taberer) Do you know that the Portuguese soldiery on the East Coast practice sodomy? – [Picannin] I have never heard of it but I have not been home for the last few years. [21 January, 5]

By comparision, Leary and Taberer found their European witnesses effusively cooperative in confirming the above long-standing prejudice among Britons. Indeed, contagion from Portuguese or Arab sources appeared to be self-evident to the British witnesses. Where the commissioners had to prompt their African witnesses with leading questions about Portuguese "habits," for example, several of the British blithely offered their personal opinions. "I dare say it is an Eastern habit," intoned one, while another claimed, "This thing comes from the East" (29 January, 7, 17).

The non-African origins of *nkotshane* were spelled out even more explicitly in a subsequent enquiry. The judicial inspector of Johannesburg, for example, submitted in 1916 that "Tropical Natives, who have been initiated to revolting practices by the Arabs, have introduced them in the Transvaal Compounds and the infection has unfortunately spread." The inspector of Randfontein South maintained, "It is certain that the practice is very common among the Latin races on the Mediterranean seaboard" and that "the spread of Mohammedism" in Africa only exacerbated it.[33] To some extent, then, the Shangaans were seen as casualities of their position on the frontline of contact with degraded non-African "races." Lack of contact with Arab or Portuguese sources of contagion is what had presumably spared the non-Shangaan Africans on the mines.

Orientalism of this nature subtly served an important though politically delicate objective that Leary and Taberer shared by virtue, if nothing else, of their positions in the colonial bureaucracy. It allowed the commissioners discreetly to reassert in an apparently neutral or scientific form one of the foundational myths of colonial rule in Africa, viz., Africans were a childlike race in need of protection by a mature ward (say, for example, the British). One sees this subtext writ in several ways, notably by the report's dismissal of evidence that pointed to an indigenous Shangaan origin to male-male sexual relations. The majority of witnesses explicitly denied such an origin, true, but the fact remains that several of the witnesses did refer to a customary relationship known as *mgane* or *mgami* (literally "friend" but metaphorically closer to the expression "bosom buddy" or the Shona term *sahwira*).[34] One European witness reported that his East Coast employees "admitted that at home a man had a boy when he went traveling. The man who carries the mat is the 'inkotshane'" (A. Norton, 28 January, 14). Intriguingly, this claim of an indigenous Shangaan origin had also been

made during the enquiry into Chinese practices (and was similarly disregarded). Ed Constable, the mayor of Boksburg, had then submitted that
"There is little doubt that the Natives from the East Coast – particularly
Shangaans – are far more addicted to the practice than the Coolies, and I
believe pursue it in their own Kraals, where they have their women folk."[35]

Whatever the nature of *mgane* or other sexually intimate behaviours
between males back home, the fact that witnesses invoked it as an analogy
to *nkotshane* is an important piece of evidence that corroborates my earlier
argument: pre-modern African society was more accommodating to discreet sexual diversity than first appearances and loud assertions to the
contrary might suggest. The fact that Leary and Taberer ruled this evidence
out of serious consideration thus suggests that they were not interested in
complicating their understanding of African primitiveness/simplicity. This
narrative of African childishness, passivity, and undeveloped or brutish
sexuality can be seen as well in Leary and Taberer's striking lack of interest
in questioning the Sokisi theory of origin. So deficient were Africans
assumed to be in the core of individual identity that supposedly defined
civilized man that if a chief ordered men to have sex with each other, then
of course they would *sans hésitation*. Similarly, it was suggested that the
mine owners themselves might have actively abetted the practice as a form
of safe sex that protected (and attracted or stabilized) their workforce.
To assert that African men needed to (and could) be directed in their
sexual desires and decisions by their white bosses was not considered in
the least unreasonable.

This is not to deny that Sokisi likely was a powerful, charismatic role
model or that European managers did perceive advantage and therefore
encouraged same-sex relations among their African workers. Some came
close to admitting as much by expressing the view that the proposed
"cures" would almost certainly be worse than the malady.[36] However,
contemporary scholars need to be very careful about uncritically accepting
Leary and Taberer's more unequivocal conclusions. In fact, on closer
inspection the idea that African men were just following orders to engage
in "unnatural" behaviour is not merely counter-intuitive but is also contradicted by the evident self-confidence of the African men and boys
themselves. Notwithstanding how opaque the mirror is through which we
see them, the African witnesses display the full panoply of human emotions
and motivations – deviousness, anger, humour, curiosity, fear, greed,
respect, disrespect, loneliness, and so on. They do not give the impression
of being passive victims or empty vessels. Rather, they are men who had
made their own choices, choices that they were willing to defend even at

the risk of incurring their white bosses' wrath. A common theme emerges that these choices were not inherently wrong or unnatural. According to one compound manager, "They do not take the trouble to report it [*nkotshane*] because they look upon it as more or less natural. It is the custom in their homes" (28 January, 13).

Many of the European witnesses and commentators afterwards interpreted this self-confidence, this lack of guilt, as evidence of African men's brutish inability to feel finer, civilized sensibilities. As an exasperated Junod later put it, "The worst aspect of the situation is that the immense majority of the Natives themselves do not consider this sin as of any importance at all. They speak of it with laughter" (Junod [1916] 1962, 495). Yet the evidence given to Leary and Taberer shows that African men *did* try to keep their behaviour discreet. With rare exceptions, the African witnesses denied that they themselves had ever been involved in *nkotshane* (although they readily conceded that it was common among others). Some responded to intrusive questions about it or clumsy entrapments in an obviously taciturn or resentful manner, while one European reported that African men had sharply rebuked him for making enquiries. Moreover, while certain rituals and talk were allowed or even celebrated in public, the actual affairs were intensely private. They took place in silence behind screens or blankets in the hostels or in the darkness underground. A sole witness could be found to have seen "men" (his word) actually engaged in the act (18 January, 5–6). Not one person, even the most hostile of the African guards and inspectors, testified to overhearing any sexual activity despite the crowded conditions of the hostels.

The claim that African men were shameless about their same-sex sexual affairs was thus expedient to affirming colonial and missionary paternalism but ultimately was not fully believed by even the most racist European witnesses. Two of the main ideas put forward during the enquiry as "remedies" in fact focused on denying the men their already minimal privacy so as to elicit (an implicitly existing) sense of shame. The first suggestion was to remove all curtains around beds, behind which the actual sex took place, and so expose the guilty parties to condemnation by their peers. The second suggestion came from the indefatigable Reverend Baker. He advised publicizing the men's behaviour to their wives and betrotheds back home. In the face of the women's "abhorrence," he argued, the men's aberration would quickly cease (18 January, 5). Junod later related a story that implied the same solution. A Shangaan miner who had taken his wife's brother as an *nkotshane* purportedly returned home to be publicly shamed and divorced by his in-laws (Junod [1916] 1962, 495). The inspector of

Native Affairs for Johannesburg East developed this idea even further with his 1916 proposal to deport the guilty back home wearing women's dresses or a "badge of shame ... specially devised to excite the ridicule, or scorn, of all beholders."[37]

Leary and Taberer did not test this assumption about African women's abhorrence by interviewing any women on the subject. They also accepted (indeed, clearly prompted) testimony from those African witnesses who expressed the strongest revulsion and asserted the harshest punishments for sex between men in traditional terms (the Zulu above all). On this basis, Leary and Taberer decided to spare the "boys" the humiliation or danger of reporting their practices back home. In retrospect, however, we know that many claims made by African men about African women's ignorance and about patriarchal customs (like the death sentence for adultery and "unnatural crime") were overstated at the time. Some later sources suggest that this was the case in this instance as well, and that African women were in fact well aware of *nkotshane*. Interestingly, for example, it was Mark Mathabane's mother, rather than male relatives or peers, who warned him to stay away from the hostels for that reason (Mathabane 1986, 68–74). Women as wives may actually have been well disposed towards it for some of the same functional reasons as the men. Pule Hlohoangwane's remarkable account of his female "co-wife" in the Orange Free State mining town of Virginia, for example, has her expressing gratitude that her husband's "girlfriend" was male rather than a real rival, as a female wife would be (Alberton and Reid 2000). Or, as "Philemon" described to Mpande wa Sibuyi (with reference to the 1930s to '50s):

They knew it! They knew that once a man was on the mines, he had a boy or was turned into a "wife" himself.

So, how did they feel about it? Weren't they angry about it?

No, why should they be angry? Besides that, even if they knew, what would they do? Nothing![38]

There are further contradictions between the Leary and Taberer summary and some of their own evidence that should cause us to exercise caution in reading both that and subsequent reports. They claimed, for example, that *nkotshane* was "exclusively confined" to Africans from Mozambique. This indeed was the predominant view among the witnesses. Other ethnic groups are nonetheless mentioned, notably men from British Central Africa (modern-day Malawi) and from "Zambezis," the latter including Shona-speakers from northern Zimbabwe and central Mozambique. One Zulu cast doubts upon the Basotho. It is important to note as well that the word "Shangaan" was often used colloquially for Ndau, Shona-speakers of southeast Zimbabwe. At least one witness did in fact come from there ("Melsetta," that is, present-day Chimanimani, Zimbabwe). James Ngonyafia was coy about his own past as an *nkotshane*. However, he did make an important point about openness of ethnic lines that Leary and Taberer did not care to listen to: "The tribes do not specialise," he explained; "the men take boys from any tribe" (18 January, 11).

Suggestively, the word *inkotshane* was thought by a Zulu witness to derive from the Zulu word *ulukutshane*, meaning, "a foul-mouthed and filthy woman or a low sort of concubine" (25 January, 15). This raises some interesting questions. Why would Shangaans have adopted a Zulu word in this way? Did they pick it up on their way through Zululand to Kimberly, or were they poking fun at their old Zulu enemies? Or, was it a Zulu-ized (or "Kitchen Kaffir") form of a Shangaan term? Junod speculated that the latter was the case, and that it was a corruption of an old word from the "Bilen country" – that is, near Delagoa Bay (Junod [1916] 1962, 493–4). It meant an unmarried girl who had slept in the boys' hut where she had presumably satisfied her lover's desire by thigh sex, against propriety. Regrettably, none of the Shangaan witnesses provide their own explanation.

Whatever the etymology, the word was unquestionably multinational in nature by 1907. A criminal court case tried that year over a thousand kilometres north of Johannesburg uncovered familiarity with the word across quite a range of African languages. Forty-year old Bisamu, a "boss boy" at a small mine near Bulawayo, Southern Rhodesia, stood accused by fifteen-year-old Lindunda of assaulting him between the thighs while he was asleep. Tesitified Lindunda, "I got up and said 'what are you doing? I am a man and not a woman.' He said it was nothing and that I was a 'ngotshana.' An 'ingotshana' is a small boy who is used by the Zambesi boys on the mine as a wife."[39] Bisamu was described in the court record as a "Tonka" or "Zambesi," that is (probably), a Tonga from the middle Zambezi valley. The constable who arrested him testified that they spoke in siNdebele. Lindunda, meanwhile, was an "Umlozi" (Lozi of Bartoseland or western Zambia) whose language derived from Sotho/Tswana. The spelling in the court transcript reflects a Shona pronunciation.

Another disjuncture between the Leary and Taberer final report and the testimony that they gathered relates to the sex acts themselves. While most of their witnesses agreed that thigh sex was the main practice, and that to stray from the norm was regarded by co-workers as a punishable offence, quite a few claimed that anal penetration was also done. The testimony of Phillip Nyampule is especially powerful on this point. Nyampule, a Chopi from southern Mozambique, was one of the few witnesses who freely admitted both to having been an *nkotshane* himself and to having used them as the dominant partner during his sixteen years at the mines (starting in 1890 or '91). He not only claimed to have done both thigh sex and anal penetration, equally and on both receiving and giving ends, but that such relations were not confined to men and boys. On the contrary, he explicitly disagreed with one of the "remedies" that Leary mooted to him on the grounds that "I do not think the separation of the boys from the men would have any effect because the grown-up men do it themselves, with each other. Because the men practice it amongst themselves the little boys also practice it with each other" (18 January, 13).

Zephania Dhlamini, a Zulu guard at the Jubilee mine, was a hostile witness who condemned the Shangaan as a "filthy lot." His testimony, however, corroborates that of Nyampule as well as the accusations made by the missionaries who had first lodged complaints about "unnatural vice":

(Mr Taberer): Do you consider that much actual sodomy is carried on? – I do not know how much, but before the war cases came to my notice when I was at the Salisbury Mine where sodomy was actually committed. It was the custom of the boy operated upon to insist on the operator giving him £5 as a present. The custom is for the boy to wash himself thoroughly and then besmear his legs and thighs with fat; this is done to facilitate the operation.[40]

Leary and Taberer declined to include this information in their final report, or to acknowledge other testimony that would have qualified their stronger assertions about the near-universality of *hlobonga*. Their determination to minimize the existence of "actual sodomy" went to the extent of challenging witnesses with leading questions, not always successfully. The following exchange, for example, took place between Leary and Ronald Tillard, the compound manager at the Meyer and Charlton mine for the previous four or five years. I reproduce it at length because it suggests that the commissioners played an active role in constructing a neat but significantly misleading picture of African men's behaviour:

(Mr Glen Leary): What is the definition of the word? – An "inkotshane" is a youngster who allows another man to commit sodomy with him.

What do you call sodomy? – I mean actual sodomy.

We have had witnesses who say that it is connection between the thighs? – No. I take it it is actual sodomy.

Has any case been brought to your notice? – Yes ...

You know that amongst the tribes in their own country the boys are allowed to sleep with girls so long as there is not penetration, and that the thing is acknowledged by the parents? – Yes.

Do you not think the same thing exists between the boys? – I cannot say I do, because one always hears the mine guards say "this boy was 'inkotshane' to so-and-so," and if I ask them what do they tell me straight away. It is purely and simply sodomy (24 January, 6–7).

Penetration where it happened would have been facilitated by the elaborate greasing of the "wife" by the "husband" described by several witnesses. As Skwaimana explained in response to a question from Taberer about whether men give their *izinkotshane* presents: "Yes and feed them well. They give almost all their money away like that. It is common in the mines and openly done for the boys before they go to sleep with the men to wash themselves and then besmear themselves with fat round their middles. They do not besmear their whole body" (25 January, 16).

Other witnesses alluded to apparently professional *izinkotshane* with numerous "husbands" (possibly prostitutes, who moved from compound to compound in search of liaisons), men with multiple "wives," public kissing, sexual jealousy, and lovers who absconded together from the mines when disciplined by managers. The *umteto ka sokisi*, in other words, seem to have been honoured in the breach to a noteworthy extent. Certainly, enough references to mutuality and reciprocity exist to make us question the rigidity of the idealized traditional husband/wife or older man/youth model that Leary and Taberer asserted. We need to be attentive here as well to the colonial discourse that often failed to differentiate between Africans who physically were boys and those who physically were men. In fact, the "boys" in question were often old enough to be considered young men by physical criteria. The preferred ages were said to be fifteen to twenty years old, but one case is suggestive of even greater maturity obscured in the language of African boy-ness: "I have a case just now where both boys were reported as deserters. *Both were grown men* and they were carrying this thing on to a great extent. I have had them repeatedly before the magistrate for being absent without leave. That is a case where they carried it on underground. I discharged the 'husband' and immediately afterwards the other boy deserted" (25 January, 8–9, my emphasis).

Such cases were memorable because they were so unusual and so unambiguous in their demonstration of male-male desire. For most men, the ultimate desirability of sexual intercourse with women was never in question.

One witness in fact maintained that the men who took boy wives were also the main consumers of sex with female prostitutes (25 January, 10). This is a noteworthy point in that it forces us to qualify the "shortage of women" explanation for the men's sexual choices. Women were available for sex, albeit in a position to make fairly high demands for their services. At Robinson Mine, for example, a Native location right on the property was home to fifty-two women; (at the time there were 2,600 men employed at the mine – 25 January, 5, 10). At Langlaate Deep, women at "a terrible place" serviced men from the neighbouring property, a short walk away:

(Mr Leary) A lot of wash boys congregate there? – Yes.
  (Mr Taberer) Are there many loose women? – Yes.
  Do the boys visit them? – Yes. (25 January, 4)

For Bande, an M'Chopi at City and Suburban Mine, the availability of women made the very idea of being or taking an *nkotshane* absurd. "If I want I go to the location and get a woman" (21 January, 3).

Why did other men not simply do the same? Some argued that the main concern was fear of catching a sexually transmitted disease from the women, potentially leading to a painful death in poverty and shame. There is little doubt that vaginal intercourse was indeed risky in the circumstances. Yet these were men who had widely practised *hlobonga* with females back home. Why would they not appreciate the prophylactic possibilities of the practice in town? Why would mature men from a strongly heteronormative society choose to have thigh sex with young males rather than females, even to the extent of defending the practice in sometimes violent competition with other men over the male "wives"?

The answer to this question probably lies more in the hegemonic construction of masculinity than in any rational calculation of health advantages. Firstly, *hlobonga* back home was primarily understood as an adolescent form of sexuality. Real men penetrated and impregnated. To do *hlobonga* with women in town was thus demeaning to the men at a symbolic level. Better than stooping to such boyishness was to raise *hlobonga* so it enabled a more appropriately masculine performance of power-over, particularly when transgressive sexuality carried strong potential for *muti* in some of the cultures involved.

Secondly, the women in town were by definition untraditional. Assertive as Shangaan women were reputed to be back home, their negotiating skills and levers were all the more effective in the context of their low numbers in town. Such women were known to parlay a pregnancy (even by another man) into long-term financial obligations. As Bande explained, "The men do not go in for the women because they cannot recover the money from the women afterwards" (21 January, 3).

For the male "wives," meanwhile, there were likewise mixed motives and sometimes-subtle discrepancies between how their acquiescence in the role was commonly explained. To begin with, the Shangaan, like other African cultures in the region, were gerontocratic. Young men and boys were expected to do as their elders told them. Some who resisted may have been raped or otherwise forced against their will to become *izinkotshane*. Most, however, seemed to have been persuaded into the relationship by the gifts and the protection that they received in return. They saw it primarily as a patron/client arrangement, rather than a masculine/feminine one. This implied an eventual graduation from client to patron as they matured and acquired self-confidence and independent earnings.

Another point at which individual agency entered was when to make the graduation or when to negotiate a more mutual relationship. Some may have calculated that remaining in the wife role was cost beneficial in comparison to relationships with relatively scarce, possibly syphilitic, and untraditionally assertive female prostitutes. The possibility of sexual and emotional intimacy free from the profound gender tensions and pressures to perform characteristic of heterosexual intercourse would also have entered into the decision. Indeed, because *nkotshane* did not involve potential impregnation and social judgment in the eyes of the community back home, the act may not have been regarded as sex at all. The intimate component of taking or being an *nkotshane* was more likely seen as recreation or play, companionship, or simple release of stress, all much needed in the otherwise dehumanizing atmosphere of compound life.

Yet *nkotshane* could lead to the development of quite strong feelings of attachment. For example, although Tail denied having sexual connection with his "husband," Jasi, he did describe the relationship in the fondest terms: "I love Jasi. We exchange presents and money. I am his 'inkotshane.' When he is cold he sleeps on my chest" (24 January, 4). Even stronger emotions were apparently at play in an earlier case described by police inspector T.E. Mavrogordate. As he told the Native Affairs Commission, "the other day a Kafir committed suicide by throwing himself down a shaft, and the reason attributed for his doing was that his boy had left him and gone to somebody else."[41]

Given what we know (or rather, know we do not know) about sexuality today, evidence of such a diversity of motivations and sentiments should hardly be surprising. One anecdote from the testimony given to Leary and

Taberer does, however, hint at the truly unexpected – sex as political theatre. Nothing in the testimony even remotely suggests the existence of a politically assertive, timeless gay archetype. Yet if it wasn't gay rights, there was at least a whiff of revolution against traditional patriarchal authority in the attitude of some of the men involved. Notably, Zephania Dhlamini's account of Sokisi makes us question the argument that *nkotshane* was a strategy to preserve nostalgic ideals of masculinity and custom among the miners. It seems that the Shangaan king, Gungunyana, had heard about Sokisi openly consorting with *izinkotshane* and had ordered him to return to Mozambique to be punished. Sokisi not only flouted the command and defiantly remained in Transvaal with his consorts: he also cheekily re-christened his principal *nkotshane* Sonile, the name of Gungunyana's chief wife (23 January, 9).

Finally, on the question of *lobola*, Leary and Taberer were correct to reject the claims by Baker (and later, Junod) that boys were formally *lobolaed*. Unlike in the traditional *lobola* relationship, an *nkotshane* earned an independent income as a mineworker. With these earnings, and with the gifts he received from his "husband," he could eventually refund any payments made to his elders and clear himself from any "marital" obligations. The fact remains, however, that gifts and payments were given to family members both as a means to overcome "wives'" reluctance and to stabilize unions that were otherwise in constant danger of fission. As James Ngonyana explained, "The boys like being 'inkotshane' because of the pay they receive *and the money their fathers get*" (18 January, 11, my emphasis). The sums of money involved were surprisingly large – the £10 one witness mentioned was equivalent to several months' wages and in excess of most commoners' traditional *lobola* payments. Others refer to payments of five shillings to £1 per sexual act and up to £5 for anal penetration, payments that could hasten the return home from the mines with savings and good health. By 1916, inflation had driven the sum for a monthly arrangement up to £15 ("a favourite amount") and even £25 (Junod, 493), not including the liquor and the animals that had to be sacrificed at the "wedding." Those elaborate weddings actually led one NAD inspector to recommend the prohibition of sheep and goat killing in compounds as a key deterrent to *nkotshane*.[42] I suggest that it further supports the claim that male-male sexual relations were not formerly as scandalous as African patriarchs have since protested. They themselves were not above either exploiting such relationships for personal gain or enjoying them for the fun that they offered.

Given the constraints under which Leary and Taberer were unofficially operating (viz., do not embarrass your employers, do not say anything that might destabilize an already difficult labour situation), and given the racist, sexist, and homophobic assumptions that they brought to bear upon their investigation, their ultimate recommendations were not very radical. Some of the bolder suggestions made to Leary and Taberer were in fact candidly ruled out of hand. It just was not on, for example, to allow large numbers of female wives to immigrate from Mozambique or other migrant labour reserves. Nor could the government be seen to condone large-scale female prostitution, another mooted "solution." Other suggestions, like shaming the men in front of their families back home or having "the boys flogged judiciously with a proper instrument," were quietly dropped from the final report. The principal recommendation of the report to government was simply to tear down the screens and blankets behind which the men conducted their affairs. The practice of the men bringing very young boys with them from Mozambique was to be discouraged.

Leary and Taberer received effusive thanks for the distasteful services that they had performed and Government Notice 292 of 1907 was duly promulgated. Screens around beds were prohibited throughout all industrial compounds in South Africa on pain of £1 for the first offence and £5 for second. Yet even this feeble "solution" clearly worried government, and it appears that high officials acted almost immediately to undermine it. Godfrey Lagden was almost blunt on this point. Within a week of the report's submission, he wrote to the governor-general to warn of the possible consequences of enforcing Leary and Taberer's recommendations. "If these Native men are driven to locations and other haunts infected with Syphilis it is bound to have its bad results upon the men, and I have no doubt that a certain number of the men who have practised this habit for some years will as appears from the evidence in the enquiry leave the country."[43]

That Lagden's caution was taken to heart is suggested by the decided lack of zeal in policing the new edict thereafter. In spot searches of the criminal register of the Johannesburg area over the period between 1907 and 1912, I did not find a single charge laid, let alone conviction made, for blanket and screen offences. A follow-up circular by Taberer and Leary in 1911 conceded as much: *izinkotshane* remained "very prevalent," and perhaps "extra-judicial" deportations might be necessary to make the men take the new law seriously.[44] Curiously, the proposed punishment would be done "without reason" (that is, without naming the offence), allowing the men to infer from silence the horror of their crime. No documentary evidence remains to attest that any such summary deportations ever took place.

Not surprisingly, this lack of zeal by government and mining officials did not impress the missionaries. Henri Junod first entered the fray with a remarkable novel, *Zidji,* published in 1911 in French and German (that is, primarily directed at a Protestant missionary readership). *Zidji* included an explicit, polemical portrayal of a violent, pederastic *nkotshane* relationship. This was followed over the next few years by pressures for an investigation into the alleged rapid spread of the practice from Mozambicans to indigenous South African blacks. The spread was all the more alarming as it appeared to affect even those (such as the Zulu) who in 1907 had voiced some of the most unambiguously hostile sentiments to *nkotshane*. A confidential 1915 investigation by the NAD in response to these allegations called for better lighting and beds but otherwise suggested little more than to keep up Leary and Taberer's good work.[45] The issue surfaced again in 1928 when the Mpondo chiefs in Transkei raised their fears of contagion among Xhosa miners.[46] Yet again, however, government appeared to be more concerned with public relations than doing anything that might jeopardize the smooth flow of migrant labour. The chiefs were reassured that "the prevalence of the alleged practices has been greatly exaggerated," but that in any case, "When delinquents were detected they were rigorously dealt with according to law. Both the Government and the Mining Industry strongly disapproved and special measures were being adopted to suppress it."[47] With that pronouncement, further public debate was for all intents and purposes shut down.

Oral evidence taken in the 1990s is obviously not reliable for events and "secrets" of the 1910, '20s and '30s. It nonetheless does strongly corroborate the view that government and mine owners effectively did nothing to suppress *nkotshane*. Notwithstanding anti-*nkotshane* propaganda and gestures towards less private sleeping arrangements, African men continued to negotiate and to participate in new forms of sexual relationship with each other over the decades in a variety of ways. Violence was sometimes involved, and cases of what we would now term rape and child abuse caution us against interpretating *nkotshane* as a totally benign means to affirm masculine identity and dignity in an otherwise dispiriting environment. That said, however, most of the physical violence associated with *nkotshane* appears not to have been in the sex itself but rather was the result of conflicts between men over access to preferred *izinkotshane* or over money. Accounts of the sex reveal that while there was indeed a big inequality of power between the husband and wife, the wife was not merely a victim. Consent, negotiation, fun, and ritual were also part of the relationship.

Contemporary oral evidence supports as well the early twentieth century view that such relationships were a *majority* practice – Zimbabwean informants typically estimated that 70 per cent or even 80 per cent of the men at the mines took male sexual partners.⁴⁸ The reasons included both the modern (rational calculations of the risks of disease and economics, rebellion against patriarchal authority, individual sensual desire and emotional need) and the pre-modern (such as belief in the *muti* of transgressive sexuality, and the re-enactment of idealized gender roles that were getting harder and harder to achieve with actual females). As one middle-aged Zimbabwean man explained, recalling South African mines in the late 1960s:

They do that because of two things [sic]. First, some do it for safe sex because in mines there in South Africa women were very few so they were afraid of STDs. The other thing was their strong medicine like *Sandawana*. For a man to be rich he was sometimes forced to have sex with a particular woman. But if he has sex with a man, he will be very rich. It's a way to make the medicine to be more powerful ... The other thing is that they do it for pleasure. If the rich man has sex with a poor young boy, the boy gets paid. But if he finds pleasure in it he will continue even without payment.⁴⁹

These men (and evidently we are talking of millions over at least seven or eight decades) did not consider themselves "gay" or "homosexual" in the sense of having an innate sexual orientation or a political consciousness of their difference from heteronormative society. On the contrary, for the majority, having sex with males was not regarded as incompatible with heterosexual norms and ideals of masculinity. It would nonetheless be wrong to assume that *nkotshane* somehow existed in hermetic isolation from homosexual desire in a modern or subversive sense. Victor Mkhize alludes to this in his research on the origins of "a gay Zulu language" (*isinqumo*) that developed at the mines. He reports how awareness of same-sex relationships at the mines attracted young men who desired sex with males and who, discreetly, pulled other men towards an appreciation of the sensual possibilities:

In the old days some of the men used to dress up like women, especially in the weekends if there was a party – a gay party, of course. I was told that the parties were nothing but a camping spot where the queens used to find their boyfriends. The queens were the young boys who came to look for work. The older men used to promise them a better life if they slept with them. Not all of them were recruited like that. Some of them already knew about gay life and were gay. These are the ones who used to tell the young ones how to sleep with a man. That is where the language comes from: the queens did not want to be understood by outsiders, by straight people and their boyfriends (Mhkize 2001).

I will return to this theme – the inability to contain the widespread adoption of *nkotshane*, and its eventual elision with more unambiguously modern male-male sexual relationships – in subsequent chapters. For now, let us simply acknowledge one final point that the early, moralistic investigations into male-male sexual crime bring out about the history of homosexuality in southern Africa. Leary, Taberer, Junod, Lagden, and other European "Native experts" show how white racism and orientalist assumptions about non-whites pervaded official and missionary thinking at the time. Among other things, they tended to understate or deny African agency. Junod makes this point with entirely typical lack of humility: "The only conclusion I would offer on this painful subject is this. As white civilisation is responsible for the introduction and the frightful development of this vice amongst the Natives, the Whites must not remain indifferent in the face of an iniquity which threatens the very life of the South African Tribe" (495). European hubris, in other words, at least as much as African self-assurance about these matters, underpins the claim that male-male sexuality was un-African.

3

Outlaws

Early reports of male-male sexuality in South Africa point to another strand in the history of same-sex behaviour in the region: prison sex. Mine officials and police identified prisons and criminal gangs as the proximate source of the *nkotshane* infection at the mines, while scholarly analysis of the period commonly conflates the two places or passively assumes that prison sex and mine marriage were analogous. In fact, however, virtually none of Leary and Taberer's African witnesses made such claims. Indeed, a gangster to whom the propagation of sexual preferences has been attributed, Nongoloza Mathebula, explicitly denied a prison origin to his "system."

Moreover, as Niehaus (2002a) makes clear, prison environments were rarely directly comparable to the mine compounds. With the exception of the closed diamond mine compounds, most of the mines were ultimately open to the veldt and surrounding communities. Not only could the men there get out to nearby locations but also passers-by might wander close enough to observe unusual activities. The witness Willie, for instance, recalled to Leary: "As I was passing the mine, I came across a lot of boys washing and some natives jumped up and caught hold of me and asked me what I meant by walking past while the 'inkotshanes' were washing ... they wanted me to pay a penalty for having walked past and looked at those boys washing, but I refused" (Leary/Taberer 1907, 22 January, 4).

If the conflation of mine marriages and prison sex is misleading, it also carries dangerous political implications for human rights activists, in the sense that prison sex tends to be portrayed in an extremely negative way in popular culture in southern Africa, as elsewhere in the world.[1] Galgut (1982), for instance, portrays a teenaged petty criminal who first witnesses and then participates in homosexual rape during his incarceration at a boys' reformatory. Moses Dlamini tells spine-chilling stories of kidnapping, all-night gang rapes, and torture on Robben Island (1984) while Duiker (2001) depicts a black gay man who is brutally raped by ex-prisoners and members of an infamously "homosexual" gang. The very first discussion of lesbianism in the popular media in South Africa focused on the female gangster and former juvenile delinquent Gertie Williams (Chetty 1994). The lesbians recalled by former female inmates in Schreiner (1992, 52, 62, 203, 240–4) are almost as tough, fight-prone, and feared as male gang members. A sensationalized article in the Zimbabwean press hinted at popular fears that the recent emergence of "known lesbians" in that country might be linked to prison culture.[2]

In all of the above cases, "normal" heterosexuals are presented as innocent victims of aggressive, predatory, and/or wily criminals. It is a powerful image implying that violence is essential to situational homosexuality, a rhetorical staple to contemporary homophobes in the region.

Zackie Achmat (1993) argued against scholarship that unintentionally condones that stereotype. He even provided an eroticized account of his own first night in the lock-up, complete with an affectionate portrayal of the gangster he bedded. This may strike some as a romanticized reaction to the predominant homophobic or heterosexist accounts. More rigorous and extensive studies from the United States, however, also challenge stereotypes about prison sexuality. Contributors to Hensley (2002), for example, show that while fear of rape is indeed pervasive in American prisons, the actual incidence of physically coerced sex is far lower than commonly imagined – affecting from as few as less than 1 per cent of inmates to as high as 20 per cent, depending on definitions. In other words, the majority of same-sex experience falls in the category of negotiated and desired rather than violently imposed. Gear and Ngubeni's research in South Africa raises a similar possibility, not by quantifying sexual decisions and acts but by querying where the lines between coercion, negotiated consent, and actual desire can reasonably be drawn.

At the other extreme, meanwhile, the South African minister responsible for prisons reportedly claimed as recently as 1995 that there was no sex in prisons: "As I travel around I ask prison commanders and warders about homosexuality in prisons. They say nothing is happening. You might as well say sex in happening in monasteries and convents."[3] A spokesperson for the Zimbabwean prison service also denied allegations made against the system. Frank Meki claimed that it was "highly unlikely for acts, such as homosexuality, to occur in prison cells as guards were always present round the clock."[4] Indeed.

Important truths about gender and sexuality are bound to lie somewhere between the extremes presented in these various accounts. In this chapter, therefore, I would like to examine what we know about the actual history of same-sex sex in (mainly) South African prisons. The evidence is scanty, to be sure, and its interpretation is beset with profound methodological questions. Seen in light of recent studies of masculinity, however, even this sketchy history may help us to tease out threads of cruelty and coercion from desire in the construction of modern black African masculinity in southern Africa. Firstly, it allows us to assess the mine hostel experience in comparative perspective. Also, studies from the West have shown that gays and closeted gays tend disproportionately to be incarcerated relative to the wider population, whether from the sodomy laws or (more commonly) from antisocial behaviour arising from internalized homophobia and childhood sexual abuse.[5] Prison sexuality is therefore part of gay history, no matter how unpleasant and non-identified with gay politics it may be. Gear and Ngubeni suggest, moreover, that trauma caused by prison sex may be contributing to homophobic and misogynist sexuality in the wider society. The danger of sexual violence in prisons is enormously increased under conditions of severe overcrowding and malnutrition such as currently prevail in Zimbabwe.[6] A close consideration of the history of prison sexuality could thus help us to better understand the development of modern sexual identities in the region, from out gay and lesbian to overtly homophobic straight.

Early in its history South Africa became a prison-rich society. Crimes against property and crimes against an idealized racial and sexual order produced a high rate of incarceration, particularly for coloured and black African males as the frontier of colonial settlement and law expanded. Isolated incidents of sex among such men in prison were recorded almost right from the establishment of the first penal colony on Robben Island in the eighteenth century. Life sentences on this desolate island enabled long-running affairs like that between Claas Blank and Rijkhart Jacobz (1724–35). For the most part, though, prisoners who had sex with each other were not "true" or "incorrigible" sodomites, in the parlance of the early nineteenth century. Rather, it was widely understood that long-term isolation in a same-sex environment led otherwise "normal" men to release their pent-up sexual energy with partners of the same sex, usually on a short-term or purely opportunistic basis. Sheer boredom could lead to sex as a pastime.

By the late nineteenth century there was also a growing appreciation that prison culture actually encouraged men to have sex with men, if not necessitating it. Typically, for example, inmates experienced feelings of humiliation and powerlessness that created in some a desire to humiliate and disempower those even more vulnerable than themselves by acts of rape. The harshness of prison conditions also encouraged sexual deal-making for the smallest of pleasures or needs – a cigarette, a ration of food, a blanket to sleep under.

Men found guilty of sodomy in prison could be punished harshly. Under the British, however, Cape officials tended to regard these cases as a basi-cally inevitable and non-threatening side effect of the maintenance of law and order. If the prisoners were discreet and it helped to keep them quiet, then male-male sex aided in the smooth, fiscally prudent management of potentially violent inmates. Making an occasional example by flogging the less discreet offenders showed official disapproval, but beyond this no spe-cial attention or expenses were devoted to discouraging inmate affairs. The lack of zeal in suppressing prison sex eventually caused some concern to higher-ups in the British colonial bureaucracy. In 1872 the secretary of state for Colonies implicitly chastised the governor of Cape Colony on this issue: "I observe that it is stated by the Chief Justice and by the Executive Council that the crime of Sodomy is practiced in the Convict Stations of the Colony. I need hardly say that immediate and vigorous steps should be taken for putting an end to such a state of things."[7]

Those steps were never specified, nor were independent Cape initiatives forthcoming to any significant extent. Not surprisingly, therefore, and similar to the situation at the mines in the early 1900s, the issue continually resurfaced. In 1881 the jury in an indecent assault trial urged leniency in passing sentence because the state had self-evidently contributed to the offence by creating the conditions that led to the assaults in question. The prison dorms, the jury foreman noted, need "considerable improvement in the interests of morality and good order," above all the way up to five dozen prisoners were crammed together in a single, un-inspectable space.[8]

News once again reached the Colonial Office in 1908 that sexual acts were continuing to take place at the convict station. This came at a time when the British government was still smarting from embarrassment over the Chinese catamite scandal in Transvaal. Cape officials attempted to deflect the blame: "These unpleasant cases crop up from time to time in any penal establishment," the attorney general wrote in his defence against a stern reprimand from the Colonial Office, "and without in any way suggesting that there is any lack of proper discipline."[9] The under colonial secretary was clearly unmoved by this argument, and he wrote directly to the superintendent of the station in question: "The fact that it was possible for such abomination as the evidence reveals to have been committed in daylight at the Juvenile Convict Station without detection by the Guard on duty has caused the Colonial Secretary the greatest concern."[10] Indeed, it was "so great a scandal" of "such a prolonged occurrence" and "such deplorable events" that it suggested incompetence, complacency, or dereliction of duty at the administrative level.

Stung by this criticism, and by accusations against government arising out of the missionary campaigns against *nkotshane* on the Rand, prison officials in several colonies began to reflect on their previous complacency. They began to wonder as well whether the prison system were not contributing to, rather than mitigating, wider problems of African criminality and sexual deviance. The mining and industrial revolution that began in the late nineteenth century had brought a huge expansion of the numbers of men passing through the criminal justice system. The conditions they faced in prison were typically squalid, crowded, and brutalizing. Public enquiries and official introspection began to identify these conditions as inflaming an otherwise containable side effect into a major new malady. The minister of Native Affairs conceded as much in 1908 in response to a request by Christian missionaries. Practices in the Pretoria jail, he observed, in particular that of piling men with simple pass law infringements into crowded cells with hardened criminals and gangsters, "is not only calculated to spread but is actually spreading the evil of sodomy."[11]

The Leary/Taberer enquiry in 1907 also made the argument that specific penal practices were interacting with urban poverty, with the pass laws, and with the migrant labour hostels to foster a new and potentially dangerous homosexual subculture among African men. Mine officials, at least, clearly did not take the connections very seriously and for the most part continued to treat male-male sex in their compounds as a basically harmless and possibly beneficial foible of the African employees. The testimony of Nongoloza made shortly afterwards, however, exposed the danger in a compelling way. Indeed, Nongoloza's indifference or contempt toward European bourgeois morality on sexual matters, and his willingness to order the murder of whites as well as blacks who stood in his way, clearly shocked the prison authorities. They took the unprecedented and politically risky step of publishing Nongoloza's statement in the government's annual report on prisons.[12]

In this report, the director of Prisons frankly admitted to an embarrassing failure of policy that had allowed the homosexual gang, the Ninevites, to proliferate. He also offered his own analysis of Ninevite organization and philosophy. He described an apparent amalgam of traditional Zulu and Boer commando structures. Where Nongoloza had been somewhat coy about gang violence, however, or had characterized it as almost African nationalist in intent, the director drew attention to Ninevite cruelty to other Africans:

The organisation comprises besides this head, a judge for major cases and a magistrate or landdrost for minor cases, a fighting general, a so-called medical officer, the warriors and the younger natives who are termed the wives and made use of for sodomistic practices by the warriors. These organisations hold trials and decree punishments in some cases even sentencing to death by stabbing with a sharpened nail through the shoulders, or strangling with a wet towel or by putting powdered glass into the victim's food. The more usual punishments, however, are "tshaya sigubu" or striking in the ribs, the balloon punishment or throwing into the air, and the knocking out of the front teeth in the case of police informers.[13]

Nongoloza himself stressed that in his pre-prison days he and his men had an implicitly equal and free choice between women or young men as sex partners, but he hinted that the preference for males was at least partially a self-conscious political act. That is, by deliberately flouting one of the strongest taboos of respectable society, they defined themselves as the fiercest of rebels. The very name of the gang was a gesture against the systemic injustice of colonial society, a biblical reference to rebels against God.[14]

No specific reforms to the penal system were proposed in this report. Greater vigilance, it was implied, would have to serve to suppress the gang system. In this, no lessons were drawn from similar calls for vigilance then being made by the Native Affairs Department and the Chamber of Mines, to little effect. The result was that the Ninevites did not merely continue to terrorize their fellow prisoners but also carried their criminal activities into the mine hostels. This had something of a domino effect as non-Zulu African men formed themselves into defensive gangs modelled upon the Ninevite hierarchy. The very first such rival was in fact a breakaway from the Ninevites (28s) led by one of Nongoloza's own *indunas*, Kikilijaan. Informants in the late 1970s recalled that Kikilijaan formed his Scotland gang, or 27s, some time prior to 1907 primarily to escape from the homosexuality of his mentor (Haysom 1981, 4).

In another case, however, Mpondo gangs called *isitshozi* emulated the Ninevite preference for sex with males. Non-gang members were recruited by kidnapping or were subjected to an extorted "tax" for engaging in sex outside gang parameters. Breckenridge (1990) emphasizes how violent this could be. A boy who refused the sexual advances of a gang leader at Geldenhuis Deep in 1929, for example, was killed in punishment, while murders by disembowelment and wider inter-ethnic bloodletting were commonly associated with rivalry over "wives." According to Gary Kynoch (2000), the Basotho gangs known as the "Russians" arose in part as a defence against *isitshozi* attempts to control and presumably to extort a tax upon them. A confidential memo from the secretary of Native Affairs shows that the Mpondo gangs were still forcibly recruiting members to their homosexual system as late as 1939 (Breckenridge 1990, 60). This was well after having been pushed out of the mine compounds (the late 1920s), at a time when their primary area of activity was the brickfields, an informal settlement with a large female population.

Despite the publication of Nongoloza's statement and official worries about the spreading influence of gangs that practised and profited from male-male sex, authorities clearly lacked the imagination and the political will to actually do anything about it. Two subsequent investigations into prison or gang sexuality reveal how this paralysis of leadership and seemingly wilful ignorance contributed to entrenching the gang culture in the interwar years. The first of these investigations came in 1921 during the trial of two young men accused of sodomy at the Porter Reformatory in Tokai, near Cape Town. Inmates at Tokai were mostly Coloured or "poor white" (meaning, for the most part, Afrikaners). They ranged in age from teens to early twenties and slept in large open dorms with minimal adult supervision. The sodomy trial of 1921 revealed that the situation had in many ways deteriorated since first reports of apparently widespread and flagrant homosexual relations among the inmates there had surfaced back in 1908.

The accused in this case were Daniel Apon, charged with five counts of sodomy on four of his fellow inmates, and another "blue cap boy" or monitor named Jacobus Stout, who had allegedly aided and abetted in one of the assaults. The first victim to testify at the trial against the two was Edward Swanson. Eighteen years old, Swanson was eloquent in describing the events and the context of his repeated rape over a period of several months. "It is a common occurrence," he explained to the court, "and has been so whilst I have been there for boys to come from one bed to another. There was a secret gang amongst the boys. There was a lot of boys who did these naughty things which happened, about 15. The accused Apon was at the head of the gang." He went on, "I have heard the word 'Canary' used amongst the boys at the Reformatory. A 'canary' is the wife one boy makes of another boy ... The big boys keep the small boys as 'canaries.'"[15]

In a dorm of thirty-eight boys, Swanson estimated that at least fifteen were treated as canaries (possibly meaning that eight boys somehow managed to avoid involvement on one side or the other of the dorm's sexual arrangements). Considerable violence, to which officials turned a blind eye, was said to account for the high participation rate: "When the bigger boys do these things to the smaller boys and the littler boys try to scream the big boys close the little boys' mouths. When a little boy does scream a warder will come to the window and shout out 'Stop that noise' but he never comes inside the ward to see what is the matter." The big boys purportedly kept smuggled canes in the dorm with which to beat their victims and to enforce silence, including from other monitors. One monitor testified that yes, he had caught others in an act of gang rape but did not report it. "I knew that they would beat me, if I interfered, and that is why I did not do anything … None of the little boys complained to me about what had happened."

The boys' silence about such abuse was not merely from terror of retribution. It also reflected an acute perception of official incompetence, complicity, and/or apathy towards the victims. Gamat Beka, for example, testified that he had been raped by Stout. They were discovered by a warder right after the act in an obviously compromising position "but [Stout] then got off because his thing was not stiff." The warder then went on his way, leaving the first accused, Apon, to take his turn with the luckless Beka. Another of the witnesses also testified that the warders were utterly useless in protecting him. Michael Carelse maintained that he had complained four times about assaults, to no avail. Compounding the authorities' negligence in Carelse's case was the fact that his rapes occurred with easily preventable regularity at the same time every Saturday afternoon.

Despite the violence of the crimes for which Apon and Stout were found guilty, sentencing was light – fourteen days of additional time for Apon and twelve strokes with a cane for Stout. The magistrate seems to have been influenced towards such relative leniency by the expert testimony of the physician who had been called to testify. Dr Percy Stubbs had presented a list of contributory, mitigating factors to the crimes. He observed that Apon "was absolutely illiterate and came from a background where right and wrong were not well-established. The immorality begins in the houses from where these boys come, where in some places you have half a dozen families living in one house. Sodomy is also being practiced today in our public schools, and elsewhere." Rather than harsh punishments, the doctor advised, "What you should do is establish better homes for these people." Indeed, as he argued in support of leniency for the accused, "Sodomy is an evil as old as the hills, and we have outbreaks of it at intervals … The system at present in vogue conduces to immorality."

Making the link between male rape in prison and the poverty, illiteracy, and sexual abuse that abounded in the wider community removed much of the onus of guilt from the individuals involved. It also deflected pressure upon the authorities to invest in more humane conditions in the prison system and to investigate the behaviour of the warders. This was ultimately the effect of a second investigation into prison sexuality coming in the aftermath of a notorious murder case from Durban in 1929. In this case the accused and witnesses were almost all Zulu. The accused, Dhlamini, had killed the prison cook, Albert, following a dispute over his *umfaan* ("boy").[16] During the trial, the incredulous prosecutor J.P. Boshoff closely interrogated one of the witnesses to the crime: "What did the prisoner [Dhlamini] mean by 'my boy?' – He meant that his 'boy' had married the cook. In the gaol a 'boy' is used in the same way as a woman, sodamy [sic] is committed on him." Mr. Boshoff protested. "I don't understand. Is this what goes on in gaol? – Yes ... Not everyone of us, others do it." But why had the superintendent of the prison not been called to testify about such an outrage?

Crown counsel replied that he did not consider anything to be gained by so doing, as sodomy in prison was such a "wellknown fact." Boshoff nonetheless insisted that the superintendent be summoned to account. "I might mention," the latter duly informed the prosecutor, "that there is a system in the convict prison of 'wives' and the probability is that in many of these cases these assaults are caused from jealousy." It was quite simply impossible to stop, he maintained, as the "convicts keep guard and give warning when the officers are coming round."

A dumbfounded Boshoff announced upon hearing this information: "I do not want to say anything about the practice here today in this crowded Court." Rather than expose the public to further scandal, he sent the dossier on to his superior, the minister of Justice, who in response commissioned an enquiry "into alleged practice of sodomy in prisons." Its goal, in the words of the director of Prisons, was to determine which "drastic measures will have to be adopted to prevent a continuation of this disgusting practice."[17]

Little headway was made towards that ambitious goal. The one clear achievement of the enquiry on this occasion was simply to preserve on paper a host of defensive responses and rationales for inaction. Particularly sensitive was the hint of suggestion that slackness on the part of the guards was partially at fault. Not at all, the Durban authorities assured their bosses. In the first place, they could not be held responsible for a problem that was notorious throughout the country and was attributable to murderous and secretive gangs like the Ninevites and Scotland. Second, the *umfaan* relationship was "not necessarily" sexual but reflected traditional African client/patron relationships. Third, however, when it was sexual, it was "brought to light only by the complaint of an unwilling passive party and is not discoverable by other means" (implying that there were few unwilling passive parties and therefore the authorities had no way to catch them). And fourth, notwithstanding the above, "whenever there is any ground of suspicion that a convict is an addict [to sex with males] he is at once isolated."[18] In sum, ergo, no prison reform was necessary.

As if to take further wind out of the sterner, blanket condemnations of same-sex affairs in prison, the courts ultimately accepted the gist of Dhlamini's defence – that it was a crime of passion and thus less blameworthy than a premeditated act. Moreover, he was never charged with the additional offence of sodomy. While Dhlamini was eventually found guilty of murder and sentenced to life, the minister of Justice himself intervened with a plea for leniency to the governor-general. Dhlamini's sentence was subsequently reduced to fifteen years.

The status quo was confirmed over the following decades. Indeed, economic depression in the 1930s, changes of government, and the outbreak of World War II all provided ample excuse for prison bureaucrats not to do anything radical. The advent to power of the National Party in 1948, backed by and spouting the moralistic bromides of the Dutch Reformed Church, then further reduced the possibilities of meaningful prison reform along the lines that were starting to gain attention in the West (conjugal visits; suspended or more lenient sentencing; humane, responsive, and accountable prison authorities; better food; private quarters; and so on). First-hand accounts in the African press that began to appear in the 1950s thus indicated that the willy-nilly dumping together of increased numbers of detainees continued to be the norm in the city jails of Johannesburg. Extortion of sex from newcomers by gangs and the selling of sex for cigarettes and food also reportedly remained endemic.[19] As in the Dhlamini case above, the prison cook at Johannesburg Fort was deeply implicated in the "system" when the gangster Godfrey Moloi was an inmate there. The cook (Mzimba) was well known not only for his sexual appetite but also for abusing his ability to barter food for other men's "brides." According to Moloi, Mzimba ultimately paid for that abuse when gang members set him up for public humiliation and punishment by the guards (Moloi 1987, 156).

The apartheid era actually exacerbated many of the conditions that allowed for such abuses. Above all, it created a huge expansion of the numbers of Africans entering the prison system for pass law violations and political charges. There was also a climate of virtual impunity for corrupt and abusive warders, with chronic hunger and a deteriorating infrastructure.

Moses Dlamini, a Pan-African Congress leader incarcerated for his political beliefs in 1963, provides an especially damning account of those conditions in the early 1960s. Among other horrors, he describes (and names) wardens who incited and seemed to take vicarious sadistic pleasure from criminal gang members who terrorized and humiliated the political prisoners (Dlamini 1984, especially pages 111 and 156). Indeed, the Robben Island prison authorities not only tolerated the homosexual system of the Big Fives but actively colluded with the gang in the selection of "wives" from the incoming prisoners.

Other accounts from men who spent time in various types of jails from the 1960s onwards confirm the bleak and deteriorating situation for inmates. According to Niehaus's informants, for example, there could be as many as hundred inmates to a single cell. "When Elleck Malatsi and thirteen other Comrades were held in custody in a storeroom at the Tsakane police station, they slept on a cement floor, were issued with only eight blankets, could not wash, and were fed only oranges and bananas ... Unlike the dormitories of the mining compounds, inmates of the prisons were not segregated by ethnicity or by the category of crime they had committed. Basotho, Shangaan and Zulu robbers, rapists and murderers shared the same cells" (2002a, 87). Female institutions were hardly better. Indeed, referring mostly to the 1980s, Barbara Schreiner's informants describe warders who mixed political prisoners with convicted murderers and used the threat of lesbian gangs to instil fear in the inmates (Schreiner 1992).

When the first academic studies of prison conditions began to appear in the 1970s and '80s, they found many of the same gangs and social dynamics as Nongoloza had described in the 1910s. Haysom (1981) found that the 28s still defiantly and violently retained their sexual preference for males over a century after Nongoloza purportedly initiated it – a longer run than the straight gangs and indeed most of the states in the region. Niehaus, and Gear and Ngubeni (2002), show that the system has continued beyond the end of apartheid.

Likewise in Zimbabwe, more than two decades of independence from settler rule appear not to have affected the dominant prison culture as described in the earlier accounts. Numerous informants describe a sometimes rough initiation into prison sex – but then, with the de facto complicity of the prison guards, an acceptance if not appreciation of the benefits of the system. According to one:

Boys were forced in the sense that he just arrives in prison not knowing about anything. By the time he receives his meat and kapenta, that's when everything started. So first night he sometimes cries but there's nothing that can be done. As time goes on that's when he will see everything getting easier for him because the husband will take him as his own brother, working for him and giving him more food. The husband will give tips to the cooks so that he will receive more meat and sadza for his wife. That's when he, the boy, starts to love him and the whole game. Even now, young men are not afraid to be taken to jail because they know how the game will be there.[20]

We need to be very careful about extrapolating back in time from these recent studies and from the oral testimony of recent graduates of the prison system. These sources can nonetheless help to flesh out the bare bones of the earlier government reports, criminal court records, and memoirs. In the following section, therefore, I focus on the specific aspects of sexual relationships in prison today, aiming to shed light on the ways that prison sexual cultures and practices of masculinity have been reconstituted over time with such striking apparent continuity.

The dominant model of sexual relationship in prison remains a harsh, uncompromising version of patriarchal marriage in the outside world. Gender roles and identities in prison are defined primarily by the ability to exercise power; those who can exercise it become the men or soldiers, while those who cannot become the *wyfies*. Also as in traditional marriages, a husband could potentially be polygynous. Because of a moral obligation to provide for all their *wyfies* fairly, however, most prison husbands remain serially monogamous.

The term *wyfie* itself illustrates an exaggerated misogyny or homophobia in that it connotes a female animal – a bitch – rather than wife or servant. These gender identities are typically established and policed by stealth, threats, bribery, gang rape, and other forms of degrading violence. They are not negotiable except in rare cases. Once marked as a *wyfie*, in other words, a man only escapes from his assigned role by the performance of an unmistakably masculine act of violence such as a stabbing or murder, with all its risk of an increased sentence or warder retaliation. He is otherwise consigned for the length of his sentence (or until age makes him unattractive) to the passive role in sex. He may be exchanged or "rented out" by his "husband," can be directed to perform certain "womanly" tasks like fetching things and cleaning, and may be ritually renamed with a feminine name. He may even be confined to his cell in the way that an idealized traditional wife would be confined to the home while her husband ventures forth to provide for her.

How do male-bodied, masculine-gendered persons become female gendered? Some, of course, never do. As former inmate "G" recalls of his own experience in jail, "Four out of ten did it there. Quite often they fought, most of the time because they compete for these young boys. They didn't bother me because I was old. They want the young boys."[21] With these younger men, however, decisions have to be made. In many cases, new arrivals in prison may be obviously "womanly" in the eyes of the other inmates. Their smaller size, demeanour, "beauty," passivity, or trusting nature immediately marks them for the *wyfie* role. In other cases the gang leadership must decide. The task, as in the days of Nongoloza's "medical officer," falls to the *ngaka*, or "doctor," "chief justice," or "blacksmith." Depending on the gang, the assessment of gender in the ambiguous cases can be done by taking the newcomer's pulse or by putting him to a test. A typical such test is to show the courage to stand up against threatened rape, facing the risk of murder for insubordination to the gang leadership.

As one informant described it to Gear and Ngubeni: "Once you are in the office of this guy called Blacksmith ... he is going to trick you into having sex ... He must classify you whether you ... are a young man or ... a full soldier ... the Blacksmith will say '*Uyangigicwalisela* – make me believe you' ... [that] you can be a young soldier... The Blacksmith will say, 'Come.' Maybe they go to the shower ... (soldiers are standing guard outside ... to keep watch for the warders). 'Take off your trousers' ... [The Blacksmith's tone] has changed now. The young man will see, 'Aish, I haven't got a chance ... I must agree with everything that this man says.'" (2002, 35)

The *ngaka* may also assign gender retroactively. Dlamini recounts the extraordinary tale of a battle in which the Big Fives capture and gang rape none less than the president of their enemies, the Big Sixes. When he reappears in public after his ordeal, that man is formally removed from both his office and his masculine status in a renaming ceremony led by the gang doctor. As Dlamini incredulously put it: "I'm flabbergasted by the endless horrors that happen in this prison. The warders and the Big Fives are jubilant. The leader of the most powerful gang has now become a wyfie of his antagonists. It's mind-boggling. But it has happened" (Dlamini 1984, 111).

In addition to "president," "doctor," "general," and so on, other ranks in contemporary gang hierarchies also correspond to those of Nongoloza's time. Gear and Ngubeni further discern a hierarchy among the *wyfies* that mirrors the men's. *Wyfies* rise and fall in this hierarchy in accordance with their loyal service and their ascribed womanliness. The latter includes physical appearance but also passivity and stoic acceptance of their lot. The most senior *wyfie*, or "queen," in Niehaus's study, also carried political functions, notably mediating non-sexual grievances among the other *wyfies* and pleading for mercy in disciplinary trials for both *wyfies* and low-ranking soldiers.

Interestingly, as Hensley et al. found in the case of American prisons (2002), "real homosexuals" are not necessarily regarded as the most "womanly" (and hence the lowest ranking) in this hierarchy. Since gays are assumed to be naturally effeminate, it does not particularly enhance a man's aura of power to take them sexually or to order them about. The womanliest in this hierarchy are rather those heterosexual men who submit to the role in a way that highlights the masculinity/power of the husband. Gays are thus not the preferred type of *wyfie*. On the contrary, because they actually enjoy sex with males, they are perceived as more likely to be unfaithful. While there is a hint of admiration in some straight men's testimony of gays' ability to barter (and to enjoy) casual sex as a means to acquire an expensive life-style (Gear and Ngubeni 2002, 59), real gays remain at high risk of victimization, particularly from men who lack the rank or the strength of character to take sex by force from unwilling heterosexual men.

Many *wyfies* experience humiliation, shame, fear, simmering anger, and other emotional traumas from being forced or tricked into their role. Murderous retribution against "husbands" after release is thus apparently not uncommon. For that reason, the *ngaka*'s advice can be crucial in ensuring that *wyfies* are not assigned to husbands from the same township or home area where they might run into each other again. Others, however, apparently grow to appreciate the protection and companionship that the feminine role can offer. Gear and Ngubeni even described cases where *wyfies* and soldiers continued affectionate relationships after release (78–9), something Niehaus (2002b) also found in a high-profile case from Bushbuckridge in the early 1990s.

A mutual type of sexual relationship within prison may also be negotiated. This relationship, known as *uchincha ipondo* ("to exchange money"), is apparently tolerated by the gangs as long as it remains covert or if, in the case of non-gang members (*mphathas*), a tax or payment in kind is made to the gang for the privilege. *Uchincha ipondo* would typically be alternating, experimental, and a way for a *wyfies* to enjoy a respite from the passive sexual role with a fellow *wyfie* or an *mphatha*. Oral evidence gathered for the present study in Zimbabwe indicates a similar pattern in that country and suggests that, in fact, *uchincha ipondo*-type sex was not just occasionally practised but was characteristic of prison: "One difference [between prison and the mines] that I experienced is that the men in prison sometimes exchange the nights. One does sex to the other today, then the one who was the wife will become the husband the next day, so each fulfils their desires for sex."[22] One of Gear and Ngubeni's informants even described a case of two cellmates discussing whether their sexual relationship should follow the husband/*wyfie* model or should restrict itself to *uchincha ipondo* (55). The proposed wife, perhaps in recognition of his inferior bargaining position, ultimately chose to request a transfer out of the cell and away from the proposing husband, who worked in the kitchen.

This leeway to discuss and negotiate types of sexual relationship stands in stark contradiction to claims about gang and prison dogmatism around sexuality. Inmates and observers alike often assert (and can give gruesome examples and anecdotes) that inflexible gang rules around sexuality are enforced by extreme violence. The Big Five gang, for example, has a rank of "spy." Spies check the anuses of all the *wyfies* every morning to ensure that they have not been penetrated. A *wyfie* who reports unwanted anal intercourse could call upon her gang's soldiers to punish her assailant, even to death. In the case of a jealous husband, she might be the one punished. Other illustrations of the rule-bound nature of prison sexuality can be found as far back as the 1929 Dhlamini case. Albert had taken Dhlamini's *umfaan* without permission, apology, or compensation. Dhlamini then smashed the man over the head with a broom, saying simply, "*Kungo mteto loko umfowetu* (That is the law, brother)."[23]

Yet gang rules appear to be broken with a frequency that somewhat belies this reputation for sexual dogmatism. The 28s are the only gang that explicitly requires male-male sex as part of their constitution and are supposedly the only ones who practise anal intercourse. But even those gangs that expressly forbid sex in prison, let alone anal sex, are known to tolerate both. Informants portray this as a fairly recent phenomenon, although, given the evidence provided to Leary and Taberer, there is reason to suspect this presentist claim. As one inmate put it, "The Big 5s are sodomists but they also like food ... and they pimp a lot ... Then [the] 26s, well they were not supposed to ... but today they've got their wives as well" (Gear and Ngubeni 2002, 13). For another, the distinguishing feature between the gangs is not the sexual activity but the willingness to fight over it: "[In] all the Numbers gangs it is happening. But the 28s specialize in small boys [and] are not like us [the Big 5s] ... and the Airforce, because ... we have sex with them, but we do not have the courage to fight for them. The only gang that fights for them is the 28s."

Bearing in mind this contradiction between gang law and actual practice, we might also want to be sceptical of gang member claims about normative sexuality in prison. With respect to actual sex acts, for example, informants in the various studies are unanimous in recognizing only two – between the thighs and anal penetration. Outside of the 28s, the latter is supposedly a recent phenomenon. The terminology used by Gear and Ngubeni's informants is suggestive, however. Among other terms, thigh sex is known as the "new road" in contrast to the "old road" into the anus. Why old? No explanation is offered except that penetrating the anus is more analagous to vaginal penetration and so recalls pre-incarceration sex with women. Anal intercourse also allows for much faster ejaculation. The customary ban put by most gangs on using the "old road" thus appears to have lapsed, at least in terms of enforcing private acts. "A lot of people are used to doing a boiler. A 'boiler' is the old way, and that's what they always do" (61). An observation confirming the practice, and the negotiated nature of anal sex in prison, comes from an alumnus of a Zimbabwean prison: "I know that they generally had sex between the thighs but could also do it through the anus if that was what they agreed beforehand."[24]

Belief in the dangerous qualities of sperm may be a constraint on *wyfies'* willingness to oblige their husbands' requests for anal penetration. It might also account for the apparently absolute ban on oral sex, a topic seemingly so horrible that it is never mentioned by non-gay identified men, even to denounce it. "The strength of the sperm causes debilitation," explained one of Niehaus's informants. "The sperms are alive. Maybe they do something inside your body. You become powerless" (Niehaus 2002a, 93). Interestingly, and in contrast to some pre-modern notions of preparation for battle, male-male sex in contemporary inmates' eyes is a cause of weakness, physical wasting, and infertility for the inserter as well as the insertee. To another of Niehaus's informants, for example, "When you have sex with a boy, your penis will suck air into your body, and there will be dirt in your lungs" (2002a, 93, 82). Soldiers (that is, rank and file gang members) are not allowed to have sex for that reason, according to one of Gear and Ngubeni's informants: "How can a soldier go to war being drunk?" (2002, 37).

Comparable studies on incarcerated women in southern Africa have yet to be produced. What historical evidence we do have, however, suggests both analogies to the men's experiences and important distinctions. As early as the 1930s, for example, the psychologist B.J.F. Laubscher (1937, 31) observed how his female patients in a prison-like institution (Queenstown

Mental Hospital) commonly and casually engaged in mutual masturbation, something that would not have been tolerated in a men's prison. Laubscher attributed this and other "perverse homosexual activities" among women to traditional forms of insanity that were the precursor to witchcraft or spirit medium status. It may also be that the mutual masturbation he witnessed was in fact simply the indiscreet, uninhibited practice of a discreet norm among adolescents in traditional settings – that is, labial stretching in preparation for marriage.

Gertie Williams's brief account of her stint in a reformatory for girls in the late 1940s, by contrast, reflects a self-conscious performance of a masculine/feminine dyad that was clearly akin to what was happening in the men's prisons. Immediately upon arrival at the reformatory, the masculine-identified Williams encountered other "men" with whom she needed to negotiate both for her independence from their aggressive attentions and for access to the "girls." The women identified as girls fulfilled the traditional tasks of wives. They were forbidden to eat, shower, or smoke *dagga* with the "men." As in the men's prisons, violence might be used to enforce this gender dichotomy. When a girl teased Williams about her masculine demeanour, for example, Williams responded sharply: "One blow to her face was enough to shut her up, and also anybody else who would speak about me."[25]

Both Elizabeth Fourie and "Pumla Mkhize" confirm a propensity to violence or even outright gang warfare among the lesbian prisoners they encountered in the 1980s. Indeed, Mkhize characterized them simply as "men, strong. Yes, they are men," while Fourie noted the very manly weapons that they used against each other – knives, sjamboks, and barbed wire (Schreiner 1992, 243, 62). Shylet Muzah's revelations about her stint in a Zimbabwean women's prison also parallel the descriptions provided by male inmates on non-physical forms of coercion. These included threats of violence and extended prison sentences in order to maintain a code of silence about same-sex practices, and the use of hunger to recruit otherwise unwilling sex partners. "Many prisoners are being forced into homosexuality in exchange for soap, toothpaste, Vaseline, bread and meat. The most vulnerable are those without relatives who bring them basic needs not supplied by the prison" (Ncube 2000).

This testimony probably represents an extreme, given that few women were imprisoned for violent crimes compared to men. The majority of female inmates in both South Africa and Zimbabwe historically were in for pass law and liquor law violations or for prostitution and vagrancy. Such violence as occurred in sexual relationships would thus more commonly be expressed through ostracism, jealousy, or verbal abuse rather than physical blows. Where overt forms of violence and lesbianism did take place, they were concentrated in specific wards or sections. As Elizabeth Fourie explained, the lesbian reputation of a section could be used as a threat by the guards to discipline inmates who feared transfer (Schreiner 1992, 52). But even this could backfire in the sense that the lesbians could not be counted upon to be violent or to humiliate the transferees. Fourie's fears about Section D quickly evaporated on the grounds that "they did have lesbians, but they were not the fighting types."

Studies from female prisons in the United States, as well as Judith Gay's anthropology of Basotho girls and young women in boarding schools, also suggest a divergence from the men's experience. Female-female sexuality could be expressed in ways that were not fundamentally different from heteronormative femininity and friendships, or even considered sexual in hegemonic gender relations. This included hugging, kissing, non-genital caressing, and intensely close emotional attachment (Gay 1985, Hensley 2002). The women themselves would likely deny that these activities were sexual. After all, as Kendall concluded about her informants' incredulous responses to queries about lesbian sex, the dominant assumption among Basotho women was simply, "no *koai* [penis], no sex" (Kendall 1999). Female-female affairs of this type in prison or other closed institutions may thus not have been "lesbian" by a modern Western definition. They do, however, raise intriguing questions for queer scholars about the nature and durability of women's phallocentric notions of physical, emotional, and spiritual gratification by sex.

At the time the phenomena of *nkotshane* and *wyfie* relationships began to surface as official concerns in early twentieth century South Africa, bureaucrats in both Prisons and Native Affairs regarded them as more or less equivalent. They even partially blamed each other for abetting "its" (singular) spread. They both condemned same-sex relationships, but they were similarly unwilling to take more than basically token or repressive steps to address the factors that they themselves understood as contributing to such relationships. Some of the same impulses towards official denial and avoidance appear to be still at work in South Africa and Zimbabwe in both male and female prisons.

These parallels and continuities are easy to understand. At first glance, mine compounds and prisons were not dissimilar in appearance and organizational structure. Some prisons may actually have had better amenities and been less physically dangerous than some of the mine compounds. On the surface, as well, the hierarchical, gendered model of same-sex "marriage" that emerged as the dominant one in the two contexts appears almost identical. Yet a closer look reveals important differences in the two relationships over time. Above all, a *wyfie* clearly had far less control over his/her fate than did an *nkotshane*. Once marked as a *wyfie*, often by an act of betrayal of trust or direct force or extortion, a man had little chance of escaping or of graduating to a masculine rank in the prison and gang hierarchies. His/her subordinate sexual and social status had its own ranks with varying degrees of privilege, as would a female wife in a village setting. The opportunity to buy oneself out of that subordinate status, however, was limited to exercising extreme violence. To be caught in a mutual, affectionate relationship was meanwhile to invite ostracism, extortion, or worse. Simply to accuse another man of "real" homosexuality – "It's an insult, it's a challenge … You can be assaulted for that" (Gear and Ngubeni 2002, 63).

For an *nkotshane*, by contrast, increasing physical maturity, an independent income, and the open-ended possibility of desertion or migration to another workplace gave him/her the power to negotiate more mutual or otherwise satisfying sexual practices. This key distinction explains why straight African men will often recall their youthful mining affairs with an element of nostalgia or amusement,[26] whereas even men who were masculine-identified in prison have evinced regret, if not shame, at the "system" as they experienced it. The Ninevite leader Nongoloza was almost wistful in reflecting on his ex-gang members' refusal to see the light. "Of course they are ignorant and have not yet learnt the lesson which I have," he told his interlocutor. "Here I was with bags of money [and lots of male sex partners!], the proceeds of the robberies of my gang, and to-day getting old in prison, when I might have had a wife with growing sons and cattle for my old age in Zululand."[27]

For men who were forced into the *wyfie* role, the regrets would have been rather stronger. Like many female rape victims, these men may well have been traumatized to an extent that reverberated throughout their lives with alcoholism, misogyny, misanthropy, and homophobia. And yet, remarkably, it is not hard to find men who recall their prison affairs with some tenderness or appreciation compared to their sexual life on the outside. Moreover, even in this hostile environment, mutual and affectionate sexual relationships did exist among men who did not identify as homosexual or bisexual:

There is no *lobola* but love and presents. You can't be tired of it in jail. Everything becomes easier and life very comfortable. At first it will be done without feelings most of the times but there's nothing that can be done but to accept it. Once you eat and allow him to be friendly, that's all. Their favours are food; help when you are given work to do as punishment, and a lot of cigarettes if you are a smoker. Everything will be easier for you. There are no rules because we don't say it out, it's private. But what we did was the husband would have sex with us between the thighs and anus-style sometimes. We were supposed to play with him, love, play and hold him nicely. As time went on we enjoyed it and even now we are not afraid to be arrested because if we find our big boyfriends life will be easier.[28]

This is not to romanticize "love" behind bars. Nor is it to overstate the importance of affectionate and relatively egalitarian relationships as counter-cultural to the dominant ethos in prison. However, the mere existence of non-*wyfie* sexual relationships between inmates who did not identify as homosexual or bisexual is powerful testimony to men's need for and ability to create intimacy regardless of other factors. This cautions us against both assuming the worst about prison sexuality and essential-izing the role of violence and power in masculine sexuality.

4

Towns

Zimbabweans rightly object to being subsumed into South African history. Zimbabwe had distinctive pre-modern African cultures and a very different modern historical experience. It was colonized much later, 1890–93 versus the 1780s-1880s for most of South Africa, and had a much smaller ratio of non-blacks to blacks: at the greatest, about 1:20 versus 1:5 or 6 in South Africa. It achieved black majority rule earlier, in 1980 versus 1994, and in a more violent way. Its economy has always been small in comparison even to individual South African provinces. The urban centres were consequently much smaller and more parochial, and were more appropriately termed towns beside South Africa's cities.

Nonetheless, the two countries do share a common heritage of British colonial rule and of heavy-handed racial capitalism structured along similar lines. The latter included dependence on African male migrant labour and the geographical division of the land into European areas and towns on the one hand and African reserves and townships on the other. Infrastructural development and services were concentrated in the modern European sector, while African reserves and townships were relatively underdeveloped, crowded, and impoverished. In both countries, anxieties about African sexuality and the desire to control it were integral to governance and the spatial division of urban areas. "Black Peril" (the exaggerated fear of black men having sex with white women), "loose women," and venereal disease were parallel obsessions throughout much of the early twentieth century.

The emergence of a vibrant gay rights movement in Zimbabwe in the 1990s, employing an indigenized version of the very same word that first appeared in South Africa meaning "homosexual wife" or "mine marriage" or "buggar boy" in the 1880s or '90s (*inkotshane*, now *hungochani*), also suggests elements of a common heritage in the two countries around male-male sexuality. This chapter examines that heritage in a comparative way, relying primarily upon the criminal court records to discern trends in sexuality and identity over the period from the 1890s to the mid-1930s. This period spans the establishment of British South Africa Company (BSAC) rule and the extension of Roman-Dutch law to the areas of white settlement in Mashonaland (1890) and Matabeleland (1894), through the attainment of self-governing status (1924), to the formalization of distinct European and African land tenure and local governance regimes.

The first known European in Zimbabwe alleged to have had homosexual tendencies was none other than Cecil John Rhodes, founder of the colony that eventually took his name. Rhodes made a fortune in diamonds at Kimberly and rose to become prime minister of Cape Colony in 1889. From that office he organized the Pioneer Column that occupied Mashonaland in 1890. A lifelong bachelor, he was often seen in the company of strapping young Aryanesque soldiers whom he called "lambs." He maintained a long-standing, overtly affectionate relationship with one of these men. With a girlish laugh and a limp handshake (Hole 1928, 128–9), he was also an ardent admirer of African warrior machismo to an extent that has raised some eyebrows about his sexual preferences. Robert Rotberg has even speculated that Rhodes may have had shipboard romances, or physical sexual relationships with African subordinates, in addition to holding repressed sexual feelings towards his white "lambs." The evidence to support such speculation is weak, however, and interpreted anachronistically. At the time neither confirmed bachelorhood, public male camaraderie, nor the idealization of masculine types like Ndebele and Zulu warriors was considered to be indicative of homosexual tendencies. On the contrary, men with such characteristics were admired as exemplifying the empire-building spirit, paragons of British military virtue. Whispers about Rhodes's sexuality are thus likelier to be a retrospective slander by some of his many enemies.[1]

We may also fairly safely dispose of the claim that less luminous whites than Rhodes first introduced same-sex practices to unwary blacks when they came pouring into the territory following the Pioneer Column of 1890. As discussed in chapter 1, same-sex sexual relations were not unknown nor even necessarily incompatible with either Shona or Ndebele customs. They were not the stuff of day-to-day conversation, to be sure, nor were they evident enough to draw the attention of the early missionaries and explorers. That male-male sexual relations were in fact quietly taking place among Africans, however, became obvious to the invaders as soon as they set up their court and police structures. Within the first full year of operation of magistrates' courts in the tiny pioneer outposts of Salisbury (Harare) and Umtali (Mutare), no less than five cases of sodomy and indecent assault by men upon men or boys came to trial. None of these involved a white man. Rather, the accused were a "Hottentot," a "Matibili," and a "Zambizi" and the rest unspecified "natives," presumably local Shona.[2] The victims of the assaults are only identified in two of these cases, both Manyika (that is, eastern Shona-speakers). By virtue of their employment by Europeans, they found themselves under Roman-Dutch jurisprudence as it began to operate alongside customary law.

These early trials were perfunctory, and the record consequently does not give much insight into the motives or history of the men and boys involved. The numbers alone, however, raise compelling questions about male-male sexuality in Zimbabwe. The five cases of male-male sexual assault tried in 1892 amounted to nearly 1.5 per cent of all criminal court cases that year, a notably higher rate of prosecution than in the regional Sodom (Kimberly), in the tavern of the seas (Cape Town), or even in the burgeoning industrial and criminal gang centre of Johannesburg. Over the same period as these five cases, there were zero cases of bestiality and heterosexual crimes such as rape, indecent assault, and *crimen injuria*. In other words, of all the "perversions" that plagued society at the moment of birth of colonial rule, assault by black males upon other black males was the most visible to the upholders of colonial law and order. While the Catholic priest F.J. Richartz may have been exaggerating when he described sodomy as "simply common" in 1896, the new judicial system was clearly catching glimpses of an apparently fairly widespread pre-existing practice.

As Salisbury, Umtali, and the former Ndebele capital of Bulawayo grew into towns and eventually into cities with well-appointed suburbs, and as new settlements sprang up across the colony, the district courts proliferated. By 1935 there were fifty-two of them covering all the lands designated for white settlement – by then, about half the area of Southern Rhodesia. Between 1892 and 1935 these courts processed approximately 450 cases of male-male sexual crimes, making this a particularly rich archive in relation to the other jurisdictions of the region. Of these hundreds of cases, only thirty-nine involved whites as the accused, slightly less than 9 per cent of the total. Close to half of this number had perpetrated their assaults on other whites. This means that only twenty-four cases of whites assaulting Africans ever made it to court in the first four and a half decades of record-keeping, about one every two years.[3] Of these, about a third were judged to have been the victims of false accusations. Asians and Coloureds were an even smaller fraction of cases – twelve, or just over 2.5 per cent of the total, with an equally high proportion of apparent blackmail attempts by their accusers. Also noteworthy is the fact that in all these years there are but three examples of non-African repeat offenders, only one of whom was considered to be white.[4]

These numbers do not support the contention that the settlers had a direct corrosive effect on the morals of African men. On the contrary, they reveal that almost 90 per cent of all recorded cases of male-male sexual crime involved African men assaulting or seducing other African men or boys. This statistic is even more remarkable when one considers that Africans comprised only a half to two-thirds of the population of the cities and towns where the courts were based. Africans, in other words, were lodging complaints against or were being caught *in flagrante delicto* with other Africans in disproportionate numbers to their population in the areas served by colonial law.

It may be argued that the small number of cases of European men indicted for sexual crimes against males simply reflects the fact that European perpetrators were more able than Africans to threaten or to buy silence from their victims and the police, and hence able to hide their disreputable acts from the public record. Southey (1997a) has shown that this was the case in at least one scandal from colonial South Africa. He has shown, moreover, that church officials were not above colluding to suppress or destroy incriminating evidence about colleagues disgraced by accusations or rumours of homosexual impropriety. The fact that only one case of a missionary abusing his power over pupils or African subordinates ever made it to court in Southern Rhodesia during the period under consideration is certainly suspicious. This could be interpreted to support the belief, widely held among Zimbabweans today, of institutional suppression of accusations of sexual assault by whites.[5] One gets a sense of this as well in a small number of politically sensitive cases involving white police who were discharged with suspicious disregard for incriminating evidence against them.[6]

Yet having acknowledged the discrepancy of power and wealth between whites and blacks under colonial rule, as well as the prodigious capacity for duplicity and hypocrisy by the colonialists, the notion of a widespread conspiracy of silence to protect white dignity is nonetheless insupportable. It is, in fact, strongly contradicted by other evidence. Africans on the whole were not shy about turning to the police to register their unhappiness with European behaviour. Thus, despite colonial racism and the sometimes dubious probity of the police and magistrates, the courts in Southern

Rhodesia entertained many hundreds of cases that called whites' self-proclaimed civilized nature into question. These included such forms of "perversion" as white women attempting to seduce black men. The white Rhodesian population also purportedly had among the highest rates of incest and heterosexual rape in the British empire, while white men's sexual exploitation of African women was the subject of intensely shaming public debate through the 1910s and '20s. Court stenographers meanwhile made little effort to protect white men's dignity during their trials for alleged homosexual assaults. On the contrary, court transcripts to some extent actually protected African dignity with euphemistic translations of words for sex acts, whereas Europeans tended to speak directly to the court in often crude, undignified language.[7]

In sum, we may safely put to rest the claims that whites introduced same-sex sexuality to black Zimbabweans and then hid behind a racist legal system to keep their shameful behaviour from the public record. At the mines, there are hints that the learning process may have actually gone in the other direction, if not in deed then at least in language. In one revealing case from 1922, a white miner was accused of assaulting an African at Genii mine near Belingwe, Matabeleland. The accused reportedly used African terms to describe his behaviour. "I want you to be my 'Nkotshana,'" Alexander MacNair was alleged to have proposed to Ranganai. After two incidents of anal rape, McNair then supposedly used a common African euphemism for sex to dismiss him – "The smoke's finished. You can go."[8]

Among Africans themselves, no one ethnic group appears to have had a special affinity for same-sex sexual relationships. Cases are remarkably well spread out among the many ethnic groups present in the country. "Alien natives" accounted for about two-thirds of the identifiable total of accused, roughly equivalent to their ratio of the African urban population. The majority of these came from various loosely defined "tribes" in Portuguese East Africa, mostly Chikunda and Sena (about a fifth of the total). Nyasaland provided about one in eleven of the total accused, mostly Chewa, Ngoni, and Tonga, while Africans from Northern Rhodesia comprised 6 per cent, mostly Lozi (BaRotse, sometimes Kololo). These were the territories that supplied the majority of migrant labourers in the industry and commercial agriculture in Southern Rhodesia, the ones most likely to get enmeshed in the colonial court system.

Among indigenous peoples, the Ndebele and related groups account for about 16 per cent of the total cases and the Shona about 17 per cent. While the latter figure would seem to suggest that the Shona did not engage in same-sex relations in proportion to their population (75–80 per cent of the whole territory), it should be recalled that the majority of Shona continued throughout this period to live in the reserves under customary law. They thus mostly remained outside the net of Roman-Dutch law. When this began to change, so too did the numbers of indigenous African men appearing in town and before the district courts. The forensic evidence suggests that indigenous Zimbabweans adopted many of the same behaviours as foreign migrants when exposed to the same "unmanning" circumstances of colonial rule and market forces. Hence, in 1921 Shona for the first time actually constituted a majority of the accused in male-male sexual crimes countrywide. In the period between 1924 and 1931, Shona men accused of male-male sexual assaults outnumbered Nyasaland men by more than two to one (thirty-six to fourteen).

Interestingly, while there is a small indigenous population of Shangaans and Shangaanized Shona in Zimbabwe (the MaNdau), and while the Shangaans were already notorious for *inkotshane* in South Africa in the first decade of the century, they are notably under-represented among the identifiable accused in cases of male-male sexual crime in early colonial Zimbabwe. Shangaans and MaNdau comprised 3 per cent of the total cases, or about half their proportion of the population in the territory as a whole. Similarly rare are other migrants from the more industrialized south ("Hottentot," Xhosa, Basotho from Basutoland, Cape Coloured, and Zulu) or representatives from South Africa's infamous gangs. None of the many cases that occurred in prison, for example, makes reference to the Ninevites or 28s, the prison gang known for its active preference for sex with males. The single case of a man who explicitly admitted to having acquired his homosexual habits in South Africa was a twenty-three year old white accused of interfering with fifteen to seventeen year old youths, also white. His case does not bespeak of a major cultural invasion from the south.[9]

The vocabulary used to describe male-male sex acts similarly does not indicate a big external influence. Versions of *nkotshane* only crop up in two cases. *Hlobonga*, the Zulu term for thigh sex that was likewise commonplace at the mines in South Africa, was used just once (by a Shangaan). The great majority of other cases where the African terms are preserved in the translation are simply variations on local terms for sex acts. Shona witnesses, for example, use words like *kurinda* or *kuswina* (meaning "to fuck," not specifying who or what) and *kubata* ("a polite word for sexual connection [that] approximates as near as possible to the English "copulate"").[10] *Shamwari* (the Shona word for "friend") appears to have been widely understood as synonymous with *nkotshane* or "sweetheart," even to non-Shona speakers.[11]

Whatever their ethnicity, the overwhelming majority of Africans both accused of and complaining about sexual assault were men and boys who were far from home. Mostly they were either employed by or imprisoned in colonial institutions. By no means, however, was male-male sexual crime confined to the mines and prisons as might be imagined. On the contrary, only slightly more than a third of all allegations of male-male sexual assault took place in mine compounds (at 22 per cent of all cases) and prisons (17 per cent). About the same number of cases as occurred in prison took place on commercial farms and in woodlots, "kraals," and other *rural* areas. The remaining cases (about half) occurred in other urban contexts, including hotels, police camps, non-mine industrial compounds, hospitals, the veldt between working and drinking places, private homes, and even in established African locations. Simonas, alias Bye-Bye, for example, was a self-employed mattress-maker with his own private accommodation in Salisbury township when he was found guilty of multiple counts of sodomy in 1923.[12]

One of the most striking illustrations of the diversity of location of same-sex crimes, and one that somewhat undermines an over-arching situational explanation for same-sex behaviour, was the 1928 case of public indecency against Bikinosi. An unspecified "alien native" working as a general servant, Bikinosi lived in the municipal compound bordering on the Kopje district of Salisbury, just southwest of the central business district. Kopje was dominated by a wooded park, fringed by some of the oldest residences in the city. It was also well known for having the oldest, most frequented working-class bars and brothels in the city. The main witness in the case against Bikinosi was Nyandora, a local resident. He testified that he was sitting with his wife on the porch of their house when around 4:00 P.M. they "saw [Bikinosi] and another native come down kopje. Both stopped. Took off their shorts. The other one lay down and accd got on top of him. Accd's private parts were exposed. His penis erect. I ran up to them. The other one got away. I arrested accd. This is a public place. My wife could see them."[13]

Similarly confounding to stereotypes of a spatially confined phenomenon is the fact that the cases were remarkably spread out territorially. The two largest urban centres accounted for about a third of all cases between 1892 and 1931, with Salisbury at about one hundred and Bulawayo eighty. Yet jurisdiction of these urban courts extended over a wide swathe of commercial farms, compounds dotted along the railway lines, and even "kraals" in the surrounding African reserves, where many apparently urban cases originated. Moreover, Bulawayo, with fewer cases than the capital city, was actually the larger, more industrialized, and more cosmopolitan of the two cities in this early period. Some of the mid-sized urban centres meanwhile produced almost no cases. In thirty-one years of operation of the magistrate's court in Fort Victoria (Masvingo), for example, only one single charge of male-male sexual assault was ever lodged.[14] Gwelo (Gweru), the third largest city in the colony, had a mere four cases over this period. Comparisons between mining towns reveal further seeming anomalies. For example, Hartley (modern Chegutu) was a small town with large mines around it and a preponderantly male migrant population. As one might expect, it was a veritable den of iniquity with forty-two cases of male-male sexual crime in seventeen years. Yet just down the road the even larger mining centre of Gatooma (Kadoma) recorded less than half that number of cases. Selukwe (Shurugwi), another mining town, reported none at all. Small agricultural centres such as Odzi and Marondellas (Marondera) were by comparison busy.

The geographical distribution of male-male sexual crime may indicate nothing more than discrepancies in the zeal of local police forces. Clearly, however, it warns us against asserting a straightforward correlation between the frequency of male-male sexual crime in any given community and the level of urbanization or type of economic activity that predominated there.

Considering the numbers over time, the evidence also further defies conventional explanations for the appearance of male-male sexual behaviour among Africans. Van Onselen (1976) and Jeater (1993), for instance, have argued that African male sexuality was transformed in the early colonial period, in part due to the declining ability of African men to produce or afford the *lobola* needed to secure proper wives. Sometimes this was the direct result of heavy taxation, loss of land, and discriminatory pricing against African agricultural produce. In other cases, it was the indirect result of the colony's enormously distorted urban demographics. The influx of tens of thousands of alien natives in town produced a high demand for commercial sex with a low supply of female prostitutes to meet it. That supply and demand ratio meant that local women could negotiate relatively high prices for their services – making as much as forty pounds a month, according to Lawrence Vambe in 1949. Indeed, some prostitutes and *mapoto* (common-law) wives have recalled the period up to the 1950s as something of a golden era of opportunity for women in town compared to later (see, notably, Schmidt 1992, Barnes 1999; also Vambe 1976). Meanwhile, as the numbers of women absconding for the bright lights and cash of town life increased, the concomitant shortage of marriageable girls in the reserves allowed parents to inflate *lobola* demands upon future sons-in-law. Some men were driven into homosexual liaisons partly because they simply could not afford otherwise.

Yet were this full story, one would expect a steady increase in the frequency of male-male sexual crime as real wages declined and as men's economic straits worsened. In fact, absolute numbers of homosexual cases in Southern Rhodesia peaked in a time of relative prosperity (in 1927, twenty-five cases territory-wide). They then fell sharply during the depression years (only ten in 1931, for example). In relative terms the frequency of the crime declined even more precipitously, from three out of a total of 228 cases in Salisbury in 1892 (1.3 per cent of all crimes) to four out of approximately five thousand cases in 1923 (0.08 per cent). That trend continued erratically downwards through to the 1940s, when male-male sexual crimes virtually disappeared from the public record. Indeed, in the three years of 1947–49, years of sharp inflation, labour unrest, and a huge increase in other crimes linked to economic hardship, the annual police report did not list a single case of sodomy.[15] However one explains this decline (and I shall attempt to below by looking more closely at the attitudes of the state), it surely rules out narrowly economistic explanations of male sexuality.

Finally, a quantitative analysis of cases of male-male sexual crime in early colonial Zimbabwe calls into question one of the key assertions of Moodie and Harries in their studies of mine marriages in South Africa, and the claims of African inmates and gang members themselves – that is, that the men who engaged in sex with other men or boys conformed to a rigid set rules including no penetration or mutuality. The evidence from Zimbabwe shows that ejaculation by the senior partner between the thighs of a passive boy or young man was indeed the predominant form of same-sex sexual practice recorded. In a startling number of cases, the accused took his satisfaction while the complainant was actually asleep (a variant upon the Shona custom of heterosexual *kuruvhurera*). Yet the position of the passive or juniour partner during the exercise varied considerably – supine, prone, on the side, and even (as I will discuss below) taking turns on top. Anal intercourse was not, meanwhile, unheard of among African men. On the contrary, nearly a third of all cases from 1892 to 1935 involved accusations of sodomy. Cases where the magistrate determined that actual anal penetration had indeed taken place account for about one in six of the total number. Reflective of this, one of the first translations of the word *ngotshana* to appear in Zimbabwe was "passive sodomist."[16]

Other types of male-male sexual practices to have come before the courts are extremely rare. Only two cases of mutual masturbation were ever alleged in the whole period of company rule, while oral sex between African men is completely non-existent in the record (to be sure, coerced oral sex is similarly non-existent as a charge by African women against male assailants). Zimbabweans may not have been quite as ignorant of the possibilities, however, as this invisibility to the courts implies. Vondo of Bulawayo, for instance, was apparently savvy enough to include attempted fellatio among his other accusations against a white man as early as 1902.[17] A case from 1929 also implicated Europeans (and Mozambicans) in the practice but nonetheless shows that a local Shona man was aware of it as a concept. As Msekiwa, a general servant at the Grand Hotel in Gatooma, explained to the court in his charge against James Battersby: "I told him that I was an Mzezuru native. I asked him why he was enquiring and he said that he thought I was a Portuguese native. I asked him what about the Portuguese and he said that they were nice boys and understood everything that he spoke. I asked him in what way were the Portuguese boys nice and he said that they know this at the same time making a motion with his finger in his mouth. Then accused put his hand between his legs."[18]

Numbers, when dealing with such an incomplete and flawed source as criminal court records, are inherently untrustworthy, and I have considered them here primarily as a springboard to asking further questions. A close qualitative analysis of the court records, however, supports many of the possibilities suggested by those questions as well as the testimony provided to Leary and Taberer and other contemporary investigations in South Africa. Further, African men's own words to the courts reveal often surprising evidence. Among the most striking discoveries are that reciprocal, relatively long term, and apparently loving relationships actually did exist in an atmosphere that otherwise appeared so utterly to militate against them; that cash was able to transform gender identities at a personal level with relative ease; and that Zimbabweans of yore were often quite phlegmatic about an issue that today causes outrage in many circles.

To begin with the situation at the mines, various sources from early colonial Zimbabwe make it clear that male-male sexual liaisons were the active choice of many of both the accused and accusers. Among the latter, a surprising number implicated themselves (and hence lost their cases) by referring to negotiations over money. The crime to them was not so much that a perverse sexual act had been imposed upon them but that the accused had not properly paid for the pleasure. Tshakusamba was quite frank about this, to the prejudice of his case against Fanyere in 1904. He told the magistrate in Hartley: "If the accused had paid me the money I should not have reported the matter. I considered I was entitled to damages because he had treated me as a woman and had spent on my legs."[19] Morenyu's brother also clearly (though mistakenly) thought that he was helping Morenyu's case against an alleged assailant when he told the court that "the acc'd should have paid the picannin."[20]

Among the accused, in no case can it accurately be maintained that they were "forced" to have sex with males. They chose to do so rather than remain celibate or seek sexual release by solitary masturbation or bestiality. They also chose to do so even though this typically meant considerably more effort and expense than simply taking advantage of a co-worker pressed close on account of overcrowded housing conditions. Commonly, for example, the accused travelled from his own hut (or bed) to that of the complainant. In some cases this involved a walk of several hundred metres, indicating both a degree of premeditation and a lack of concern about being seen by others. In one Umtali case, a man travelled all the way from Penalonga (more than thirty kilometres away) to have sex with a former "room-mate" who had moved to the city.[21] Even within the mine compounds themselves, offences did not always take place in cramped quarters but also at the back of wagons, in the open veldt, and in underground shafts.

The accused in most of these cases chose to have sex with males even when women were available in the vicinity. An important point to underscore here is that Zimbabwean mines in this period did not have closed compounds. As a rule, the mines were much smaller than those found in South Africa. They also generally had lower profit margins, significantly lower wages, and minimal investment by the mine-owners in infrastructure. They tended, as a result, to be seen by migrants as little more than stepping stones on the way south. Passing through, the men erected temporary huts of their own or to share with two to three others in the vicinity of work. Undoubtedly cases occurred when snuggling under a shared blanket for warmth in these huts on chilly winter nights caused "accidents" to happen, as well might happen in a traditional bachelor's hut in the rural areas.

The very primitiveness of labour camps in colonial Zimbabwe, however, meant that men were mostly free to wander in and out and to seek sex with females elsewhere. This was not as difficult as sometimes portrayed. As revealed to the Leary and Taberer enquiry, even in South Africa small but increasing numbers of women made themselves available to mineworkers for commercial sex, often on nearby farms. In Zimbabwe, where the power and determination of the state to exclude women from town was relatively weaker, some mining compounds were veritable villages with wives, children, and "prostitutes" mingled among the workers' informal accomodation. A common lament in the testimony of complainants and witnesses in male-male sexual assault cases was that such assaults were not necessary. "If you want a woman, I will fetch one for you," pleaded Murisell as he tried to fend off his boss's amorous advances. Objected another, "Why do you not get yourself a woman instead of doing it to this boy?"[22] In a similar vein, several defendants scoffed at the charges lodged against them: "If I wanted to have a woman I can get plenty in the location"; or "there are plenty of women"; or "I could not have had connections with the picannin. I have my own wife."[23] Several of the accused were in fact locally married men with children.[24] In one unusual case from Dawn Mine in the Hartley district, the accused was said to have entered the hut where the complainant was sleeping *beside his wife* – and mounted the man![25]

One oral informant also recalled the Jumbo Mine just north of Salisbury before World War II in terms that colourfully undermine the "they-were-forced-to-do-it" explanation of male-male sex: "My son, life in the compounds was full of comedy. We liked it. We had our way of entertaining ourselves. Those who came from Malawi like me organized traditional dances called *zvinyawo*. I tell you also that I quenched my sexual desire by going to prostitutes. Prostitutes were always there in our compounds. Prostitution was the nature of the compound. There was nothing to be ashamed of in being a prostitute. Some of the prostitutes were better off because they charged exhorbitant prices. Mine owners even supported prostitution because then we would not go out looking for women."[26]

Old men are probably wont to romanticize their youthful days, and it is important to put this particular recollection in the context of the constant danger and exploitative conditions of work and the racist, abusive bosses who were part of compound life in the early twentieth century. Clearly, however, anger and stress from work in the context of a transient, cosmopolitan population did give rise to a culture of hard-drinking, ribald, and sometimes sexually transgressive fun among the men. Lawrence Vambe alludes to "unnatural" and "irresponsible" behaviour among the migrants around Arcturus in the 1920s (1976, 233) without elaborating. His description of their impact on the local Shona villages, however, bears quoting at length:

They came, young and old, men from all parts of Nyasaland and Mozambique, men who had left their relatively poor countries in search of the proverbial wealth, bright lights, and beautiful women of Southern Rhodesia. Travelling in big or small groups and out for a good time, they created a new atmosphere and transformed our surroundings into a kind of weekend fair, with much drinking, animated conversation and, of course, that very African habit of dancing and singing, right through Saturday night until late Sunday afternoon ... Our visitors had the village rocking with songs, dances and rhythms which were fascinating, being so different from our own. They seemed to be more expert in harmony and dancing than ourselves, allowing for the fact that they did and said things on a slightly exaggerated scale, both to get rid of their pent-up emotions and to impress the local people, especially the women whom they fell for heavily (225–6).

Men in urban locations (as opposed to isolated mining centres) similarly cannot be construed as absolutely deprived of the opportunity for sex with women. The early gender imbalances in town were fairly quickly evened out. Teresa Barnes maintains that by the 1930s, there were "often just as many women and children in the larger compounds" as men, (1995, 100). One police report from 1929 Bulawayo maintained that "most males are living with women in the location," while in Que Que by 1943 "all [men] have a woman" (Barnes 1993, 75–6). Barnes is referring to the very end or after the period that I am considering here. However, the frequency of court cases involving women in the urban locations between the late 1890s and 1923 (rape, liquor violations, infanticide, abortion, and so on) supports her contention that women were a significant presence in and around the towns from as early as the turn of the century. This presence was not incompatible with homoerotic dancing among the "mine boys." Women and children appear in an account of public indecency in a 1917 Bulawayo township, for example. "This dancing" – with the men's genitals exposed and garishly painted – "happens practically every Sunday," according to a police witness, and for that reason the man accused of indecency expressed perplexity at his arrest.[27] Homoerotic *gure* dances performed for the wider community's enjoyment were also recalled by an oral informant from the sewage works on the Mukuvisi River, Salisbury (Scarnecchia 1994, 78).

For many migrant men, the women in the audience at these dances would not have been available or desirable for either short-term sexual affairs or for longer-term *mapoto* marriages (too expensive, likely too "uppity," and probably a bit too risky, health-wise). For many others, the homoerotic dancing was likely a displacement of sexual energy, a way to attain emotional and physical release without consummating the activity. They did contribute to a "gay affirmative" ambience, however, that made the option of male-male sexual relations relatively socially acceptable, if not downright attractive. Indeed, for those men who considered self-masturbation a childish thing unbecoming to their sense of masculine dignity, taking a younger male as a "wife" was a rational decision and an affirmative choice. "Ingotshana" was being described as early as 1907 as a "common practice on the mines" in Zimbabwe, indicating that a significant minority of the men, and perhaps even a majority in certain locations, were involved.

The testimony of potential witnesses against the alleged assailants in homosexual cases also seems to suggest a fairly blasé attitude towards a commonplace occurence. Hence, a frequent difficulty encountered by complainants was the inability to rouse co-workers in their defence at the time of the alleged assault. Jim found this out to his dismay after being awakened one night in his hut at a railway camp near Bulawayo. The penis of a certain Mwangala was working up and down between his buttocks. "I was very cross," he told the court. When one of his companions shouted for assistance, however, "the natives in the next room laughed and told him to shut up."[29]

Several types of male-male sexual relationship among Africans can be documented from colonial Zimbabwe. At the one extreme were cases that today we would consider child abuse. "I have emitted semen on you and it does not matter because you are only lad," explained Bisamu to his unhappy *ingotshana*, Lindunda.[30] Other men justified sometimes horrific acts of violence, including anal rape resulting in bloody internal damage, with the casual defence, "I was only playing"; "Oh it does not matter"; or "It was nothing." One Shona man used the word *kumanga* to describe his assaults on a juvenile, meaning to "tease a child or helpless person."[31] This contempt stemmed in part from the discrepancy in power between the partners, of which "husbands" were often all too willing to remind their "wives" and their families. Sometimes the boys put up with virtual slave labour and demeaning, painful sex because of fear. They feared either the physical violence that their "husbands" could inflict or the "husband's" ability to hurt them financially. A servant could be dismissed (back-pay withheld), a "boss boy" could refuse to sign an employee's work ticket, and an employer could refuse to condone the pass that every African needed to remain in town. In a typical such case, twelve-year-old Mumbera explained how he had put up with over a month of relentless use by Sitwala out of fear of not getting paid: "I consented because I saw another boy whose ticket was not marked because he refused to go to the accused's hut."[32]

It is no surprise to find evidence of violence or threats of violence in the proceedings of criminal trials. What is surprising in this archive of several hundred cases stretching over decades is that violent acts do *not* predominate, a fact that seems to support the findings of Leary and Taberer in South Africa. Oral evidence also tells us that the dominant type of male-male sexual relationship was in fact closer to that described to Leary and Taberer: hierarchical marriages modelled on heterosexual common-law unions or marriages of convenience – that is, *mapoto* marriage. This relationship was predicated on almost reciprocal gift-giving and favours. Gifts ranged from significant cash outlays to a few pence, a bar of soap, a notebook, pen knife, or ratty blanket. The only constant was that the husband always gave more than he received from the wife. As in heterosexual relationships, the husband sometimes had to be seduced to make this happen. Twenty-sex year old Matshela, alias Stein, a general servant in Sebungwe, actually tried to defend himself against charges of indecent assault on those grounds in a 1924 case. He did not deny the assault. But, he explained (unsuccessfully), "I did it on invitation ... For three days complainant played with my penis."[33]

This type of relationship could of course be violent, exploitative, and demeaning to the "wife" – just as heterosexual marriage could be. Yet it could also entail real affection:

They do love each other because they were doing the same as husband and female wife – the wife always wanted to walk with his husband. They chat, they play, they enjoyed everything. The boys gave favours of cooking for the husband some other times but the husband always gave favours like food, shelter, and a comfortable place to live. They started giving favours from the first day. Like what they did on my 1st day at that compound [a tobacco company in Salisbury, 1947]. I was welcomed by a handsome old man and he showed me his room and he ran to the shops to buy me some groceries and nice, nice things. I ate a lot, 'til I was full. When the night came he just asked me to share his bed with him and that's when the whole game began. There was nothing I could do after such a nice welcome so I gave him some days to have me. When I quit the game, he was very disappointed but I paid for the food I ate.[34]

Oral informants for this study were unanimous in denying that such exchanges took an equivalent form to heterosexual *lobola*. Clearly, however, some husbands sought to establish a kind of marital stability with their *ingotshana* that exceeded the usual informal *mapoto* arrangements. In one case from Kanyemba mine near Gatooma in 1915, the husband (Singame) appears to have actually negotiated directly with his "father-in-law" for a *lobola*-like exchange. The marriage came to court because the "wife" (possibly instigated by his father) had decided to up the ante – ten pounds! – which Singame refused to pay.[35] In another case, an affair in prison led Siamasari to pledge a *lobola*-like payment in more customary terms – two pounds and a cow. In addition, according to the complainant Mutambo, "He said that when we returned to Wankies [Hwange] I should stay with him as his wife and he would give me many things."[36]

Another type of same-sex sexual relationship was closer to prostitution in the form of servicing another man's immediate, short-term desires for a negotiated price. There are hints that this was happening in Bulawayo as early as 1907. In a case of assault with intent to commit sodomy that year, the alleged assailant (Hlahali) successfully defended himself with a counter-accusation: the complainant had first solicited him with an offer of sex for money to buy meat and cigarettes.[37] In another case from Salisbury the following year, Miabe actually implicated himself in this way. His accusations were against a drunken Italian traveller: "I demanded 30/. He refused to pay this amount."[38] But who could blame Signor Umberto for balking at such a demand? The price asked for individual acts of thigh sex more typically ranged from three to ten shillings, an amount equivalent to the rate most commonly demanded by female prostitutes for their basic service.[39] Miabe thus appeared to be either attempting extortion or demanding the higher rate expected for anal intercourse.

The price for anal penetration was certainly inflated compared to thigh sex or sex with a female prostitute. It was nonetheless still significantly below the level of fines traditionally levied as "damages" for heterosexual misbehaviour such as adultery or impregnating an unmarried girl (which, after all, could have long-term financial implications to the victim's family). Yet in the minds of many of the men who came to court, the two concepts of buying sex and offering compensation were often virtually indistinguishable. The accused typically only offered to pay "compensation" after having taken their gratification, for instance, rather than negotiating the amount beforehand. Some men also demanded sex in lieu of unpaid debts. In one particularly nasty case, Jack claimed his due from the father by anally raping the man's three-year-old son.[40] In other cases, the sense of economic entitlement could entail sometimes baffling logical connections. As Manswa, a thirty-six-year-old miner from Northern Rhodesia offered in his defence against a sodomy charge: "I admit the offence, I slept with Shilling because I had given money to Tom and a friend of Shilling had killed a dog of mine some time ago."[41]

The going price for a single act of "connection" could also be parlayed into the equivalent of traditional damages or more if fear of public exposure was an issue for the accused – blackmail, in other words. A complainant could apparently make as much as ten to fifteen pounds by threatening to report an assault, an amount equal to several months' wages as a general servant.[42] As early as 1900 clearly spurious charges were being brought against "boss boys," whites and Indians – that is, men with relatively good incomes and high professional or social status. Boys and young men also lodged highly suspicious accusations, often in concert with one another, to exact revenge upon their superiors for unpopular decisions at work or out of "tribal" animosity.[43] From the court transcripts it is often difficult to tell when these extortion attempts were based on totally fabricated incidents or whether the extortionist entrapped his target with a real seduction. It is clear, however, that even quite young complainants could be astute about these matters. "The picannin laid the charge against me," complained Siangara of his thirteen-year-old servant in a typical case, complete with intimate descriptions of anal intercourse, "because he refused to do the work I told him to do."[44]

Finally, in cases that took place in prison or isolated labour camps where it truly could be said that neither women, "piccanins," nor cash were available, sex was sometimes negotiated between men or youths of similar age and status. In such cases there were no "damages" but the mutual exchange of favours. By no means were these favours strictly functional or entirely lacking in *joie de vivre*. On the contrary, it appears that the fun sometimes got out of control. As one prisoner complained to the Bulawayo magistrate about two of his cell-mates, "they were both lying on their side laughing and wriggling and making a noise and Mbwana told them if they went on like that he would call the guard."[45]

How did the men who engaged in sex with males regard themselves or the acts in question? We may plausibly surmise that some were "gay" in the sense of actually preferring sex with males for sensuous reasons and that a small number of repeat offenders was driven to repeated indiscretion at least in part by strength of their desire. The first of these repeat offenders was "Suzie," a thirty-something migrant labourer from Gazaland

(Mozambique) hauled before the courts because of his insistence on having sex with males on three different occasions between 1900 and 1903.[46] Simonas, alias Bye-Bye, also made his preference quite clear to one of his many "victims" in a case from Salisbury township in 1923. Simonas allegedly told Mapanda that "he preferred piccanins to girls,"[47] a preference that entailed anal intercourse on a daily basis. In several other cases, the innocence of the "victims" was called into question by medical testimony: "I am of the opinion as the result of my examination that the act of sodomy has been committed both parties consenting thereto," intoned one doctor; "sodomy might have been committed frequently previous to this," or "habitually," two others posited.[48] France, a juvenile Shona servant in Salisbury, "appeared to me to be a youth accustomed to the practice of sodomy," said a fourth.[49]

Manwere (alias Antonio, alias Joe or Jonas) deserves honorary mention at this point as the single most frequent guest of colonial hospitality for this tendency. A Sena originally from Port Herald (Tete province in Mozambique), Manwere first appeared before the courts as a precocious "victim" in Umtali in 1900. Although he claimed to have been sodomized for the first time by his employer (a compatriot from Mozambique), the medical doctor thought otherwise: "from the appearance of the anus I would say that he has been the passive agent before."[50] By the following year, still probably only ten or eleven years old, Manwere had graduated to the status of accused and was found guilty of sodomizing a co-worker on a commercial farm in the Salisbury area. Over the next sixteen years Manwere then found himself before the courts on similar charges no less than seven more times in various locales around the country, including industrial compounds, a hotel, and prison. On every occasion he denied the charge.[51]

A man closely fitting Manwere's description made a final appearance before a Rhodesian judge in 1919. Manwere had by this time left the migrant life to settle down in a "native kraal" near Mvuma. He was even married to a local woman and appeared to have given up his errant ways. The charge against him this time was in fact not sodomy at all but stock theft. Still, testimony that was offered in his defence hints at suspicions around his sexuality. Perhaps doubtful of his testimony on account of the long string of prior convictions against him, the court called Nawu, a five-year-old boy, as a character witness. This was a highly unusual step in itself, but even more striking is what the boy volunteered. Nawu explained that "acc lives at the kraal – my mother lives with acc but I don't know if he is my father although I call him father."[52] For a young child in a patriarchal society to publicly express doubts about his paternity suggests that his parents' relationship may have been a fictive marriage, a customary type of cover for Manwere's non-normative sexuality.

Of all the cases that came to court in the history of British South African Company rule, however, few more poignantly illustrate the possibility of love between African men than that of Mashumba and Njebe, referred to in chapter 1 because of the strange way their case came to light. These men identified themselves as BaSili (Bushmen), but they lived in a stable, settled, mainly agricultural community administered by an Ndebele chief. Their self-confessed behaviour can in no way be said to represent a throwback to some ancient hunting and gathering past or peculiar Bushman ways. The accused, Mashumba, was established to be about forty years of age. His wife had died four or five years earlier, and he claimed to have been unable to remarry thereafter. "I want to say that it was the need I was in through not being able to get a woman that tempted my heart and I made the boy Njebe agree to become a woman for me," he said.[53] For his part, the sixteen-year-old Njebe explained that "Accsd is my uncle. I live in the same hut with him. I sleep with him always and have done so for a long time. I have no blanket. Accsd has one. We sleep under the same blanket. Accsd has been committing sodomy with me for a long time. Accsd has no wife, his wife died some years ago at the time of the influenza. Since then I have been accsd's 'wife.'"[54]

Njebe went on to say that "We loved one another." Indeed, the relationship as it had developed over three years was qualitatively more egalitarian and mutual than what one would expect from the usual *nkotshane* model, despite the differences in age between the partners. "Every time accsd had connection with me he allowed me to do the same to him. We did it in the hut and also in the veld ... I never objected to accsd doing what he did before because it was not painful and I did it to him." This arrangement ended amicably, not because of dispute over money or the principle of sexual love between males. Rather, Njebe began to fret about the health consequences: "Were it not that I was afraid I might become pregnant I would have let accsd go on doing the act always." Mashumba accepted the worry as legitimate.

Njebe's expressed fear of pregnancy may have been literally true. It may also have been meant in a metaphorical sense, however, reflecting anxiety about the power of semen as *muti* or *divisi* (magic, protective charms). As seen in the previous chapters, semen could act as *divisi* bordering on witchcraft if put in the wrong place. Such *divisi* appeared to explain, for instance, the otherwise surprising success of Nyasaland (Malawian) migrant labourers in adapting to their hostile work and social environment in Southern Rhodesia. The Shona of colonial Salisbury and environs often condescended to these men, so that "MaNyasa" and "MaBlantyre" became synonymous with country bumpkins. They were also despised for occupying the dirtiest jobs, such as cleaning lavatories. The Shona word for public lavatory cleaner (*matanyera*) actually derives from a Malawian (chiNyanja) word for an extremely disgusting type of excrement, and carries with it highly derogatory connotations.[55] Even despised workers earned money, however, and with their earnings the Malawians early on acquired a reputation for seducing the wives and daughters of local men. How did they do it? To many Zimbabweans the answer to that question was (and still is) implicit in a second meaning attached to the word *matanyera* from at least the early 1920s: "for one male to have connection with another male between the thighs."[56] In other words, the Malawians managed to survive and even prosper in colonial Zimbabwe in part because of their powerful *muti*:

Nyaradzo Dzobo: What kind of men practiced *ngochani*?

Sekuru (grandfather) Nyabonda: The men who did this are like any other men in Zimbabwe, I mean the way they look and speak. But I do know that those who come from Malawi and Mozambique were more famous for it, in fact it seemed like they all did it. I was living in hostels and they were doing it there ... They do it to make their *muti* strong.

ND: What did the whites think about it, your bosses?

SN: We were afraid to report such things because the *ngochani* used strong herbs. They could use these to kill us or for making themselves powerful. That was why they became homosexuals ... otherwise the *muti* would not work very well. It's not necessarily that they didn't love women but that by loving boys the *muti* would work better. This could increase their power at work so they could earn more money. No one told the bosses because we were afraid of that *muti*.[57]

Migrants from Malawi who have settled in Zimbabwe do not dispute this. As Sekuru (grandfather) "D" explained, "My dear, note one thing. This thing was and is extremely private, especially in our Malawi tradition. Some have strong medicine for work or boxing and this has the strong rule that for it to be effective and to last a long time, you must have sex with another man and to show your power that way ... Here in Zimbabwe they do it but only after some of them were taught when they were used as boyfriends or were given this *muti* [by Malawians]."[58]

Other indigenous Shona and Ndebele may also have learned the practice from simple observation of high-profile public figures such as Dhuri or

James Mabala. Dhuri originally hailed from Nyasaland, eventually becoming a champion boxer and much-admired scofflaw in 1930s and '40s Salisbury Township. According to Scarnecchia, he lived as an "open homosexual" throughout his boxing years. His success as a boxer and his courage in flouting colonial police were widely attributed to his regular sexual consumption of young men. That Dhuri was never actually accused of sexual assault on males or punished for his "truculence" and "excitability" with colonial authorities only proved the efficacy of such *muti*.[59]

Dhuri was at the forefront of popularizing boxing and its attendant youth culture. By 1939 it had become "the private pre-occupation of countless houseboys ... [who] pursued the sport in any secluded grove of trees or distant space that offered.[60] This development was regarded with great ambivalence by Europeans and "respectable" African opinion, some of whom felt it a worthy distraction from criminal activity while others saw it as conducive to "vice," "sin," and "truculent spirit" (that is, anticolonial attitude). Ranger (1987) does not consider homosexuality in his analysis of the controversy, nor does it crop up in contemporary government documents or newspapers accounts. Dhuri's charismatic role in the boxing culture may, however, help to explain why missionaries and the African middle class were so sternly opposed to an African sports initiative.

James Mabala, meanwhile, was the leader of the Zvibengu gang in 1929 Bulawayo. According to the police, the Zvibengu was an offshoot of the Ninevites or 28s. Mabala himself was identified as Shona, and while little else is recorded about his history or activities, his sexuality is implicit from what we know of the Ninevites in South Africa. Intriguingly, Mabala was said to control a thriving illicit trade in *mangoromera*, a powerful *muti* imported from Mozambique that the police believed was fuelling gang violence. *Mangoromera* reputedly gave strength in battle and as such was "much sought after by youths in town."[61] By the late 1930s *mangoromera* was the *muti* of choice on the boxing scene (Ranger 1987, 205).

African men charged with sexual assaults upon males showed a wide range of reactions to getting hauled before the courts. Many had nothing to say at all. Others expressed frank surprise at the charges. "I admit the offence. I did not know it was a crime," conceded one thirty-two-year-old Ndebele man accused of anally raping a twelve-year-old boy. Since when was play (*d'hlalisa*) anybody else's business, let alone a matter of concern to the *mlungus* (whites)?[62] Those who did defend themselves most commonly either denied the charges altogether or portrayed the assault as a wet dream. Many sought to pass the buck to the demon drink. A Shona man employed at the Mazoe Citrus estate calmly explained this when informed that he was facing imprisonment for indecent assault upon a

young boy: "I might have done these things. I don't know, I was drunk."[63]
The accused in sodomy and indecent assault cases also frequently pleaded
that they had only done it after being advised to do so by their superiors
or after seeing it practised by others.[64] One defendant justified his actions
by simply stating that "in Beira [Mozambique] the big boys always had
connection with the piccanins and paid them for it."[65] Why shouldn't he
do it as well? Mangwire also seemed to be surprised that he was being
held responsible for his actions in a suburban police cell. "Prisoners often
do it," he justified himself. "It has been done to me in the same gaol."[66]

Those men who showed remorse for their actions commonly attributed
their behaviour to extreme loneliness, Satan, or even, in one case, "the
Supreme Diety." Marital status, as well, was sometimes cited to excuse
behaviour that would have been outrageous in a pre-modern setting.
Rubore, an indigenous adult, was caught by an African constable openly
masturbating in a residential area of Bulawayo. When approached he
reportedly said, "It was allright as he had no wife."[67] In another extraordinary case, a Chewa man even defended himself on customary grounds.
Kamtengo volunteered the statement to the police that "I do not [illegible]
deny the charge. In my country it is the custom to commit Sodomy when
we are unable to get a woman."[68]

Aside from sometimes dodgy defences, one of the most striking aspects
of the testimony of the accused in these cases of male-male sexual assault
is that they often did not concede that they had anything to be defensive
about. On the contrary, some were positively brazen about their right to gratify
themselves as men with violence if necessary. Thirty-year-old Siagwaka,
challenged for sodomizing Siatiki, said simply, "I have done it and I don't
care."[69] Others expressed a hint of sadness at having been brought to court
by unhappy (or ambitious?) "wives." "[H]e was my friend," Sitwala
plaintively told the court after his betrayal by Mumbera, "I called the
piccanin my friend."[70] "Friend" (shamwari in Shona) was indeed one of
the main euphemisms for ingotshana. As the police reported in a case of
two adult miners in 1913, "The accused [thirty-six-year-old Manswa] seem
to think that the act he had done was not serious as the Native Chimbango
was a friend of his."[71]

What was the attitude of the colonial state towards the emergence of new
and at least potentially subversive sexual practices? Unlike in South Africa,
in Southern Rhodesia there were no enquiries into, public debates about,
or policies directed at male-male sexuality. We can infer attitudes, debates,
and change over time, however, from examining the sentences meted out

to the men caught in the legal system. For example, in the early days and in some jurisdictions throughout the whole period, male-male sexuality was clearly regarded as highly repugnant and was consequently prosecuted with considerable zeal. Where guilt was established to the magistrates' satisfaction, punishments ranged up to five years in prison with hard labour or one year with one hundred lashes. This was light in comparison to "Black Peril" sexual crimes, which as late as 1934 still drew the death penalty, or to the harshness of punishments in earlier times in the Cape and Natal. It was quite severe, however, when compared to other gender or sexual crimes in Southern Rhodesia. Wife battery resulting in death, notably, could earn an African husband as little as three months' imprisonment if there were extenuating circumstances (such as she was a poor cook or a nag or had denied her husband his conjugal rights).[72] In light of that sentence, six months in prison with hard labour for having non-violently emitted semen onto another man's legs seems disproportionately harsh.[73] Sentencing in cases involving white men assaulting African males suggested even greater animosity on the part of colonial officials. At a time when white men could almost literally get away with murdering their African employees or got a slap on the wrist for raping African girls, and at a time when skilled white labour was at a premium, blacksmith George Burgess earned himself five years behind bars for his crime of raping an African male.[74]

Africans themselves only rarely alluded to their perception of European attitudes toward male-male sexuality. When they did it was mostly to invoke the white man's disapproval: "Please don't tell the White people," Muridzo allegedly pleaded of Magaya in 1925.[75] Zaza's defence against the accusation of indecent assault was simply that "my heart would not let me sleep with that boy, I am frightened of what the Government would do to me if I had slept with that boy."[76] To suggest that whites did *not* disapprove of such behaviour in fact swam strongly against the current of common sense. Yet on at least one occasion the surprising idea of white approval was used as a "seduction" gambit. "Picannin" explained in 1912 that Sangoma had prevailed upon him to allow thigh sex by claiming that "'even the white people know about that,' meaning that it was not wrong." The court reassured Picannin that this was not the case, sending Sangoma to prison for nine months.[77]

On the other hand, and again unlike in South Africa, Southern Rhodesian officials seemed almost determined not to know what was going on. The Leary/Taberer report does not seem to have circulated as far as Zimbabwe, and no archival record remains of even a confidential discussion of it.

Magistrates, meanwhile, were never given explicit guidelines to follow in their dispensation of justice on this matter – "punishment rests with the judge" was all the 1904 *Handbook of Colonial Criminal Law* had to say.[78] The police for their part did not even list the category of sodomy or unnatural crimes in their annual reports until 1927, despite the fact that sometimes dozens of cases came before the courts every year. Even confidential internal debates on prison conditions avoided the issue.

The first allusion to male-male sexuality in an official policy discussion on prisons only appeared in 1934. The question was how to reduce the number of African men being crowded into prisons.[79] As we saw in the previous chapter, this issue had been raised in South Africa as early as 1908, with overcrowding and the indiscriminate mixing of men convicted of petty offences together with hardened criminals identified as contributing to the spread of homosexual gangs. A single memo from the native commissioner of Sinoia (Chinoyi) hints at this risk only to dismiss it, confident of the heterosexual purity of "his" natives. Writing in support of the status quo, he argued "There is a risk of contamination in gaols for natives charged with petty offences, but for reasons peculiar to native life, the risk is small compared with that which a European would be in peril of amongst European convicts."[80]

This striking reticence to talk openly about situational homosexuality among Africans in colonial Zimbabwe, let alone do something about it, was not merely a conspiracy of silence among ass-covering bureaucrats. Rhodesian discretion about such matters triumphed as well over market forces. That is, newspaper editors throughout the colonial era did not run stories about even the most salacious homosexual scandals. A striking example of such restraint was in the case of James Noble, superintendant of Thabas Induna mission school near Bulawayo. Noble was charged in 1929 with nineteen counts of indecent assault against one of his teachers and no less than thirteen of his pupils.[81] Despite the sensational nature of the accusations and the fact that the case resulted in Noble's imprisonment, the case was not reported in the *Bulawayo Chronicle* (nor even, tellingly, in the published annual report of the British South African Police). Same-sex relations among migrant workers were not revealed by Lawrence Vambe in his 1949 piece in *African Weekly* on "shameful practices at industrial sites and power station compound." Indeed, the first published report of a homosexual incident in then Rhodesia was not until 1969, telling restraint in comparison to sensationalized accounts and public debates around Black Peril. The first official police comment on homosexual-related crime did not appear until 1972 – in a single sentence published in the annual report.[82]

It may be that this silence around male-male sexuality reflected a combination of sincere blindness on the part of Southern Rhodesian officials, unusual prudishness around the topic, or even chauvinism about the heterosexual "manliness" of "their" Natives versus those of the neighbouring colonies. A clue to a further possibility comes from Vambe's description of the migrant labourers passing through his village near the mining town of Arcturus:

Once they were in the country, Nyasaland and Portuguese East Africa became little more than accidents in their lives and their romantic search for the El Dorado and the fleshpots of white-controlled southern Africa went on. When their lusty, rough voices were raised in song and poetry, they did not recall their distant homes, wives and children, but such places as Gatooma, Que Que, Selukwe and Bulawayo in Southern Rhodesia, and the supposedly "heaven on Earth" cities of South Africa. The Arcturus mines and dreary farms and Herrenvolk-type employers were mere stepping-stones to the greater splendour of the Union of South Africa. As the Crusaders of old were drawn to the Holy Sepulchre in Palestine, these men were irresistibly drawn to the south, and with such a compelling urge that the hazards of the trail seemed not to matter. (Vambe 1972, 229)

This is to say that the shortage of labour in Southern Rhodesia was so acute and the economic health of industry and commercial farming so precarious compared to South Africa that officials simply could not allow themselves to brook the slightest doubts about anything that helped to stabilize the labour situation. This was what van Onselen (1976) meant when he referred to "sex in the service of industry." Powerful self-censorship about the sexual eccentricities of these migrants was one small way to contribute to slowing the haemorrhage of cheap labour from the country.

Fear of stirring up a hornet's nest with dangerous ramifications for labour stability should not be underestimated. Remember that even the Christian missionary who first broke the scandal of African men's behaviour in South Africa conceded that he had suppressed his concerns for years because of his worries about disrupting the flow of labour to the mines. A further factor in Southern Rhodesia, however, may ultimately have been more decisive: the liberal tendencies of the magistrates who were left on their own to interpret the law. Some of these men were eminently retrograde in their views on gender and race. Yet as a whole and with some outstanding individual examples, they confound the stereotype of reactionary settler. Indeed, the magistrates tended to see themselves at the vanguard of building a relatively liberal, pluralist, and tolerant colonial society. Southern Rhodesia had been founded with those ideals in mind, particularly as they applied to British-Afrikaner relations but also in terms of enlightened native policy. With respect to same-sex practices, the magistrates therefore tended to keep in line with a long-standing trend in the Cape Colony and in Britain itself, that is, to interpret the law in increasingly liberal ways. As early as the 1900s, for example, courts began to differentiate between cases involving violence and those in which the complainant either enjoyed or profited from the act. If the latter were demonstrated to have been the case, the charge was usually downgraded from sodomy or attempted sodomy to indecent assault.

Some magistrates began to dismiss cases altogether as soon as they suspected that there had been prior consent to the alleged assault. "It seems to me no offense has been committed," ruled L.F.H. Roberts in 1913 in dismissing a case where the complainant had repeatedly accepted payment for intracural sex but came to court after the accused had attempted anal penetration.[83] The attorney general simply declined to prosecute a case of another case of consensual sex in 1915: "As complainant was old enough to appreciate what was being done, and consented, no crime was committed."[84] The solicitor general, Clarkson Tredgold, overturned a conviction for indecent assault in a local court because, as he phrased it in 1922, the evidence "points almost directly to a case of consent."[85] Tredgold also reduced the sentence levied by the native commissioner of Gutu upon a court messenger accused of sodomy. The "whole affair was so trivial," he ruled, that it should never have come to court in the first place.[86] A total sentence of fifteen cuts with a cane, which in 1892 had been the daily prescription for men convicted of indecent assault on males, was reduced to seven by the attorney general in 1925 on the grounds that such an amount "savours I am afraid of brutality."[87]

That African men observed this liberalizing tendency, and so progressively stopped bringing their more routine cases to court, is implied in some of their testimony. One *ingotshana* defended his tardiness in reporting an assault as arising from his belief that the police no longer cared. "I did not report it because they said the white people know these things we are doing," he said, meaning that they no longer cared about it and could not be relied upon to see justice done in the hoped-for manner.[88] The overall decline in the number of court cases after 1912 suggests the same. How else can the virtual disappearance of male-male sex crimes from Hartley be explained? From an average of one case every two months in the mid-1910s, the number coming to court dwindled in the late 1920s. A single case of sodomy between 1928 and 1931 was discharged as a false allegation, while in the first three years of the 1940s not even indecent assault charges were laid.[89] Had African men suddenly found virtue and abandoned their lusty ways? More likely they found that lodging a complaint on such matters had become a waste of time.

Colonial Zimbabwe clearly was not a heterosexual enclave. Indeed, despite important differences with the colonies that became South Africa, Southern Rhodesia experienced many analogous changes in male sexuality. In both cases, male-male sexual behaviour involving adults was probably rare before colonial rule but became common soon after, at least in certain contexts. "Unnatural crimes" in both places similarly occurred overwhelmingly between African males and not as a result of "instruction" by Europeans, Indians, Arabs, Portuguese, Coloureds, or any other supposedly decadent and morally degraded people.

The evidence from Zimbabwe, however, suggests that Moodie and other historians are wrong to identify this development so closely with mining compounds or prisons. In fact, male-male sexual crimes were committed throughout the country – on rural commercial farms, in the administrative and agricultural centres, in police camps and prisons, in urban households, in hospitals, and even (albeit rarely) in "native kraals." Although prisoners and "alien natives" do comprise a disproportionate number of those accused, indigenous men and boys were a significant and generally increasing minority over the first forty years of colonial rule. Almost all of these were internal migrants. Yet a sufficient number of cases of men with female wives or prostitutes nearby exists to call into question the "sexual frustration" explanation for men turning to men for sexual release.

Similarly, African men's sexual attraction to men cannot be explained simply by the conditions of accommodation. As van Onselen has suggested, this may indeed have been the case in many instances. In cramped huts or workers' quarters, men's and boys' naked bodies were often pressed together in the most intimate contact. The common defence that "I was only dreaming" is surely plausible under such conditions. However, cases of men travelling some distance seeking sex from a specific person are also found throughout the record. These men had their own quarters, their own beds, and their own blankets. They clearly were not forced or even unconsciously enticed to commit "indecent acts." They chose to do so.

This element of agency is brought forward by Moodie, Harries, and other recent scholars. Yet in doing so, they assert that mine marriages were rigidly structured, hierarchical, and, at root, functional for the maintenance of both patriarchy in the rural areas and profits for the big corporations. The evidence from Zimbabwe is ambiguous on this. Certainly, cases of older men preying upon "piccanins" were the most common type of male-male sexual crime to be reported. In these cases the men may well have had some of the motivations stereotypically ascribed to them: fear of sexually transmitted disease or the desire to pass the humiliations structured into their work experience down the social hierarchy. But many other cases that bear witness to the existence of male-male sexual relationships simply cannot be categorized in functionalist terms. These include relationships between men and adolescents of rough parity in age and employment status. Actual sexual practices also varied to an extent that forces us to question the dominance of a strictly rule-bound sexuality. There is testimony as well to mutual consent and enjoyment and to emotions such as love, affection, and jealousy. That these emotions can be discerned even through so opaque a mirror as court records suggests that they were quite powerful.

Finally, the role of the state in policing male homosexual crime was ambivalent. At one level there was hostility and revulsion. To Africans' own reluctance to admit to such behaviour, however, was added colonial officials' rigorous self-censorship or averting of eyes to make *ingotshana* virtually invisible to the public record. In the absence of any clear-cut policy, then, magistrates adjudicated individual cases according to their own prejudices and on an ad hoc basis. This evolved over the period to witness a growing tolerance of consensual male-male sexual relations. Although the courts continued to be highly intolerant of interracial homosexual relations (just as they were of interracial heterosexual relations), magistrates and police were increasingly inclined to turn a blind eye to non-violent sexual affairs between African males.

We cannot know how common such affairs were, nor how enduring the emotions that they involved. We can safely conclude, however, that historically a much more significant proportion of Zimbabwe's black male population engaged in sexual relations with other men than has hitherto been acknowledged.

5

Fear and Loathing: Settlers

European men did not introduce male-male sex in southern Africa. They were, however, the first to unabashedly admit an actual preference for sex with males than with females for reasons of sensual desire. As George Snell, a twenty-nine-year old Englishman living in Cape Town, responded defiantly to the accusation of sodomy in 1891, "Yes, I do like men, I love men, and hate the sight of women. I am willing either to commit an unnatural offence upon a man, or to allow a man to commit the same upon my person."[1]

Joseph Carey of Durban was even more forceful about his preferences. A sailor, he allegedly boasted how "he had been in the habit of fucking every man on board the ships on which he had been." An accomplice in one of his homosexual rapes told the court that Carey had told him it was a "common thing" in the American navy. "He learnt it there. He did it there and does it wherever he goes. He preferred having a boy to fuck than a woman. Then I asked him whether he could call himself a respectable man. He said yes. I told him he was a disgrace to his country, to his countrymen, to the vessel he was on board and to everyone with whom he was on board. I asked him whether he should like the lady who was aboard to be made aware of such a conduct by one of the officers of the vessel. He answered me with an oath. He did not care a goddamn if she knows it."[2]

Very little about female-female sexuality is documented from this early period. A fragment of evidence from the 1930s, however, hints that white women could also express self-confidence in their attraction to women, despite the enormous social pressures to deny it. "People can say what they like," wrote Moira to Alma in one of a series of passionate letters from the eastern Cape dated 1931, "but I don't believe that there is anything sick or unclean about our love. Is it so unnatural to want you not a husband or babies?" An admiring sketch of Alma's naked breasts in another letter, and a closing salutation of "your loving wife" in yet another, make it clear that she felt that this was indeed not an unnatural desire.[3]

Europeans like Henri Junod who decried Africans' supposed shameless-ness about *nkotshane* look rather foolish in light of such bold assertions by Europeans. Those African men who took or became *izinkotshane* in fact almost always disavowed a sensual, sexual preference for doing so. Many claimed that they did not consider ejaculating between someone's thighs to be sex at all. Sex, by customary definition, was rather an act that served to propagate the lineage, to connect one politically to another family, and to connect one metaphysically to the ancestors. This notion of what constitutes a "real" sex act is still reflected today in an inability among many Zimbabweans to conceive the purpose of homosex. A sense of apparently sincere bafflement comes through strongly, for example, in some of the speeches of Zimbabwe's parliamentarians at the time of President Mugabe's denunciations of homosexuality. "We have asked these men whether they have been able to get pregnant," intoned Mr Border Gezi. "They have not been able to answer such questions. Even the women who are engaging in lesbian activities, we have asked them what they have got from such practices and no one has been able to answer."[4]

Comments like this have been interpreted by some observers from the West as evidence of a deep, perhaps essential homophobia in African culture. Yet if homophobia is understood as an active loathing or fear of same-sex sexual behaviour and desires, then such comments do not truly warrant the term. They represent incomprehension, to be sure, but possibly also the echo of an ancient de facto tolerance for sexual eccentricities. Provided the person was discreet and that the sexual activities did not threaten the interests of the extended family, then what he or she did in private was not a particular concern. Mr Gezi expressed this in the same debate as cited above. He told parliament that his rural constituents "hear that there is homosexualism and lesbianism going on. They have asked us and said that this is not a good practice. They say that if homosexualism and lesbianism is to go on, *it should be done privately*."[5]

The following exchange between a GALZ researcher and a seventy-two-year-old female Shangaan *n'anga* makes a similar point. Her words also reflect a stark disjuncture between the incitements to homophobic violence by Robert Mugabe and his chief supporters on the one hand and elderly guardians of tradition on the other:

W: Do you see today's society in modern day Zimbabwe accepting homosexuality at all?

Mbuya: It all depends where one is. *In the rural areas where culture is deep rooted, I think this is understood*, but the best way to deal with it is being quiet about it as I said.[6]

Such fear of the public transgression of sexual norms (rather than of the sex acts themselves) is more accurately termed transphobia than homophobia. Transphobia can be offensive and oppressive to individuals who seek to freely express their sexuality or to challenge restrictive notions of matching physical sex to gender identity to sexual orientation or conduct; nonetheless, it implies a passive de facto tolerance of discreet same-sex physical and emotional intimacy that in important ways has been an ally of gays and lesbians in the region. K. Limakatso Kendall (1999), writing about contemporary Lesotho from a lesbian perspective, warns that this element of tolerance has been undermined in recent years. The transphobia in African culture is now coming out in explicitly homophobic terms in response to various aspects of colonial rule/apartheid, Christian missionary propaganda, and the structures of the racial capitalist economy. One of her arguments, therefore, is that homophobia, not homosexuality, is the real "white man's disease" in the region. The imported, derogatory language used by some of the more vocal of Zimbabwe's anti-homosexual vigilantes supports this possibility. Certainly, there is no indigenous Shona or Ndebele word for "poofs."[7]

In this and the following chapter I would like to explore Kendall's largely intuitive argument through empirical evidence relating to the origins of explicit forms of homophobia in southern Africa. In addition to the sources used so far to uncover the early history of same-sex relationships, I will be considering representations of homosexuality as they appeared in the popular press and literature of South Africa and Zimbabwe right up to the 1990s. The present chapter looks at contestations around the meaning and appropriate reactions to same-sex sexuality among whites, while the next looks at how these debates "trickled down" or were interpreted by black Africans.

The word *homophobia* was coined in 1969 at the time of the emergence in the United States of the modern gay rights movement and sharp political reactions against it. To apply the word to the historical past therefore is, strictly speaking, anachronistic. The attitudes and behaviour it describes, however, clearly existed long before they had an explicit name. They can easily be discerned in the rich documentary evidence attesting to sexuality in medieval and Renaissance European history. Portugal, for example, which later earned the reputation for being a place that was relatively tolerant of homosexuality, has crudely anti-homosexual literature dating from the fourteenth and fifteenth centuries. The Portuguese and Spanish Inquisitions from the sixteenth to eighteenth centuries together resulted in hundreds of public executions for the "nefarious sin" of sodomy. According to Mark Jordan, as many men were put to death for sodomy during the Inquisition as were for heresy, usually by the agonizing method of being burnt at the stake.[8] This cruelty was justified by select reference to Christian texts and the imputed will of God. As Portuguese Inquisitorial law in the sixteenth century expressed it: "Above all other sins, the vilest, dirtiest and most dishonest is Sodomy and no other is as abhorrent to God and the world that the mere mention of this sin without any other act is already so serious and abhorrent that it putrefies the air and because of it God sent the flood over the earth, destroying Sodom and Gomorrah and the Knights Templar" (Mott 2000, 471).

The Calvinist Dutch also performed executions for "monstrous lust," including at their colonial outpost of Kaap Stadt. That brutality was continued by the British after they took possession of the Cape Colony, albeit in reduced numbers and with relatively humane despatch by the gallows. Yet the same religion that justified capital punishment provided an alternative discourse that promoted tolerance or acceptance of diverse sexual natures. The Christian ideals of forgiveness, "love thy neighbour," and submission to "God's plan" (which might include God's having planted innate feelings of homosexual orientation in thy neighbour if not thyself in the first place) all undermined the consistency of anti-sodomy persecutions in the name of Christ. Noel Annan even argues that within the Anglican church at least, a "cult of homosexuality" developed in the late nineteenth century that idealized male-male sexual love as a way to attain a purer knowledge of Christian love than the heterosexual vocation could allow (Annan 1990). Lane (1995) has also argued that repressed homosexuality was idealized among the colonial officer class as a way to inculcate appropriately masculine warrior discipline and camaraderie.

Adding to the confusion was the emergence in the mid-late nineteenth century of new, secular explanations of same-sex sexuality. The new "science" of psychology in particular, most influentially through the work of Sigmund Freud after 1890, saw "sexual inversion," "uranism," and other categories of neatly demarcated "perversion" not as the outcome of a free will to sin but as the result of a combination of natural human bisexuality and misguided parenting. These new theories allowed fear, hatred, and contempt to give way to some extent to pity and condescension. While still stigmatizing, they complicated the old fire and brimstone condemnations of the individual transgressors, increasingly so as the power and social influence of the Christian churches waned in the metropoles. Long-standing religious prejudices and the ferocious application of the law thus ebbed over the course of the century. Catholic Portugal actually led the way in this respect in 1852 among the powers that colonized southern Africa by dropping all mention of same-sex sexuality from its new criminal code (Howes 2000). In the British colonies, sodomy and other supposedly unnatural acts remained criminal offences, but by the 1870s "the ancient severity of the law had fallen into desuetude." By the 1910s and '20s in colonial Zimbabwe, there was not only a clear tendency towards more lenient sentencing for male-male sexual crimes but also for the police to ignore all but the most flagrant cases.

Men and boys who were truly affronted by homosexual solicitations or who were victims of actual sexual assault would have noticed this liberalizing tendency in the courts. In the prisons and mine hostels especially, it became increasingly obvious that the state might punish the complainant as much as the assailant if the former's own behaviour were not absolutely faultless. Considering the shame of being victimized by sexual assault, as well as the expense or dangers of lodging a complaint in the first place, fewer and fewer men took the risk. Rather, the possibility of encountering a lack of sympathy in the court system helped to turn victims away from the courts and police in favour of private avenues of redress. The Scotland gang (27s) purportedly had its origins in South Africa as a defence against the homosexually predatory 28s. The first evidence of privatized violence against male sexual assailants in Southern Rhodesia comes from just a bit later. Nyama in 1927 appeared in court with a broken collarbone inflicted upon him by the complainant and his friends in retribution for an alleged sexual assault.[9] Another "victim" of indecent assault explained his tardiness and reluctance to bring charges against his assailant. As he explained to a Salisbury judge in 1931, he had not initially reported the incident but had simply "decided to get up a gang to give accused a hiding."[10] In this case, the gang was white.

Ultimately more significant to the history of homophobia than these isolated acts of defensive or vigilante violence against men thought to be homosexual was the internalization of hostility towards same-sex sexuality, or indeed, any kind of intimacy that might call into question sharply dichotomous gender roles for males and females. In this internalization process, elite and official revulsion against same-sex sexuality became "common sense" among the mass of the population, policed by self-censorship or peer pressure rather than by church or state. The need for internalized markers grew in importance as the old external markers of masculine gender identity eroded through loss of land, of artisan or self-subsistence skills, of authority over children and women, and of certainty in simple, externally defined codes of moral behaviour and masculine ideals – or, as Swart (1998) puts it in reference to dispossessed Boer republicans, loss of gun, wife, and horse. The internal markers were inculcated into men's consciousness by propaganda trickling down from the emerging scientific discourses around gender, sexuality, and psychiatry and by the idealization of role models of unambiguously heterosexual heroism. An effect was to conflate private sexuality with public gender identity. In other words, over time the notion became common sense that if a man had sex with a male he was not merely a sinner (who could be forgiven or rehabilitated): he was effete by nature and character. Even if he took the masculine (inserter) role in the sex act, by virtue of his transgression of the heterosexual norm for sex object, he could not be truly masculine. As such, he was not deserving of all the rights and privileges that that gender identity entailed. In order to ensure access to those rights and privileges, he therefore had to thoroughly expunge from his behaviour and consciousness all those traits or desires that might be interpreted to call them into question.

This conflation of sexuality and gender identity accompanied and supported the ideology of "familialism" – that is, the idealization or naturalization of male-dominated, nuclear family units with women largely confined to unpaid labour in the household (Barrett 1980). As Michel Foucault first argued, and has since been both demonstrated and debated in a huge academic literature, familialism/internalized homophobia could be linked to the exercise of political power by men of a specific class and racial background. While never planned with conspiratorial foresight, it was undoubtedly functional to the accumulation of industrial capital. Internalized homophobia emerged as a social norm that helped whip working-class boys into narrow, repressive stereotypes of manliness. The invention of "the homosexual" in appropriately scientific terms also served to buttress the claims for political and social power of western Europe's rising class of bourgeoisie (virile, healthy, self-disciplined) over both the aristocracy (foppish, unhealthy, self-indulgent) and the working classes (brutish and needful of state intervention to improve behaviour).

Scholars have since extended this Foucauldian analysis to the colonial world, arguing that debates (and silences) around same-sex and interracial sexuality tended to serve not only the bourgeoisie but also Europe's larger imperial interests. Rudi Bleys (1995), for example, has shown that it was

European ethnographers, not Africans, who first insisted that homosexual behaviour was exotic to most of Africa south of the Sahara. Why such a consensus in the face of often contradictory evidence? Bleys argues that the one hand, the stereotype of black Africa lying outside a sodomy-friendly Sotadic zone was useful to preparing public opinion in Britain, France, and Germany for the abolition of the slave trade by force, if necessary (viz., black Africans are exclusively heterosexual and therefore basically moral and so deserving of our protection against sodomistic Arabs and Portuguese). The stereotype of exclusively heterosexual black Africans was also useful in buttressing the new, rigid ideologies of masculinity and femininity within Europe and within the men charged with building empire abroad (viz., even black savages don't do this thing, so why do you, you beast).

The struggle to redefine masculinity among whites was especially fraught on the frontiers between white settlement/missions and non-white societies. Ann Stoler's observations about intimate aspects of Dutch colonialization in Java are pertinent to southern Africa in this regard: "The colonial measure of what it took to be classified as 'European' was based not on skin color alone but on tenuously balanced assessments of who was judged to act with reason, affective appropriateness, and a sense of morality" (2002, 6). Gail Bederman's 1995 analysis of the "renaissance" of virile manliness in late nineteenth century United States also has particular resonance for southern Africa, beset as the two societies both were with the problems of incorporating often hostile, culturally distinct Others and mixed-race populations within an expanding frontier of white settlement. White men needed to be disciplined into a commanding, "naturally" awe-inspiring force. The law was one element in this, of course, reflected in the disproportionately severe sentences meted out to white men found guilty of sodomy with African men. But the renaissance of virility among white men, and of a parallel domesticity among white women, also took place in the sphere of everyday activity and socialization. Robert Morrell (1996, 2001b) has shown how the sport of rugby was actively and self-consciously promoted among white youths in late nineteenth century Natal in order to train and demarcate a clear, elite class of masculinity. Shirley Brooks (2001) has also looked at this process of creating a white, leader ideal of masculinity through the hunting and conservation movement in Natal. In both Natal and Southern Rhodesia, the sex-segregated "public schools" were a critical element in transforming sexually unruly boys into refined gentlemen who could fulfil "Rhodes's ideals" – ambition, polish, stability, discipline, initiative, efficiency, and such (Summers 1994, 251). As Morrell's informants recalled, this process demanded that suspected "real" homosexuality be mercilessly thrashed or mocked out of pupils, as much by each other as by school authorities.

Health and medicine were invoked in this process through countless speeches, sermons, and journalistic reports. The neat distinctions of personality disorder tended to get blurred in the process, and implicitly tolerant (if patronizing) psychological theories were susceptible to demagogic simplifications and elisions in the popular imagination. Typically, for instance, "situational" and "congenital" homosexuality were conflated. Also common was the notion that homosexuality was indicative of if not equivalent to paedophilia. New stereotypes replaced the old.

At the turn of the century the main areas of concern in the shaping of proper white sexuality included as well interracial sex and masturbation. The former was especially feared as leading to miscegenation, the "pollution" of the supposedly natural purity and strength of the master race. It was also thought to bring whites into disrepute among the non-whites who participated in the unseemly exchange of bodily fluids and emotions. Masturbation, meanwhile, was believed to cause both psychological and physical debilitation. In boys it was said to cause hair to grow on the palm of the hand or blindness, in girls hysteria and weakness. That masturbation was becoming more common was taken for granted in light of the breakdown of the old rural moral economy and of stern, religious upbringing. In the context of rapidly industrializing South Africa, this was not merely the concern of Christian missionaries and schoolteachers – it actually became possible for a doctor to earn his living by providing white people with advice on how to cultivate their dignity by repressing children's urge to fondle themselves.

Dr Karl von Oppell put it this way in his address to white Transvaal children around 1896: "As I have seen in my medical practice already many children becoming sick, nay, even dying, through playing on the lower part of the body, I will warn you against such doings in this paper. The parts out of which the urine flows are of the most sensitive and delicate nature, and are as much in danger of being injured as the eye by pressing, rubbing, or any other irritating usage. You must, therefore, guard against every unnecessary seizing of those parts of the body, and warn other children against doing the same, and inform their parents if they will not be advised by you."[11]

As it turned out, southern African white men proved their mettle as warriors in World War I, and anxiety about the ill-effects of masturbation or even limited same-sex intimacy appeared to have been proven wrong. Indeed, although his evidence comes from Canadian troops and deals mostly with World War II situations, Paul Jackson's research (2002) on homosexuality among soldiers fighting in Europe suggests that men who had sex with men in the armed forces were not necessarily shunned or even punished. In many cases they were shielded by their commanding officers and fellow soldiers alike, their worth as fighters and comrades-in-arms superceding popular fears about their sexuality that may have been learned on the home front. Something to this effect was actually the "come-on" line of Superintendent James Noble with Jeremiah Hlabangana, one of his teachers at Thaba Induna mission school near Bulawayo. According to Hlabangana, prior to sexually assaulting him Noble came to his room and "told me stories about the men in the trenches during the War."[12]

However, wartime homosexual experiences did not translate into a more tolerant society in the postwar period. On the contrary, by the 1930s overtly homophobic fascist ideologies of masculinity and race were well known and considerably admired in much of white South Africa. Popular perceptions of lax official attitudes towards homosexuality thus likely played a role in sparking the region's first "moral panic" around homosexuality among white youth in 1939. A second world war was obviously imminent. How would the local boys stand up this time? Not very well, it was feared, following revelations of the existence of an organized male prostitution ring in Johannesburg. "AMAZING SOCIAL SCANDAL," screamed the *Sunday Mail* as it broke the news. Almost daily, sensational articles and letters in the Johannesburg press thereafter demanded stern action be taken to root out the evils that had apparently crept into urban life. These evils clearly stemmed not just from the system of juvenile detention houses scattered around the city ("Juvenile Devil's Islands," as the *Sunday Mail* put it on 5 February 1939). There also appeared to be a "conspiracy of silence" by civic officials and church leaders that had allowed the rot to spread.

A Freudian psychiatrist came forward to testify at the trial of the man at the centre of the accusations, to answer the terrible questions about racial decline in a scientific-sounding way and propose a solution.[13] Dr Louis Freed argued that the root cause of the corruption was poor mothering, and that the state should intervene to counsel white mothers on a mass scale so as to nip future perverts in the bud. The state would need to ensure that white mothers did not undermine their sons' virility by, for example, excessive displays of affection. In this analysis Freed probably took at least partial inspiration from the American Psychiatric Association, which, contrary to the views of Freud himself at this time, had formally declared homosexuality to be a personality disorder.

Freed went on to build a career out of "explaining" male homosexuality in these terms and popularizing the blame-the-mothers school of psychiatry. In the 1950s he extended his analysis to Africans as well, joining a growing pool of Freudians who sought to link African sexual behaviour (and hence unfitness to rule) to African child-rearing practices. As in the earlier ethnography, there was a clear message for whites implicit in this mass psychoanalysis of African populations. Sometimes this held Africans up in a positive light. B.J.F. Laubscher, for example, observing the rarity of overt homosexuality among Africans in the kraals, as he put it, attributed this to the custom of male circumcision, which "solves the Oedipal complex" (1937, 283). John Ritchie of the Livingstone Institute, by contrast (1943), argued that "excessive" breast-feeding of male infants by African mothers fatally undermined the benefits of initiation by derailing the boys' transition from infant neediness to psychological adulthood and manliness. This he held to account for the African male's inability to stay monogamous, save money, work, and a whole host of other "typical" African failings. The lesson was clear and suitably scientific-sounding to appeal to the modern-day ruling race: White parents who cared that their sons became culturally white, civilized, and virile would do well to avoid the mistakes of African parents. Breastfeeding should be minimized, and emotional distancing and hardening should commence as early in infanthood as possible, especially between father and son.

With the advent to power of the National Party in 1948 and the institutionalization not just of apartheid but also of moral conservatism backed by the state and the Dutch Reformed Church, the climate for white gays and lesbians worsened dramatically (as indeed it did for any dissident expressions of sexuality such as interracial affairs). By no means was the new regime swimming alone against the world tide in this respect. Pseudo-scientific and political arguments in favour of repressing homosexuality emerged with renewed vigour from the United States in particular. American military medical doctors and psychiatrists sought to understand why there had been a dramatically higher rate of post-traumatic stress syndrome ("battle fatigue") in World War II compared to previous wars. Freudian theories blamed over-protective mothers for weakening, effeminizing, and ultimately homosexualizing their sons. In the context of the Cold War, such mothers and the men they reared came to be regarded as a weak link in the defence against communism. Not only did homosexual men supposedly lack the moral fibre of Real Men but also (and this was demonstrably true in a number of cases) their illicit desires made them disproportionately susceptible to blackmail by Soviet spies.[14]

These ideas percolated into official policy in the United States and many of its Cold War allies. Bureaucratic witch-hunts and suicides of accused homosexuals were among the results. Homophobia also permeated American popular culture, which, via Hollywood, was avidly consumed in South Africa. Katie Mooney (1998) has directly linked American popular culture to the rise of an explicitly homophobic white youth subculture in South African cities in the 1950s. At a time of increasing state efforts at social engineering, of repressive sexual morality, and of family dislocation caused by rapid urbanization and suburbanization, these gangs emerged as an important way for white youth to develop and express their identity independently of parents, state, and church. The young men cultivated a machismo that rejected social norms by embracing violence and despising monogamy, yet stressed conformity of style and heterosexual display.

"Moffie-bashing" or "bunny-bashing" was one such display. According to one of Katie Mooney's informants, these gang expeditions could be exceedingly brutal: "they got hold of a few pig's tails, they shave it so it's only got a bit of hair on it – now with the pig's tail all the hair lies one way – They went into Hillbrow that night and they hunted down the *queers* and each *queer* they found they grabbed and took one of these tails and they rammed it up their backside and they couldn't pull it out, it goes in one way and you couldn't get it out ... The Duckies were very anti-*queer* ... one of the boys ended up in Hillbrow hospital and the tail had to be cut out" (1998, 771).

This long century of homophobic inculturation also had a profound effect upon men and women who felt they were not "normal." An indication of internalized homophobia is provided by the gay argot that emerged among South Africa whites after World War II. *Moffietaal* or *Gayle* was a secret language used by gay-identified people to find each other without calling wider attention to their sexuality. As Ken Cage points out, Gayle is often overtly homophobic in its terminology. The word "queen," for example, is used as an intensifier of stigma, ("what a Nora [drunk]" compared to "what a Nora Queen [fucking drunk])." Gayle nouns also often dehumanize homosexual lovers ("piece," "number," "stuk," "pomp," "fuck"). The effects of internalized homophobia in fact comprise a recurrent theme in gay men's writing from South Africa.[15] In this writing, men's repressed homosexual feelings or self-hatred is deflected by public performances of homophobic rage, including the rape of women as a "cure" or the rape of men to show contempt. For some gay men, to be victimized by such rape, or even to overhear such merciless homophobia, confirmed their feelings of self-loathing or hopelessness. Suicide and other forms of self-destructive behaviour were ways to escape those feelings. To the extent that sexual orientation became known to the public as a contributing factor in the alcoholism or the suicide, it fed back into the public stereotype of homosexuals as an inherently weak link in the chain of being.

Nick Southey eloquently describes the emotional turmoil that realization of his own homosexuality in such a homophobic society caused. His account of how the headmaster of St Alban's College (Anglican) dealt with a homosexual scandal in the 1970s vividly captures the trauma and the rhetorical overkill to which white boys were subjected:

Summoning the entire school into emergency assembly, he icily and bluntly delivered a tirade against perversion, corruption and immorality. This was an offence unto the laws of God, the laws of the state, the laws of the natural order, even more despicable among elite boys such as ourselves, destined as we were to offer leadership within society by right of birth and by example. It was a threat to the very foundations of the school; other offenders would be hunted down and expelled; future deviants could expect the harshest retribution. It was a *tour de force*, this definition of codes of masculine behaviour, and went straight to the core of my being, for I realised then, with blinding clarity, that I was indeed different, and that I was damned. (1997b, 45–5)

The stigma attached to male-male sexuality made it susceptible to exploitation for political ends. The temptation to use accusations of homosexuality to advance ethnocentric or nationalist agendas was particularly strong. Nick Southey (1997a) has documented the first such instance in the region, a close study of how protestations of revulsion against male-male sexuality were transparently a means to score political points against an ethnic group/political enemy. The case unfolded in the independent Afrikaner republic Orange Free State in the mid-1860s. The Free State at that time was under the relatively liberal regime of J.H. Brand, and the capital city, Bloemfontein, was seen as something of a melting pot where old enemies – the Boers and Brits – could live together harmoniously. Indeed, the English-speaking population of traders, missionaries, and settlers was growing so quickly that an Anglican bishopric was created to cater to its spiritual needs. The first man to take up the position was Edward Twells. Twells seems to have begun unspecified same-sex acts soon after his arrival in 1863. This was known or suspected by colleagues who for years remained mute about it. In the context of the climate of good relations that then existed between the British minority and the Afrikaner majority in the state, discretion around a potentially inflammable topic seemed advisable.

Those good relations deteriorated rapidly after 1865, and the Brand government began to face increasing criticism from Boer hard-liners who resented the British presence and British imperial policy. When Britain openly sided against the Free State by declaring a protectorate over neighbouring Basutoland (1868), the hard-liners seized their chance. Free State police issued a warrant for Twells's arrest, and over the next few days, the Afrikaner press howled its denunciation of him. By association, it also condemned the British and the British-friendly Brand regime. "God-defying," "shameless and God-forsaken," "satanic lust," "animal-like behaviour," "pollute our children," and like sentiments sought to mobilize Afrikaner nationalism, perhaps to drive the British out, perhaps to justify a war to finish off the Basotho. By contrast, the English-language press was restrained. It, and Twells's superiors, at first tried to give Twells the benefit of the doubt. His demonization quickly gained ascendancy, however, as it proved useful to his superiors' own enemies within the Anglican church, then riven by deep doctrinal disputes. The charges against Twells were never proven (nor even made explicit), but his disgrace weakened the dominance of the High Anglican or Anglo-Catholic faction within the church. Twells fled the country.

A comparison between the Bucknill and the Leary/Taberer investigations of 1906 and 1907 provides another glimpse of how the level of official revulsion against male-male sexual activity was partly dependent upon the political context in which accusations were being made. In other words, it made a big difference who precisely was doing what to whom and what else was happening at the time. That African men were having sex with each other and their "umfaans" at the mines was well known from at least the 1890s but had not been subject to close official enquiry or suppression. On the contrary, given the critical shortages of African labour, "their vile practice of 'hlabonga'" seems to have been tacitly condoned, if not defended. This went to the extent (in 1902) of official collusion in blocking diplomatic representations about conditions at the mine hostels from (ironically) the supposedly sodomy-tolerant Portuguese.

The situation changed dramatically after 1904, not because African men's activities suddenly became more vile but because of the importation of large numbers of Chinese labourers. Unlike Africans, the Chinese were regarded by white labourers as more or less civilized and, as such, a direct threat to their relatively well-paying jobs. They made many attempts to have the Chinese deported, and the flurry of accusations about Chinese catamites in 1906 clearly arose from growing frustration among white workers that their other forms of protest were failing. Indeed, when the scandal first broke, British officials immediately suspected it was a cynical ploy, the invention of a self-serving American missionary among the white workers. One official, hinting at a Republican plot, cast withering scorn upon the allegations and the motives of the man behind them. "[C]an he produce a creature so vile as to give evidence to the effect that he has seen a man in the act of committing the crime of sodomy and having seen did not take summary action in the matter?" he asked, rhetorically answering himself, "of course not."[16]

In the context of postwar reconstruction, however, even cynical ploys had to be dealt with and democratic appearances maintained. The allegations of unnatural vice among the Chinese had caused an uproar – angry town-hall meetings, politically dangerous posturing by parties claiming to represent the interests of the white working classes and Afrikaner farmers, and heated debates in Westminster. The Bucknill enquiry was called in part to calm things down. It, and the summary deportation of about one hundred alleged catamites, comprised a public performance of official action suited to the political needs of the specific situation.

The 1907 Leary/Taberer enquiry into "unnatural vice" among Africans was necessitated by this public performance rather than by any sudden changes in African behaviour at that time. The scandal, such as it was, was largely driven by missionary concerns and generated little interest to the wider white population, except for the fodder it provided for racist ideologies about Africans (and Portuguese). The issue was not debated in Westminster. In fact, subsequent splutters of official indignation at African men's behaviour appear to have been largely token. Despite occasional confidential expressions of concern about unnatural vice in the hostels and prisons, by the 1920s officials were publicly minimizing the existence of such behaviour, if not actively blocking rural African patriarchs from making too-close enquiries. Those patriarchs were key to maintaining the flow of migrant labour to the mines, and it simply would not do that they be alienated from the system by frank discussion of its social impact. One particularly blatant example of this ingenuousness came after some Mpondo chiefs expressed shock at learning about homosexuality among migrant labourers in 1928. While flattering the chiefs for their "courage" in broaching such "a very unsavoury" topic, South African officials reassured them that sodomy was "practically non-existent on the Gold Mines."[17] They conceded that "some immorality" took place in the form of *ukumetsha* (thigh sex) but maintained that delinquents "were rigorously dealt with according to law. Both the Government and the Mining Industry strongly disapproved and special measures were being adopted to suppress it."

The confidential discussions among British officials shed further light on this disjuncture between private knowledge or opinion and public sentiments. In private some officials allowed for a certain amount of tolerance for human fallibilities. They did so on the grounds that male-male sexuality was a universal phenomenon to which they themselves were not inherently immune. "Very likely it does exist to a certain extent with either [Chinese or African]," offered the acting mayor of Roodepoort-Maraisburg in 1906, "as indeed it does in almost every race, including Englishmen in England."[18] British and later South African officials were, however, deeply sensitive to accusations that they did not take the issue seriously. Public pronouncements therefore stressed a homophobic unanimity that did not exist in private. This homophobic posturing helped re-affirm the dignity of the native administration and justify its civilizing mandate to a sometimes sceptical public – and even to themselves. Lord Selbourne wrote to Lord Elgin at the time of the Chinese scandal, for example, to insist how "the greatest indignation prevails amongst his inspectors that insinuations should have been made that they could have been so far forgetful of their birth and traditions as in any way to connive at any suppression of fact relating to this subject."[19] Reputation was at stake.

Heterosexual reputation and identity were also at the core of rival Boer-British masculinities, according to Sandra Swart's analysis of the 1914 rebellion by Afrikaner men in Transvaal and the Orange Free State (1998). Although Swart does not discuss sexuality per se, the nostalgic Republicanism that she describes as fuelling the rebellion was assertively and explicitly hetero-patriarchal. Defeat and humiliation by the British in the Anglo-Boer War, plus the widespread poverty and landlessness that followed the commercialization of agriculture in the war's aftermath, had created a crisis of meaning for many Afrikaner men. Government efforts to prepare South Africa for war with Germany were then one emasculating policy too many in that they attacked some of the key symbols of Afrikaner patriarchy. Thousands of Afrikaners rebelled specifically against the imposition of British-style military discipline, which included shaving of facial hair and submitting to a rigidly hierarchical chain of command. At military school the proud Afrikaner commando was dressed and housed in a dormitory like a "schoolboy." Men who refused to comply were required to surrender their guns. Several of the rebels equated this affront to their masculinity to being cuckolded. As one of the leaders of the rebellion explained his motives, "'A

Boer and his gun and his wife are three things always together.' A gun is his 'second wife, his sweetheart'" (Swart 1998, 750).

The nostalgic republicanism of Afrikaner rebels held little appeal for Southern Rhodesia's relatively prosperous Afrikaner minority. Indeed, the colony was conceived in part as a place where Boer and Briton could co-exist harmoniously. Once the African resistance to colonial rule was crushed, no other ethnic or racial group posed a threat to white domination or privilege, and consequently there were no comparable scandals or public debates over the sexuality of specific ethnic groups. Only once did the state actually broach an anxiety about the diminution of imperial white masculinity specifically due to a foreign homosexual element in the population. It happened on the eve of the greatest test of that model of manhood yet: World War I. The Immigration Act passed that year included a clause that explicitly prohibited persons convicted of sodomy or unnatural offences from settling in the colony. But so self-evident was the wisdom of this exclusion that no public debate was deemed necessary or took place.[20]

Notwithstanding homophobic propaganda and laws, small circles of men who enjoyed homosexual relations and did not regard them as sinful or criminal began to grow in the urban centres of the region. Harry Weincier, for example, was a twenty-three-year-old storekeeper in Kwekwe, Southern Rhodesia, when he was caught fondling the genitals of three white adolescents in 1931. He defended himself, "I have been doing this sort of thing in Johannesburg amongst boys and nothing was thought of it ... It is through mixing with other fellows in Johannesburg before I came up to Rhodesia. I did not want to break the law in any way. Yes, I know I have been foolish to do so as I had no idea it was against the law." One of his "victims" thought much the same way: "I allowed accused to play with my penis. I don't know why I did this. I do not know whether I consented or not. I did not agree to him doing it. I allowed him to do it without thinking."[21] Sentence was £10 or three weeks in the lock-up.

The first flourishing of a true gay scene in the region coincided with World War II. The huge military encampment at Joubert Park, Johannesburg, where thousands of transient, young, virginal men gathered in preparation for departure to possible death or mutilation in battle, was its geographic focus. The bars and cruising spots remained after the boys came home from war, and indeed began to spread northwards and upwards into the self-consciously urbane suburb of Hillbrow.

With the advent to power of the National Party in 1948, however, the climate for white gays and lesbians immediately worsened, as it did for any dissident expressions of sexuality such as interracial affairs. The apartheid state began to intervene increasingly forcefully to police white sexuality. The first evidence of this came in the late 1950s with periodic raids on private "bottle parties" and known male homosexual cruising areas. Official homophobia intensified as Cold War tensions mounted and were linked to African nationalist struggles against white rule. Beginning in 1960, the South African Defence Force instituted a quixotic thirty-year crusade to "cure" homosexuals in its midst with drug and electro-shock aversion therapy and mandatory counselling.[22] As in the United States, the military establishment regarded homosexuality as indicative of psychological weakness or unfitness for the coming battle. It also suggested vulnerability to communist blandishments or political opposition to apartheid. Proof of the link was embodied in Cecil Williams, a prominent gay member of the South African Communist Party, who was imprisoned and then deported from South Africa in the mid-1960s.

The most spectacular state intervention against homosexuality among whites, however, was the Forest Town raid of January 1966. Undercover police infiltrated a gay party in a quiet suburb of Johannesburg where they found no less than 350 mostly white men dancing, kissing, and cuddling each other. They made arrests and sparked a huge public outcry. Undercover operations were launched to infiltrate and round up suspected homosexual networks. A parliamentary debate followed in which the danger was spelled out in breathless rhetoric. As Retief (1994, 102) describes it, the minister of Justice, P.C. Pelser, invoked the ghosts of Rome and Sparta as a warning: "Formerly glorious civilizations were lying in the dust and South Africa should beware of a similar fate. The canker of Sodom had to be sliced out before it ruined the moral fibre of the nation." Not a single parliamentarian raised a voice against this biblical diatribe.

One outcome of this uproar came in 1968 when the government introduced a proposal to define "immoral, indecent or unnatural acts" in terms so broad that they would have empowered police to harrass private social events and to imprison errant men and women for up to three years for offences. Although some of the more extreme recommendations were staved off by gay rights and civil libertarian lobbyists, the amendments to the Immorality Act that did become law in 1969 drove nascent gay communities into tighter and more geographically isolated spaces. The new provisions for the first time explicitly acknowledged state hostility to lesbian sex by banning dildos. The state's determination and ability to root out "immoral and indecent behaviour" among females continued to be strengthened in law as late as 1988 (Cameron 1994, 91).

An indication of the climate of the times was the sudden discovery of South Africa's first known white hermaphrodite (intersexed person). Prior to 1970 this condition was thought to occur primarily among blacks and "mixed races who share Negro ancestry" (Grace and Edge 1973, 1553). When it was identified by doctors in a white child in Durban, the male genitalia were surgically removed and the child "completely oriented as a girl" through therapy. Tellingly, the doctors did not recommend this apparently successful operation be applied in the black community, despite their own suggestions that it was much in need there. Ostensibly this was because the resources for post-operative counselling essential to the procedure were lacking in the black community. In fact it provides yet another example of how medical science and sexuality could be used both to rationalize white privilege and to create ever-clearer lines between the races.

Ironically, the South African government in the apartheid years aggressively sought to burnish its image in the West as an outpost of modernity and freedom on a dark, communistic continent. Medical triumphs such as the operation above were part of this. But Hillbrow and Cape Town, whose flashy Westernness and vibrant cultural life were significantly fuelled by the barely underground gay scenes that thrived there, also emerged as useful to the state for that purpose. The cosmopolitan cities appeared (albeit without mention of the homosexuals) in South African propaganda in the West as exemplars of democracy and development under apartheid.

A similar contradictory culture of intolerance against homosexuality among whites coalesced in Southern Rhodesia for many of the same reasons. After World War II, and particularly after a huge industrial strike in Bulawayo in 1948, political pressure to move towards black majority rule grew rapidly. The influx of white immigrants from southern and eastern Europe as well as working class Britons, meanwhile, was diluting the relative homogeneity of the white Southern Rhodesian population. For those whites who sought to resist decolonization or democratization, it was increasingly imperative to create a distinct settler identity that cut across the ethnic and class divides in the white population and that could be mobilized politically. The need became almost an obsession of cultural and political elites. Gender and sexuality featured prominently in this national identity. It drew upon flattering images of rough and ready settler manliness from a mythologized pioneer period, as well as the elite derring-do of those Rhodesians who fought in the Royal Air Force (future Prime Minister Ian Smith among them). It celebrated a muscular, Christian, hard-drinking, heterosexually lusty, at-ease-in-the-*bundu* (wilderness), at-ease-with-Natives masculinity. Idealized Rhodesian masculinity stood in stark contrast to the socialistic, effeminite, treacherous, and wimpish liberalism that was presumed to be sapping the morale of the West (and abetting Native and white female uppityness). Rhodesian-ness in that sense was fostered through an exaggerated stigma of supposedly homosexual behaviour that was internalized in white boys from a very young age. As in South Africa, this was policed, usually by peers and often with considerable roughness, at school and through the country's flourishing hyper-masculine sports. At the same time, a hyper-feminine Rhodesian girl was "finished" in schools and through housecraft courses to take her romanticized place in society as a settler wife. This sexualized nationalism was endlessly reiterated through the popular media, including by clumsily didactic humour that idealized horny heterosexuality and mocked gender-bending in the West.[23] The smallness and tight-knit nature of the white community made it even more stultifying to gays and lesbians than South Africa; Salisbury lacked a Hillbrow or Sea Point (Cape Town) to disappear into.

White immigration to Southern Rhodesia was solicited world-wide with images of the good life and frontier-taming men and women. Just to be on the safe side, however, the Immigation Act of 1914 was revised in 1954 to prohibit anyone who was deemed to practise prostitution or "homosexualism" from entering the country even as tourists (let alone settling in and polluting it).[24] The law was also tightened to catch those homegrown perverts who otherwise were almost impossible to convict or even harass under sodomy and indecent assault charges. In 1964 the Miscellaneous Offences Act made it a criminal offence to wear gender-inappropriate clothing, empowering the police to arrest transvestites, queens, and trouser-wearing lesbians (HRW 2003, 262).

The outbreak of the bush war in Rhodesia in the late 1960s and the consequent militarization of white society in the 1970s combined to bring public sentiment about those who "let down the side" to a violent boil. Kaarsholm's study of Rhodesian war novels shows how murderous male fraternity was valorized through often crudely drawn dualisms of Rhodesian manliness on the one hand and a communistic, sadistic, and/or homosexual enemy on the other. The latter was defeated in graphic bloodbaths time and again in these novels. John Gordon Davis's 1967 *Hold My Hand I'm Dying*, for example, depicts the Rhodie protagonist reacting in dismay to the sexual corruption of urban society. He reconstitutes his masculine wholeness by moving to the wild Zambezi valley where he can battle terrorists. The heroic policeman in Robert Early's 1977 *A Time of Madness* first rescues a South African man from debauchery in Johannesburg, then goes on to defeat in battle and to humiliate in wit a whole range of communists, terrorists, stupid, liberal, meddling whites from overseas, and homosexuals (Kaarsholm 1991, 44–8).

The ultimate expression of this culture of masculinity occurred in 1972 when two white men, one a police constable, hunted down and beat to death a middle-aged gay white man. "We don't like you or your way of life," they were overheard to say as they commenced their assault on Cyril Durrant. "What's more, you're a poof and you sleep with kaffirs." Rosemary Johnson, a coloured woman who lodged in the same Salisbury flat, was also beaten by the two men (apparently because of her complexion). She told the court: "I heard Mr. Durrant say to them, 'Please forgive me. Forgive me. I am dying.' But they showed no pity at all. They carried on kicking him just as if he were a football."[25]

Durrant's death was the only reported incident of homicidal "gay-bashing" (the term used by the press) in Rhodesia. Nonetheless, by the following year the climate of hostility against suspected gays was so bad that the commissioner of police almost expressed sympathy towards them. He promised to take greater efforts to protect discreet homosexual men from juvenile extortionists.[26] Perhaps conscious of the de-listing of homosexuality as a mental illness by the American Psychiatric Association in 1973, or perhaps identifying as "modern" in relation to South Africa's puritanical regime, the police did not aggressively enforce the anti-homosexual laws at their disposal. The modicum of tolerance of a discreet gay scene that this provided nonetheless remained fragile. Indeed, rather than any real concern for gays as citizens, the de facto blind eye the police turned to the small homosexual scene may have simply reflected a desire to protect whites from victimization by non-white extortionists – especially international visitors who might demean Rhodesia's precarious image after a bad experience. The state certainly proved quick to react with a public performance of homophobic intolerance the moment that de facto tolerance was exposed to public ridicule. This was occasioned in 1977 when a story appeared in *Illustrated Life Rhodesia* (Bond-Smith 1977) that criticized police indifference to a gay-friendly nightclub in Salisbury. According to Keith Goddard (2004a), police raided the club and permanently shut it down almost immediately after the article appeared.

The willingness of colonial states to torture and put men to death for "unnatural crimes" began to diminish as early as the mid-1800s. Nonetheless, the deep revulsion against such men continued to be worded into the charges laid against those so accused. Hogoza (the last known person to be executed for sodomy in South Africa) was thus not simply charged with sodomy: rather, he "did commit and perpetrate that detestable and abominable crime of buggery (not to be named among Christians)."[27] Even as late as the 1920s and '30s, well after homosexuality had begun to be de-stigmatized in scientific terms, charge sheets in Southern Rhodesia continued to emphasize that the crime was of a uniquely horrible and threatening quality. Not only were male-male sexual assaults indecent, lascivious, and abominable by definition (that is, even before evidence in the case was heard) but they were "contrary to the order of nature." The language used by magistrates *after* the evidence had been heard could be even stronger, a tradition that continues among the upholders of Roman Dutch law today. State, church, and the academy alike often fomented contempt and hatred against perceived homosexuals to advance specific political objectives, including the promotion of ethnic nationalisms.

That said, homophobia among whites was never as consistent in practice as it may have sounded in rhetoric, and indeed was often contingent upon factors other than the sexual acts in question. Moreover, both Christian dogma and secular explanations of overtly homosexual behaviour were open to non-stigmatizing interpretations, allowing for the emergence of small, discreet subcultures where homosexual desire could be openly expressed. For some men in the majority culture, the emergence of a gay scene and the idea of tolerance of homosexuality in a time of such rapidly changing, often violent gender, class, and race relations added to insecurity about their own masculinity and may have contributed to fear or violence against perceived homosexuals. For others, however, and probably for Rhodesian women as well, even if only subconsciously, that scene helped foster a feeling of modernity or liberalism that linked small outposts of white civilization in Africa to the West.

These contradictory messages and behaviours unfolded over the course of more than a century of colonial rule before the gaze of African populations that were by turns admiring, aspirant, and resentful towards Western culture. In the following chapter, we look closely at some of the specific ways that Western discourses around homosexuality were heard and interpreted by those Africans.

6

Fear and Loathing: African Transitions

African cultures of discretion or denial around same-sex desire could be oppressive in crude ways. Several witnesses from various nations in the region told the 1907 Leary-Taberer enquiry that the death penalty was imposed for flagrant and persistent indulgence in male-male sex; Sokisi himself, role model *extraordinaire* of "mine marriage," was purportedly sentenced to death by his king *in absentia* for his behaviour. Similar claims about African tradition have also been asserted in contemporary Zimbabwe to justify deportation, rape, castration, cutting off of the penis, and even execution of unrepentant lesbians and male homosexuals.

Yet capital punishments in the pre-modern past were only rarely carried out with the zeal that modern homophobes would have liked. Given the many mechanisms by which same-sex sexuality could be explained or plausibly denied, and given the terrible risks of avenging spirits in any case of unjust death, communities tended to avoid extreme reaction. Moreover, the cultural power of gender socialization obviated much of the need. Both girls and boys learned from the youngest age that sexual pleasure required male penetration of the vagina and ejaculation therein, and that the purpose of sexual pleasure was not to satisfy individual sensual desire. Rather, it was an obligation to one's health, to one's partner's health, and to one's family, the latter understood to extend well beyond the grave. For girls to pull at each other's labia to lengthen them was thus not pleasurable per se (though they might do it daily and as much as possible), but a service to their future husbands and, hence, to extended families and ancestors. For boys and young men, masturbation, physical intimacy with peers, and even sex with animals were likewise not sensual ends in themselves but preparation for marriage and fatherhood. Upon marriage, the extended family then watched closely and could intervene in cases of sons failing to fulfil their duty to provide children for the lineage. The family could, for example, demand that a son divorce, provide a second wife if the first appeared infertile, or arrange for the "raising of seed" by a brother if the husband rather than the wife were suspected to be at fault for the lack of offspring. The highly gerontocratic nature of southern African societies, meanwhile, meant that the young had to be seen to obey the old in these and other demands.

Publicly conforming to heterosexual conjugal expectations is not, in fact, especially time-consuming in terms of the actual sexual acts involved. Indeed, it left considerable time for private experimentation or play as people's sexual natures, curiosity, and desires prompted. Provided that appearances were maintained and formal relationship not disrespected, neither shame nor guilt attached to such behaviours such as premarital sex play (*hlobonga*), girls' manipulation of the labia from young age, lack of concern about nudity, and "wife-loaning" between male friends or to patron/client or to a guest. For Europeans, whose own sexuality was governed by the internalized voice of an omniscient god, Africans' relative casualness about sexuality was extremely unsettling to observe. African heterosexual "immorality" thus became the object of concerted attack by Christian missionaries from the onset of their respective missions in the region. Implicit in much of this Christian propaganda – and in some cases almost explicit in its relief – is that the appearance of exclusive heterosexuality was one of the few truly admirable qualities of African society.

Shock at learning that African men were in fact amenable to sex with males under certain circumstances mobilized missionaries and secular authorities alike when the fact belatedly came to light in the early twentieth century. African men working in the mines in the Johannesburg area were then subjected to direct propaganda against same-sex sexual practices on a mass and embarrassingly explicit basis. The message was not just that such conduct was bad. It was also that morally reprehensible sexual acts would be punished, regardless of whether they were witnessed and reported by another person. They would be punished whether or not compensation was paid to the one upon whom the act was done. And they would be punished whether one was the active partner or a consenting, passive one. How was that possible? Easily, since the crime would be witnessed by an omnipotent and omniscient being no matter how thick the curtain around the bed. Moreover, punishment would not be a short to middling stint in the lock-up or a few stripes from a cane. It would be everlasting torment at the hands of the sadistic minions of the devil, being perpetually flayed, roasted, frozen, or otherwise made to rue the day that one had ever been born.

Many African men regarded the Christian vision of hellfire and damnation as nothing less than deranged. However, evidence given to Leary and Taberer suggests that it was beginning to have an impact among African migrant labourers as early as 1907. Non-Christian African witnesses to the enquiry into "unnatural vice" were for the most part phlegmatic or even a bit curious in describing the sexual behaviour of their fellow workers. Expressions of disgust and contempt for male-male sexual practices, by contrast, were most commonly voiced either by the European witnesses or by Christianized Africans like the Fingoes. In one of the few cases of physical coercion and resistance to *inkotshane* reported to Leary and Taberer, Christianity as much as the proposed sex was the focus of violence. The witness, Concertina, explained how "all the guards came to us in fives and tens and asked me and the last witness to love them. They said that we must love them and that they wanted to make us their wives. We refused and said that we were believers in the Lord Jesus, and then they got sjamboks and beat us" (Leary and Taberer 1907, 22 January, 2). The testimony of Bob Zandemela, a Chopi miner, then makes the connection between his conversion to Christianity and to exclusive heterosexuality completely plain: "I was an 'inkotshane' myself once; I gave it up when I heard it was an evil thing. I practiced this both at the Chimes and at this compound. When I learned in the Book [the Bible] it was wrong I stopped it. I submitted to being an 'inkotshane' because I did not know better" (21 January, 1-2).

Christian missionary intolerance towards same-sex sexuality is recurrent as well in the rare works of southern African fiction that touch upon the subject (Junod 1911, Lanham and Mopeli-Paulus 1953, Mokhoane 1995, Duiker 2001). Yet it would be wrong to attribute the emergence of explicit homophobia among Africans today merely to the trickle-down effect of Christian propaganda. More subtle cultural influences arising out of European discourses around sexual morality, economic progress, and science were also at play. The contrast between the tolerant attitude of a non-Christian *n'anga* and the sharp intolerance of an African doctor familiar with modern psychiatric explanations of homosexuality in one account from the 1920s is suggestive of this emerging scientific homophobia. The South African psychiatrist Wulf Sachs tells that the *n'anga* "John" had walked from Manyikaland in Southern Rhodesia to Johannesburg in 1918. John subsequently got into a discussion with Nkomo, a Xhosa *sangoma* who worked under Sachs at the Johannesburg African hospital. According to Sachs, Nkomo had denounced as madness "the abnormal ways of lovemaking practiced by many of his patients in the asylum." John, however, came to the patients' defence. He "just laughed, declaring that if this were true, hundreds of natives in the compounds and in the crowded city yards would need to be put into asylums, for in such places love-making between men was quite usual, as it was between women also." Since most nevertheless eventually got married and had children, why the fuss? (Sachs 1937, 193). A contemporary of Sachs (Laubscher 1937, 284) alludes to this same contrast between supposedly primitive and modern paranoia around homosexuality in clinical terms. African patients who had same-sex affairs did not engage in "homosexual masking by means of rationalizations and projections." European patients, by contrast, were modern in their denial of the obvious.

Direct connections in intellectual history on this issue are almost impossible to discern. One of the few, unambiguous assertions made by an African nationalist intellectual about male homosexuality in Africans, however, does reveal a startling indebtedness to European sources and prejudices. This comes in an article by the influential Kenyan academic Ali Mazrui. In what amounts to an apologia for Ugandan dictator Idi Amin and other supposedly virile African "warriors," Mazrui (1975) plumbs a version of the Shaka myth that first surfaced in 1929. He begins his analysis, "Legend has it ..." and then proceeds to "explain" how Shaka's violence and poor political judgment ultimately stemmed from his small penis size and confused sexuality. To back this claim, Mazrui quotes an obviously fictionalized anecdote about penis size published by an ex-colonial official from Natal, E.A. Ritter (1957, 14). Ritter's anecdote is meanwhile plagiarized almost verbatim from the Christian missionary Alfred Bryant (1929, 62). Bryant's own sources are identified only as "Many stories are extent ..." but none of these in fact appears either in James Stuart's compilation of actual Zulu oral histories (Webb and Wright 1982, 1986, 2001) or in other African accounts of Shaka.

Mazrui further cites the white South African anthropologist Max Gluckman (1974), whose claim that Shaka was a latent homosexual is apparently derived from the same European authors, embellished by Freudian speculation (see Golan 1994, 91–6). Mazrui cites non-African scholars to support his theory of the link between "sexual inadequacy and a policy of brutal assertiveness." None of these (J.D. Omer-Cooper, Desmond Morris, and V. Walter) conducted original research into the histories they concocted; indeed, Walter's account of "the historic insult" against Shaka's penis size that supposedly launched his bloody career can be traced straight back, once again, to the missionary Bryant via Ritter.

Jeater (1993, 1995) has also shown how the hegemony of modern values was not merely achieved by incessant, blunt propaganda and a steady diet of didactic Christian or scientific, historical literature coming from the

West. Rather, she argues, lessons were imparted more insidiously and more enduringly by the penetration and cooptation of indigenous languages. The subtleties of "Deep Shona" that allowed the language to maintain certain social fictions, or that allowed empirically contradictory evidence to co-exist in thought if not in the very same spoken sentence, were lost in missionary translations. These imposed the literalist, positivist values of the golden age of colonialism. The word *nkotshane*, to give the most obvious example, originally included the meaning of "servant." For many of the witnesses who testified before Leary and Taberer, it was neither pejorative nor necessarily entailed a sexual relationship (moreover, where it did the latter, it connoted thigh sex only). Yet the missionary translations that wended their way into popular understandings of the word stated its meaning baldly as "sodomy." Where African languages lacked an explicit word equivalent to the English ones, missionaries did them the service of inventing biblical neologisms – *isono samadoda ase-Sodom* in McLaren's 1923 Xhosa dictionary, for example, or *mosodoma* in Hamel's 1965 Sesotho dictionary.

Jeater does not specifically address European fears about homosexual perversion in her work on colonial Zimbabwe. But those fears were communicated through material culture as well as through language. Notably, living spaces in institutions like boarding schools, hostels, and prisons were restructured over the course of colonial rule according to European sensibilities that conveyed strong messages about sexual propriety. Thus, where it had been considered entirely normal, non-sexual, and non-threatening for African men to sleep together under the same blanket in the nude in the early days of urban development (as had been the case in pre-colonial days), by the 1950s almost all institutions and public housing provided for separate sleeping arrangements. While this was never done with a stated intention to save men from perdition, nonetheless the notion of homosexuality as a contagious thing that could be resisted by proper spatial arrangements was strongly implicit. Such arrangements were admired for that very reason by a South African "expert" on African sexuality. Southern Rhodesia, he maintained, was a model for Johannesburg in the post-World War II era precisely because its superior urban planning supposedly protected African men from homosexual temptation.[1]

Attire was another way that powerful colonialist messages about sexuality were conveyed. In traditional terms modesty could be achieved by covering the genitals and often little else. The missionaries, by contrast, regarded virtually the entire female body and even words that evoked thoughts about it as sexual. Modesty, and hence progress towards civilization in their eyes, demanded a full cover-up for females. The unseen, the forbidden, in this way became eroticized. One elderly Shona man recalled, "We grew up swimming with girls, without clothes. There was nothing sexual about the exposure. When I worked in Harare in the 1930s I realised for the first time that the female body was sexual."[2] Vambe (1976, 20) has also described how women who put *more* clothes on were regarded as *less* modest in the 1930s: "Some of them had a highly developed sense of dress, the result of European influence, and those who had taken to using sopa [soap] and other beauty aids were hard to resist." We may assume that some African girls and women as well as boys and men noticed and took a heightened interest in this sexualization of female bodies.

Burke (1996) provides a seminal study of the process of the internalization of European values and tastes among black Zimbabweans through the lens of soap. Early European travellers had observed that African societies in Zimbabwe placed a high value upon personal cleanliness, often more so than their foot-weary selves. But as the settler population in the colony increased, and as Africans as servants came into close daily contact with Europeans of both sexes in the domestic and the wider urban sphere, a discourse of African uncleanliness became entrenched. African men in particular were said to smell so badly as to be physically repulsive to civilized persons. White women (and in one unusual case, a white man) successfully used this argument to defend themselves against accusations of sexual impropriety with black men.[3] The argument could be extended even further. As the *Salisbury Citizen* put it as late as 1956: "the native African is not clean enough, physically, to make social intercourse with him pleasant or even hygienically safe" (cited in Burke 1996, 20).

That message was drilled into African boys and girls in boarding schools, often with violence at the hands of older acculturated boys and girls. Nationalist leader Maurice Nyagumbo recalls about his arrival at St Faith's mission in 1936, for example, "All the 'oldcomers' were carrying long sticks. From here, we were told to march to the stream called Jordan, and as we marched along we were told to sing ... 'We are the newcomers / We are dirty / We are dirty / We do not know how to wash outselves / We have not acquired education' ... At the stream, we were told to undress and to jump into the water." After lights out, the newcomers were beaten (Nyagumbo 1980, 24).

Burke does not consider whether such fetishization of body odour could be homoerotic. The barrage of propaganda, however, plus advertising, pseudo-science, and often deeply humiliating personal instruction about Africans' intimate personal hygiene conveyed an erotic subtext. Freshly scrubbed genitals, when constructed as a signifier of modernity and thence conflated with sexual/marital fitness and material success, certainly implied the possibility of same-sex desire to a much greater extent than older rituals of cleansing. Thus it is that the showers of boarding schools and hostels, rather than cramped sleeping quarters, are remembered by many contemporary black gays as the scene of their first awakenings of homosexual attraction. Shimmer Chinodya's description of a boys' boarding school in 1960s Southern Rhodesia is highly suggestive in that respect, fraught as it is with homoerotic tension (1990, 89–93). Responsible authorities, teachers, and parents were likely often well aware of this "danger." Yet because compromise about the imperative of showering was simply not allowable, alertness to and dogmatism against its homoerotic implications had to be meticulously cultivated in the consciences of individual pupils.

Structural changes to African society that flowed from colonial rule and racial capitalism also profoundly affected attitudes towards sexuality as well as opportunities to express it (see Schmidt 1992, Barnes 1999, Kaler 2003). Most obvious to contemporary observers were dramatic increases in African fertility and heterosexual promiscuity. Young men gained access to cash that enabled them to circumvent parental control and either to pay *lobola* for a wife themselves or to negotiate sex with women on less formal bases – prostitution, in many commentators' eyes. Women gained the means to escape rural patriarchy and to negotiate partners and remuneration directly. Even in the rural areas, customary constraints on very high fertility gave way to increasingly unbridled reproduction. Notably, in the first two to three decades of the colony at least, capitalist-minded male peasants in Southern Rhodesia had strong market incentives to increase the labour available to them through polygyny. More wives meant more children, which meant more profits from selling produce in the new urban centres. More children were also desirable in that they could earn cash in town to provide inputs for agricultural improvements. Changes in rural governance abetted this tendency. Under the colonial regime the chieftaincy was transformed into a subordinate and sometimes venal branch of the tax-collecting bureaucracy. As the traditional function of chiefs as redistributors of wealth waned, pressure increased on individual families to have more children who could support the family in times of economic hardship.

Christian propaganda and secular law contributed to the rising fertility of African women by deriding as primitive, and in some cases by criminalizing, the medicines (such as abortificients) and practices (no sex during lactation, infanticide) that had traditionally limited family size to what a woman's health could bear. Likewise derided as quaint if not foolish were those customs that honoured "witch doctors" who for spiritual reasons did not marry. For educated young men who aspired to advance in the few modern careers open to them, bachelorhood was equivalent to being blacklisted. Domestic Christian marriage was a prerequisite to "prove" civilized status (Summers 1999). State-backed education and development projects that fostered an idealized femininity centred on the hearth and home further narrowed the scope for respectable African women to control their fertility or to fulfil roles outside that of repeatedly pregnant mother. As that role acquired overwhelming dominance in colonial society, pre-modern notions that valued celibacy or sexual restraint began to seem "unnatural." It was a short mental step to regarding control or neglect of maximum fertility as unpatriotic.

Yet as we saw in previous chapters, a contradictory tendency emerged in the early colonial period. While enabling and effectively condoning increased fertility and heterosexual promiscuity or prostitution among Africans, colonial rule and racial capitalism also progressively emasculated African men. "Emasculation" is meant here in the sense of undermining men's ability to attain the signifiers of social manhood. This emasculation occurred as a result of changes in the political economy, of racist laws that incarcerated large numbers of Africans in dehumanizing conditions, and of ideologies that infantilized or pathologized African men and their sex-uality. On the ideological front, colonial discourse characterized an African male as a perpetual "boy" irrespective of his age or marital status or achievements within the colonial education system.[4] *Mabhoyi* as such were subject to innumerable indignities, including white men helping themselves sexually to African men's wives and daughters. African men seeking employment were required to submit to genital and anal examinations, often in the utterly humiliating presence of elders or youths. Compulsory, semi-public vaginal examinations were imposed on African women in town ("*chibeura*" or "open your legs" – Jackson 2002), to identify "loose women" and deport them back to rural areas. Averting their eyes from their own transgressions, meanwhile, white men and women assumed for themselves the power to debate, define, and legislate black sexuality. Through a host of discriminatory legislation such as the Native Marriage Ordinance (1901) and the Native Adultery Punishment Ordinance (1916), the colonial state asserted its power to control and re-shape African sexuality in ways that it deemed suitable. Some African patriarchs benefited from, and indeed, influenced the colonial state in these assertions of power over young men's and women's sexuality. In Ibbo Mandaza's analysis, however, and even more so by Lawrence Vambe's account, white men's cavalier attitude towards the sexual exploitation of local African and

Coloured women, and hypocritical prescriptions about appropriate sex objects, created a lingering pool of resentment in the African and Coloured communities. To paraphrase Vambe, referring to the 1940s, whites interference in other people's sex lives was the possible main root of racial problems (1976, 107).

The discursive and legal unmanning of African males by whites took place against a backdrop of the steady erosion of the material base of traditional African masculinity. In Southern Rhodesia it was felt first and worst by migrant labourers from the poorer neighbouring colonies, the Malawians and "Zambezi boys" above all. Many of these men had been driven by economic desperation to take the most despised jobs available. Yet even that work was not sufficient to earn them the wherewithal of social manhood – *lobola*, a submissive wife, fields, children. For some of these men, taking a male wife in town was thus not simply an accessible way to assuage loneliness or achieve sexual release: it was also a strategy to attain masculine status in customary terms. It allowed the "husband" to exercise power and moral authority over a "wife" in an intimate relationship. It enabled savings that otherwise might have gone to female prostitutes. And it preserved health for an eventual triumphant return home. In some cases, having sex with a male was also held to generate *muti* that could get one safely through the trials and tribulations of life in Salisbury.

The word to describe the Malawians' need to resort to such strategies – *matanyera* – may have been coined as black humour among themselves. Derived from a chiNyanja word for a painful, smelly diarrhea caused by worms, it could be translated as "those who shovel the most disgusting kind of shit known to mankind."[5] A second, figurative meaning of "homosexual" was also assimilated into chiShona to make it one of the most insulting epithets it the language. Vambe, who avoided naming their homosexual behaviours, described *matanyera* as "the lowest of the low," a kind of man "who caught syphilis just as easily as he caught the common cold" (Vambe 1976, 196). The word subsequently made its way southwards with the migrants where it was Sotho-ized and Zulu-ized. For a man to "eat *matanyola*" or "*matanyula*" in much of southern Africa today thus means to have sex with a male, usually in exchange for money or favours. Referring to practices at the mine hostels in the Johannesburg area in the 1960s and '70s, Mark Mathabane defines the word simply as "male prostitution" (Mathabane 1986, 74).

If the Malawian *matanyera* were initially regarded as an inferior, despised Other by Shona men, the same forces that had socially unmanned them were also increasingly at work upon the Shona. By the 1920s, it could take

many years of "boyhood" for a biological Shona man to earn the wherewithal to become a social man in traditional terms. The chances of
acquiring all or even any of the traditional signifiers of masculinity declined
further over time. Growing land shortages, declining real wages, imprisonment for petty offences, and the interference of colonial bureaucrats in
daily life all combined to extend the period of social boyhood to a
permanent condition for some men. Vambe recollects the shock of realization that this had come to his people, the VaChishawasha, when the first
of the community's sons left for good in 1923: "The reason for the fear
and despondency at Nhawu's departure was the possibility that it could
trigger off an exodus of their educated young men for the El Dorado of the
distant South Africa. They were afraid of the development of a Nyasaland-
type situation, with its deserted wives and children, frustrated virgins and
neglected fields. Until Edward Nhawu made this break, they had thought
that only inadequate, unpatriotic and deprived Africans from abroad could
be attracted to this extreme form of vagabondage" (Vambe 1972, 242–3).

Assertive town women, meanwhile, often added to insult to injury by
exercising hitherto unimaginable degrees of independence from men. Notwithstanding that colonial states throughout the region tried to buttress
the legal powers of African men *vis-à-vis* African women, the tendency
was for women to challenge, if not outright mock, the respect for masculine
authority that custom expected of them.[6] Reflective of these rising gender
tensions, women in town became virtually synonymous with *mahure*
(derived from "whore") and were increasingly considered to be the legitimate object of physical violence.[7] A modern Shona aphorism captures this
development – "*Ihure rego rirohwe*" ("it is a whore, let it be beaten") (Shire
1994, 153). We know from criminal court records and oral testimony that
the anger behind such sentiments was increasingly acted out through
violence and sexual exploitation of women by men.

African men in this era of rapidly changing gender relations did devise
new ways of signifying or performing social manhood. These included
sports, clothes, faction fighting, heterosexually predatory gangs, ostenta-
tious consumption of European products (notably liquor), and achievement
in the white man's terms (school, church, police, master farming, hygiene,
and so on). Yet racially coded discourses continued to define even successfully Westernized African men's achievements as necessarily inferior,
imitative, or childish. In fact, by the early 1950s some of the most respectable avenues to social manliness were being closed down in direct and
intensely alienating ways. The Native Land Husbandry Act of 1951 and
population control programs in particular were perceived by many Africans

as an intolerable assault on the rural and sexual base of indigenous masculinity. This assault sparked the first stirrings of anti-colonial rebellion in the countryside since 1897, stirrings that nationalist leaders sought to harness to their own emergent agenda. As we shall see in the following section, the struggle for independence from white rule then added a further, political incentive to conflate high female fertility, male virility, and African identity. As that conflation grew tighter, the social space to concede discreet alternative expressions of sexuality grew less, and traditional transphobia elided into assertive homophobia.

Overt expression of anger against colonial injustice was extremely risky for Africans throughout colonial southern Africa. For many African men, however, a certain amount of satisfaction could be had by exposing and mocking white men's sexual foibles and perhaps even exploiting them for monetary gain. As early as 1907 the courts bring us a hint of the possibilities of "remasculation" in this sense. Robert Cox, a married white man, had taken Zita, a thirty-six-year-old Zulu man, for a walk along the beach at the Umgeni River in Durban. Two African constables watched them disappear behind some bushes and followed them. They continued watching as the two masturbated each other for a bit, then stripped. Naked, Zita got down on his knees and elbows to allow Cox to enter him. At that point the police intervened. "Are you a dog?" Constable Mkonto challenged the white man. Mkonto explained to the court how the "European stated that the boy was excreting and I asked if it was usual for him to excrete through his penis as they were both erect. They both cried as we took them along to the Depot."[8]

The first documented public remonstrance against male-male sexuality by African leaders in southern Africa was not, however, made against white perverts preying upon hapless blacks. It came during a brief debate in the Transkeian Tribal General Council in 1928 in response to rumours of the spread of *inkotshane* among the Mpondo. Councillor Mbizweni moved that a delegation be struck to "visit the Compounds at Witwatersrand for the purpose of lecturing to their own people on immoral practices obtaining among labourers working on the mines." Interestingly, the chiefs were of mixed opinion about the wisdom of such a course of action. Thus, while Mbizweni felt that "It was very painful to see their sons doing those things," Mr Bikitsha "said he did not see why they should waste time over that matter ... He personally did not see how the Council could fight against the evil."[9] In the event a delegation did travel to Johannesburg but was rather easily fobbed off by Chamber of Mines officials. The topic, embarrassing to almost one and all, then disappeared from black Africans' public discourse for more than two decades.

When homosexual behaviour among African men re-emerged in public discourse, it did so in a way that shows ambivalence rather than knee-jerk reaction. The novel *Blanket Boy's Moon* broke the silence in 1953. Based upon a story by A.S. Mopeli-Paulus interpreted by a white South African author, Peter Lanham, *Blanket Boy's Moon* is questionable as an example of "authentic" Mosotho voice. It nonetheless provides the first case of public acknowledgment of "bestial lust" in the prisons by an African to a wide, international audience. Yet the novel also hints at mixed feelings by an African man towards some forms of homosexual attraction. The protagonist, Monare, first of all admits to familiarity with "that friendship of men which is born of a great love, much as marriage springs from a great love of woman," and that this familiarity comes from his youth in rural Lesotho rather than from his adult life in town (Lanham and Mopeli-Paulus 1953, 77). He then goes on to ruminate upon his own loosening inhibitions in the city:

He found, too, that his fancies increasingly strayed in the direction of handsome youths. He was not ignorant entirely of this side of life – no African who had lived on the mines could be – he had himself passed through phases in his friendship with Koto, in which great affection and loneliness had led to very minor adventures in homosexuality. But this new craving which possessed him was not founded on love, friendship, or a solitary life – it was merely an appetite directed at any good-looking youth who had a graceful figure and a compliant, wanton disposition. But these things, which most men know, but which even the rude speak not about, were, Monare knew, *against the white man's law, and, according to the Moruti Lefa, were frowned on by God* (132).[10]

Ambivalence towards same-sex sexual relations or gender inversion is also reflected in the sensationalized but not necessarily hostile coverage of the "moffies" – drag queens – of Cape Town in the black press beginning around this time (Chetty 1994). The leading English-language magazine for black readers, *Drum*, reported the story of Gertrude Williams in 1959 as "the sensitive suffering of a person who feels misplaced in her sex."[11] Williams was the Coloured cross-dressing "gangster" in Cape Town who admitted to seducing and having sexual affairs with women, some of whom continued the affairs even after they learned of Williams's true identity.

Recalling an incident from 1963, Moses Dlamini also points to a degree of tolerance if not celebration of same-sex sexuality among Africans of peasant background that stupified him, a respectable city man. The two male lovers who were caught and thrashed by their fellow political prisoners on Robben Island refused to be blamed for their long-standing affair (five years). Moreover, they claimed that homosexual marriage – with a "dowry" to friends and relatives of the *wyfie* – was "tradition" in the mine compounds (Dlamini 1984, 132; see also Buntman 2003, 241–6).

Oral testimony from gay men who lived in the mine compounds or in black townships since the 1950s similarly attests to an absence of overt homophobia there. Mkhumbane, a booming informal African settlement in Durban, came to be known for its homoerotic dances and public male-male wedding ceremonies (Louw 2001). But Mkhumbane was not a gay ghetto subject to derision or hostility by the wider African community. On the contrary, as one elderly informant told researcher Ronald Louw (2001, 291), female wives from the rural areas would sometimes visit. In deference to their husbands, and perhaps enjoying help with domestic labour, they maintained cordial polygynous marriages with the junior male wives (*isikhesana*). According to "Boy," to give an example from Soweto, he and fellow homosexuals were never harassed but were regarded by co-workers as "jolly people with tendencies."[12] An openly lesbian woman, referring to Soweto as recently as the early 1990s, also told researchers for the play *After Nines!* that it was "nice" in the shacks, and that she never experienced insults or harassment on account of her sexual preference. Even her mother "never had a problem with it."[13]

Two recent studies of the coverage of homosexual topics in *Drum* provide insight into the ambiguous ways that same-sex desire was represented and understood in popular culture from the 1950s to early 1980s. *Drum* was founded in Cape Town in 1951 by a white businessman who sought to tap into the black market, much as *Ebony* was doing in the United States. While most of *Drum*'s authors were black, and the advertisements and articles were specifically aimed at a black audience, the editors were white. They largely avoided the difficult political questions of the era in favour of questions of style, popular culture, and the changing nature of interpersonal relationships. So successful was it that separate editions were launched in the 1960s in newly independent Ghana, Nigeria, and Kenya. By the 1970s, over 300,000 copies sold every month, with each copy estimated to be read by (or read to) a further eight to fifteen consumers (Mutongi 2000, 2; Burke 1996, 140). As Flora Veit-Wild's study of the first cohort of African nationalist leadership in Southern Rhodesia attests, it would be a mistake to understate the influence of *Drum* (and emulators like *African Parade*) in shaping urban African opinion about style and society. "The general trend was to teach correct behaviour to the rural African who comes into the city and to point the way to success" (Veit-Wild 1993, 70).

Drum was the first mass publication in which homosexuality among black Africans was openly discussed and debated. There are suggestive differences in the ways it did so between the editions circulating in white-ruled southern Africa and those that were published in independent black African states. Lindsay Clowes's study (2002) of the South African edition argues that the editors sought to propagate their own homophobia to the readership, either by shaming men who wrote in for advice about their uncertain sexuality or by creating the impression that homosexuality was confined to the Coloured "coons" and "moffies" of Cape Town. The first direct mentions of homosexuality among black Africans came in the February 1954 edition. In a rant otherwise focused on urbanized African women's sexual immorality, an anonymous "expert" described homosexuality in passing as an "evil which is spreading among Africans in cities."[14] Another contributor (Manalil Gandhi) mentioned the same "evil" in a letter denouncing the atrocious conditions he encountered during his stint in prison. That the "unimaginable" took place in jail was further alluded to in an excerpt from A.S. Mopeli-Paulus's autobiography published in 1955. But tellingly, none of these references, nor the 1961 revelation by a letter-writer of male-male marriage in the mine compounds (June 1961, 87, 89), sparked investigation or reader reaction. Not until 1963 did the editors respond to a reader's further enquiry about the mine-marriage allegations. *Drum's* editors acknowledged that such relationships did indeed exist but that they were a "disgrace" (February 1963, 7). Subsequent rare mentions through the 1960s also characterized male-male sexuality as a pathology. It was caused, variously, by shortage of women or, in the case of a notorious paedophile and murderer in 1969, by childhood in a broken home. One man who confessed in a 1964 letter that he felt sexual disgust towards women was shamed by the editors for being queer, abnormal, and possibly hating his own mother. He was advised to repress his feelings (December 1964, 64).

The paucity of letters to the editor by South African or Southern Rhodesian readers who wanted insight into their own confused sexual feelings stands in marked contrast to what Mutongi found in the other African editions of *Drum*. In independent black Africa in the 1960s to '80s, as many as one in eight letters to the personal advice column "Dear Dolly" enquired about same-sex desire. While Dolly was always disapproving, "she" clearly distinguished between real homosexuality, criminal offences like sodomy, and situational or temporary homosexual feelings. The latter could be tolerated, even among females, provided they did not become a permanent condition. In one remarkable response to an enquiry from Nigeria in 1965, for example, Dolly almost condoned male-male sex as long as it was done the right way: *"It would not be so bad if you had one male friend*, but if you chase after different boys all the time, you are promiscuous and morally wrong as well as breaking the law" (my emphasis, Mutongi 2000, 17). To Julia of Nairobi, who confessed her growing attraction to women in 1978, Dolly was even more accommodating: "What you feel is quite natural. Accept your new feelings and do not feel guilty. There are quite a lot of men and women who feel the same way as you do. They have husbands, wives, or lovers of the opposite sex but turn to people of the same sex for a sexual relationship."[15]

What this contrast between the two editions of *Drum* suggests is that outside of the pressure-cooker of apartheid and colonial rule, African patriarchy was well able to accommodate even public displays of same-sex sexuality. Indicative of this de facto tolerance is the fact that very first unequivocal public denunciation of male-male sexuality by a non-white in southern Africa did not come from an African chief or even a black intellectual but rather from "A Coloured Student." The occasion was the Coon Carnival in Cape Town, an annual celebration of cross-dressing by Coloured moffies that had its origins in the inter-war years and that was regarded as harmless fun by the straight citizens of the port city. With the outbreak of war with Germany, however, and in the context of the recent abolition of the franchise for Africans in Cape Province, planning for the 1940 parade inspired a furious exchange of letters in the *Cape Standard*. "A Coloured Student" started it with a full-page diatribe against the "idiocy" of the "sexually abnormal," "hermaphroditic," "pitiable" moffies: the "very thought of them should be repulsive to all but the scientist," he wrote.[16] He demanded an end to the disgraceful spectacle in the name of the dignity and political aspirations of non-white people. This evoked a lively debate over the following weeks, to which the author eventually responded in a detailed defence of his original letter. Revealingly (and incorrectly), he claimed that among his critics "Everyone seems to be agreed that 'Moffies' are 'no good,' so I will pass over this phase of the subject."[17]

The false claim of unanimity reflected the opinion in a small but growing circle of articulate society. Bessie Head's tormented novelistic reflections on her racial and gender identity shed light on how that homophobia gained currency in the wider society under apartheid. In *A Question of Power* (1974), Head's dream images of "weak," "disease[d]," and dying

Coloured homosexuals embody a sense of racial humiliation at the hands of whites. They provide a vehicle for the protagonist, Elizabeth, to express her anger at the apartheid system. Yet at the same time Elizabeth feels a certain empathy for the men that confuses and ultimately shames her. Unlike the white South African woman in Nadine Gordimer's *Burger's Daughter* (1980), for example, who is empowered in the struggle for racial justice by defining herself as virile in contrast to decadent, self-absorbed, European lesbians, Head's Elizabeth "feels contaminated by her recognition of her affinity with the disempowered homosexuals of her nightmares" (Jolly 1996, 115). The shame she feels comes from an imagined authentic African voice. Indeed, Head, via the character Elizabeth, attributes to black Africans a stern homophobia that fundamentally alienates them from the Coloured, ambiguous side of her heritage. Elizabeth's fears about Africans' negative judgment of her recur as an internal song in which she chastises her Coloured compatriots: "Dog, filth, the Africans will eat you to death" (Head 1974, 45).

A similar theme of failure to conform to the high ideals of heterosexual performance of African society is central to the works of Tatamkhulu Afrika, an Egyptian-born orphan adopted by a white family in Cape Town. For his first forty-four years of life Afrika was considered "white." But he converted to Islam in 1964, changed his name, and established a radical anti-apartheid movement that later merged with the armed wing of the ANC, UmKhonto we Sizwe. His poetry and novels, published after the end of apartheid, predominantly deal with the theme of winning acceptance or legitimacy from blacks in the struggle years. His characters typically express disgust or denial of homoerotic feelings, using often brutal language. Yet they also constantly bring those feelings up as if in mortal combat with them. Indeed, in Chris Dunton's terms, for Afrika "masculinity is seen as being proven both in the field of struggle and in sexual performance, two realms that are interlocked both metaphorically and in terms of the construction of objects of desire" (Dunton 2004).

Head and Afrika were mistaken to project homophobia and heterosexual purity onto African society in general. The links that they illuminate between intolerance of homosexuality or homoeroticism, racial and masculine dignity, and the struggle against apartheid were, however, unquestionably gaining currency among the leadership of the anti-apartheid political parties in the 1960s. Prison warders who used criminal gangs to rape and traumatize political prisoners no doubt contributed directly to making those links. But as early as 1963, the political prisoners at Robben Island took violent umbrage against comrades who were seen to betray revolutionary discipline and racial dignity by engaging in consensual homosexual relations (Dlamini 1984, 131–2). Harsh lines then began to be drawn by black Africans in the wider popular culture in the mid-1970s. The churches, beginning with a national conference on migrant labour in 1970 and at another in 1976, renewed their commitment to target the "atrocious vices" caused by the compound and hostel system. Their hostility to situational homosexuality was thus part and parcel of their opposition to apartheid more generally (Berglund 1970, 75; AIM 1976). The characters in *After Nines!* also assert that a change in public opinion happened in this regard, which they associate with the Soweto student uprising in 1976 (Colman 1998). This would agree with Dunbar Moodie's observations as well. In the racially charged context of nationalist struggle where the need for black men to maintain or to project hyper-masculine appearances in opposition to the state became exaggerated, the possibilities for tacitly admitting and tolerating sexual ambiguities were drastically reduced. Intriguingly, Moodie further claims that this whittling away of de facto tolerance for same-sex sexuality among black South Africans was abetted by the arrival in those same years of large numbers of migrant labourers from Zimbabwe, where nationalist homophobia was already more developed (Moodie with Ndatshe 1994, 247). The Zimbabweans brought with them an assertively heterosexual struggle masculinity that purportedly inspired the emerging generation of South African "comrades." By the 1980s, the years of the toughest government repression, criminal gangs joined that struggle in their own way. "Bongie" in Sam (1994) refers to the rise of Jackrollers, who would "go particularly for [suspected] lesbians" to "put right" by gang rape.

African men's anger against colonial rule and racial capitalism in Southern Rhodesia took many forms after 1897, including cultural associations, lawsuits, trade unions, social banditry, and fisticuffs down the mine shaft. It also began to be displaced onto "uppity women" from at least the 1920s. Many Zimbabwean men perceived women to be taking advantage of colonial laws, cash, and the migrant labour system (those Malawians!) at their expense. In most cases their rhetoric remained ostensibly respectful of women in idealized domestic roles. It elided all too easily, however, into barely disguised violence against women who stepped out of those roles. Ian Phimister and Charles van Onselen (1997, 15–16) have noted hints of politicized, modern misogyny from as early the 1920s when the Watch Tower movement at the Wankie colliery targeted "loose" African women. Several other scholars have also noted how many men approved of or even abetted the colonial state in cracking down on women's freedoms or violating urban women's dignity.[18] Ndabaningi Sithole, one of the founders of the modern nationalist movement, hints at this politics from the early 1940s. In his memoirs he recalls with pride how he "soundly thrashed" a schoolgirl who "always smiled whenever I told her not to smile" (1968, 17). He construes this act of violence as a modern, liberating one in relation to her father's rather pitiful traditional beliefs that led him to defend the girl's behaviour.

The modernity of Sithole's relationship with white men is also articulated in a striking allusion to shared virility: "African males fell down at the feet of white madonnas and forgot all about their black ones. This should not surprise us because both the African male and the white male have the same thing in common, and that is the 'male principle'" (161). The "white magic spell" that had been maintained by forbidding African men to have sex with white women had to be broken down, he argued.[19]

World War II contributed much towards that goal, but in important ways it exacerbated tensions between African men and women. Increased female migration to town and the advent of new, overtly sexualized female fashions and cosmetics in particular laid the ground both for intensified reaction against "uppity women" and for the growing conflation of male virility with African nationalism. The somewhat higher profile of gay life brought about by the war as happened around Joubert Park in Johannesburg may also have given a new, disturbing visibility to black gays in Salisbury. A tantalizing early hint of this was made in a letter to *African Weekly* in October 1946, in which the author sneers at Africans who "look down on themselves" by aping Western culture. In addition to women and men who try to lighten the appearance of their skin, he notes: "There are some blacks [men] who spend Sunday wearing women's dresses, which shows we are hopeless."[20]

The first big industrial strike to invoke African nationalist rhetoric (Bulawayo, 1948) gave an even stronger indication of this latent anger when the strikers lashed out with seemingly gratuitous acts of violence against African women passers-by.[21] The state responded with repression and duplicity. Over the course of the 1950s its actions served to discredit moderate or liberal African nationalism and to encourage a hard masculinity that could stand up to the settlers' "cowboy" maschismo. Prominent nationalist leaders began to go on record with misogynist statements couched as attacks upon Western fashion, the mini-skirt above all. They also used rhetoric that explicitly equated compromise or political moderation with femininity. Sithole's nationalist mentor, Obed Muteza, put his decision to go to prison this way: "[T]he honourable choice is the life of hardship, even death, than to go down in the annals of a nation as a collaborator or indeed a woman. The choice before me is simple; am I a man or a woman?"[22] Muteza further emphasized that real African men not only repressed any ascribed feminine instinct to laugh or smile but cultivated "distance between man and man" as a way to ensure seriousness, inner discipline, and self-confidence in battle.

This masculinist message was also strongly implicit in leaders' refusal to condemn followers' violence against women or indeed their retroactive approval of it. Undoubtedly the most dramatic demonstration of the latter came at the time of the mass rape of young women in Harare's female hostel in 1956, an atrocity that was tacitly pardoned by prominent nationalist leaders. The women, including some who were injured trying to escape from second-storey windows, were said to have provoked "unruly youths" because they had refused to participate in a bus boycott to demonstrate anti-colonial solidarity. Some had purportedly scorned the orders of the boycott enforcers (young, unemployed males) on the basis of having an independent income. To Maurice Nyagumbo this was an intolerable affront to the men and to the nationalist movement as a whole: "Personally I had no reason to feel regret for the incident. I actually believed the girls deserved their punishment" (Nyagumbo 1980, 104–5).[23] The aggressive expression of African men's virility as a counter to white racism and political violence was also implied in the symbolism of the two main nationalist parties in the 1960s and '70s – the cock and the bull. "Tea-drinkers" (softies, sell-outs, stooges, and "women") began to fall by the wayside of the struggle in this context.

One of those tea-drinkers was Charles Mzingeli, the first and only African leader known to have publicly broached the topic of homosexuality in this period. Mzingeli was the founder and leader the Reformed Industrial and Commercial Union (RICU) and a towering figure in the movement by Harare citizens to obtain decent living and working conditions in the postwar period. In 1952, these were under threat as the city government stepped up its efforts to rid African residential areas of undocumented illegal residents. One effect was constant police harassment of suspected female prostitutes in the Old Bricks section of Salisbury township – most women, in other words. Mzingeli took up their cause. Rather than harassing and deporting African women, he argued, the authorities should allow them free entry into town and provide them with secure accommodation so that the men who lived there could enjoy their company. "Most of these men in the Old Bricks have wives but when they visit their husbands they are arrested, how do you expect the men to survive?" Mzingeli is purported to have challenged municipal officials. "Do you want the men to be homosexuals?" (Barnes 1999, 143).

Mzingeli himself may not have been homophobic. His rhetorical question was aimed to shame homophobic white officials out of their arrogance and complacency towards Africans. It failed both in that and in preventing the self-styled radicals from undermining his leadership. The *coup de grâce* came in 1956, just prior to the mass rape incident, when Mzingeli was unseated from the Salisbury African Advisory Board by members of the City Youth League. The leadership of the nationalist movement then passed to those "radicals" who went on to build a mass movement disciplined by modern political parties. It was this generation that took up the armed struggle for liberation or *chimurenga*, won independence for Zimbabwe, and today still, through the person of Robert Mugabe, cling to power. They did not make homosexuality an issue of public concern at any time during the liberation struggle. We know from their pronouncements in the 1990s, however, that strong feelings of disgust and xenophobia towards homosexuals are part of their political worldview. This they claim primarily in the name of African culture. Yet a close look at the geneology of homophobia in the "second generation" of Zimbabwean nationalist leadership reveals a more complicated picture.

To begin with, these men mostly came from rural, peasant backgrounds. Mugabe himself herded goats as a boy. They would have learned much of the customary understanding of sexuality – strongly heteronormative, transphobic, and policed by shame rather than guilt. An internalized sense of guilt at transgressions from the heterosexual ideal came later, principally from Christian education. Indeed, almost without exception these men attended mission schools. Mugabe was educated at a Catholic school run by the Canadian Marist Brothers. Joshua Nkomo, president of the Rhodesian African National Congress after 1957 and a founder of the Zimbabwe African People's Union in 1961, described himself a proudly monogamous, tea-totalling Christian (Nkomo 1984). Ndabaningi Sithole studied under Garfield Todd at Dadaya mission, and so on. Their moral compass was attuned by their missionary teachers to the dogma of Leviticus and Corinthians and away from the ambiguities of VaNyemba and other traditional spiritual figures. Moreover, unlike a traditional education, the modern education they received did not include frank instruction about sexuality, as per government as well as most mission policy.[24] Despite their later appeals to African traditions and the manipulation of pre-colonial religious symbols to win popular support during the liberation struggle, these men were thus highly ambivalent towards many of those traditions.

We can presume as well that they were relatively ignorant about the range of sexual behaviours that people, including Africans in the pre-colonial era, accommodated within their cultures.

So equipped intellectually, the future leaders of the liberation struggle graduated to become members of Zimbabwe's aspirant middle class, commonly as teachers or ministers in mission schools. As Michael West (2002) has shown, this was the class that was most obsessed with achieving "respectability" in bourgeois terms, and the most heavily influenced by the colonialist discourses around hygiene, progress, body image, attire, and sexuality. Zimbabwean novelist Tsitsi Dangarembga (1989) has also portrayed them as the class most affected by "nervous conditions," that is, the psychopathologies that Frantz Fanon identified as springing from colonial emasculation. This becomes immediately apparent from political leaders' statements on gender during the liberation struggle. In contrast to the revolutionary rhetoric about class and race, gender policy was often infused by a conservative Christian idealism or even, at times, a puritanical preachiness and dogmatism that reflected mission school education.

Naomi Nhiwatiwa, a Zimbabwe African National Union official, for example, told a Western audience in 1979 that ZANU had abolished *lobola* and that it facilitated monogamous marriage among its fighters.[25] Men who fathered children were required to marry the mother. The guerrilla leadership also purportedly prohibited divorce and adultery and condemned beer-drinking. An internal report prepared by the ZANU Commissariat Department in July 1979 makes this gender conservatism even more explicit. The unpublished document, "On Marriage," does not discuss rape, homosexuality, or masturbation but concentrates its ire on boy-girl affairs in the guerrilla camps. It describes marriage as "natural," then lists the "disastrous consequences" of allowing women or men to refuse it, including prostitution and more prostitution. Its remedy is to "intensify orientation on our culture with emphasis on marriage and 'internal discipline.'"[26]

Perhaps the most striking examples of this implicitly homophobic analysis can be found in the writings of the Reverend Canaan Banana. The man who became the first president of independent Zimbabwe, and who later became the first African president ever to be convicted of sodomy, authored a number of homilies on how to build a revolutionary society. This included the dismantling of capitalism in favour of scientific socialism, the rejection of European luxuries and habits in favour of African traditions of modesty and community, and the need for men to dominate women, as explained in the Bible (Banana 1980, 147). In *The Woman of My Imagination,* he actually adjures wives to be subject to their husbands by citing St Paul. He then blames boys' sexually irresponsible behaviour on "the poor upbringing of the girls" (9). Pervading the nationalist movement were anti-contraceptive attitudes that were similarly justified in both anti-racism and biblical terms, counter to traditional practices that allowed for child spacing (Kaler 2003).

In addition to their Christian beliefs, Nkomo, Mugabe, Banana, and others in the mainstream of the nationalist movement in the 1970s articulated much of their revolutionary analysis in Marxist-Leninist or Fanonesque terms. Both movements aspire to female emancipation from customary and capitalist male domination. Both, however, also have socially conservative, pro-natalist traditions with respect to sexuality. This was particularly true in Communist China and the U.S.S.R. at the time Zimbabwean leaders began travelling there for ideological training. Similarly pro-natalist were the fraternal frontline African states that provided haven and education for the comrades in exile – Tanzania, Zambia, and post-1975 Mozambique (see GALZ 2004). Fay Chung, who went on to become minister of Education in independent Zimbabwe, described the effect of this education when "puritanical, idealistic, Marxist 'VaShandi' [workers]" allied themselves with puritanical traditionalists in the Zambian guerrilla camps to oppose those guerrillas who took an indulgent view of sex.[27] And while the focus of this alliance was on heterosexual affairs, we can infer the VaShandi's intense disapproval of homosexuality from pejorative interpretations found in both Marxism-Leninism and Fanon. In the former tradition, homosexuality tended to be regarded as bourgeois or aristocratic decadence, hence to be despised as counter-revolutionary. For Frantz Fanon, the French-trained analyst of colonial psychopathologies, homosexuality among blacks was a function of black men's debasement by white men, likewise to be despised (1967, 156). Crude versions of Fanonesque homophobia were particularly popular in the African-American community and among "Afrocentric" intellectuals in the United States during the 1970s where several Zimbabwean leaders (Canaan Banana, for instance) went to school.[28]

How (or even if) this garbled, derivative homophobia was ever communicated from the nationalist leadership to the masses or to the cadres in the guerilla armies has yet to be discussed in the memoirs of African combatants. What is known, however, is that nationalist discourses around African male virility were often distinctly undermined by the actual practices of nationalist struggle. During the war of liberation in the 1960s and '70s, young men with guns and scant respect for the niceties of the old patriarchal order daily heaped humiliations upon the majority peasant population. This included the public beatings of husbands accused of mistreating their wives.[29] Young girls also took advantage of the presence of guerrillas and Rhodesian soldiers alike to escape patriarchal controls and flout tradition. Some cited the propaganda of the liberation forces about women's equality to assert their sexual independence. In the guerrilla camps, a high degree of sexual indiscipline took place. Paulos Matjaka Nare's reflections on this in a camp high school provide a wonderfully understated account: "In the absence of their real parents and relatives, the children lacked proper guidance and counselling. Strange manners and habits were evolved" (Nare 1995, 137).

The war years also witnessed an enormous jump in rape statistics, up by a third in the single year of 1965 alone (that is, the year that white Rhodesians unilaterally declared independence from Britain in order to frustrate African men's demands for the vote). Many factors may have contributed to this surge, but it is striking how it continued, virtually unabated, until the end of the war of liberation in 1979. By that time, the number of arrests of African men for rape and attempted rape had nearly tripled over 1964 (to 923 from 343). As the police put it, the rapes were the result of "the general lawlessness that arose amongst the young thug element recruited and incited by nationalist elements."[30] We are rightly sceptical of police analysis from this period. Nonetheless, the official explanation for this precipitous rise in sexual assault cases against African women was also tacitly conceded even by some African nationalist leaders. Pervasive public gender and sexual violence in the townships that reflected the deteriorating political situation in this period is also vividly described in the works of Dambudzo Marechera.[31]

In the bush, meanwhile, the overwhelmingly young male guerrillas were under orders to keep their hands off peasant girls, on pain of execution in some cases. This was not merely to preserve a cooperative peasant sea in which the guerrillas could swim. It was also couched in the "traditional" imagery of sexual taboos. One former *mujiba* or scout explained their eventual victory to anthropologist David Lan in these terms: "[O]ur forces didn't make love to girls but Muzorewa's [Rhodesian] forces did this very much. If our forces had done this the country would never have been taken by the blacks" (Lan 1985, 158). To another, "If a pregnant woman came to our camp, sure that camp would be destroyed" (ibid., 159). These taboos extended to the women who prepared food. To eat something touched by a menstruating woman was thought to be especially dangerous.

No one has yet seriously claimed that these enforced homosocial environments resulted in homosexual ties among the comrades. A new generation of fictional and autobiographical accounts of the war does, however, portray the young men who took to the bush in intensely confused, fearful, and shaming sexual situations. Chinodya has portrayed masturbation among the guerrillas and Hotz refers to child rape and murder (Chinodya 1990, 206; Hotz 1990, 197 and passim). The film *Flame* and female war veterans have also begun to reveal that shameful rape was endemic on and behind the front.[32] Even the military violence of the war is depicted in these accounts as far more sordid than heroic or humanizing in the Fanonesque sense. Moreover, those who were unlucky enough to be captured by the Rhodesians sometimes spent long years in incarceration, in some cases together with hardened criminals and gang members. Nkomo notes how much he and fellow political prisoners "hated" the tense, confusing, and presumably humiliating conjugal visits that the Rhodesian jailers finally allowed (Nkomo 1984, 132).

In short, while the war unquestionably did force a negotiated transition to black rule and an end to state-sanctioned racism, the violence of the struggle, including sexual violence, generated a great deal of alienation. In traditional terms it also created innumerable "avenging spirits" (*ngozi*). According to traditional religion, *ngozi* are one of the main causes of incurable sexual identity problems. In the eyes of many Zimbabweans today, failure since the end of the war to appease the *ngozi* with the proper rituals quite straightforwardly accounts for the apparently sudden emergence of out gays and lesbians in the 1990s.[33]

Independence came in 1980. The new prime minister, Robert Mugabe, was a devout Catholic who espoused Marxism-Leninism yet advocated reconciliation with white commercial farmers and capitalist entrepreneurs. Under his leadership, Zimbabwe experienced a flowering of democratic governance, freedom of speech, rural economic development, huge expansion of the health care and education systems, and the legal emancipation of women. The oppressive Rhodesian past began to be shed in cultural life as well. Thus, notwithstanding the moral conservatism of much of the leadership and its indebtedness to rural patriarchs from the bush war, the new regime was initially self-confident enough to allow an unprecedented degree of sexual emancipation to pass without negative comment. According to Evan Tsourillis's memoir (2001), the period beginning from the 1979 ceasefire (and the arrival of Commonwealth peacekeepers) was almost a golden age of gay life. New nightclubs sprang up, exiles from South Africa and the West returned with experiences there of out gay life, the first-ever lesbian group was formed (1982), and gay men could almost openly cruise in downtown Harare's Cecil Square. Even the state-controlled press

advocated tolerance of homosexuals. "Homosexuals break through barri-
ers," Harare's *Sunday Mail Magazine* reported as it broached the topic in
a substantial article for the very first time in 1983. It advised readers not
to be fearful of homosexuals since they were probably born that way and
therefore not contagious.[34]

This relative golden age, however, was fragile. To begin with, the old
colonial laws against sodomy were never questioned. They not only
remained on the books but cases that came before the new cohort of
Zimbabwean magistrates were frequently characterized by stern moralizing
that in many ways exceeded the Rhodesian regime. Oliver Phillips cites a
magistrate's pronouncement in 1991, for example, that might have caused
missionaries a century earlier to blush. Describing sodomy between consenting adult men in private, "Such unscrupulous acts," the lower court
judge thundered, "do in my view stink in the nostrils of justice, above all
society does look at such offences with abhorrence" (Phillips 1999, 195).
No attempt was made to challenge such attitudes in the new school
curricula, and indeed, considerable propaganda emerged to convince
Zimbabweans to return to idealized, sharply dichotomous gender roles.

The major media also fostered the stereotype of homosexuality as a
white man's foible. Identifying blacks as homosexuals remained taboo –
all the individuals described in the *Sunday Mail* article mentioned above
were white or Coloured gays and lesbians. To suggest any other possibility
was deemed so absurd as to be hilarious. Thus, the same paper that advised
readers to be tolerant or to pity white and Coloured homosexuals at about
the same time blatantly pandered to transphobic humour with a cartoon
depicting a feminized Joshua Nkomo in drag. The "father" of the nationalist struggle and a rival with Mugabe for political power, Nkomo was
drawn with panties and ample, womanly buttocks exposed to heighten his
disgrace.[35] Similar mockery was fostered by occasional coverage of gay
rights activism in the West in a regular column entitled "It's Weird Weird
World." A report on Zimbabwe's first gay wedding ceremony in 1986 was
played for titillation or amusement rather than taking a hostile tone.[36] The
emergence of black gay activists in South Africa in the mid-1980s meanwhile simply passed without comment, so as not to complicate a picture
that allowed proudly independent Africans to mock their former colonial
masters. Even the daring novelist Dambudzo Marechera hedged his bets
in this respect. While his 1984 novel *Mindblast* contains Zimbabwe's first-
ever description of an erotic lesbian encounter, the Shona woman who
enjoys it is portrayed as highly Westernized. She is also the passive object
of an American woman's seduction (Marechera 1984, 70).

The shift from sexist, transphobic, and mildly xenophobic humour and imagery to state-sanctioned backlash against sexual freedom was not long in coming once the post-*chimurenga* euphoria began to wear off. Independent women were the first to feel the brunt when in 1983 hundreds of alleged prostitutes in Harare were arrested and deported to work camps in the rural areas, a round-up that would have dismayed Charles Mzingeli three decades before.[37] Gay men's activity in Cecil Square was roughly closed down soon after, although whether by freelance gay-bashers or by pro-government thugs is unclear. As Tsourillis recalls, "It was sometimes dangerous. Once in a while gay-bashers would try and muscle in. Most of the activity stopped around 1986 when the Spanish ambassador was murdered. There was a lot of speculation amongst gay men at the time that the ambassador was murdered by a trick picked up at The Square. But that is one of Zimbabwe's untold stories" (Tsourillis 2001).

The chilling climate was partly reflective of a growing realization that black men were surreptitiously engaging in the disapproved activities. The phenomenon was sufficiently common that a new sneer entered popular slang for black homosexual – "clear-drinker" (that is, a black man who exchanged sex for money to buy relatively expensive, European-style beer). But blacks were evidently not just opportunistic tricks but consumers as well. Whispers spread about no less prominent a person than the (ceremonial) president of the country, Canaan Banana. Banana was made redundant when the ZANU-dominated parliament amended the constitution in 1987 to create an executive presidency. For years afterwards, however, police followed his activities closely, keeping "numerous intelligence reports" of his alleged criminal acts from "many parts of the country."[38] This secret surveillance suggests that there was considerable anxiety about Banana's potential to embarrass the ruling party. His behaviour was reportedly discussed at the highest levels of cabinet in 1986.[39]

Growing harassment of male homosexuals in the mid-late 1980s was also linked to an economic downturn and rising popular disillusionment with the regime. Frustrations at the slow pace of land reform, shortages of consumer goods, political repression including mass killings in Matabeleland, and economic stagnation were all undermining public enthusiasm for the ruling party. The Economic Structural Adjustment Programme (ESAP) adopted in 1990 exacerbated the sense of disempowerment, particularly for men. Indeed, by abetting de-industrialization, by the steady erosion of real earnings among those who avoided retrenchment, and by the creeping imposition of user-fees for government services, ESAP undercut several of the principal stays of masculinity in Zimbabwe – the ability to provide for a wife and children above all. Workers in public administration by 1991 earned only slightly more than half of what they would have taken home in 1980, while agricultural workers earned about two-thirds of their 1982 wages (Dashwood 2000, 47). Alcoholism and prostitution flourished in this context, as did a hitherto unimaginable population of unwanted African "street kids." It was a fertile field for the leadership both to shift the blame from its own errors in judgment onto convenient scapegoats and to reassert its old Christian moralism.

Sensing a lowering homophobia, a small number of mostly white and coloured gays and lesbians came together in 1990 to form GALZ, the first public association to promote gay rights in Zimbabwe. By 1992 it had a constitution and was actively seeking to advertise its counselling services and propagate anti-homophobic arguments in the national media. While it was blocked from access to the state-controlled press, it found an eager ally in an increasingly outspoken independent press hungry for stories that highlighted corruption and bigotry in the ruling party. Papers like the *Zimbabwean Independent* ran GALZ advertisements, extolled the emergence of a democratic and gay-friendly South Africa, and published sympathetic stories on local gays and lesbians. In March 1994, for example, the *High Density Mirror*, a newspaper circulating in the former black townships, ran a story discussing the plight of local black gays, an implicit criticism of the ruling party (Goddard, 2004). In 1994 Ngoni Chaidzo was formed, the first association for black gays and lesbians in one of the historically black townships.

Such unprecedented assertions of individual freedoms, gay identities, and the right to criticize if not outright mock one's elders were seen by the ruling party as a dangerous foot in the door heralding wider attacks from civil society. But the state backlash against women's and gays' sexual liberation also needs to be understood in the context of the gathering HIV/AIDS epidemic. The effects of HIV/AIDS were becoming visible, reported in grim, growing tallies of deaths – 600, 700, 800 per week! They were also demonstrably linked to the culture of masculine virility and sexual entitlement that the Rhodie-"radical" dialectic had fomented so much since the 1950s and '60s. With the Rhodies now long gone as a significant cultural and political force, HIV/AIDS stood as a deeply damning indictment of the "radicals'" social policies. It was also seen to be contributing to the emergence of dangerous sexual behaviours. These included women's and men's predation upon younger and younger children (supposedly to avoid HIV but also, in the case of men, to assert the power to refuse to wear a condom), the rape of virgins (to cure the disease), and a fatalistic sexual consumerism (we are all going to die anyway, so why not indulge in the most conquests possible?). In addition, long-standing fears about "uppity women" began to manifest themselves in a virulent misogyny expressed most shockingly in public strippings of women in short skirts.[40] Men's anxieties about women's ability to escape male control (or even to assert control over men) were widely expressed in articles in the popular media about women "raping" men, as well as through whispered fears about *mupfuhwira* – husband-taming herbs that could render a man helpless, penis-less, or even dead (Goebel 2002).

In this context, apparently growing numbers of men and women who identified as heterosexual turned to prostitutes of the same sex for what they considered to be relatively safe and uncomplicated sex. For young unemployed men and women or for street kids, the possibilities of earning or extorting money from such bisexual or closeted gays and lesbians were attractive enough to draw them into homosexual relations regardless of their actual sexual orientation. As one Shona woman admitted about her preference for rich white women, "I am not afraid at all because I am not a genuine lesbian" (Chigweshe 1996, 29).

Sexual opportunism of this nature was deeply upsetting to traditional and Christian moralists (not to mention many GALZ members). To fully understand the anti-homosexual campaigns after 1995, however, we also need to appreciate how worrisome homosexual opportunism was in a material sense to Zimbabwean women. The majority of African women still aspired to stable, heterosexual marriage, as without it their legal rights to property and their moral rights to income were sharply circumscribed. Women's anxieties that their tenuous rights were further endangered by men's sexual irresponsibility (for example, income siphoned off to the husband's girlfriends) were expressed in a wide variety of media (see, for example, Kala 1994). That those same anxieties also underpinned a growing, angry homophobia among women is revealed in Charles Mungoshi's remarkable short story, "A Marriage of Convenience." In this story, first published in 1997 in the popular magazine *Parade*, Shamiso bitterly resents having to share dwindling family resources and the affections of her husband with his long-standing male lover. The bitterness she expresses sheds light on why few groups in Zimbabwe were more strident and vituperative in their support of Mugabe's denunciations of homosexuals than the ruling party's Women's League.[41]

The appearance of openly homophobic statements and threats by ruling party officials in fact began in early 1994. The minister of Home Affairs, Dumiso Dabengwa, reportedly described homosexuality as illegal and directed police to "warn homos – net is closing in."[42] In January 1995, Dabengwa denounced homosexuality as "abhorrent," while Harare's state-controlled *Sunday Mail* ran an article denouncing foreigners who meddled in and sought to pervert Zimbabwean culture.[43] President Mugabe himself first waded into the fray the following month with a speech in Bulawayo that equated prostitutes and homosexuals. This speech occurred at the start of his long, nationwide campaign for re-election as president. It inspired the editors of the Bulawayo daily newspaper to praise fellow Zimbabweans who "loathe foreign ideas on morality" and to sneer at "pseudo-campaigners for people's so-called rights."[44] Mugabe raised the issue several more times over the next few months, culminating most notoriously with his denunciation of homosexuals at the Zimbabwe International Book Fair in August 1995. In September the Zimbabwean parliament voted overwhelmingly to endorse the principle of increased persecution of homosexuals.

Mugabe's characterization of homosexuality as a threat to an idealized patriarchal culture and national values, frequently and explicitly linked to Western imperialism and "reactionary forces," allowed his supporters to portray him as "brave." The harsh rhetoric may also have been a pre-emptive move against Canaan Banana, who was rumoured to be thinking about re-entering politics after a stint at the university. That option, serious or not, was decisively foreclosed by the implied threat to out Banana's secret. Mugabe thus went on to an easy electoral victory, following which he left the topic of homosexuality alone. He did not, for example, make a statement at the time of the 1996 International Book Fair imbroglio, in which vigilantes forced GALZ to abandon its display. Nor did he comment when Banana was finally outed by a former aide in 1997. When challenged internationally, he even made some mildly conciliatory statements. Asked whether gays and lesbians were allowed in Zimbabwean churches, for instance, he allowed that "if they have come as individuals to pray to enhance their moral entity as human beings and desist from the Gay way of theirs, well, well and good. This is the church."[45]

Mugabe's minions in the state-controlled press were not so gracious. They continued without hesitation to use homosexuality to score political points against Western imperialism. The *Harare Herald*, for example, briefly mentioned Banana's "alleged indiscretions" when the case first broke. It then immediately launched into an attack upon the "establishment media across the Limpopo," coded language for white South Africans.[46] Zimbabweans who were members of the ruling party or who were dependent upon ruling party patronage put their career ambitions at severe risk if they spoke out against such views. Some, like "Leonard Chaza," publicly ventured expressions of tolerance only under a pseudonym out of fear of victimization.[47] Conversely, jumping on the nationalist, "anti-homo" band-wagon was a clear route to curry favour with the nationalist old guard. The brief re-emergence of washed-up politicians like Michael Mawema in 1996, thumping Leviticus and Corinthians for attention, was one example; contributors to the breathless rhetoric of the *"Sunday Blackmail"* (as GALZ members call it) were another.[48] Banana himself, in an unsuccessful, des-perate attempt to save himself from the charges of sodomy and indecent assault made against him, added to this rhetoric wild allegations of racist conspiracies couched in nasty homophobic language.[49] Even black men who identified as gay contributed (anonymous) denunciations of "Western deviants" as a means to win public sympathy for their preference of a discreet, "traditional" homosexual identity. In the words of "A Homo-sexual," "We are fully aware that we have an unfortunate condition and only wish to continue our lives in our own quiet way, without publicity or persecution."[50]

Mugabe himself eventually returned to take up the cudgels as the eco-nomic and political crisis in Zimbabwe deepened in 1998. His post-election statesmanship had seemingly been rattled at a personal level by British activist Peter Tatchell's attempts to conduct a citizen's arrest, and at a political level by increasingly outspoken British criticism of his land reform policies and human rights abuses. In 1999 he took to describing the British government as a "gay government" or "gay gangsters" who "wanted to impose homosexuality." He also brought the topic up without provocation in a series of speeches to traditional chiefs. The main objective of the speeches was to garner support for seizures of land from white farmers. "Unlike pigs and dogs," he digressed to an audience of two hundred chiefs from around the nation, "which knew their females and could naturally become intimate with them, gays and lesbians could not differentiate between males and females ... we, as chiefs in Zimbabwe, should fight against such Western practices and respect our culture."[51] The state-controlled press also used clumsy homophobic innuendo at this time in an attempt to vilify one of the regime's most outspoken African critics, Roman Catholic Archbishop Pius Ncube.[52]

Ironically, one of the first real victims of this resurgence of anti-homosexual rhetoric was a prominent member of the ruling party. Alum Mpofu was chief executive of the Zimbabwe Broadcasting Corporation and had allowed the state television and radio channels to disseminate homophobic opinions and incitement to hatred during the 2001 presidential campaign. He scored an own goal in April 2002 with his arrest for allegedly fondling and kissing a young man in a quiet corner of a public restaurant. GALZ reacted to the incident by venting anger not against homophobia specifically but against people who knowingly served a government that was so increasingly contemptuous of human rights in general terms. "His betrayal is not that of an active campaigner against homosexuals but that of a deep silence and quiet acquiescence to state-led physical and psychological violence against defenseless minorities, including lesbian and gay people."[53]

The nuance here was apposite, extending GALZ's political message to a much broader audience than the usual gay rights one. Indeed, the worst-hit victims of the renewed incitements to homophobic violence have not been members of the overwhelmingly urban, internationally connected out gay community at all. They have been heterosexual villagers in the countryside where most of the land reform and electoral turmoil has been concentrated. In particular, a national militia known as the Border Gezi Youth or Green Bombers has acquired notoriety since 2001 for perpetrating sexual crimes against political opponents. Reports spoke of widespread heterosexual rape by the Green Bombers, and of forced acts of public sex intended to traumatize the villagers, including fellatio by women upon men and sexual acts between men. Beginning in March 2002, the human-rights organization Amani Trust began to report "incidents where men were forced to commit sexual assaults on one another, to the amusement of their tormentors."[54] By 2003, male rape had become an apparently common-place terror tactic. As reported in the British press, this speaks to a profound criminality in the state:

It has also emerged that boys of 15 are being raped at youth-training centres in what appears part of the government's plans to crush dissent. The Sunday Times has interviewed 52 male Zimbabweans who have fled to South Africa after claiming to have been tortured; of them, 38 said they had been raped or forced to engage in anal sex with other victims ... Sekai Holland [the Movement for Democratic Change's secretary for international affairs] said this showed the use of male rape as a weapon. "This is not casual sex," she said. "It is a concerted campaign to terrorise our members. Even one of our MPs was raped by 10 men. We are trying to counsel him to go public about the attack." Her concerns were echoed by a doctor in Johannesburg providing free medical treatment to 14 of the exiles. The man asked not to be named for fear that publicity would deter others from seeking his help. "In their culture rape is worse that death and all my patients are being treated for depression and mental trauma," the doctor said. "In my 35 years as a doctor, I have never seen such brutality."[55]

The emergence of a politicized, violent homophobia and of internalized homophobia among gays and lesbians in Zimbabwe is a fairly recent phenomenon. Its roots lie in a combination of pre-modern transphobia, Christian missionary propaganda, structural changes occasioned by racial capitalism, Western media, and imported fetishes of previously non-sexual parts of the body. While the Western influences are clear, however, it cannot be explained as simply the internalization of Western values or as a cynical electoral contrivance of Westernized political elites. The sudden upsurge of invented homophobic "traditions" has clearly resonated among the wider population, particularly among those people most threatened by the rapid changes in gender relations, by economic collapse, and by the demoralizing breakdown in health and extended family obligations. Unemployed and disaffected male youth are at special risk in this regard due to their widespread recruitment into the Green Bombers and their exploitation there as weapons of political terror.

This latest phenomenon aside, homophobia in Zimbabwe has in some ways been overstated in the international community, evoking defensive reactions even from proudly nationalist gays and lesbians. Offensive and oppressive as it sometimes is, homophobia directed against gays and lesbians in Zimbabwe rarely approaches the level of violence often encountered in the West. African traditions of discretion and tolerance in fact remain strong. Nonetheless, the many pressures and incentives to act out homophobic sentiments are unlikely to go away in the near future. On the contrary, a breakdown in law and order, the HIV/AIDS pandemic, and deepening economic crisis in the years since Mugabe's first incitements to homophobic intolerance all bode ill in that respect. Homophobia (and misogyny and ethnic bigotry) are likely to intensify under such conditions of stress. The use of homosexual rape as a political terror tactic against heterosexuals, for example, is an abhorrent development that may, as has sometimes been observed in cases of coerced prison sex, feed into a vicious cycle of internalized homophobia and repressed sexual trauma.

7

Contagion!

One of the foundational fears underlying homophobia is that homosexuality is contagious and therefore threatening to the majority of the population (Fone 2000). The very first enquiry into "unnatural crime" on the Witwatersrand in 1906 was predicated on the assumptions behind this fear. If Chinese catamites were present at the mines, as alleged, then they posed a danger of infecting their African co-workers, and a key justification for empire (civilizing the natives) would fall away. In the event, the catamite allegations were found to have been exaggerated. The contagion thesis was nonetheless reaffirmed in the course of the investigation when it was revealed that a certain section of the African workforce *did* practice male-male sex. How could savages, so close to nature in their brutish, heterosexual lustiness, behave in this depraved and sinful way if they had not learned of it from the Chinese? They must have caught the habit from the Portuguese, a belief duly acknowledged (despite the lack of evidence) in the Leary/Taberer enquiry into African men's behaviour the following year.

The new intellectual disciplines of psychology and sexology had begun to challenge this contagion metaphor even by the late nineteenth century. In Leary and Taberer's time, the jury was still out among colonial officials. By the 1910s – '30s, however, the metaphor had lost much of its persuasiveness in South Africa and colonial Zimbabwe. Bureaucrats and magistrates there increasingly turned a blind eye to behaviours among African men that in practice appeared not only to be self-limiting but, all in all, preferable to many of the men's other leisure-time pursuits. In this, modern science was getting closer to "traditional" African beliefs than it might have cared to concede. Indeed, a blasé attitude towards contained, discreet, or situational same-sex activity distinguished the transphobia that predominated among Africans at the time from the homophobic attitudes found today.

Gays and lesbians themselves, meanwhile, have tended to dismiss the contagion metaphor out of hand: since homosexual orientation is something that a person is born with or is bestowed by God or the ancestors, it cannot be transmitted against the will or instincts of the majority. From a gay rights perspective, the absurdity of fears of contagion (or recruitment of heterosexuals to a gay life-style) is even more pronounced, given the prevalence of homophobic attitudes in society today. One GALZ pamphlet was droll about this, if somewhat hyperbolic: "Can you imagine how gay and lesbian life might be advertised to potential recruits? 'You, too, can be a member of a despised minority. Join us and your parents will reject you, your boss will fire you, and absolute strangers will call you names or physically assault you'" (undated).

The dramatic re-emergence of inflammatory rhetoric about disease and contagion in political discourse in southern Africa over the last decade is thus remarkable, even considering the possibilities of cynical political opportunism or popular anxieties about gender relations and health in general. "The homosexuals are the festering finger endangering the body," parliamentarian and historian A.S. Chigwedere of Zimbabwe said in 1995.[1] In this view, an idealized blend of traditional and Christian gender roles should act as a prophylaxis. The sharp, disciplined polarization between masculinity and femininity that is purportedly inherent to "African values" and Christian fundamentals should protect African girls and boys from homosexual infection and other forms of contemporary Western imperialism. And yet, if heterosexuality were as natural to robust Africans as claimed, how could they possibly be susceptible to something as supposedly unnatural, self-defeating, self-indulgent, diseased, and purposeless as homosexuality?

The answer to that, of course, is that Africans' cultural "immune system" has partially broken down through the history of colonialism and racial capitalism. We have seen that urbanization in colonial and apartheid southern Africa did indeed facilitate the emergence of new expressions of sexuality including heterosexual female prostitution but also homosexual mine marriage, prison sex, and tentative gay orientation or preference. There is, moreover, considerable evidence to support the argument that the men and women who "succumbed" to these new sexualities were precisely those who were most emasculated, "demoralized," or "detribalized" by the living and working conditions they faced under racial capitalism (*matanyera*, for example). This argument implies that an African people who retained their sense of independence and cultural integrity would have been able to resist the contagion.

In this chapter, I would like to test that argument with a close study of an assertively heteronormative culture in the region that appeared to have all the ingredients supposedly needed to resist homosexual infection – Sesotho. Sesotho is the language and culture of the Basotho people of Lesotho (Basutoland under colonial rule), also formerly known as the "British Basutos" or the "Moshesh tribes" in distinction from other Sotho-speakers who fell under South Africa rule. Same-sex behaviours are rare in the ethnographic record about pre-modern Sesotho even more so than among the Shona, Ndebele, or Zulu. As a protectorate and then a High Commission Territory, Lesotho experienced almost none of the infrastructural development that came to be associated with male-male sexuality in South Africa and Zimbabwe. It had no white or Asian settlement beyond tiny, isolated "reserves," very little tourism, no mines, no hostels, very few boarding schools, prisons, or hospitals prior to the 1950s, precious few liberal-minded magistrates to interfere with or interpret the law, and precisely one kilometre of railroad. In common with other African "reserves," Lesotho did develop very high levels of male migrancy and enforced, long-term separation of the sexes. The men who migrated, however, asserted a fierce attachment to idealized heterosexual practices. By the 1920s Basotho gangs known as "the Russians" (MaRashea) had become notorious for predatory sex upon women. They even rejected heterosexual *hlobonga* as a mere boyish thing done by tribes they regarded as their inferiors. The Native Economic Commission of the government of South Africa in 1932 found that Basotho men were, in consequence, "much more syphilized than the Union labourers on the mines."[2]

From evidence such as this, one historian has recently argued that the *nkotshane* so widely noted among other Africans at the mines "was an impossibility for most if not all Basotho migrants" (Maloka 1995, 306). Moreover, an American lesbian scholar who by her own account went "looking for lesbians" in Lesotho encountered sincere bafflement among her informants at the very concept of women having sex with women (Kendall 1999). Even a contemporary gay journalist, Bart Luirink, concerned to show the universality of homosexual orientation and having had notable success in that goal in his wide travels throughout the region, came up virtually empty-handed from his trip to Lesotho (2000). It seems that if any group had managed to hold the heterosexual line in the face of the dramatic changes occasioned by the development of racial capitalism in southern Africa, then it was the Basotho.

But did they really? Twenty-four hours after first asking this question, I found a small, lively, and openly gay community in an urban village on the outskirts of the capital city, Maseru. What I learned there and through subsequent research challenges some of the key assumptions behind both the contagion theory and the idea that heteronormative culture is necessarily opposed to homosexual activity. Might a close historical case study of same-sex sexuality among "traditionalists" such as the Basotho also shed light on the tradition versus modernity trope, as well as the presumed opposition between "African values" and Western imperialism? Lines that were first drawn in the colonial era may on closer inspection be blurrier than commonly understood.

The Basotho consolidated as a people from diverse groups of refugees, migrants, and indigenous Bushmen in the 1820s to the 1860s.[3] Under pressure from Afrikaner settlers expanding from the neighbouring Orange Free State, they sought protection by the British in 1868. Britain then passed responsibility for actual administration on to the Cape Colony. The Basotho briefly regained de facto political independence in 1881 after inflicting a military defeat upon the Cape, but they returned to the British fold in 1884. Their status thereafter enshrined or even expanded many of the powers of the hereditary chiefs to the point where the form of colonial administration came to be described as "parallel" rather than indirect rule. Basotho men took considerable pride in this military and diplomatic success and in their ability to preserve what they (mistakenly) regarded as political independence. Often to the considerable chagrin of their neighbours, they were strongly chauvinistic for having maintained a high degree of cultural integrity in comparison to other Africans in the region.

Men's ability to control women's sexuality was a key element in that culture. The early missionaries, their first Basotho acolytes, and the first colonial government in fact all believed that Basotho men's ability to dominate and exploit Basotho women largely explained both the men's reluctance to embrace Christianity wholeheartedly and their frequent lack of cooperation with British imperial interests. Once a woman had been properly "paid for" with *bohali* (*lobola*, bride price), it was said, a Mosotho man was free to use her as he desired, including giving her away as a gesture of hospitality to male friends and travellers. Her labour went to enrich his household and decrease his own responsibilities. In addition to polygyny on a sometimes-grand scale, Basotho men appeared to regard adultery as a sport to be boasted about, with no regard for the dignity or safety of the wives involved (who, indeed, often suffered the consequences of harsh corporal punishment). A priority of the Protestant missionaries and the first colonial regime therefore was to emancipate Basotho women from such degradation. As one Basotho Protestant convert described it in 1871: "When a natives talks of 'Sesuto' ... he refers especially to marriage, the property in women, and the consequent rights and customs. Take them away and the whole fabric is broken in pieces – the native heathen customs become meaningless ... In our attempts therefore to introduce and propagate Christianity, our chief blows should be struck at this system" (Mohapeloa 1971, 96).

Basotho men themselves upheld this aspect of culture through the medium of heroic or praise poetry and travellers' songs or *lifela*. The masculine *braggadocio* in these is somewhat qualified by an admiration for intelligent opportunism (running away when appropriate, for example). Thus the joys of seducing other men's wives are enhanced by the close getaway. Masculine achievement in the accumulation of *linyatsi* (lovers or concubines) or in the exercise of stern authority over "children," including wives, were meanwhile (ideally) tempered by men's moral obligation to protect their "children" and to respect the family into which they were married. Nonetheless, the poems and songs constantly affirm the Mosotho male's "need" for multiple mistresses (Coplan 1994; see also Bereng 1982). Gary Kynoch's interviews with retired MaRashea (members of the Russian gang) make this clear as well. Not all Basotho men on the Rand became Russians by any means, but MaRashea lore and image were unquestionably central to the formation of working-class masculinity since the 1920s. According to Kynoch's old gangster informant "LT," "Women are the support people of *Marashea*, they help us socially and economically. Women are the cause of most fighting in *Marashea*. In fact they are the foundation of *Marashea* – if there were not women the *Marashea* would dissolve" (Kynoch 2000, 101).

Basotho women did not necessarily find this culture oppressive or exploitative. On the contrary, they often appeared to missionaries, government officials, and even other, non-Christian Africans to be disconcertingly willing to cater to the demands for sex made upon them. As Kendall found from interviewing Basotho women, sex in the popular culture was conceived as coterminous with phallic penetration of the vagina. No sex on a regular daily basis, moreover, no health: according to some of the earliest missionary accounts of Sesotho, both men and women believed that regular intercourse was essential to maintaining mental, spiritual, and physical well-being. In traditional terms sex was a means for an individual to connect with the ancestors and to cool the blood against dangerous hot tendencies (Murray 1975).

Possessed of beliefs such as this, Basotho women had by the 1920s established a "notorious" reputation in urban South Africa as prostitutes and illicit liquor brewers. This was not just a concern of moralistic colonialists. Other African women worried about the Basotho as well, especially the imputed effects of the *labia majora* that Basotho women so assiduously lengthened: "If your husband is in love with a Shoeshoe woman he will certainly desert you. Don't you know they have 'traps' for men!"[4]

Conspicuous heterosexual behavior or reputation is obviously not incompatible with discreet same-sex behaviour. Yet here too the Basotho acquired a reputation that placed them among the ethnic groups most admired by homophobic European observers. The absence of same-sex traditions was asserted as early as the very first official enquiry into Sesotho law and customs in 1873. Commissioners heard, and accepted without further interrogation, that "unnatural crime" was "of rare occurrence and I have never heard of any punishment for them" (Cape Colony 1873, 40). This view is implicit by the almost total absence of cases of male-male sexual behaviour from the ethnography.[5] Likewise, the magistrate courts that were set up in 1871 do not appear to have encountered any cases until the 1890s, after which they remained extremely rare through to independence in 1966.[6] This makes a striking comparison to early colonial Zimbabwe, or indeed, "European" cities like Cape Town.

The invisibility of same-sex behaviour in the documentary evidence from Lesotho cannot, however, be taken too literally. A similar invisibility in the African reserves (or "tribal trust lands") of Zimbabwe and in Malawi reflects African discretion on the topic, the nature of the dual (Roman-Dutch and customary) legal system, and the simple fact that there were so few magistrates to adjudicate and hence to preserve a record of Roman-Dutch cases. We know as well that, notwithstanding Basotho "truculence," the British administration and the Christian missionaries both had political incentives to present the Basotho to the world as a model, "civilizable," fundamentally moral African people. Pressures from successive hostile South African regimes were alone a strong motive to underplay or deny contradictory evidence. At a time when the Afrikaner press of the Orange Free State was loudly accusing the British of pro-sodomite tendencies (Southey 1997a), it would have been most impolitic to probe too deeply into the claims of two aging Basotho patriarchs about the non-existence of unnatural vice among the Basotho.

Yet a fragment of evidence from colonial Natal shows that Basotho men did in fact negotiate sexual arrangements in this period. It can be found in an 1878 sodomy trial from Belair, a suburb of Durban on the railway line to Kimberly. Moba was "a Basuto under no chief" working as a railway labourer and sharing a tent with three other countrymen. He allegedly had thigh sex upon another labourer named Maseane. As Maseane explained to the court: "When I said to prisoner that I would report the matter to my master he said don't do so as I will give you what money you want. *I said I would take a pound sterling. I would have taken a pound but he refused to give it me*" (my emphasis). A witness, Umschweshwe, corroborated that the two had haggled over money the following morning, only after which did Maseane lodge his accusations.[7]

The court docket in this case does not specify Maseane's age, although there is a suggestion by one of the witness that he was a juvenile. If so, this would conform to the pattern later described as prevalent among Shangaans and "Zambezis." It would also help to explain the infrequency of male-male sexual charges coming to public attention. Boys in Sesotho were taught from a very young age that silent endurance of physical pain and humiliation was one of the more admirable qualities of masculinity. Respectful submission to the authority of elders was another. These masculine values were not simply inculcated through daily socialization but were ritualized through an exceptionally tough circumcision school, a period of several weeks during which boys were initiated into manhood. In short, boys and youth who were subjected to coercive homosexual attentions far from the watchful eyes of home would be expected to keep quiet about it. Indeed, Basotho informants told me that assaults (or seductions) of this nature occurred far up in the mountains and independent of the influence of mine culture. "M," notably, described his own repeated rape as a herd-boy by other herd-boys. There was, he said, "nothing to do but learn to like it."[8]

Two cases from Southern Rhodesia also suggest that Basotho migrant labourers were acquainted with patterns of behaviour supposedly confined to the Shangaans in the first decade of the twentieth century. Both involved "John of Lesotho," also known as Shubela, a thirty-something "boss boy" at Old Hartley mine near modern day Chegutu. In 1908 he allegedly anally raped a Shona youth named Kadzwiti.[9] This case was dismissed on the grounds that Kadzwiti may have misunderstood Shubela's pronunciation or intentions with the word Shona word "chamoiri" (*shamwari*, that is, "friend," also a euphemism for *nkotshane*). The very next year, however, Shubela was charged again with indecent assault upon an even younger (nine to ten years old) herd-boy. The assault this time took place in the veldt near Inez Mine in Matabeleland. "Come and work for me and we will sleep in the same bed," he allegedly proposed before attempting to mount the unnamed boy. In his defence Shubela explained that he was very drunk, besides which he was "only playing."[10]

The first serious enquiry into male-male sexuality in the region nonetheless reiterated the absence of such behaviour in Sesotho. The witnesses who testified at the Leary/Taberer enquiry – including Africans from other ethnic groups who had historical reasons to want to slander their rivals – almost unanimously exonerated the Basotho of "unnatural vice." The Basotho were one of the few ethnic groups to be so clearly distinguished. On this basis, several mine inspectors recommended using Basotho as compound guards in place of the compromised Shangaans. They, and perhaps the Zulu and Christianized Fingoes, could be counted upon to police the less reliably heterosexual behaviour of their fellow Africans. It may be coincidental, but one of Henry Taberer's first tasks following the submission of his report was to travel to Basutoland specifically to stimulate the recruitment there of more Basotho men for the mines (Mohapeloa 2002).

Yet evidence given to Leary and Taberer may be suggestive of a potential instability to heteronormative sexuality that in retrospect somewhat belies the confidence of Basotho boosters. Only two Basotho actually testified to the commissioners. The first, Jerry, repeatedly claimed total ignorance that the word *nkotshane* had any sexual connotation (Leary/Taberer 22 January 1907, 7–8). Yet he had been living in a hostel for three years at Ferreira gold mine together with 2,100 other workers. The majority of these were "East Coast boys" among whom at the time sexualized *nkotshane* was "pretty general," "very prevalent," or "very common," according to other witnesses. In this context the flatness of Jerry's denial rings suspiciously hollow. Japtha, a Zulu guard at the same mine, casts a shadow of doubt as well: "The Zulus and Xoxas do not do it; I am not sure about Basutos. I see them sleeping together and the men buying food and things for the boys" (22 January, 9). Mlambo, the other Mosotho witness, did admit to his interlocutors that he knew quite a bit about *nkotshane* as a sexual practice. He did not express particularly strong disapproval. On the contrary, he described the "old custom" of "playing with boys as with women" in phlegmatic terms. He also freely acknowledged his own curiosity about it: "After enquiry I have come to the conclusion that this custom does not exist at their kraals because the Shangaans say that there they use girls, but here as they are away so long from their homes and have no girls they make use of boys ... I cannot see any [way] by which the thing could be stopped" (30 January, 4–5). Regrettably, the original interview in Sesotho is not preserved. In the English transcript, however, Leary asked Mlambo directly and without explication whether "actual sodomy" took place. Mlambo did not hesitate to reply in the negative, apparently not needing an explication of the concept.

Could it be that the example of caring, fun, rebellious, and utilitarian homosexual relationships among the Shangaans and other African men at the mines was attractive to Basotho migrant men, notwithstanding the lack of any such traditions in Sesotho? Evidence from Premier Mine taken only a few months after Leary and Taberer's report hints that this may indeed have already been the case in 1907. Premier was one of the biggest mines, with a workforce that included 2,900 Basotho, 4,175 "Transvaals," 1,200 Shangaans, 481 men from Blantyre, 345 Zulus, and 394 men from miscellaneous groups. For the most part the mine management tried to keep the men separated from each other by their tribal affiliation. In this case, however, the "Moshesh tribes" occupied the same compound as the Shangaans.[11] On 6 September 1907 the Basotho attacked the Shangaan and their allies in a pitched battle that left one dead and 71 injured. "Faction fights" such as this subsequently came to be an almost regular feature of compound life. Intriguing in this specific instance, however, is that one of the Basotho witnesses called to testify in the aftermath suggested that something else was becoming regular: this man (no age given) gave his name as, simply, Nqochane.[12]

Whatever the origins of same-sex sexuality among the Basotho, allegations began to surface soon after the Leary/Taberer report that the Basotho were not as immune to *nkotshane* as had been so widely assured. On the contrary, to the great scandal of Swiss missionary Henri Junod and the historian William Scully, all kinds of African men were adopting ever more elaborate and brazenly public celebrations of mine marriage. Junod fired the first shot across the bow of Sesotho integrity. Contrary to received wisdom that the Shangaans were infecting other Africans with knowledge of *nkotshane*, Junod's novel *Zidji* portrays a world-weary Mosotho forewarning a young Shangaan of the fate that awaits him at the mines. In a scene that is central to the novel's plot and Christian message, "unnatural vice" is introduced to the protagonist (and the reader) using a Sesotho spelling of the word, *la boukontchana* (Junod 1911, 254). The Basotho were also singled out by Scully the following year: "I fear that Natives from Basutoland have, to a certain extent, been demoralized by the example of their northern room-mates [the 'addicted' Shangaans]" (Scully 1912, 234).

In response to such public allegations, the director of Native Labour instructed his inspectors to investigate: "Sodomy or similar unnatural practices have recently become somewhat prevalent among the Basutos and it is suggested that it has its origin to a considerable extent [in] the dissemination of natives from the Premier Mine."[13] Could this be true? To the government's dismay, it was. The inspector for Johannesburg East described the situation in his jurisdiction in early 1916: "It is even alleged that in certain compounds, there is actual competition for certain youthful Zulu lads, amongst East Coast natives. Feasts of lemonade, bananas, and cake are provided by the successful competitors ... Within a short three years, the Moshesh tribes, were more, or less, free from the vice. Now it is spreading with rapidity."[14] In fact, the inspector rued, "all are inoculated [sic, infected?]," the honour of being least so now going to the Batswana. The inspector at City Deep Mine, commenting on a rare case that was coming to trial, observed that the accused "the crime is rife amongst the Moshesh."[15] The inspector at Germiston even noted an apparently new Sesotho word to describe a new homosexual ritual. Each recruit upon arrival at the mine had to "*Komba-E-Kehle,*" that is, "choose a husband who will look after him and his interests."[16]

The final summary of the various reports to government in 1916 is worth quoting at length not only because it acknowledges the spread of *nkotshane* but also as it suggests some inventiveness on the part of the Basotho (that is, new depredations hitherto unheard of even among the Shangaans):

Basutos from Basutoland, who, formerly were practically free from unnatural vice have now adopted in the Compounds revolting practices which however do not constitute Sodomy as defined by law. – Reliable natives emphatically state that the practice originated among B[ritish] Basutos at the Premier Mine where the conditions of seclusion are responsible for it. It has been imported into the Rand Compounds by Boys coming from there. It consists of of [sic] using such viscera as sheep's lungs, wind pipes, hearts and liver of beasts, which when half cooked and still warm, are placed between the thighs of a complacent friend. Etc ... The consequence is that the demand for such viscera has considerably increased and has enhanced their mercantile value. From frequent references to this vice in open air services held in the Compounds by native Preachers one is forced to the conclusion that this practice is general and from the attitude and tacit acquiescement of the hearers, the allusion sometimes bringing on their faces a kind of bashful smile, it may be gathered that it even exists among natives attending religious meetings. – The natives seem to think that it is a necessary evil when away from their homes.[17]

As in the case of the 1907 enquiry, a wide range of recommendations was made with appropriate huffs and puffs of indignation. Again, however, it does not appear that anything substantive was actually done. The risk of strikes, desertions, and riots that would probably result from aggressive state intervention on this matter was judged to be too high, particularly given the Basotho reputation for prickliness. There are, as before, strong hints of passing the buck back to the Portuguese ("Let these officials enjoy some of the odium attached to such an Order"). Oddly, no one thought to blame, or apparently even to alert, colleagues in the Basutoland administration or Christian missionaries among the Basotho. No record remains of any discussions among the missionaries, nor in the Basutoland National Council, the main advisory body of chiefs. Indeed, so delicate was the issue that two inspectors hand-wrote their submissions. The inspector of Eastern District explained to Pritchard, "I have addressed this Report to you in order that these highly-flavoured remarks may not, inadvertently be opened by, or fall into the hands of, your Lady Typists."[18]

Quaint as this discretion may seem to us now, the dangers at the time seemed all too real from the perspective of mine owners and government officials. Long-standing problems of instability in the African labour force were being exacerbated by wartime inflation, the militancy of white workers, and a new, demonstrable, terrifying ability of Africans to organize on a proletarian scale: nine thousand mineworkers had struck for three days in 1913. In 1919 the Industrial and Commercial Union was formed, followed the next year by a strike of seventy thousand African mineworkers. In Basutoland, African men's resentment of the colonial system and the deteriorating conditions of labour in South Africa led to the establishment in 1919 of Lekhotla la Bafo, or the League of the Common People. Lekhotla la Bafo was highly critical of the British and their allies (or puppets, as they claimed) in the chieftaincy.

A shocking incident around this time made evident the theoretical potential of even minor interference with *nkotshane* to disrupt production or to incite political reaction; it also demonstrated the weakness of the state. Albert Maama was the son of Chief Maako of Makgalene (Mohale's Hoek district of Lesotho) and a "police boy" at Brakpan Mines. In October 1919 a juvenile Mosotho named Mokete laid a charge against him of kidnapping and indecent assault. It seems that Maama had accosted Mokete almost from the moment of his arrival at the mine compound. Mokete eventually submitted out of fear of Maama's status. He endured a month of nightly exertions and emissions upon him by Maama in the hostel but then ran away to another room. Maama promptly dispatched a troop of fifteen of his men to give Mokete a thrashing and return him to his bed. Mokete escaped again, however, and this time informed the mine manager. Maama was promptly dismissed on the grounds of "neglect of duty" – that is, failure to report the kidnapping, there not being sufficient evidence to uphold the indecent assault charge. His men immediately threatened to go on strike, while no less than forty-four deserted the mine en masse to accompany Maama home. They were arrested before they reached the border but, far from being punished, were all reinstated, including Maama, when he agreed to pay a fine of three pounds.[19]

Government officials next confidentially conceded the growing popularity of male-male sexual practices among Basotho migrants in South Africa in 1941. As in the Maama case, "immoral practices" at East Geduld compound were not brought to official attention because of scandal about the actual sex but because of their potential to disrupt mine production. A group of twelve Basotho "boss boys" had been accused of organizing homoerotic dances, which included the greasing up of the "girls'" crotches in apparent anticipation of further delights. The twelve were dismissed. Trouble immediately arose, when an estimated four to five hundred Basotho men violently demanded their return. The words of Police Inspector L.D. Doubell of Boksburg show that the protest was not only a remarkable display of mass solidarity by common miners with their leaders but a direct rebellion against mine authority: "the Basutos are in the habit of holding dances in the Compound during the night and ... at these dances the young natives are dressed as women and squeezing and kissing are resorted to. Such dances are foreign to native custom and the Compound Manager warned the Basutos that these dances must stop. Later it was found that the dances are being continued and on the 20th October, 1941, twelve of the ringleaders and organisers of these dances were dismissed and sent to Johannesburg. *They all admitted that they continued the dances and disobeyed the instructions*" (my emphasis).[20]

Sensitive to the delicacy of chief/commoner relations, and perhaps fearful that "communists" in the Lekhotla la Bafo would get wind of the incident and exploit it to rouse opposition to government, no representations were made to the Basutoland authorities. Had they been, however, it seems likely that the fate of the Mpondo chiefs' curiosity in 1928–30 would have been repeated. That is, it would have been silenced by profuse expressions of official concern and disgust toward male-male sexuality, by assurances that matters were not as bad as they seemed and in any case were getting better, and by blaming the Portuguese. The issue thus disappeared again from the public record. It did not reappear until 1946. At that time, Bishop Joseph Bonhomme, the man who first openly denounced Basotho men's same-sex sexual practices, was summarily deported from the colony and placed under a lifetime ban upon interference in its affairs.

Bonhomme, the Roman Catholic vicar apostolic of Basutoland, had admittedly done much to irritate the British since his arrival in 1933. His attacks on white traders who exploited the Basotho were particularly galling. Bonhomme was out of the colony during the war years, but when he returned he immediately resumed his self-appointed role of gadfly. Changes that had happened in his absence shocked him in many ways – above all, greater depths of poverty but also the apparent further entrench-ment of *nkotshane*. He wrote an extensive, rambling diatribe to the Colonial Office in London denouncing the situation. Among the many grievous sins of the Basutoland government he included: "The Mines! A calamity for the Basutho people. Sent there by the Government they inherit all the lowness of the outcast. The N.R.C. [Natives Recruiting Corporation] admit themselves that the compounds have become dens of sodomy, scan-dal and immorality."[21] Bonhomme proposed to remedy this with, among other things, greater cooperation between the government and the Catholic church as well as the prompt dismissal of the "incompetent and inefficient" officials whom he claimed predominated in the administration and had abetted the immorality.

Bonhomme's anti-sodomy, anti-colonial rant did not persuade London to intervene as he hoped, and indeed, Bonhomme was undoubtedly naïve in many respects. Whether he reflected on this from exile in Quebec, we do not know. That he was correct about the embrace of same-sex rituals and sexual practices by Basotho men, however, is corroborated by more recent research, including that of the only Mosotho historian ever to have written upon the topic. Notwithstanding his moralistic tone, J.M. Mohapeloa acknowledges both a Sesotho and a Sesotho-ized version of the common term for homosexuality at the mines in the inter-war period of such practices: *maotoane* and *ngotshana*, respectively (Mohapeloa 2002, 272–3).

The near-banality of such practices in the postwar period is also sup-ported by depictions in Lanham and Mopeli-Paulus's *Blanket Boy's Moon* (1953) and by oral history from that era. One of Vivienne Ndatshe's Mpondo informants, for example, fondly recalled a Mosotho "wife" from the 1940s or '50s: "My girlfriend was a Basotho young lad. I was not ill-treating him as other boss boys did. I was very nice to him, did everything for him, and he was very polite" (Ndatshe 1993, 47). A sociological study based on interviews in the 1970s found that "sodomy is very common" among migrant men (Blair and Gay 1980, 109). Pule Hlohoangwane, whose testimony is discussed further below, carries the narrative into the 1980s with his account of a loving polygynous marriage to a Mosotho miner (Alberton and Reid 2000, Achmat and Lewis 1999), as does the more cynical Mookameli Nyakama in Don Edkins's examination of migrant life (1992). Mpapa Mokhoane's fictional depiction of mine life is also remarkable, coming as it does in a novel published in Swaziland for high school students in the former high commission territories. In *Teba*, Mokhoane depicts the "secret love" between young married men of equal age in undated but apparently near-contemporary times (1995, 64).

Although these references span seven or eight decades, two constants are drawn fairly emphatically. These are the lines between Basotho behaviour at the mines and Basotho behaviour at home and between expedient or playful same-sex acts and homosexual preference or orientation. As long as those lines are not crossed, the hegemonic construction of masculinity is not in question. Mookameli Nyakama is especially clear about this in his interview with Don Edkins, constructing his countrymen's homosexual choices strictly as a response to heterosexual desire. "The feelings of a man for a woman can take control over your actions here in the mines," he explains. "These feelings come when I think about my wife. I am lying in bed here, thinking about what I could be doing with my wife. Then I see a young man who is well built and fit. I look at his buttocks and I am already thinking of a women. Gee, he is really pretty. This makes me think again of what I have been imagining. And then I can't avoid wanting to turn him into a woman although he is a man" (Edkins 1992).

Maloka's claim that male-male sex was a virtual impossibility for the Basotho is clearly unfounded. So too were early official and missionary fears that the spread of male-male sexuality from the Chinese or Portuguese might undermine African patriarchal institutions upon which "morality," the migrant labour system, and colonial governance all partially depended. These fears were not realized. The main lineage of the "traditional" chieftaincy in Basutoland actually gathered powers to itself through the 1930s to '50s, while Basotho men flowed into South African mines and other industries in steadily increasing numbers up to the mid-1960s. Far from unmanning them, the experience of migrancy became a new form of initiation or test of manhood in idealized customary terms. As a small but revealing illustration of this, when the British were seeking more detail on Sesotho customs around inheritance, one chief advised them simply "to find means of reaching places in the Union where Basotho live in large numbers, who are the ones who love custom more than any others."[22]

Moodie (1994, 2001) has identified male-male sexuality as a widespread response of African men to the conditions of racial capitalism that they encountered in South Africa and that enabled them to preserve their dignity as men in traditional terms. Of course there were cases of violence and humiliation in *nkotshane* relationships, just as was true, abundantly, of heterosexual marriages, abductions, rapes, and prostitution in this period. Yet on the whole, African men's and youths' dignity was preserved by a widely known and respected code of etiquette that included the exchange of presents between partners, the possibility of negotiated and amicable exit from the relationship, the tacit and sometimes even open recognition of the legitimacy of such relationships by peers and relatives, and provision for modesty. Privacy was achieved through screens around beds and in some cases distinct rooms for male-male sex, but also through collective agreement to avert prying eyes and ears. This conforms to snippets of evidence about Basotho at the mines. Coplan's informants thus seem amused or even boastful rather than guilty or ashamed of their mine affairs and erotic dancing (1994, 140–1). Mokhoane's fictional depiction of his narrator's reaction to a Christian preacher's denunciations of homosexual relationships is also revealing of a determination not to feel guilt: "Was it possible that Peter [the missionary] knew about what had happened between him and Khepho, his secret love, a few days ago? No. He did not think he did. Anyway, the fellow was mad. Oh no, he could not be made to feel guilty about himself ... not only did he preoccupy himself with suppressing this guilt but also with encountering Khepho again. They did meet secretly as before and, after every such encounter, whatever traces of guilt were there were wiped out" (Mokhoane 1995, 64).

Because these relationships arose more out of the specific conditions faced by industrial labourers than out of an innate homosexual orientation, they were relatively amenable to change as those conditions changed. Moodie makes a convincing argument that 1973–75 was a turning point in that respect. The sudden withdrawal of large numbers of Malawian and Mozambican labourers for political reasons, a dramatic rise in the price of gold on the international market, and the consequent ability of the mining companies to pay higher wages combined to undermine both the functionality and the material base or "practical foundation" of mine marriage as a mass practice or system (Moodie 1994, 278–9). More men were recruited locally than previously, and consequently were able to return home more frequently than long-distance migrants could; some even commuted to homes in surrounding townships or reserves. More women also moved to town, making it possible for men to strike up relatively stable urban families. This became an increasingly attractive option as deteriorating conditions in the reserves made the traditional ideal of retirement to a rural home less and less realizable. Indeed, political repression and widespread violence in Lesotho in the 1970s added to the poverty there to increase the numbers of men and women who permanently turned their backs on the country.

Moodie notes as well the effect of a brief period of recruitment of Zimbabweans at the mines in the mid-1970s: "[W]ith their superior education, flashy dress, violent homophobia, and liberation politics they were not unlike many of the younger new South Africans who later came to be known on the mines as 'comrades'" (1994, 247). To these men, mine marriages were not merely offensive on moral grounds but were seen as politically dangerous, in that they ultimately served the interests of the mine owners. Adding to the pressure from increasingly militant and well-organized trade unions was a renewed campaign by the churches against what they denounced as the dehumanizing effects of the migrant labour system, explicitly targeting homosexuality among the miners. A former Lesotho-based Anglican deacon made a particularly strong presentation to a national conference of Christian leaders on the need to confront the "whirlwind" of that "evil" system. To Desmond Tutu at that time, homosexuality was equivalent to crime, prostitution, and illegitimacy (AIM 1976b, 20).

The mine companies responded to these criticisms and pressures by scrambling to modernize working conditions. As they did, aspects of the old system that had particularly abetted mine marriage all but disappeared – above all, the *induna* or boss-boy system that had been so prone to abuse. Skills-based promotion and relatively transparent channels to grieve acts of violence removed much of the ability of traditionalist patriarchal authorities to abuse their power and coerce or entice younger men into sexual service. Electric lighting, better-spaced beds, and even video surveillance made it increasingly difficult to conduct affairs in the hostels. Mass redundancies of Basotho miners since the early 1990s and the conversion of many of the male-only hostels into family accommodation since 1994 further reduced the opportunities for mine marriage in the "traditional" form. Also, with the appearance in political discourse of explicitly homophobic rhetoric, a whole new and subtle language of evasion or denial developed that removed male-male sexuality from the commons. This new language, known by the Zulu word *isinqumo* (Olivier 1994, Mkhize 2001), added to the impression that homosexuality at the mines was disappearing.

Despite these changes, recent research reveals that the mines have nonetheless continued to be known for the space they provide for relatively non-controversial homosexual liaisons, and even attract men to them because of this. "M" informed me (1996) that yes, indeed, "there are some men who travel to the mines to earn money [by providing sex to mine workers]. To this very day, say, on the weekend they just go there and charge a certain amount. Then they return to here, perhaps with some fancy things from town. And when the money runs out, they go back. The men there are willing to pay." Meanwhile, agents at the main recruiting centre for mine labour in Maseru were reputed to have illegally engaged under-age youth for employment and "marriage" well into the 1980s.[23] Edkins's 1992 film, *Color of Gold*, by contrast, emphasizes that no juveniles were involved. Rather, mature Basotho men with wives back in Lesotho enjoyed gratifying themselves upon the shapely buttocks of their fellow workers. They did so, at least in the early 1990s, without the kind of violence that would warrant analogies to prison sex. In Mookameli Nyakama's words, "But the worst of it is with money you can achieve exactly that [orgasm]. You offer him fifty rands, and he will in turn agree and say, 'What have I got to lose?'"

Interestingly, the construction of "married quarters" and the expansion of proper townships also presented new possibilities. These arrangements did not just allow for growing numbers of miners to settle down with their wives; they also made it possible for some men to move out of the compounds and come out as unabashedly gay men, as the following remarkable testimony of Pule Hlohoangwane reveals. Hlohoangwane, a South African Mosotho, was born in the mining town of Virginia in the Orange Free State. A fully out queen, Hlohongwane spoke candidly with researchers "Zakhi" and Graeme Reid:

It was my first day in the mining industry in 1987 ... I started underground. What happens is you are looked at, "Ooo, oww, look at this young one." So he proposed me for almost a month and I realized that there is nobody that can run after you for so long being just making a joke so I said I agreed to the terms. [But] it is very difficult for gay people to stay in the hostel because you have to bath with men, forty-two men around you naked, it's something, it was very irritating ... So he realized that I had a problem and he said to me it's better for me to hire a flat in town because you are a real homosexual person (Alberton and Reid 2000).

Hlohoangwane makes clear that the problem in the hostel was not homophobia among his co-workers but his inability to shower without getting constant erections. He goes on to touch upon another issue that the historiography has not explored very well – what real (female) wives thought about their husbands having sex with men:

My husband is a bisexual. He's married in Lesotho, he's got a wife with two children and I'm accepted as the second wife of the family.

The first time when she realized that I was maybe going out with her husband it was a little bit confusing because she used to visit the hostel where the husband was staying but only to find that the man is no longer staying in the hostel but in town. "With whom, who is that lady who has taken my husband?" Then he brought her to my house. "Here is the person I am staying with, meet her." She said, "Oh, is it you? I'm very lucky that my husband is going out with a gay. I thought maybe he is going out with a woman whereby maybe he can make other children and all that stuff."

Hlohoangwane's relationship may be an unusually harmonious and stable one – she even had an adopted son who lived with them in town. However, a Tsonga miner named Philemon described a similar lack of scandal about *nkotshane* among Tsonga women in the 1930–70s: "They [the women back home] knew it! They knew that once a man was on the mines, he had a boy or was turned into a 'wife' himself." When asked if the women were they angry about it, he said, "No, why should they be angry? Besides that, even if they knew, what would they do? Nothing!" (Sibuyi 1993).

Back in Lesotho, "P's" case further suggests that women's awareness (and acceptance) of men having sex with men was not unusual: "I know that many men who come here [to this bar to pick up men for sex] are married. Their wives know. In fact their wives don't like me. Sometimes they shout at me, but I just shout back. Then we get to understand each other."[24] When pressed to clarify if he meant that married men actually sought male sex partners in Lesotho or had sex with men unwittingly, he maintained that it was both. Some married men were "real gays" like him, but others "don't know at first, they think I'm a woman until … then they know. They do it, even though they may be surprised. Then they come the second time, the third time and they like it."[25]

Basotho men's widespread adoption of *nkotshane* at the mines occurred at a time when the population of Basotho women in the locations around the mine compounds was burgeoning. Indeed, so many women left Lesotho for urban South Africa between 1936 and 1946 that the population of the territory actually declined. By virtue of their increasing supply, these women made it easier than ever for young men to afford heterosexual relationships in the townships or en route to the mines. At first glance, this would seem to undermine the argument that links situational homosexuality among men to an absolute shortage of women. When we recall, however, that the Basotho women who migrated to South African cities tended not to be of the type that the men aspired to marry, the mystery is solved. "Proper wives" stayed home and did what they were told. Town women, by contrast, often forcefully challenged traditional ideals of demure, respectful, and fecund wives and daughters.

Nor was the phenomenon restricted to Basotho women in town. One of Ntabeni's male informants recalled that in the 1940s even within Lesotho women could be dangerously, innovatively assertive when it came to sex. The few young men that remained in the territory during the war found it was prudent to avoid walking past female work parties lest one be "eloped" by man-hungry women (Ntabeni 1996, 168). Women also asserted themselves in untraditional ways with other means at their disposal, including "witchcraft," prayer and pious associations, and turning to gangs for protection.

While fear of disease among town women was thus no doubt a factor in some men's decision to take *izinkotshane*, perhaps it should not be overstated. Indeed, contemporary attitudes towards HIV should make us highly sceptical about claims that people can be rational when it comes to sexual health risks. Moreover, to the extent that rational calculation did enter into the sexual decision-making process, there were several ways to have relationships with town women that would have allowed men to protect themselves against disease. Heterosexual *hlobonga* was one. A man could also pay "protection" money to the MaRashea to ensure that his local wife remained faithful while he was at work. In any case, cheap medical treatment for syphilis and gonorrhoea became widely available by the mid-1930s. Niehaus's informants thus do not cite disease but rather the expense and social complications of women's uppitiness as the most compelling reasons to avoid town women (2002a).[26]

Further complicating matters were the new, modern ideas about sexuality being propagated by missionaries and implicit in much consumerist discourse – notably, romantic love. The context of intense gender conflict made it difficult, to put it mildly, for young men to learn or to practice the new ideas safely with young women. Heterosexual dating was difficult, expensive, and full of the risk of humiliation.[27] Same-sex relations, by contrast, provided a way to experiment with the new ideas and practices and to prepare oneself in relatively safe way for a future modern-style marriage with a woman.

Changes that have been observed in female sexuality back in Lesotho support this interpretation. We know from the early ethnography that Basotho women and girls shared with men and boys both the desire for and the means to express intimate friendship and sexual experimentation without the dangers of heterosexual play or dating. The culture of Sesotho in fact condoned a limited amount of this, provided it was discreet. Sesotho recognizes, for example, that some women might experience possession by male ancestral or other spirits that excused them from sexual intercourse with men. They, and married women in general, were allowed to express close physical affection including kissing and snuggling with an intimate female friend or a co-wife. Sesotho in fact enabled several types of formalized female-female marriage. Most commonly, a widow could assume the role of *ntate* (father, sir), pay *bohali* (brideprice), and take a young woman in marriage. The young woman was supposed to get pregnant by a discreet arrangement with a male lover, but the female *ntate* was entitled to have and to show affection.

The Sesotho word for female-female intimacy of this nature was the very same as that which was applied to neglected wives who had extramarital sex with men: *setsualle* (Nthunya 1996, 69). Obviously the physical acts were different in the two situations, and *setsualle* was further differentiated as to whether it was "fat" (that is, was beneficial to the cuckold, as adultery could be if it added children to the household) or "yellow" (had no material benefits, as would normally be the case in female-female intimacy). Nonetheless, the word implied an equivalency of meaning in emotional terms. The word recognized female-female physical intimacy as necessary or desirable in a context where brides moved away from their childhood friends and family into the groom's village. It almost certainly gained greater sympathy in the public imagination through the colonial years as so many married couples were torn apart by men's migration.

Girls meanwhile could manually assist each other to lengthen their labia majora. The ostensible reason for this was to enhance their future husbands' pleasure. It is difficult to imagine that there were not other, less androcentric aspects to the custom as well. Mosebetsi Damane, interviewed in about 1965, claimed as much. The practice was a means for women to learn to experience orgasm so that they could enjoy the sex act as much as men ("*afin qu'elles puissent procurer la pleine jouissance*").[28] A Roman Catholic priest also recorded his impressions based in part upon girls' confessions dating from the 1920s: "Enlarging of the genitals, when does she do it? Often. Why? So men can find it, also men say women have more pleasure; does she do it to herself – usually but sometimes others will do it. When the girls go to the river (ba ile nokeng) what do they do? General rule: they develop their genitals" (Chévrier n.d., 73, my translation).

Sesotho did not label *ba ile nokeng* as masturbation or self-indulgence. Nor did it have a concept of "lesbian" in the sense of a woman who chooses to have sexual intimacy with other women out of individual preference or orientation. Girls were socialized to expect, indeed, to demand regular sexual intercourse leading to pregnancy as their right and as intrinsic to their identity and health as women. Non-phallic activities that stimulated the genitals fell outside the category of "sex" and consequently *ba ile nokeng* was not a cause for parental or wider societal concern.

The first girls to break decisively with cultural expectations around their sexuality did so in the late nineteenth century by becoming nuns. This typically came at the cost of painful ostracism from family and community. We can assume that the decision for most reflected a spiritual calling. For others, by their own admission, the path of celibacy within the church was a means to avoid the burdens and heartbreak that often accompanied marriage, particularly as gender relations modernized in the colonial era.[29] It may be, and certainly is much rumoured, that some took advantage of the cloistered environment to explore their sexuality with other women. No record of such scandal appears in the archives of the Catholic mission. Judith Gay has shown, however, that with the widespread development of girls' boarding schools after the 1950s, the opportunities to explore new forms of female *setsualle* hugely increased. The most common lesbian-like relationship among the girls was known as "mummy-baby." As with the lengthening of labia, and in fact much like *nkotshane* among the men, "mummy-baby" relationships were modelled on heterosexual norms of courtship and marriage. The girls and women themselves typically described them as preparation for romantic, companionate marriage by allowing the girls to develop their kissing, petting, and flirting skills. Gifts were exchanged with a moral code of mutual obligations attached. The relationship could continue beyond school years and even after one or both partners married a man.[30]

The mummy-baby relationship, or the analogous *amachicken* among the Zulu (Sam 1994, 186), helped African girls learn to be heterosexually attractive and appropriately responsive women in a context where heterosexual courtship had become much more dangerous and individualized than had traditionally been the case. Yet despite the untraditional partner and the modern discourse of romantic love, these relationships were fundamentally conservative. That is, they reflected an attempt to apply new ideas about romantic love and individual sexual gratification while preserving old moral values and hierarchies. The possibility that male-male sex could also function to enrich the emotional quality of heterosexual relationships while maintaining conservative structures needs to be considered. Indeed, why should we assume that same-sex sexual relationships were necessarily "immoral" or degrading when the men themselves (that is, those who identify as "normal" heterosexuals) do not regard them that way? To one of Moodie's informants, for example, the homosexual relationship was almost more moral than the alternatives. When asked if taking male lovers impeded men's ability to find female wives back home, he explained, "No, it actually helps because you understand the woman's point of view. You learn to be more gentle" (Moodie 2001). Hlohoangwane's female co-wife was even more affirmative of this. She reportedly told the cross-dressing Hlohoangwane she was grateful that his love and patience were teaching their shared husband to be more caring and more responsible with money: "And since you came into my husband's life, there is some [positive] changes that I see. Thank you very much. Please, if you've got any problems with my husband let's come together as a family and sort it out, completely!" (Alberton and Reid 2000).

Evidence from Lesotho on the adoption of same-sex sexual relations enriches our understanding of similar developments elsewhere in the region. Above all, it seriously undermines both the "they-were-forced-to-do-it" thesis and the view that same-sex sexual relations are necessarily immoral. Basotho men, and later girls and young women, did not passively catch a homosexual infection because they were exposed to conditions or abusive bosses that left them no choice. Of course there were instances where force or intense peer pressure was applied. However, for the most part the individuals involved actively chose to maintain sexual relations with members of their own sex because they appreciated the manifold advantages. These advantages were not limited to sexual release or safer sex but included developing emotions, social skills, and a sense of moral obligation or anchor that was otherwise under profound threat in the dominant culture, by poverty or prostitution, for example. The strong heterosexual norms that defined masculine and feminine gender roles did not protect the Basotho against same-sex sexuality. On the contrary, they may have facilitated and been enriched by caring same-sex relationships.

Same-sex relationships among the Basotho were not static. Indeed, infrastructural developments alone have been constantly creating or closing down opportunities and incentives to engage in same-sex sex. New highways, for example, have made the hitherto unimaginable easy – a weekend trip from the heart of the Maluti Mountains to Johannesburg and back. The numbers of men who do this, however, is surely the less interesting question than what was the quality of the relationships that they engaged in. Here, evidence supports the intuition that changes took place in the sexual/emotional content and politics of same-sex relationships over time, just as they did in modernizing heterosexual relationships. This will be the focus of the concluding chapter. But it is appropriate here to end by reflecting on "M's" experience with the heterosexual-identified, often married, men who came to his bar to have sex with men in the early 1990s. In the past, he told me "It used to be just feeling [that is, lust] but there is love now. There is love."[31]

8

Politics

The coming out or modernization of South Africa's and Zimbabwe's gay rights movement has been well described and analyzed in various media elsewhere.[1] My objective in this final chapter is therefore a modest one. I would like simply to review the recent political history in these two countries as a means to underscore a point that I have already made but which I believe is important for the majority population to appreciate and share with those around them. This is that dissident, minority sexualities are not an irrelevant sideshow to the great dramas of underdevelopment and racial conflict in Africa. On the contrary, as few, troubled, fractious, and uncertain as they have been in the past and to a significant extent remain, southern Africa's "queers" have played disproportionately important roles in the general development of civil society over the past three decades or so. Given the looming catastrophe of HIV/AIDS in the region, as well as the widespread deterioration of economic and political conditions under aging, anti-feminist, and homophobic leadership in the Zimbabwe case, their work on behalf of the vulnerable *majority* population deserves appropriate recognition. Reflective of this, Zimbabwean and South African gay rights associations have begun to attract the attention of HIV/AIDS service organizations across Africa more broadly and of staid international donors like the World Bank (Goddard 2004b).

Small, geographically contained subcultures where men and women could discreetly but more or less openly express non-normative gender identities and sexualities existed in South Africa from at least the 1920s, most famously with the "coons" and "moffies" of Cape Town. World War II enormously boosted the populations, visibility, and vibrancy of these urban subcultures, particularly in the case of white lesbians. By the aftermath of the war, a true gay and lesbian scene had been established in downtown Johannesburg. In the 1950s and '60s, however, a political discourse that linked homosexuality with vulnerability to communism or radical African nationalism emerged in the dominant white society. It did not stimulate a counter-discourse of tolerance in either the newly independent black nations elsewhere on the continent or in the mainstreams of Zimbabwe's and South Africa's liberation movements. On the contrary, African nationalists tended to respond to settler racism and intransigence with a hyper-heterosexism of their own. Local expressions of transphobia or latent homophobia in African nationalism for the most part remained subsumed within or implicit to generalized masculinist discourse. Combined with "cowboy" settler culture and state repression of non-normative sexuality of all types (including inter-racial sex), by the mid-1960s this masculinist discourse pushed same-sex sexuality in the region deep into the closet or into isolated ghettoes.

That said, inklings of change could nonetheless be sensed in the growing self-assurance of gay rights advocates in the West and in the gathering liberation of the rest of Africa from colonial rule. The gay rights movement in sub-Saharan Africa dates from this time of political transition. South Africa led the way, haltingly, for a variety of reasons. It had a large, affluent white population that was attentive to international trends or even, in the remarkable case of novelist Mary Renault, helped to set those trends. Renault was an Englishwoman who settled in Durban in 1948 with her lifelong partner, Julie Mullard. Although she had alluded to lesbian sexuality in earlier writing, her 1953 novel *The Charioteer* was one of the first in the English language to deal frankly and non-judgmentally with a male homosexual love affair. Her treatment of male-male sexuality as normal in subsequent historical fiction about ancient Greece and Persia made her an iconographic figure in the nascent gay liberation movement in the West, albeit a somewhat reluctant champion of gay rights and sexual liberation in South Africa itself (Sweetman 1993).

Well-heeled South African universities meanwhile supported research that destigmatized homosexuality, notably through the work of another lesbian, the psychologist Renée Liddicoat. The world of Johannesburg theatre then produced one of the leading lights of the early anti-apartheid movement, Cecil Williams. Williams's communist politics and unapologetic homosexuality in the late 1950s and early '60s combined to profoundly influence the thinking of future African National Congress leaders.[2] Other African nationalist leaders who were incarcerated in prisons where male-male sex was widespread were challenged by African men with experiences of loving homosexual "marriages" at the mines. Some of these leaders began relatively open-minded consideration of the issue of gay rights as early as 1963, notwithstanding the dominant homophobic ethos in the nationalist movement (Dlamini 1984, Buntman 2003).

Also, however attenuated by the effects of apartheid, South Africa had a judicial system that remained relatively independent from executive interference and therefore capable of protecting individuals threatened by homophobic violence or extortion. This may have contributed to an exaggerated confidence among white gay men in the affluent northern suburbs of Johannesburg in the mid-1960s. In January 1966, they indiscreetly spread the word of a large celebration of gay society to be held at a private house in Forest Town. When the police caught wind of it and crashed the party, the ensuing scandal sparked a government commission of enquiry into this perceived danger to the state. Yet it also led to the formation of an articulate lobby group seeking to end state harassment of homosexuals (Retief 1994).

The Homosexual Law Reform Fund (or Reform Movement) consisted of mainly white, middle-class liberals. It drew upon the latest medical and psychological theory and civil rights debates in the West to refute the arguments for the criminalization of homosexuality as proposed for an amended Immorality Act. Some of their logic resonated even among the police, no doubt worried about the practicalities of having to regulate citizens' private thoughts and urges. But the reformers did not succeed in stopping parliament from passing many of the proposed amendments into law or even in winning unequivocal support from other white liberals such as the Black Sash, which refused appeals from one of its own leaders (Mary Renault, discussed in Sweetman 1993, 249–50) to take up the cause.

The reform movement disbanded soon afterwards. However, the fact that an articulate opposition could come together on this issue under a repressive, moralistic regime seems to have dissuaded the police from actively enforcing the new laws at their command. This reluctance, in the context of a surging economy and rapid urbanization, allowed for the emergence of a progressively bolder and more out gay voice over the next few years. A revolutionary (expansive rather than defensive) approach to gay rights was first enunciated in 1972 with the establishment of the (ephemeral) South African Gay Liberation Movement based at the University of Natal-Durban. In 1978 *Equus* became the first commercial gay magazine. Discreet night and social clubs catering to gays and lesbians began to spring up in the smaller cities of the country, eventually linked by the national Gay Association of South Africa (GASA) in 1982. While

GASA at this stage disclaimed a desire for political confrontation, it did create a network that came to facilitate often-heated debates about the interconnections between racism, misogyny, and homophobia under apartheid. In 1984 it facilitated the first Christian homosexual study group and worship meeting, which eventually became the Gay Christian Community with its own gay-friendly magazine, *Perspective* (Stuart 1997, 86–7).

Conscription in these years played an unintended role in propagating a modern gay identity. As had been the case in World War II, conscription brought tens of thousands of young white men and women into an institution that ardently promoted homophobia and sometimes cruelly punished offenders against compulsory heterosexuality. Yet military service also allowed for the emergence of significant pockets of de facto tolerance for homosexual activity, including drag shows and quickie sex. Ironically, one of the most reputedly gay units in the South African Defence Force was at the mental hospital where homosexuals were sent to be "cured."[3]

North of the border, the heating up of the bush war in the 1970s similarly brought together large numbers of young white and Coloured Rhodesian men for military training. Numerous American and other Western mercenaries joined the fray on the government side. In that way, the state unintentionally facilitated the expansion of off-duty gay networks. Drag contests began in the late 1970s, with at least one gay nightclub and a "thriving" underground scene (Goddard 2004a).

With the collapse of the Rhodesian regime in 1980, exiles were able to return to the country from abroad and from the "pink ghettoes" of South Africa. Gay-positive nightclubs suddenly blossomed in the capital city. These were private affairs and spaces, disproportionately attended by whites, Coloureds, and non-Zimbabweans, not least of all white South Africans hoping to escape the draft there. They nonetheless represented the beginnings of a public expression of an African gay identity. Black men who self-consciously identified themselves as essentially different from heteronormative culture and who were no longer content to hide homosexual behaviours behind customary fictions and closets began to come out in this scene. Lesbians also began to organize in the early post-colonial period as white society emerged from the stultifying atmosphere of Rhodesian nationalism. The first regular group, consisting of ten white lesbians, began their meetings in 1982 in what they eventually called the Women's Cultural Club (Clark 1995).

These early attempts at organizing public associations were riven by deep, often debilitating fault lines. The economic, linguistic, and cultural divide between whites, blacks, and other racial minorities or ethnic groups some-times caused bitter recriminations (as, of course, they did in the non-gay community). Racism, sexism, or misogyny among male gays, excessive per-formance and reactionary gender politics among drag queens and butch lesbians, substance abuse, and internalized homophobia among many gays and lesbians were all at times deeply alienating to different individuals striving to unite under the umbrella of gay rights. Alienation for these reasons contributed to a high turnover in membership, but it also stimulated much-needed internal debate and reflection. For instance, Bev Ditsie, one of South Africa's first out black lesbians, organized a black lesbian beauty contest to draw attention to the hurtful and divisive behaviour among some members of the community. "Our biggest problem among lesbians," as she put it to journalist Mark Gevisser, "is that our butches feel they need to behave like real men, and in our African culture this means beating up their girlfriends and of course – just like any 'real' African man – practicing polygamy and having as many 'wives' as they choose" (2000, 134).

The early days also saw sharp disagreements over whether the focus of organizing efforts should go towards partying and the development of personal self-esteem or towards partisan political activism. The former view clearly predominated in South Africa up until the mid-1980s. Indeed, for the majority of gays and lesbians who joined the movement in the first half of that decade, simply coming out, having fun, and trying to heal from the experience of growing up in a sexually repressive society were politi-cally radical acts. Even then, though, a minority worried that freedom to be gay could never be achieved without first achieving freedom to be human – a freedom fundamentally denied for most South Africans by both apartheid laws and crushing poverty. This minority grew more vocal as the economic and human rights climate in the region deteriorated.

GASA was the first big casualty of this divergence of opinion. In 1986 the association fragmented and died over its leaders' apparent hesitancy to take a principled stand in opposition to the harsh state crackdown on black township activism that had begun the year before. Blacks who split from GASA then formed the Rand Gay Organization, while whites who felt frustrated by the party/self-esteem politics formed Lesbians and Gays Against Oppression, later the Organization of Lesbian and Gay Activists. A decisive step to heal the racial split came in 1988 when the various groups melded into the Gay and Lesbian Organization of the Witwatersrand, or GLOW. Where GASA had tended to shy away from politics in the partisan sense, GLOW embraced the social democratic ideals of the anti-apartheid

United Democratic Front (UDF) and the ANC. Simon Nkoli, an openly gay black man and UDF member who had been imprisoned for treason in 1986, quickly emerged as a leader who symbolized for gays their multi-faceted struggles for freedom.

ANC leaders also took note of Nkoli's courage and of the support given by international gay and lesbian groups to the anti-apartheid struggle. In his short memoir, Nkoli describes the initial uproar in the Congress of South African Students following his coming out in 1981 (Nkoli 1994, 253). Comrades nonetheless voted 4–1 in favour of his continuing as a movement leader. Similarly, despite initial homophobic reactions, his co-accused during the Delmas treason trial publicly stood by him. Future President Thabo Mbeki stated that year that "the ANC is very firmly committed to removing all forms of discrimination and oppression in a liberated South Africa. That commitment must surely extend to the protection of gay rights."[4]

This commitment remained little more than rhetorical in a period when the political landscape was dominated by intensifying violence, the unbanning of opposition parties, and the start of constitutional negotiations. Its first real test only came in 1991 during the high-profile trial of Winnie Mandela for assault and kidnapping. Mandela, "the mother of the nation," adopted as part of her defence strategy the argument that she was just trying to protect African boys from a white man's sexual predation. Outrage from gay activists at home and internationally was only somewhat appeased soon after the trial by a letter of support, described by one activist as "warm," from the ANC for the Lesbian and Gay Pride march (Holmes 1994, 291).

Winnie Mandela's subsequent divorce from Nelson Mandela symbolically distanced the mainstream of the party from her brand of African nationalism and opened the way for the ANC to move decisively to embrace the demands of gay activists. Most importantly, the party decided in May 1992 to include in its manifesto a commitment to entrench sexual orientation as a category of identity that would be protected against discrimination in South Africa's post-apartheid constitution. The proposed clause equated sexual orientation with race, colour, creed, and gender among types of discrimination. It thus implied a political will both to radically rewrite South African law and to challenge public prejudices against homosexuality. The other major parties, meanwhile, all quickly conceded to the sexual orientation clause without serious dispute. Even the National Party, responsible for first introducing the notorious Immorality Act and then, as recently as 1988, extending it to enable police to ban dildos and to arrest lesbians for "indecent assault," now saw advantage in accepting the principle of gay rights. This obviously did not spring from any new-found ideological commitment to non-discrimination. Rather, the Nats and the other minority parties appear to have been motivated by the coolest of political calculations: the concession of vague civil rights for the tiny, openly gay minority might be parlayed into specific political rights for the ethnic groups that they represented.

In this atmosphere of hard-headed political horse-trading among deeply distrustful rivals with well-publicized homophobic sentiments, the sexual orientation clause was in constant danger of being negotiated away, more so as new opponents sprang up during the constitutional negotiations. The African Christian Democratic Party (ACDP), notably, arose to trumpet the kind of homophobic "African family values" that Winnie Mandela had earlier voiced in the ANC. Gay activists responded to the threat by forming, first, the Hope and Unity Metropolitan Community Church (HUMCC) in February 1994 and then the National Coalition for Gay and Lesbian Equality (NCGLE) in December 1994. The HUMCC grew out of Johannesburg's only gay bar with a predominantly black clientele (Reid 1998). Its leader was the Reverend Tsietsi Thandekiso, a theologian whose homosexuality had led to his disgrace and removal from the Student Christian Movement. Thandesiko aimed to provide a safe forum for black homosexuals to openly express their Christian spirituality, including offering to sanctify homosexual marriages and to allow the kind of dignified mourning for deceased members that the mainstream Christian church denied. He also opened a direct dialogue with the ACDP and with other Christian leaders who espoused discrimination against gays and lesbians. According to Graeme Reid, the HUMCC succeeded in convincing the ACDP to remove some of the most offensive expressions of homophobia from its political platform. It has also been successful in encouraging Christian parents to mend their relationship with ostracized gay children.

The major front of gay activism in South Africa, however, has been fought by NCGLE. NCGLE coordinated the many local LGBT associations (including the HUMCC) to counter ACDP propaganda, recruit new members, and politicize those members who still did not appreciate the urgency of achieving explicit constitutional protection. It lobbied to stiffen the determination of the other parties not to crumble on this issue. And it expanded its contacts internationally to maintain pressure on the ANC. Through these means it achieved success. In December 1996, South Africa's first democratically elected president formally enacted the new constitution with the sexual orientation clause intact, the first national jurisdiction in the world with such a clause.

Following this victory, NCGLE sought to extend the theoretical principles of the new constitution to actual legal practice – to spearhead, in other words, the process of overturning discriminatory laws case by case. Its first and arguably biggest triumph in that effort came in 1997 when it convinced the Constitutional Court unanimously to declare that the old Roman-Dutch sodomy law discriminated against gay men and hence was unconstitutional. NCGLE won another important case in 1998 representing Jolande Lagemaat, a police officer who sought spousal benefits for her lesbian partner. In the following year it succeeded as well in convincing the High Court to chastise the Ministry of Home Affairs for discriminating against non-South African gay and lesbian partners of South African citizens.[5] Meanwhile, it expanded its contacts within the ruling party to win explicit commitments with respect to the eradication of homophobic attitudes. At its 50th Party Conference in December 1997, the ANC adopted a platform that promised to secure the legal recognition of same-sex relationships including custody and adoption of children, equal employment opportunities and benefits for gays and lesbians, protection from harassment and hate speech, recruitment of gay and lesbian comrades as members of parliament, an equal age of consent and the equal right to marry. In 2002 the Constitutional Court confirmed that same-sex couples could legally adopt children, and on 17 March 2003 it upheld a High Court ruling that same-sex couples should receive the same benefits as married heterosexual couples.[6]

NCGLE was also proactive in seeking to educate the police about the problem of extortion and gay bashing. Not surprisingly, given the vehemence of homophobia in the apartheid-era force and the terrible pressures the police have been under to deal with other criminal activity, success in this regard has been mixed. The gay press in South Africa is nonetheless now full of remarkable praise and stories of police heroism in protecting the gay community. Police now even have a website providing "hints on safer cruising for gay men"![7] Following the gruesome massacre of eight gay men at a club in Sea Point, Cape Town, in January 2003, the police assigned their top investigator to find the perpetrators even before the outpouring of sympathy that came from politicians across the political spectrum. Indeed, a telling sign of the changing times was that Winnie Madikizela-Mandela joined in with an offer to extend financial assistance to the families of the massacre victims.[8]

Gays and lesbians in Zimbabwe followed a similar path to political engagement, although with less dramatic success. Notwithstanding the post-liberation flowering of a gay scene in Harare, Zimbabwe remained a country with fewer democratic traditions to build upon and a less cosmopolitan culture than South Africa's. The first formal gay rights association was thus not established until September 1990. GALZ aimed principally to bring diverse informal social groups together to support each other in the face of homophobic laws and a worsening climate of backlash against post-1980 democratic freedoms. Non-whites were welcome and present in the association from the beginning. Membership nonetheless tended to be white and urban, in part because of the dominance of English as the language of business. Efforts to change this, and to recruit blacks as active members, were given a fillip when Tina Machida and Poliyana Magwiro (Tsitsi Tiripano) joined up as Zimbabwe's first publicly self-identified black lesbians (1992–93).

The increasingly black African composition of the association partly explains the growth in government hostility. Yet GALZ has not only survived the vicious rhetorical campaign against it but has prospered. Since the 1995 Book Fair controversy in particular, it has built up a network of international supporters, significantly increased membership, professionalized and "indigenized" its executive, and assisted in the opening of regional associations in smaller cities and black townships around the country (GLOB, for instance, Gays and Lesbians of Bulawayo). GALZ took ownership of a house in Harare that now serves as a secure, permanent counselling and social centre and as a refuge for LGBTs who have broken with their families. GALZ provides legal assistance to members threatened with extortion and has scored a number of important legal victories against censorship and police harassment.

As in South Africa, these successes were accompanied by setbacks. A notable loss for GLOW came in 1996 when long-time activist Bev Ditsie left the organization over male leaders' seeming lack of commitment to lesbian concerns around homophobic rape (Ditsie and Newman, 2001). The increasing blackness of GALZ's membership has meanwhile prompted some whites to leave the organization. In some cases, as in the formation of GayZim in 1999, the split was amicable.[9] In others, however, the temptation to use inflammatory accusations of racism has caused bitter recrimination and further splits within GALZ. Some members also left in fear or in opposition to the higher public profile, opting instead for the presumed safety of the closet or neo-traditional means of denial/discretion. Still others exploited the controversy to win political asylum in the West by exaggerating the actual state of repression. Goddard is frank in assessing the damage that such "playing the victim" has had upon GALZ and other LGBT associations in Africa. They have "led to division and suspicion," "drained the continent of leaders with experience, disrupted activities and wasted scarce resources, [and] given the general impression, in some quarters, that LGBT organizing is largely geared towards opening up escape routes from the continent" (2004b; see also Luirink 2000).

GALZ nonetheless remains multiracial and committed to representing a modernized African rather than West-aping gay identity and politics. Towards that end, it has forged collaborative links with (and indeed has inspired) similar organizations as they have appeared elsewhere in the region. These include the Rainbow Project and Sister Namibia in Namibia, and Lesbians, Gays, and Bisexuals from Botswana (LEGABIBO). Together with the Johannesburg-based website Behind the Mask, GALZ has spearheaded efforts to organize a pan-African network of LGBT groups from as far afield as Nigeria and Ethiopia. Such a network would aim to respond to human rights crises in Africa with a unified voice, and to share experiences that could lead to greater self-confidence and reduced dependence upon Western gay rights associations.

The implications of gay rights activists' struggles in all these countries go far beyond concerns around sexual expression or gender identity. Indeed, the often arbitrary ways by which governments in the region have sought to repress emerging gay rights groups have profound negative ramifications for civil society as a whole. The 1996 decision by the Zimbabwean government to ban the participation of GALZ from the annual international book fair, for example, was predicated on the claim that GALZ had to be prevented from displaying "obscene" materials. In other words, the government claimed the right to censor publications sight unseen.

Similarly, the ruling handed down in the case of the sodomy and indecent assault charges against the former president of Zimbabwe, Canaan Banana, established a legal precedent that directly threatens women's efforts to win greater protection from sexual assault. Banana was allowed to avoid the bulk of his sentence by paying compensation in a "bizarre" (to quote from GALZ's legal advisor) muddle of modern jurisprudence and customary practice, "riddled with contradictions and inconsistencies."[10]

On a more positive note, in November 1996, when the Zimbabwean High Court ruled that the police had unlawfully detained a GALZ member, not only was he awarded monetary compensation but the police were required to apologize. This was an exceedingly rare event in contemporary Zimbabwe that may be appreciated by citizens in general (GALZ 1996).

Legal victories for a small minority in one country have meanwhile had sometimes profound implications for the majority population in another. NCGLE scored such a victory in 1999 when the Cape Province High Court overturned the law that discriminated against immigrant partners of South African citizens. In its judgment the court criticized the Department of Home Affairs as "tardy and uncaring" on this issue. This was an important statement of principle against xenophobia in general that should resonate well among the hundreds of thousands of Zimbabwean and other African migrants in South Africa.[11] South Africans' courage in speaking out to a broader audience is also unquestionably inspirational to gays and lesbians worldwide. When Bev Ditsie became the first woman to address a United Nations conference as an out lesbian in Beijing in 1995, she exposed the hypocrisy of governments that claim to support women's rights and empowerment, yet deny the same to lesbians. And while noisy demonstrations against visiting African leaders like Robert Mugabe have apparently not been hugely persuasive, one leader at least was compelled to backtrack from a homophobic statement by the storm of criticism he raised by South African activists. Uganda's President Yoweri Museveni did not exactly apologize for baiting homosexuals in an earlier speech, but during a visit to Durban in 1999 he did allow that homosexuals should not be persecuted as long as they did not "flaunt" their sexuality. Shortly after, a discreet Gay and Lesbian Alliance of Uganda was established in Kampala.[12]

NCGLE eventually folded itself into a broader coalition, the Equality Project. In combating discrimination in Zimbabwe, GALZ has also sought to position itself in alignment with other, sometimes reluctant feminist and human-rights organizations. It has criticized Western-backed structural adjustment policies, Zimbabwe's crippling war in the Congo, and abuses in the land-reform process. It has repeatedly called for an independent judiciary and free and fair elections. GALZ also played an important role in sinking the proposed new constitution in February 2000. During the gathering of public submissions, the abusive way that the commissioners treated GALZ members alerted observers to the dubious nature of the exercise.[13] As it turned out, the proposed constitution contained no real human-rights protections against expansive presidential power. As "a sop to the international community" and "a gigantic fraud" (in GALZ's words), the proposed constitution was subsequently defeated in a national referendum.

Interventions such as the above make GALZ a frequent critic of Robert Mugabe's regime. Yet by no means is GALZ dogmatically hostile to the president or an uncritical parrot of Western or partisan political propaganda. On the contrary, consciousness of the hypocrisy of the West is high among GALZ members. Evershina, for example, as quoted by Margrete Aarmo, deplored Mugabe's attacks upon gays and lesbians but said, "I still admire the president for his courage to tell the West to go to hell" (1999, 269). Similarly, while the defeat of the proposed constitution in 2000 hugely strengthened the main political opposition party (the Movement for Democratic Change, or MDC) GALZ cautioned the MDC against statements that could contribute to political violence or that equivocate on the issue of human rights.[14] GALZ has also been explicitly critical of the cultural imperialism of Western gays and gay rights associations (Goddard 2004b).

Another promising area of activism has been on the health front, above all in the struggles against HIV/AIDS. HIV first appeared in the region in much the same way as it did in the West, among white gay males. While the main body of GASA initially downplayed the danger, the Cape Town branch established the region's first AIDS Action Group (1982). When the epidemiology began to transform in the mid-1980s and HIV/AIDS began to strike predominantly at the black, heterosexual population, Simon Nkoli founded the AIDS Township Project. NCGLE dynamo Zackie Achmat and other homosexual leaders were also prominent in the establishment of the National Association of People with AIDS, Positive African Men's Project, the AIDS Law Project, and, in 1998, the Treatment Action Campaign (TAC).

Spurred by the charismatic Achmat, TAC has since scored several astounding legal and propaganda victories. It spearheaded the campaign to force Western drug companies to make unprecedented price and patent law concessions in the supply of anti-retroviral drugs to South Africa and neighbouring countries. It then sued its own government for refusing to take advantage of these concessions.[15] It conducts research and provides community outreach services to improve local knowledge of treatment among the poor. It also relentlessly exposes tardiness, ineptitude, or duplicity in official efforts to tackle the crisis. In February 2003, for example, TAC exposed dangers in U.S. President Bush's otherwise vaunted "gift" of $15 billion to HIV/AIDS work in Africa and Haiti, notably the emphasis on proven inappropriate and ineffective abstinence campaigns. In a letter to the president and the U.S. Congress, TAC also expressed its "concern, regret and anger that your government has failed in its commitments to the Global Fund Against HIV/AIDS, Tuberculosis and Malaria." It called for the urgent negotiation of a new global patent regime that would enable the production of generic drugs in the developing world. At the same time, it organized the "largest march in the history of the AIDS epidemic, not only in South Africa but in any developing country."[16] Beginning in March 2003, it embarked on a national civil disobedience campaign to maximize the pressure on the South African government to take action, and to remind the ruling party of its social democratic roots.

Mission statements from gay rights associations elsewhere in the region now almost all prioritize HIV/AIDS education as one of the central defining services they offer. On this basis, and under this cover, fifty-five representatives from twenty-two LGBT groups in seventeen African countries met in Johannesburg in February 2004 to launch the All Africa Rights Initiative (Goddard 2004b). Their willingness to broach taboo topics in frank, accessible language stands in such stark contrast to mainstream media outside of South Africa that GALZ, for example, devotes a significant amount of its counselling work to ostensibly straight people. Indeed, in the context of widespread denial about the extent and nature of the crisis, HIV positive activism on the part of gays and lesbians has repercussions that go far beyond the discrimination they may feel as HIV positive individuals. In its March 2000 ruling in favour of Andrew Barnes's right to donate blood, for example, South Africa's Human Rights Commission pointed out that gay men were actually one of the lower-risk categories for the transmission of HIV in southern Africa, and that the highest risk was faced by young heterosexual black women in KwaZulu Natal.[17] Simply affirming this fact may eventually prove to be life-saving to many of those young women.

The issue of stigma against people living with HIV/AIDS may be contributing to a wider appreciation in southern African societies of the seamlessness of gay rights with human rights. Stigma has resulted in the abandonment, ostracism, and even murder of individuals who have come out about their infection, including the stoning to death of HIV/AIDS activist Gugu Dhlamini in a Durban township in 1999. Stigma thus directly impedes efforts to contain the spread of the disease and to provide dignified lives to the millions of *hetero*sexual people, including children, who are living with HIV and AIDS. Many straight human-rights activists know this at an intellectual level but remain incapable of overcoming the shame and denial in their personal demeanour. By contrast, LGBT persons know about stigma at the most profound level. They have in consequence adopted a forthright role in identifying the correlation between stigmatizing individuals because of HIV status and the rampant spread of the virus.

A recent press release from GALZ (8 June 2001) makes brilliantly clear this correlation, and its further interconnectedness to bad governance in general. The occasion was a speech in which President Mugabe honoured Chenjerai Hunzvi, the outspoken racist and leader of the invasions of white farms by so-called war veterans. Mugabe used the occasion to deny that Hunzvi's untimely death was caused by AIDS. To suggest as much,

Mugabe claimed, was to pander to anti-Zimbabwe sentiments. GALZ immediately chastised the president for his damaging rhetoric. Alone of the human rights associations in the country, it drew attention both to political corruption and thuggery and to the irresponsibility of leaders who failed to recognize the social aspect of the HIV/AIDS pandemic: "It is deeply unfair and irresponsible to stigmatize and blame people living with HIV or AIDS ... It is the duty of our national leaders to set a good example and support those within our nation living with the HIV virus and to concentrate their efforts not on apportioning blame but providing access to affordable treatment for all people living with HIV and AIDS regardless of their social background, their gender or their sexual orientation."[18] These are brave words at a time when even HIV/AIDS service organizations have been reluctant to challenge a political leadership that has all too willingly incited violence against its critics.

One of the many ironies of the gay rights movement in southern Africa today is how gays and lesbians will commonly acknowledge that the continent's most outspoken homophobe plays a positive role for the movement as it seeks to overcome the many obstacles it faces. GALZ's first black African member, Herbert Mondhlani, expressed it this way: "Mugabe is our inspiration. His sacrifice during the war of liberation is what is inspiring us to fight for our cause."[19] Others point favourably to Mugabe as their most effective publicist. His rhetoric has drawn international attention and money to support GALZ and other gay rights organizations region-wide. He has introduced homosexuality into Zimbabwean discourse in a far more powerful way than GALZ could ever have achieved on its own. However negative and abusive in intent, this discourse has broken the taboo that existed against the frank discussion of sexuality in traditional and colonial discourses. In a similar way, confusing and often stigmatizing rhetoric by Thabo Mbeki and some of his ministers around HIV/AIDS has drawn gay rights activists into leadership positions and key alliances with other civil society organizations, notably the powerful Congress of South African Trade Unions. Hostile or recalcitrant politicians have thus unintentionally helped to win gay rights activists a higher, more widely respected profile in South African society than otherwise would have been the case.

All of the above should not be taken as lionizing the gay rights movement for its role in challenging anti-democratic political and social culture. To be sure, elements of that culture permeate the gay rights movement as well as the wider society. Incidents of extortion, petty corruption, fraud, homophobia, misogyny, and political opportunism within the community have thus sometimes derailed idealism. For now, however, the "abomination" of gay rights (as Mr Mugabe put it) clearly remains one of the brighter lights on the developmental scene in southern Africa. There is solid reason to suppose that the movement will to continue to spread regardless of, indeed even on account of, the efforts of elites to discredit and suppress it.

Conclusion

Historical evidence from southern Africa does not support grand claims about a distinctive and timeless "African sexuality" that was exclusively heterosexual in nature. Rather, it appears that black African men and women in earlier times made a wide range of sexual decisions in response to the full gamut of human emotions. This included youthful curiosity, affection, physical lust, altered consciousness on account of alcohol or other substances, altered consciousness on account of deep feelings of spirit possession or enchantment, desire to humiliate or hurt others, hopes for economic or political gain, fear, laziness, and ignorance. It seems a shame to have to say this as we start the twenty-first century but my one big, general conclusion to this study is therefore simply this: with regard to sexuality, Africans in the past did have ideals. But in practice they were as confused, needy, hopeful, shy, bold, sordid, wonderful, awful, charming, frustrating, fickle, scared, ribald, and interesting as people anywhere else one might care to look.

A number of specific conclusions may also be drawn. First, southern Africa did not possess the kind of complex urban societies that are associated with overt same-sex sexuality elsewhere in the classical world, including other parts of Africa such as the Swahili coast or northern Nigeria. Contemporary homophobes in the region are thus substantially correct when they assert that heterosexual reproduction was of paramount importance to the rural, pre-modern societies of southern Africa. Producing children was, as a result, the defining characteristic of social adulthood for both women and men in the dominant cultures of the region over the past thousand years or more. To remain childless in these cultures was in most cases to remain a perpetual child oneself and a potential danger to the community. That community was understood to extend well beyond the living generation, implying metaphysical sanctions against those people who offended the sensibilities of the living community. Thus, few societies could admit childlessness as a legitimate option open to individual preference, even if this were only done implicitly by naming same-sex sexuality in order to denounce it. Homosexuality as an identity or an exclusive life choice did not exist when the pressures to have sex for reproduction were so over-determined by material, political, spiritual, and other cultural considerations.

Yet notwithstanding all of the above, same-sex sexuality was known in pre-modern southern Africa. Moreover, it did not necessarily invoke scandal, shame, or explicit denial. Customary ways of explaining and dealing with it varied widely but often showed a sophisticated appreciation of human diversity and frailty. The desire to preserve community harmony and people's sense of dignity was also strongly evident in African responses to same-sex behaviour. They thus do not support contemporary claims by African nationalist leaders about dogmatic and extremely harsh retribution or intolerance in the pre-modern past. As noted in a Zimbabwe case, for example, a Zezuru headman told a magistrate that "native custom" dictated a fine of one beast for attempted sodomy.[1] Such a fine bespoke a misdemeanour rather than a serious felony. The same would appear to be the case from the testimony of an Ndebele man tried for indecent assault in 1917. When charged, Tayisa said simply, "I admit the offence. I did not know it was a crime."[2]

In part, this de facto tolerance of sexual difference and individual nonconformity was possible because "sex" in pre-modern contexts was not sex the way that it is usually construed by modern Western discourse. Real sex was that activity that potentially resulted in pregnancy. Activities that did not involve the penetration of a woman's vagina by a man's penis resulting in his orgasm could in fact be construed as non-sexual, and hence non-threatening, provided that they were discreet and did not interfere with ultimate sexual obligations to the family. This ability to distinguish between real sex and other sensual acts involving genitals was an important element of culture that deeply disturbed early European observers. It did, however, enable Africans to "play" in ways that served the interests of social stability in the context.

Second, Africans on their own initiative developed new types of same-sex sexual relationships, behaviours, and vocabularies in the modern era. In this they were responding to the introduction of colonial rule and apartheid, a monetized economy, modern infrastructure and institutions, and new ideologies like Christianity and secular progress or development.

The new behaviours included male-male mine marriages, transvestism, prison sex, female *amachicken* or mummy/baby relationships, same-sex prostitution, homosexual romantic love, and (probably) some specific sexual positions and acts like oral sex. The ways in which different "tribes" adopted and adapted these new sexual practices varied according to differences in pre-existing culture, as well as the specific circumstances of class, ethnic, gender, and other struggles in which people found themselves.

Some groups, notably Shangaans from Portuguese territory and Chewa from Nyasaland, were quicker than others to change. Over time, however, the nexus of modernity expanded to include more and more Africans in increasingly similar conditions. Behaviours that were originally mostly confined to young men of a certain culture in a certain class position (Shangaan migrant miners, for example, or Chewa urban sanitation workers) began to appear among men of other ethnicities, age brackets, and employment as the opportunities, role models, and incentives or pressures arose.

Highly dichotomous gender roles and identities do not seem to have offered any particularly effective "defence" against same-sex sexuality where the opportunities arose and pressures favoured it. Conversely, specific sexual "perversions" in specific situations do not appear to have undermined pre-existing dichotomous gender roles and identities to any noteworthy degree. The opposite may in fact have been the case. That is, the dominant forms of same-sex relationships found in colonial and apartheid southern Africa actually seem to have strengthened "tradition" by allowing relatively safe opportunities for young men and women to practise modernized (but still highly dichotomous and hierarchical) heterosexual relationships.

Third, dogmatic revulsion against same-sex behaviours, acts, relationships, and thoughts (that is, homophobia) was introduced into the region by European colonialists and preachers. Sometimes this came in the form of explicit propaganda and draconian punishment. More commonly, however, it was inculcated through fairly subtle discourses, clothing, and the reorganization of living spaces that combined to fetishize certain parts of the body and to imply the need for defence against sexual temptations that were hitherto unimagined as sexual. Africans were encouraged through these discourses to equate homophobic constructions of sexuality, sensuality, and gender with civilization or progress. Ironically, as a counter-discourse of tolerance for homosexuality emerged in the metropoles in tandem with more liberal forms of colonial rule in the 1920s to the 1940s, Christianized Africans often asserted a hyper-respectability or hyper-masculinity in opposition. Over time, and in relation to frustrations in their struggles for political independence and economic security, this respectability among African elites and African nationalist leaders elided into explicit, violent expressions of homophobia. The Zimbabwean evidence in recent years of post-colonial crisis in particular confirms what Dennis Altman offers about the links between corporate globalization and changing notions of sexuality: "Increasingly sexuality becomes a terrain on which are fought out bitter disputes around the impact of global capital and ideas" (2001, 1).

Fourth, some black gays and lesbians in the region deployed Western discourses around rights and identity to fight against this homophobia. This flowering of an indigenous gay rights movement in southern Africa is a very recent phenomenon – the mid-1980s in South Africa, the early 1990s in Zimbabwe, and only in the last few years (if at all) in the other countries of the region. Superceding white or Coloured dominated gay and lesbian social clubs or associations, often employing Western-sounding language or Western-looking imagery, and often directly supported by international donors, the gay rights movement in southern Africa is understandably perceived by many people to be a straightforward product of Western cultural imperialism.

This is a mistake. The gay rights movement includes proudly nationalist black leaders and has won the support of some of the major African nationalist parties. These successes owe much to both modern Western discourses around civil rights and to activists' carefully, tactfully nesting their struggles for minority rights within the wider struggles for majority rights, whether the anti-apartheid movement or constitutional reform in Zimbabwe. But they also owe some success to submerged African traditions and knowledge. Indeed, an irony of contemporary homophobic "African family values" is that some black gays and lesbians have turned to local traditions like spirit possession to explain themselves to their families and to help them to live non-normative lives with dignity, away from the glare of publicity that attaches to the out identity.

Same-sex sexual practices in the mining compounds, prisons, and boarding schools, meanwhile, clearly did not reflect a progressive or liberal consciousness, nor can they be directly linked to the emergence of the modern gay rights movement. Nonetheless, the evidence given to Leary and Taberer and subsequent enquiries suggests that millions of African men over the course of a century – and almost certainly many of their wives and mothers – knew that sexual relations between men were taking place on a large scale. They may not have talked about it very much, and some of their Christianized and educated comrades who went on to form the leadership of the liberation struggle might not have been entirely privy to the knowledge. But clearly these millions of African men and women did not see discreet, discrete sexual relations with people of the same sex as a particularly great threat to their fundamental cultural beliefs or even to desirable rates of heterosexual reproduction.

The above should not be taken to diminish the courage of individual pioneers in the modern gay rights movement or the role of Western discourses on human rights. But the fact of this submerged knowledge within the working-class African population is clearly important to our understanding of the rapid progress of South Africa's gay rights movement. It may help to explain how South African leaders have been able to introduce legal rights that fly so blatantly in the face of idealized African traditions. It may help to explain as well how small gay rights associations in Zimbabwe and other black African countries have been able to establish themselves and even to flourish in the face of elite Christian hostility.

Fifth, while proudly out with their sexual orientation and while cognizant of the power of the dominant discourse to shape their lives, many gay rights activists in the region have begun to turn away from narrowly conceived identity or sexual liberation politics. Their political energy is instead primarily directed to the broad political, economic, and health challenges affecting the region, including HIV/AIDS, structural adjustment programs, and state corruption and repression of citizens' rights. To that extent, gays and lesbians in southern Africa may provide some inspiration to comrades in the West who have remained obsessed with individual sexual freedom or winning symbolic victories. The engagement of southern African gay rights activists in mundane struggles over patents, development assistance, international trade law, and such is also a sharp reminder to those in the West who have allowed the availability of effective anti-retrovirals in the West or the legal right to marry to blind them to the criminal inequities of the global political economy. It is those inequities, more than gay pride marches, that underwrite much of Western gays and lesbians' individual sexual freedom.

The implications of all this history for contemporary struggles are both daunting and encouraging. On the one hand, it is my belief that African nationalism and other expressions of African dignity are critically important to world politics, as much today as ever in the colonial past. Africans, and people of colour worldwide, desperately need a politics of opposition to the racism and neo-imperialism that continue to impoverish their lives in ever-new and depressing ways. White folks in the West also stand to benefit by the principled resistance to corporate globalization and from the imagining of alternative models of international development, community, and connection to the environment that African nationalism potentially offers. Yet when the main ideals of African nationalism can be as deeply compromised by homophobia and misogyny as has sometimes been the case, their potential to contribute to democratic civil society on a global scale is weakened. Some of the attitudes and behaviours within African nationalist discourses revealed in this study, particularly many men's sense of entitlement to sex and their willingness to resort to sexual violence to make political statements, are also deeply worrisome in health and economic terms as well as in political ones in the present context of the HIV/AIDS pandemic.

On the other hand, if Africans' sexuality was negotiable and could change in the past, so then it can change towards healthier patterns in the future. That lobbying for such change is taking place and is linked to broader debates about human rights is further grounds for optimism. Such lobbying draws in part upon indigenous traditions of tolerance of difference and is now significantly driven by black African activists, giving additional support for believing that the movement is sustainable rather than a passing developmentalist fad flogged by the West. It is also tremendously encouraging that the research for this study was not only possible but was fun to do and that evidence that counters demagogic assertions about African identity can fairly easily be found. All of it suggests that further careful research has the potential to contribute to current struggles for democratic political development and good health in the region. Bleak though the situation might sometimes feel in Zimbabwe and elsewhere in southern Africa today, the history of dissident sexualities gives good cause for hope.

The Gay Oral History Project, and Other Notes on Research Methodology

Euphemisms and discreet language, including unrecorded body language, odours, and eye contact (or lack thereof) are among the hallmarks of human communication around sexuality. Moreover, the nature of the language and the level of discretion vary enormously according to the relationship between interlocutors (or "cuties"). This is not a postmodern insight. On the contrary, the missionary David Livingstone was perceptive of the difficulties, and of the self-imposed constraints of research into "immorality" issues in Africa well over a century ago. Writing about the Kololo (Lozi) people of what is now Zambia, he candidly acknowledged how: "By pointed enquires, and laying oneself out for that kind of knowledge, one might be able to say much more; *but if one behaves as he must do among the civilized and abstains from asking questions,* no improper hints ever will be given by any of the native[s]" (Livingstone and Livingstone 1865, 284, my emphasis).

Queer theorists have developed methodologies to discern and interpret the self-censorship, opacity, subtlety, double entendres, and (sometimes) crude hostility or slanderous misrepresentations that occur in the main sources that we have around same-sex sexuality.[1] Because queer research is rather new in Africa, and because potential researchers may be unduly anxious about the feasibility of tackling some of the more sensitive questions that arise from it, I would like in this appendix to alert readers to the main specific difficulties with the main specific sources that I encountered. I would like as well to offer as a possible model one of the methodologies used to challenge those difficulties. In so doing I want to encourage future researchers to ponder other effective ways to lead us beyond Livingstone's notion of civilized behaviour.

My research into the history of non-normative sexualities among Africans in southern Africa began with the European magistrates' criminal court records that commenced in Mashonaland in 1891. The courts are one of the few places where the voices of the "lowest of the low" are recorded in detail, often verbatim. Where else can one gather the testimony of petty criminals, landless peasants, unemployed labourers, perverts, outcasts, drunkards, and prostitutes on issues that affected their daily lives? That said, however, the court records introduce numerous biases and limitations that need constantly to be borne in mind. Above all, they are relentlessly androcentric. The definitions and presumptions about the laws on sodomy, indecent assault, and *crimen injuria*, and the requirement of establishing "lascivious intent" meant that in practice only an erect (or presumably erect) penis met the burden of proof.[2] Lesbian-like affairs or sexually charged aggression between females could thus well have taken place but remained invisible to the people who kept the records and who commented on such matters.[3]

Among the men who came to court, a number of other biases are structured into the record. Most obviously, people who love each other or who have made satisfactory monetary arrangements between them do not normally bring their sexual relations before the public eye for posterity to record and judge. With the exception of a small number of cases where the accused were caught *in flagrante delicto*, therefore, cases on record stem from a complaint lodged with the police by "the victim." The latter clearly had a vested interest in characterizing his assailant as violent or mercenary and himself as helpless and guiltless. As a result, this source provides only the barest hints of the existence of consensual same-sex relationships. That these hints exist at all in a source so hostile to them is itself a remarkable piece of evidence.

An ethnic bias in the record also emerges due to the nature of the colonial judicial and land tenure systems. Soon after white settlement began, the administration divided the colony into so-called European lands and African reserves, or "tribal trust lands," as they were later called. Throughout the period of colonial rule, the majority of Shona and Ndebele continued to live in these reserves. There, most minor infractions of law were dealt with by African chiefs and headmen on a predominantly oral basis. These chiefs were appointed by the colonial administration and were ultimately subject to the authority of the local Native Commissioners (NCs). The NCs, however, were generally swamped by a host of administrative duties and the need to attend to more serious crimes of property and violence. Indecent assault among the Shona and Ndebele majority thus rarely made it to their attention and hence into the documentary record, even when they involved cases that were by all appearances truly scandalizing (for example, cases involving bestiality or outsiders to the village). Headman Nyamaka admitted to this silencing when confronted by a frustrated European magistrate about a Coloured man alleged to have "copulated" with a dog in a village under Nyamaka's jurisdiction in 1921. "I did not report this crime to our Chief Sipolilo nor to the Native Dept.," Nyamaka defended himself. "I thought it was too small a case to report. I did not report it to the police."[4]

The flip side of this silencing of indigenous Zimbabwean behaviour by the dualistic legal system is that the record tends to overstate the prevalence of criminal behaviour among non-Zimbabweans. Local Shona and Ndebele preferred as much as possible to avoid labour in town or on European farms and mines, although the Ndebele were less successful in this due to earlier dispossession from their own lands. White farmers and miners thus faced an almost perpetual local labour shortage that they tried to fill by importing migrant labourers. These were recruited from even poorer colonies, mostly Nyasaland, Northern Rhodesia, and Portuguese East Africa. The majority of Africans in the urban or European farming areas where law was administered by the magistrates therefore consisted of these so-called alien natives. As late as 1956, for example, nearly two-thirds of the African population of Salisbury originated from outside the colony (Raftopolous 1995, 82), while the lingua franca among Africans in Salisbury was chiNyanja, the main language of central Malawi. Shona and Ndebele were ethnic minorities in their own capital city.

Europeans, Asians, and persons of mixed race were also disproportionately found in the urban areas, and this demographic imbalance further contributes to the impression that male-male sexual crimes were mostly an alien issue. By virtue of their relative affluence, moreover, these exotic groups were the prime targets of false accusations and blackmail attempts. Non-Africans, especially whites, tended as well to have the wherewithal to challenge an unfavourable decision in the lower courts. Africans unlucky enough to get caught in the European justice system, by contrast, tended to resign themselves to their fate in part due to the prohibitive expenses of lawyers and legal appeals. The accused in cases that made it to the High Court and gained media attention were thus almost entirely white. Scholars who confined their research to the higher courts or the media would consequently come away with a very skewed view of who was doing what to whom.[5]

The reliability of forensic evidence with respect to Africans in colonial Zimbabwe suffers further from the fact that at least two translations stand between the researcher and the testimony of those Africans. The first one (or even two) translations were from the indigenous languages into English, with all the potential for misrepresentation that this entailed. A further translation then occurred from English into a type of legaleze that homogenized the acts committed. Euphemisms such as "have connection," "fundamental orifice," and "obtained his purpose" combined with a phlegmatic, businesslike tone to erase nuance and emotion from much of the testimony. English-speakers, by contrast, typically spoke directly to the record with the liberal use of words like "fuck," "bugger," and "jiga-jiga" or "jigger" (a pan-African crudity). That the African translators themselves may have played an active role in censoring lusty or violent language from the testimony of their countrymen is at least hinted at in some cases. For example, when pressed by the judge to clarify Maponga's choice of words in his defence in a 1921 case, the translator explained "For 'to hold' accused uses word 'kubata.' This is a polite word for sexual connection and approximates as near as possible to the English 'copulate.'" In fact, the word is defined by Shona dictionaries and by my oral informants as meaning "rape."[6]

Frustratingly, while the accused in these cases were allowed to cross-examine their accusers and other witnesses, their cross-examinations for some inexplicable reason were not recorded in the transcripts. One can therefore only guess from the reactions of the complainants how the accused specifically sought to challenge them and to defend himself, often with implicit counter-accusations. One can also only guess at the validity of the verdict. Were the men actually guilty of the crimes for which they were tried and convicted? Or was the magistrate – in his haste, in his racist prejudice, or perhaps even in his prurience – prepared to entertain the feeblest, concocted evidence about African "perversion"? We simply cannot know with certainty.

Cases of male-male sexual crime are buried in the mass of other, non-indexed cases generated by the racist colonial system (liquor, bicycle, and walking-on-the-sidewalk violations, and the like). This necessitated a physically demanding trawl through thousands upon thousands of dockets. The testimony is buried, furthermore, in "common-sense" assumptions that made male sexuality outside the realm of comment for the most part, that naturalized male lust, or put male sexuality beyond the need for explication (nudge, nudge). Men fuck because they must, end of story. Similar presumptions about male "nature" and "needs" pervade as well the scholarship that touches upon male sexuality from the Rhodesian era. They have the effect of lowering standards of enquiry. Zimbabwe's *only* anthropological enquiry into "homosexuality" among the Shona may in fact provide an object lesson in how *not* to do anthropological enquiry (Gelfand 1979, 1985). A white man during a time of brutal, racialized military conflict gathers testimony from fifteen senior male chiefs on a subject that to many would cast aspersions on African dignity. He also mentions an anecdote from a university colleague, rather than asking gay people themselves or even *n'angas* who specialized in "cures." He does not indicate which language or using which specific terms he communicated the meaning "homosexuality" to his Shona informants, allowing him to conclude with a homily to supposed virtues of the culture in relation to the West. Symington's (1972) Kinsey-esque research is even less tenable, based as it was on a written questionnaire and a sample size of 119 semi-literate men and sixteen women.

My search for indicators of male-male sexual desire consequently often felt like looking for a needle in a haystack. Nonetheless, as Mokhoane's stern missionary character in the novel *Teba* warns after a rambling and obscure diatribe against "sin" (which is actually directed specifically against homosexuality), "Those who have ears will hear" (1995, 63–4).

Oral history is one means that Africanists, femininsts, and queer historians have all used to help to attune their senses to coded language, assumptions, and blind spots in the documentary record. Indeed, some recent attempts to investigate sexuality and gender relations among black Zimbabweans using oral history and quantitative sociological methods like focus groups and Participatory Rural Assessment have been quite successful in revealing the importance of hitherto understated or unknown practices and attitudes – dry sex, birth control and abortion, husband-taming herbs, and so on (Burke 1996, Ray et al. 1996, Armstrong 1997, Kaler 2003, Goebel 2002, for example). The potential for these methods to silence minority or dissident opinion is strong, however. For that reason I opted for feminist/queer oral history techniques that place particular emphasis on facilitating the free expression of minority and dissident opinion, and on "empowering" informants by involving them in the construction of the research project.[7]

These methods had to be adapted to minimize the distorting effects of the specific conditions in Zimbabwe. Few people would disagree with Gelfand, for example, that Zimbabwean cultures place a high premium on discretion when it comes to the open and frank discussion of sexual matters. Simply finding people who knew about and were willing to share their knowledge of non-normative sexuality was thus tricky, particularly in light of growing fears of state retribution. Neither myself (foreigner) nor out gays and lesbians (perceived enemies of the state) were well placed to win the necessary confidence of "traditional" (straight, rural-based) Shona-speakers. For the bulk of this task, therefore, and to reassure potential informants of the non-threatening nature of the research, I employed a straight, married, rural-based female Shona-speaker, Nyaradzo Dzobo. Ms Dzobo had already been trained in feminist oral history methods and indeed had established a reputation in her district for the interviews she had done for an earlier project. So good was she with her informants that widows, in particular, came from miles around to tell her their stories (Goebel 2003). I directed Ms Dzobo to seek out men and women in the rural districts around her home (Hwedza and Buhera) who had had homosexual encounters in their past. Her tact in doing so and then in diplomatically asking the boldest of questions made her interviews among the richest of all the researchers' on the project.

Separately, I trained a number of straight Zimbabwean researchers who were sympathetic to gay rights to conduct interviews in their home areas. Melusi Sibanda, an honours student in the University of Zimbabwe theology department, aimed both to gain his degree through this research and to fortify GALZ's submissions to the World Council of Churches conference in 1998. In addition, as part of course requirements, I had my History of Southern Africa students conduct oral research on topics of their choice during their term breaks. Several successfully accepted the challenge of finding older people who had migrated to South Africa to interview them about the social and sexual life there. I myself conducted a small number of interviews, including in Lesotho, although these are probably more appropriately described as "conversations."[8]

Self-identified gays and lesbians were another obvious source of oral evidence. Yet self-identified gays and lesbians do not necessarily offer reliably queer insights into homosexuality, to say the least. Their testimony was often clouded by the same fears and ignorance found in the wider population – fear of state retribution, lack of an oral history tradition, reliance upon foreign terminology, and an internalized homophobia with which they grew up and continue to wrestle. Moreover, in a political situation where people are almost desperate to confirm their existence, the old Africanist problem of informants telling you what they think you want to hear is pronounced. "Paraliterate feedback" from the few published sources could also be pronounced. Particularly disorienting for me was to have informants tell me bowdlerized versions of my own earlier research.

The Gay Oral History Project was designed to address these research problems and to take into account the divided nature of Zimbabwean society as a whole. Those divisions were significantly reproduced within the gay community. Pre-existing social tensions had then flared up under the enormous stress of sudden publicity and donor funds that followed in the wake of President Mugabe's rhetorical campaign against homosexuals. Accusations of white racism, black opportunism, cowardice, insensitivity, corruption, homophobia, misogyny, and more may have been overheated. The bottom line, however, was that a rift opened that threatened to tear the association apart, between the more affluent, literate, and internationally connected white members of GALZ and the growing numbers of less literate black gays living in the townships without even taxi fare to make it into meetings in town. By early 1997, nasty gossip and backbiting had become endemic, with several ugly scenes played out in public, including drunkenness and fighting at the new centre. Particularly embarrassing politically was the defection to Holland of GALZ's first black president. The principal international donor, HIVOS, finally threatened to withdraw financial support unless GALZ reformed its internal dynamics.

GALZ eventually adopted a plan of action to deal with the crisis by reaffirming its original commitment to human rights ideals. These included anti-racism, anti-sexism, and democratic governance as well as anti-homophobia. The first practical result of this plan was the resignation of the mostly white volunteer leadership and its replacement by an elected mostly black and mostly professional executive committee. An "Outreach Committee" was also struck, with a mandate "to create a space for people of colour to express themselves fully in their own tongue ... and to facilitate self empowerment so that they can build self confidence which would help them grow as individuals with responsibilities to themselves and to society."[9] Its long-term goal was to foster an environment within GALZ – democratic, professional, idealistic – that would militate against the manifestations of racism, sexism, and self-loathing that had nearly destroyed the organization. As one witness phrased it, "I feel at long last the light has dawned and GALZ has finally started putting its house in order."[10]

The Gay Oral History Project was conceived as part of this reorientation of GALZ. The proposal came from me but was debated, accepted, and modified by the Outreach Committee. Its specific objectives were to:

1. Conduct interviews with gays, lesbians, bisexuals, transgendered, and any other people with knowledge and sympathy toward people whose sexuality does not conform to the heterosexual norm or ideals and whose views have historically been silenced. Life histories would be gathered from all the districts and among all the different cultures of Zimbabwe, including migrant labourers from neighbouring countries where possible.

2. Create an archive that could be a resource for people wishing to learn about the diversity of historical experiences of sexuality, and which could contribute to GALZ-members' own sense of community in a political and social milieu that otherwise tends to divide and demoralize them.

3. Publish materials that summarize the above in English and in Zimbabwe's two main indigenous languages, Shona and Ndebele. These would become part of an information kit intended to influence debates at the World Council of Churches conference in Harare (December 1998), could be part of an HIV/AIDS-awareness or other educational package, and/or be published in sympathetic mass media.

4. Bridge the chasm that commonly exists between professional scholars and local activists and provide a model for shaping a research project in a democratic manner that would involve the "ivory tower" directly in social and political activism.[11]

The last point I added as a gesture to GALZ and to keep myself honest, so to speak. GALZ by this time had already had its share of visiting and basically exploitative Western researchers and media-hounds. Local intellectuals, meanwhile, with a few rare exceptions had not taken a vocal stand against state-sanctioned homophobia. There was thus a significant pool of distrust that needed to be overcome. Crucial to winning trust was that I be seen to take an unequivocal public position in support of GALZ. I had been working on this since starting the research by, for example, writing letters to the editor for publication in the popular media, presenting my documentary research in public forums, and writing non-academic versions of it for the GALZ membership. Nonetheless, the temptation for bourgeois intellectuals, particularly foreign ones, to "gap it" or to do the "chicken run" in a deteriorating situation like Zimbabwe is a constant and strong one. An explicit commitment to remain engaged in the local political struggle was a small nod in the direction of resisting that temptation.

The project as such began by training GALZ volunteers in research skills and ethics and gathering their input into the types of questions to be asked. Considerable time was spent negotiating the financial side of the work. In order to keep mercenary feelings out and to free up resources to gather the maximum number of interviews, everyone accepted that remuneration would remain essentially token. A project coordinator (Rodgers Bande) was then elected and his specific duties and remunerations were defined by group consensus. The former included liaising with the researchers, coordinating travel, keeping a diary of the project's progress, keeping track of finances, checking for fraudulent or sloppily written submissions, entering data onto floppy disks, and keeping the Outreach Committee informed of any legal or other types of harassment encountered by researchers. My own role was defined as a resource person on technical questions about social science research and as the one who would eventually distil the raw data into publishable form.

I hesitate to claim that the evidence so produced meets the high standards set by some of the feminist historians in Africa cited above. The research did, however, result in anecdotes that enliven the more "expert" sources of information and in expressions of opinion that abundantly confirm them. Designing the project and doing the interviews was also empowering to at least some of the researchers, who have gone on to apply confidence and skills in subsequent work (Rodgers, for example, went on to be an advisor to the nascent LEGABIBO in Botswana). Three sample interviews from the GALZ researchers are reproduced in Appendix 2 to show how some of the informants also gained a degree of personal satisfaction, if not empowerment per se, from sharing their insights with GALZ.

This type of project is by its nature risky, and it would be misleading to suggest that it was entirely successful. Numerous problems emerged in the course of the project that ultimately contributed to the premature (temporary) collapse of the Outreach program. For example, everyone underestimated the rigours and costs of conducting social-science research in rural Zimbabwe, the intensity of suspicion around homosexuality issues, and the risks to personal security. Soon after interviewing got underway, notably, the state-controlled press and police renewed their campaigns of harassment and slander against GALZ. This made the presence of confidential interviews on GALZ property highly problematic. But then where would they go, who would "own" them? Certainly not me. Indeed, suspicions about my own motives as consultant were raised almost immediately after I left Zimbabwe to return to Canada in mid-1998. The money, modest by Western standards but hard to resist by Zimbabwean ones, also sowed divisions. By the end of the year it became apparent that two key members of the Outreach Committee were embezzling funds. When this was discovered, they loudly alleged racism to distract attention. They were unanimously expelled from GALZ, and the accusations of racism by whites against blacks were sharply repudiated by the majority black membership. It was a painful process, however, that brought this particular strand of the historical research to an end.

These difficulties are part of the record. I include them here as a caution against assuming that feminist/queer/participatory oral history methods are necessarily more reliable or "easier" than other sources.

Finally, the kind of feminist theory that I draw principal inspiration from enjoins that a high level of critical attention be paid to audience, and to the presentation of the data in the writing-up phase. Queer theorists are wont to neglect this aspect of research production, for example, by inventing new words and by writing so densely and abstractly that they lose the ability to communicate to all but a tiny, select academic audience. My approach has been to respect the need for intellectual sophistication but to balance that with accessibility as much as possible. "Homotextuality" is thus not merely the double reading of our sources applied during the gathering of evidence. Homotextuality also demands that our choice of words to interpret that evidence resist as much as possible the classism as well as heterosexism and other oppressive constructions of identity that are implicit to so much of our language and choice of audience. This, it needs to be reiterated, is at least as difficult as the gathering of evidence. It was extremely helpful in that respect to present research to a wide variety of audiences, including non-academic ones in Africa and North America. The range of audiences and critical input alerted me to occasions when turn of phrase or choice of words that at first seemed uncontroversial to me in fact suggested meanings or imposed Westocentric and elitist categories or logic that contradicted the emancipatory or empowering objectives of the research.

This remains an academic monograph intended for primary use at the level of university research. But the issue of the class bias inherent in that particular choice of audience implies an obligation to rewrite the material in a way that makes it accessible to less elite readers. A final stage in the methodology, therefore, has yet to come. This will be a translation of the academic language that you have just endured into a more popular form, employing the skills of local authors. I should remind readers, as well, that if you yourself would like to contribute to the struggles for gay, women's, and human rights generally in southern Africa, please check out the website Behind the Mask for ideas and further contacts. Thank you so much for reading this book!

Sample Interviews Conducted for the Gay Oral History Project, February–June 1998

WALTER ZIMUNYA INTERVIEWS MBUYA CHIKWIZI, CHIPINGE DISTRICT

Mbuya Chikwizi is a traditional healer (*n'anga*) in the middle Sabi area of Chipinge. She was born and bred within the Shangani culture and has lived with Shangani people up to now. Mbuya asked the interviewer not to mention names of the people that she mentioned. She would only give an interview after assurances that this would not at all get her involved with the police since she was afraid because of utterances by Mr Mugabe over the gay/lesbian issue.

WALTER ZIMUNYA: In your childhood days did you ever hear of *nkotshane* or men who sleep with men or women who sleep with women?

MBUYA CHIKWIZI: I was born seventy-two years ago here in Chipinge, and I remember that during my early childhood, I would say I was twelve or fourteen years old, we had a woman in our area who was called "Sa Changana" where we would go as girls to get advice. At her place we also learnt that there were girls who did not have any feelings to sleep with men and they would get their own advice about how to deal with their way of life. However, since I was not one of them, I cannot tell what type of advice they would get. This situation was never really talked of within society, but we would know who these girls were. The same with men or boys. They would seek advice on what to do as well, so I would say gays have been around for a long time. Before, though, it was taboo to talk about it.

WZ: What was your understanding of what these people would do in order to appease themselves sexually?

MC: What I understood is that the men who slept with men had one of them who would act as the wife. They would really act like people who were in a relationship just like a man and a woman. As to the actual sexual acts, I cannot give details to that since as I said earlier this was an issue that no one was allowed to talk about. The same would happen to women who would sleep with women. Overall, the elders in the area would really recognize these marriages. I would want to believe that the elders would discuss these issues, though as children we would not be allowed to. I took note of the fact that in these relationships one partner would perform all the daily duties of a man, while the other would perform the duties of a woman.

WZ: Were there any other words that were used to describe these relationships?

MC: Yes, I remember words like *murumekadzi* and *mukadzirume* in reference to the man who acted as the woman in an all-male relationship and the woman who acted as the man in an all-female relationship respectively.

WZ: Can you recall any queens or other out gay men from the past, and were they outgoing?

MC: As I previously said, this was a taboo, and you would not really find these people [highly effeminate men] outgoing with their sexual preference identified.

WZ: Were there any acts or rituals that would be carried out in order to change the sexual behaviour of these people?

MC: I would want to believe that there was something that would be done to try and change them, though I cannot tell for sure if it worked. But with a lot of *n'angas* in our culture, certainly, yes, they would try. In my opinion, when the men would stay together as husband and wife it would only be after failure to change the sexual acts of these people as society would find no other way of dealing with them.

WZ: Are you saying then that this was a sign of tolerance by the society?

MC: To a certain degree I would say so, but you know very well that even in the past no one had the right to take away another person's life so they had to live as well.

WZ: Did the question of killing gay/lesbian people ever come up, since you mention that no one had the right to take any other person's life?

MC: To some circles in the society, these people were considered as a bad omen to the family and society, and there was no reason for keeping them. But to a greater part they had to live as they were born the same as all other people, though they were to some taken as disabled.

WZ: Did society at that time view these gays/lesbians as a threat to the younger generation?

MC: When you talk of society, you are talking about a lot of people. I cannot conclusively say the society as a whole, but part of it, in fact those who were closest to these relationships, would find in most cases that they posed no harm to the younger generation. But of course to those that were far from these relationships, they would at times advocate the removal of gays/lesbians from the area and find them a place to stay that was secluded.

WZ: Was there any *lobola* involved in acquiring another man as a wife?

MC: I never heard of anyone paying *lobola* at all during those days. It may have happened, but I never heard it.

WZ: Today there has been an anti-homosexuality campaign by the government. What is your comment on this?

MC: I don't want to talk of the government. Probably there is something they find bad about these practices.

WZ: What about yourself – do you see anything bad?

MC: I've known that this happens, and so I see nothing bad as long as it is done within closets.

WZ: What would be your advice to the gays/lesbians so far as their relationships are concerned?

MC: I would urge them to be quiet and keep their relationships a secret. We have a powerful government, and once it says no to anything, it keeps to it. Look at the *Gukurahundi* era [civilian and so-called dissident massacres by the army in the mid-1980s] – do you know it?

WZ: Do you see today's society in modern day Zimbabwe accepting homosexuality at all?

MC: It all depends where one is. In the rural areas where culture is deep rooted, I think this [acceptance] should be understood, but the best way to deal with it [homosexuality] is being quiet about it, as I said.

WZ: What about in the cities?

MC: There are too many people in the cities who think they are very learned, and these people may be a problem. They are only just shy of getting a dead man back to living. They will certainly think homosexuality is a mental problem, but it is not.

ROMEO TSHUMA'S INTERVIEW OF DUBEKILE NXUMALO, MATOBO DISTRICT

RT: I did my research in Matabeleland South Province Matobo District on the 2nd of May 1998. I managed to get hold of Dubekile Nxumalo who was born in approximately 1924. She got married in the same area. To make my research easier I decided to use my own questions.

RT: Was there ever anything called homosexuality in your days?

DN: Yes, those people were there.

RT: In our Ndebele culture, was there a word that referred to homosexuality?

DN: There was a word, but people today think it does not mean "homosexuality" exactly. It literally meant a human being with both a male and a female organ. The word in Ndebele was *incukubili*.

RT: I also realize that people in Matabeleland use the other terms from Zulu to refer to gay people, words like *isithabane*.

DN: That is true.

RT: How were gay people treated in those days?

DN: It was accepted, but it was never discussed in the open. I want to emphasize to you that it was not a controversial issue. People formerly strongly believed that a person like that had the biggest spirit medium of the family. This person would not get married. The family would build a small hut for him, and then he would be given a nephew who would help to fetch water and do the cleaning. It was always believed that something sexual was happening, though nobody proved it.

RT: Surely this will be called child abuse today?

DN: This applied to people who were *sangomas* and to those who were possessed by the biggest medium spirit of the family. Therefore, the idea of child abuse would not apply, since the whole family respected the role of those persons.

RT: Do you mean that other people who were not possessed did not have this problem? I mean, were there other ways to be gay than to be possessed?

DN: There were. When the family was faced with such problems, the elderly people of the extended families would call a meeting to discuss the matter. The first thing they did was to hand him/her over to a *sangoma* find out why. If he/she was not possessed, they would try and treat [cure] the person.

RT: Could they in fact be treated?

DN: Well, not really. Let me give you a very good example. There was a certain man whom everyone thought had been cured by proper treatment, but after five years he was caught by his wife sleeping with a small boy. Which means that it never got cured, although that the elders had always tried.

RT: In situations where a person did not change, what was then done?

DN: In those days there was a high degree of confidentiality. People would sit for a meeting again to try and come out with a solution. The solution would be if he was a man he would get married and they would arrange with the other brother to sleep with the wife and have children. The husband would meanwhile be given a boy to stay with at home as a servant. It was always believed that one day he would be possessed by the spirit medium [retroactively erasing the family shame]. The children had to grow up and get married without knowing what was happening.

RT: What was the situation with women at that time?

DN: The beliefs were somewhat similar. For example, I remember a woman who lived with young female servants only. She was a *sangoma* and did not get married, but to do so was easy then because people believed that she was possessed.

RT: Mrs Nxumalo, do you agree that being gay was a taboo in our African culture that time?

DN: I don't know, but it was considered as a sad situation to be in because members of your family wouldn't be proud of you as a man. They would try and keep it a secret so that the neighbours won't know about it. The other thing was, if you were a man, every man was expected to have children and to build his own huts with his wife. General people could pass bad comments if they heard about the failure to do this from other families.

RT: In your times, Mrs Nxumalo, were there any stories that were said by your elders about homosexual behaviour?

DN: Yes, there were scaring stories. My grandmother used to tell us about her uncle who was killed by the villagers for being gay because at that time men were given wives. Her uncle did not want to get married, although he was not a *sangoma*. Then they had to find out that he was gay. He was just killed, just like that, but that was long back. Things like that did not happen in our time. I don't know why they did something horrible like that.

RT: Things like that did not happen in your time?

DN: No.

RT: What was being done if a man or a woman was found having an affair with another man?

DN: It was normal with young boys to be caught doing that, because it was part of their training. With elders, to sleep with a male was also possible if they were worried about impotence. So to sleep with a male would be to prove that they are man enough. But with elderly men, there was a minor charge paid. Mostly it was a goat given to the other family, but I am not sure exactly what was that for.

RT: You said something about young boys being trained to be real men. What training was it?

DN: Boys were trained on how to handle women, but there were no women when they were being trained which means they were trained on other men on how to sleep with women. It was okay with young boys to sleep with each other since it was considered as a phase that they were going through, and it was always believed that they were going to change.

RT: Was the same thing done with women?

DN: Yes but not sleeping with other women. Women were taught how to sleep with men. Elderly women would use their fingers to play around with their private parts, training them how to move their bodies when a man is making love to them.

RT: According to my understanding, when lesbians make love to each other, they also use their fingers.

DN: Perhaps, but in the times I am talking about that was not considered as making love to each other but as preparation for a good marriage.

TINA MACHIDA'S INTERVIEW OF AN ELDERLY MALE N'ANGA, GOKWE DISTRICT

TM: Do you know about the word *ngochani* and where did it originate from and how gay people were viewed in those days?

N'ANGA: I have known about the word for a long time after people who had gone to the mines in South Africa came back. That is where the word *ngochani* originated from. But I also knew about gay people since I was a young boy. My grandfather told me about it when I asked about my grandfather's younger brother who had never married and stayed in the outskirts of the village with his friend [*sahwira*]. This was in the old days before people went to the mines. This friendship had no name and it was something that was never discussed publicly or talked about.

My grandfather told me that his brother was bewitched by people who wanted him to marry their daughter, and when he refused, they wanted to shame and embarrass him by turning him into someone whose desire was to have sex with other men. He said that his uncle died living with his *sahwira* and the community there knew what was happening but never commented or talked about it. They all wanted to believe that he had an evil spirit and felt sorry for him. When he died, he was buried with a rat, as it is the tradition to bury a childless person this way so that they do not come back from the dead and haunt other people's children.

TM: How common were such men?

N'ANGA: In my home village where I grew up, there were several men staying in homosexual relationships, and the community never talked about it.

TM: But why not?

N'ANGA: That is because gay people were regarded as unstable and/or bewitched and/or witches themselves. So, either people did not talk about them because they felt sorry for them, or they were afraid that they may be violent because of the assumed instability, or that they were afraid of being bewitched by these witches. So basically they were left alone. Sometimes, however, the accusation would be a mobilized issue so that in the end the chief of the area would call for a *dare* [court day] and they would be tried and judged.

TM: Were there punishments?

N'ANGA: The judgment would be different according to how many people wanted them to be killed or to pay a fine. For these people to be killed, it would have taken the village elders a long time, going to several traditional healers to find out the truth, but sometimes some traditional healers would refuse to find out because they would not want to be the cause of someone's death.

TM: Were there ever women who might have been lesbians?

N'ANGA: There were women in the village as well who stayed together, especially women who were accused of being witches. I don't really think they would be lesbians as those of today, but some of them were simply considered too ugly to ever find a man to marry them. These women were famous for their knowledge of herbs and curing a lot of ailments so that in the end they were accused of bewitching the people so that they would need to cure them. A lot of the village people used to go to these women at night so that they would not be seen going there seeking help. A lot of people believed that the reason these women and men knew a lot of cures to any ailments was because of bewitchment. The belief also was that these men who were having sex with other men had so much power either to heal or cast an evil spirit on other people.

TM: Does this mean they were feared?

N'ANGA: But I would prefer to say they were well respected in the community because that their power to heal was greater than those traditional healers who were having sex with women. But there were those who were staying on their own, and these were considered to be pure. These people's use in the village would be to brew beer for the spirits to appease them if they were known to be angry with the villagers – for example, when there was a drought or an unnatural event took place like when a goat had a two-legged kid.

In addition, some men and women in the culture were not allowed to get married at all. The reason was that if a man has a female spirit and the spirit who is coming to him had died before she got married or never married, then she would want to have sex with a male through the person she lives in. This also applies to women who lived with other women but who were not traditional healers. The family would want to protect themselves by not offending the male spirit by having the woman he lives in have sex with a female.

TM: It is said that such matters were really taboo.

N'ANGA: Yes, because of the harshness of African culture there are some issues which needed to be talked about so as to understand them better, but in fact they were never discussed. These issues are, for example, *makunakuna* [incest]. People were suffering in silence because there was no way they could report it to the elders without embarrassing the family, and if the issue came out, the elders would blame all the misfortunes of the village to what had happened. They would punish the culprit either by a fine, which usually was a cow and a goat which in those days it was a lot. But mostly they would be driven away from the village forever.

The other silences were homosexuality, sex, and so on. The elders have known about homosexuality for a long time, but because the issue was a total silence, they regarded it as an issue of no concern.

TM: But now it is becoming an issue in the newspapers.

N'ANGA: Yes, but the elders are not denying the fact that this has been in the culture for a long time. The problem now is because the young generation is now bringing it out in the open, which the elders consider to be an embarrassment and degrading to the culture. The other issue is that of the young generation now taking the issue as something you are born with instead of having respect for it culturally. The new generation is trying to change the way the elders have taught themselves to believe about this issue for a long time.

TM: Do you yourself have to deal with cases here in Gokwe?

N'ANGA: Yes, there are some families who are coming to me to try and cure either their daughters or sons of the evil type of spirit. They are going from one traditional healer to the other until they either run out of money or they get tired of trying to cure something that does not have a cure. Some families end up forcing their children to marry a partner of their choice, and for the sake of family peace, the children will go along. But they do so not because they are cured. What happens is that if it's a man who is gay, the brother would sleep with the wife so as to have children, and the community will never know the truth. If it's a woman, then she will be stuck in that marriage for the rest of her life unless she does something that will make the husband divorce her, which usually is adultery.

TM: Are these traditional ways changing?

N'ANGA: Well, because of the homosexual issue coming out, a lot of the older gay and lesbian generation and some of the young ones who are afraid of being victimized are now pretending to be traditional healers with the opposite sex of a spirit medium. Some families have come to me so that I would try to convince them that their offspring has got a spirit medium [rather than a bewitchment]. I have also helped a few young gays and lesbians in that respect so that their families would not keep on pushing them to get married. In fact, I do also have some gays and lesbians that I am teaching to be herbalists so that the society would see that for sure they are traditional healers who cannot get married to the opposite sex. I charge them a fee, because it's different from having a real spirit medium. Still, they will be welcomed in the traditional healers' circle because of their knowledge of herbs, despite their sexual orientation.

Notes

INTRODUCTION

1 Zimbabwe National Archives (ZNA) D3/6/42, case 995 of 22 April 1907.

2 See, for example, GALZ (no date, 2000), Goddard (2004a) as well as other GALZ publications such as *The Avid Queer Reader* and *Galzette* and the newletter of GayZim, www.angelfire.com/zine/gayzim.

3 GALZ (1998, 1999, 2000) press releases that respectively denounce the verdict and Banana's homophobic defence. The case was widely commented upon in the Zimbabwean media.

4 Anonymous, quoted in Weinstock (1996), 40.

5 "Zimbabwe's Mugabe renews attack on 'rotting' Britain's Blair," SAPA-AFP, 20 November 1999, and "Mugabe's New Year Address," SAPA-AFP, 3 January 2000. See also Dunton and Palmberg (1996), Murray (1998), Hoad (1999), and HRW (2003) for analyses of the earlier attacks upon homosexuals set in regional context, and Goddard (2004a) for an insider's perspective.

6 "Homosexuality Okay, Just Don't Flaunt It: Museveni," SAPA-AFP, 15 November 1999; "Ekanjo Is Unfit for Office; Human Rights Group," SAPA-AFP, 2 October 2000; "Homosexuality, Alcoholism Top Govt Enemies – Nujoma," *The Namibian*, 23 April 2001.

7 Jerry Ekandjo, cited by SAPA-AFP, 10 September 1998.

8 The second being Ethiopia, as Johnson (2001, 144) reminds us.

9 Ruling of the Constitutional Court in the case of National Coalition for Gay and Lesbian Equality, unopposed, 9 October 1998. This recent history is the subject of considerable scholarship, discussed in the final chapter. Please also refer to Cameron (1994) and Botha and Cameron (1997) for compelling insider accounts. A South Africa-based website that draws together gays rights activists

and reports on developments from around the continent can be found at www.mask.org.za.

10 "The Prevention and Eradication of Violence against Women and Children, An Addendum to the 1997 Declaration on Gender and Development by SADC," published as Appendix 3 in Kethusegile et al. (2000).

11 This ethnography is discussed below.

12 See, for example, Burton (1885) as mentioned above, plus Ashe (1890) and Cureau (1915) for several of many examples that can be found in all the major imperial languages.

13 See, notably, Vignal (1983), Dunton (1989, 2004), and Desai (2001).

14 See also van Onselen (1982, 187). A contemporary of Nongoloza made similar observations about the effects of labour migration and economic development in French Congo. Interestingly, Adolphe Louis Cureau believed those effects to include perversion among the women left behind (Cureau 1915, 166–7).

15 Here let me point to the work of Paul Zeleza (1997) and the passionate radicalism of Patricia McFadden (1992 and 2000, for example, and as voiced in editorials of the feminist journal SAFERE or her columns on gender issues in the monthly magazine out of Harare, SAPEM).

16 See also Gibson-Graham (1996–97) and Hennessy (1995), whose queer theory draws much of its inspiration from materialist or socialist feminist critiques of capital, themselves ultimately indebted to Antonio Gramsci as much as Foucault (1978). MacLean and Landry (1993) offer a respectful, critical overview of the Marxian credentials of materialist feminism, and Murray (2000) a sweeping, and at times combative, survey of the state of queer theory internationally. This is also discussed in relation to Marxist, Freudian, and feminist theory in Altman (2001) and to subaltern and cultural studies in Arnaldo-Cruz and Manalansan (2002).

17 As Southey (1997a) suggests happened in one notorious case from mid-nineteenth century Orange Free State, and as I myself discovered in the case of a well-remembered video documentary on Swazi traditions (produced by and aired but subsequently taped over or destroyed by the Swaziland Broadcasting Television Corporation). Reid (2002) also notes how even professional archivists have destroyed important documents thought to impugn the memory of the authors.

18 The term "homotextuality" seems to have been coined as far back as Stockinger (1978), according to Bleys (1995, 11–12). Butler (1990), Sedgwick (1990), Wrathall (1992), Erlich (1995), and Sandoval (2002) provide other insightful expositions of this and related concepts in queer epistemology. For a fuller discussion, please see appendix 1.

19 See Boswell (1980), Bérubé (1990), Abelove (1992), Chauncey (1994), Stychin (1998), Blackmore and Hutcheson (1999), and Terry (1999) for a very select sample of this, by now, huge literature.

20 Again, this is a rapidly growing literature of which I will only mention the handful of studies that helped me to view the African material in comparative perspective. See Carrier (1995), Lumsden (1996), Prieur (1998), Parker (1999), and Nanda (1990), as well as chapters in Arnaldo-Cruz and Manalansan (2002). African and Africanist intellectuals who have made the same call include Achmat (1993), McFadden (1992), Zinanga (1996), Nfah-Abbenyi (1997), Amory (1997), and Reddy (2001), the latter addressing queer theory as it may specifically be applied to contemporary South African research and activism. For important discussions of the interrelationship between the African or Oriental sexual Other and the development of gender, race, and class structures in the modern West, refer to Stoler (1995, 2002), McClintock (1995), Hoad (2000), and Hawley (2001).

21 See, in particular, the work of Robert Morrell (1998, 2001a, 2001b), as well as edited collections by Ouzgane (2002) and Miescher and Lindsay (2003).

22 For example, GALZ (2002), Clark (1995), Camara (1997), Brooks and Bocahut (1998), Jara (1998), Achmat and Lewis (1999), Alberton and Reid (2000), Luirink (2000), Johnson (2001), Tilley (2001), Duiker (2001), Ditsie and Newman (no date), and Njinje and Alberton (2002).

23 Anonymous, no date, "Thanks to the efforts of a group of Norwegian researchers ..." Behind the Mask, www.mask.org, accessed 21 January 2001.

CHAPTER ONE

1 Telephone interview by author with Peter Garlake, 12 November 1996.

2 The following draws on pre-colonial histories offered by Beach (1980) and Huffman (1996), as well as regional overviews by Guy (1990) and Davison (1997).

3 Traditional or pre-modern Shona culture is described in rich detail in Holleman (1969), Gelfand (1964, 1965, 1968), Bucher (1980), Bourdillon (1976), Schmidt (1992), Beach (1980, 1994), and Shire (1994). Additionally, oral testimony was gathered from a select number of *n'angas* for the present study as part of a "gay oral history project," samples of which interviews are reproduced in appendix 2. See Kesby (1999) for appropriate cautions about the problematic nature of data around gender and sexuality, and Maxwell (1999) for the use of terms such as "tradition," "custom," and "modernity" (I choose "pre-modern," for example, to allow for continuities from before and into the colonial era. The term "pre-colonial" suggests a much sharper break with the past directly linked to a political

change than was often the case). Let me also reiterate cautions both about extending the ethnographic present into the past and about homogenizing Shona-speakers. The various ethnic groups that came to be known as the Shona in the nineteenth century did not consider themselves a cultural or national entity even when they were more or less unified politically. Bearing these cautions in mind, the commonalities and continuities are nonetheless strong enough to warrant the following generalizations and cognitive history.

4 See Gelfand (1964) or Huffman (1996), for example.

5 The totems themselves are an ancient aspect of Shona political organization, although attributes as recalled in the ethnography could well reflect modern influences (Fortune and Hodza 1974, 70–2; Shire 1994, 156–7).

6 See in particular the accounts of Portuguese travellers reproduced in Theal (1895–1903). Guy (1990) remains a useful description of the process of class formation through the control of women in general southern African terms; Davison (1997) adds nuance through her discussion of gendered symbols of production and ethnicity, while Musisi (1991) gives an analogous history from eastern Africa.

7 Archaeologist Thomas Huffman has conjectured that the ancestors of the Shona had circumcision and "pre-marital training" schools in which the principle of elders' control over young people's sexuality was elevated to ritual (1996, 195–204). In fact, such schools are neither remembered in Shona oral tradition nor noted in early Portuguese documents. It appears that Huffman has extrapolated to the Shona from evidence taken from the neighbouring Venda (see Beach 1998). If these initiation schools ever actually did exist among the Shona, they were moribund by the sixteenth century.

8 What constitutes "regular" or "sufficient" is obviously open to interpretation, but it is worthwhile to note that the frequency of sexual intercourse claimed by male African informants made a deep impression on modern European commentators such as Gelfand (1964, 175) and Symington (1972, 263). My own extremely unscientific enquiry suggests an ideal of sex at least once per day, somewhat like the apple that in North American lore keeps the doctor away.

9 Gelfand (1965), Shire (1994, 151), and for a comparative, historical overview of masculine sexuality in South Africa, Delius and Glaser (2002).

10 Interview, G.M. Chavunduka cited in Phillips (1997a, 476) and Solomon Mutsvairo cited in "Whose Culture Is It?" (*Woman Plus* 1996, 17) – both informants highly respected academic experts on Shona culture, confirmed in oral testimony for the present research. See also Bourdillon (1995), Shire (1994), and Chigweshe (1996).

11 Personal communication with the author, 15 March 1998.

12 Men, it should be noted, could commit adultery with a non-kinswoman without any sanction as long as they informed their wives (and so endured whatever

shaming and verbal abuse that might entail). It was an infraction only when the man kept his adultery secret, thereby offending the ancestors and threatening the health of his children.

13 Sekuru Muyambo (*n'anga*) interviewed by S. Bruce and Epprecht, Odzi, 10 March 1998. See also Schmidt (1997).

14 Mbuya Chikwizi interviewed in Mutare by W. Zimunya, February 1998; *N'anga* (anonymity requested) interviewed in Gokwe by T. Machida, February 1998. The one major ethnographic study of the plateau Tonga of Zambia (closely related to Zimbabwe's third-largest ethnic group, the valley Tonga) mentions a similar phlegmatic acceptance of mixed gender identity presumably linked to a physiological condition (Colson 1958, 139–40).

15 Zimbabwe National Archives, D3/5/74, case 3838A of 10 January 1927 (Rex v. Nomxadana alias Maggie).

16 Rex v. Jenwa, D3/10/2, case 149 of 1921. See also Posselt (1935, 59). For a comparative case among the Xhosa and other Bantu-speakers along the frontiers of Cape Colony, see Cape Colony (1883) and MacLean (1906, 62). The magistrate Mr Brownlee testified in the latter that the fine for "sodomy" among the "Kaffirs" was five to ten cattle.

17 Mr Makoni, interviewed in Chigweshe (1996, 45).

18 *N'anga* interviewed by T. Machida, Gokwe, February 1998. Possession by a male *shave* spirit in fact was one of the most common types of possession for unhappy or neglected wives, who typically behaved as men (including performing lewd men's dances in public) until appeased by food and proper attention.

19 "Baba Itai," interviewed by author, Magamba village, Wedza district, 8 December 1996.

20 Bullock (1912, 42) refers to this, or a variant of it, as a "temporary husband" (*ku puwa munhu*) with the initiative coming from the wife.

21 To the shock and disgust of Shona purists – see GALZ (2002).

22 Rex vs. Mashumba, 311, of 1 December 1923 (ZNA D3/37/8).

23 Suzie Bruce, interviewed by Epprecht, Odzi, 8 December 1997; see also Epprecht 1998b.

24 Bucher (1980, 32), citing Michael Bourdillon's doctoral dissertation. See also Latham (1972) and, for an example of the same ritual among the Swazi, Kuper (1947, 203).

25 According to an anonymous Portuguese document, c. 1794, cited by Beach (1994, 154), confirmed to me by A. Runganga, personal communication, 28 March 1999, and by oral informants in Maxwell (1999, 232).

26 *Gogo* Nguni (pseudonym requested), interviewed by Epprecht and T. Machida, Epworth, 19 June 1997. "*Gogo*" means "grandmother" in Shona and Ndebele, and this young male *n'anga* personified the point in his demeanour. For a

comparative perspective, see the interviews of Zulu and Sotho traditional healers that are being conducted for the Sangoma Project of the Gay and Lesbian Archives of South Africa; also Njinje and Alberton (2002).

27 Mr Nyabonda, interviewed by Nyaradzo Dzobo, Goto village, February 1998. In the interview Mr Nyabonda called the spirit a *tokolosh*, an imported South African term now often used by Shona-speakers in a generic (and technically incorrect) sense. I have edited the transcript here to correct his anachronism in line with Gelfand (1964) and Bourdillon (1976).

28 ZNA, Archives of Oral History (AOH) 40. Interview of Gariwa Chigwedere and Gariwa Chigwedere, Dawson Munjeri, the interviewer in Chihota TTL, 5 May 1978, 29–30 of the English transcript; AOH 3, interview with Chief Willie Samuriwo and Isaac S., Chihota TTL by Dawson Munjeri, 10 February 1979, 45.

29 Posselt (1935, 198); Mr Nyabonda, Goto village, interviewed by Nyaradzo Dzobo, February 1998; personal communication, A. Runganga.

30 Kirby (1942, 349); also noted (as a dying custom in the 1930s) by Esterman (1976, 197).

31 Purchas (1625, 587, 590); and Burton (1885, 246–7) referring to a 1558 Portuguese witness. These and other early accounts are discussed in Murray and Roscoe (1998, 146–8).

32 See, for example, Matory (1992) on the Yoruba, Thornton (1991) on the Matamba state, and Reid (1999) on Buganda.

33 Beach (1980, 106), citing Portuguese accounts from 1516–18, 1631–39, and 1696.

34 The consensus among anthropologists who have studied this and similar woman-woman relationships elsewhere in Africa is that the queen or female husband remained celibate and that there was no homoerotic element to such marriages. As Carrier and Murray have pointed out, however, the denial of any sexual connotation to woman-woman marriage is mostly "not based on actual inquiries with or observations of the individuals involved" (1998, 262). It is, rather, an assertion. In the absence of actual evidence, and bearing in mind the undefined nature of the sex so denied, we are probably on safer grounds to accept Herskovits's entirely reasonable musing that such a relationship might have been used by some women to gain sexual satisfaction ([1938] 1967, vol. I, 319–20). We cannot know for certain, but it is worth noting that this is certainly the belief among black Zimbabwean lesbians today.

35 Interviews in Wedza and Buhera districts by Nyaradzo Dzobo, February 1998. See also Chigweshe (1996, 45).

36 Isaacman (1975), but see also Elbl (1996) on official and Vatican anxieties about the heterosexual misbehaviour of Portuguese travellers in Africa in the fifteenth to eighteenth centuries.

37 See Golan (1990, 103) and oral testimony reproduced in Webb and Wright (1982, 1986, 2001). As to whether these innovations and the cruelties that ensued were the result of Shaka's "latent homosexuality" or humiliatingly small penis, as several European authors have postulated – notably Bryant (1929, 62) – that may of course have some truth in it and so warrants proper research. For now, however, the evidence provided is so poor that it merely underscores the power of homophobic/heterosexist assumptions in the dominant discourse. I discuss below how this "legend" (sic) was put to polemical use by a leading African nationalist historian in the mid-1970s (Mazrui 1975).

38 Wallis (1945, vol. 1, 69). On modern interpretations of Ndebele warrior masculinity, see Shire (1994) and Lindgren (2002).

39 I do want to be careful with this claim, particularly as, noted above, it has been made about Shaka in conjunction with very dubious Freudian analysis and without documentation of sources (indeed, in contradiction to the voluminous and otherwise often sexually explicit evidence presented in the James Stuart archives, possible exception, Webb and Wright 2001, 69). Nonetheless, oral evidence tentatively offers it as well (Dube 2000; Romeo Tshuma, who conducted interviews with elderly *izisangoma* in Matabeleland, interviewed by author, 12 December 2000; and interviews reproduced in appendix 2 below). Research from Swaziland, another warrior state based on the Zulu model, also claims this tradition ("Dhlomo," interviewed by the author, 15 July 2002). Although far away, there are striking parallels with the militaristic Azande famously observed by Evans-Pritchard (1970) but also described earlier by Martin (1913, 164). The only documentary source that comes close to this topic in Zimbabwe that I have been able to find is Bullock (1950, 254–5). Bullock is coy but does not rule out the possibility when he describes sodomy among the Ndebele as "not prevalent," whatever that means. Its existence is explained in terms of lack of heterosexual opportunity by the warriors rather than out of active choice or strategy. Bullock, it should be noted, was a fluent speaker of siNdebele and an assistant magistrate in Belingwe, Matabeleland, in the 1920s. As for the Ngoni or Shangaans, the main ethnographer of the Tsonga (that is, the people of southern Mozambique colonized by – and often conflated with – the Shangaans after their migration from Zimbabwe) does not consider this militaristic past. He does, however, strongly implicate the Shangaans for spreading homosexuality at the South African mines (see next chapter).

40 In addition to Moffat (Wallis 1945, *passim*) see the Livingstones' (1865) observations on the neighbouring and similarly "Nguni-ized" Kololo (latterly the BaRotse or Balozi).

41 Sekuru H. interviewed by N. Dzobo at Madya village, February 1998.

42 Father F.J. Richartz, "Report about the Character and Customs of the Mashonas in Connection with the Rising in 1896," cited in Schmidt (1992, 101).

CHAPTER TWO

1 Notably, Falk ([1926] 1998) and Schapera (1963, 242–3).

2 Genealogical Society of South Africa, extracts from the précis of the archives of the Cape of Good Hope Journal, 1652–1732: "No name or surname. Died 13–05–1728. Two slaves to be drowned for sodomy."

3 Cape Archives (KAB), Graaff-Reinet 1/2/1/8, case 13 of 1831, and Swellendam 1/2/1/48, case 8 of 1852.

4 Natal Archives (NAB), AGO 1/1/31, case 58 of 20 February 1868.

5 KAB, GH 23/31 #135, Henry Barkly to the Earl of Kimberly, 28 November 1871. With respect to the Afrikaner republics that had been established beyond British jurisdiction, this is another research project. It appears that the death penalty for sodomy remained on the books but may have been de facto in abeyance, at least in the case of the Orange Free State circa 1860s (Southey 1997a, 57).

6 See, for example, Cape Colony (1873) for the Basotho, Cape of Good Hope (1883) for various, MacLean (1906) for the Xhosa, Junod ([1916] 1962) for the Shangaan, and Webb and Wright (1982, 1986) for the Zulu. We need, of course, to be highly cautious with these early, amateurish, moralistic ethnographies. More modern professional anthropologies, however, confirm many of the essentials, as well as documenting parallels in other cultures – Krige (1974) for the Lovedu, Kuper (1947) for the Swazi, Ashton (1952) for the Basotho, Ngubane (1977) for the Zulu, and Huffman (1996) for the Venda, for example. With all due respect to the notion of diversity in African cultures, there are strong parallels arising from historical links between these societies and the Shona and Ndebele. The ancestors of the Shona probably came from what is now the Northern Province of South Africa; the Venda and Lovedu were southbound offshoots of Shona-speaking Karanga or Rovzi, and the Ndebele were a mix of Zulu, Sotho, and other South African ethnic groups who migrated into Zimbabwe in fairly recent times. All shared fundamentally the same cattle- and agriculture-based political economy.

7 NAB, AGO 1/1/70, case 12 of 20 February 1880. These were, it should be noted, youths of an estimated thirteen and sixteen years respectively. See Niehaus (2002, 82) and Campbell (2003) on how similar beliefs linger today among South African mineworkers.

8 Cape Colony (1883), appendix D, Wm. Girdwood, reply to Question 17 of Circular 2.

9 NAB, "Sodomy by Udelela, Native, 16 February, 1860," the complainant in this case unspecified. It may be that earlier cases happened but were destroyed by a fire that consumed a large part of the Natal government archives in 1890.

10 NAB, I/BLR 8 P64/1887, "Crimes of Rape and Indecent Assault committed by Natives – Cause and Means of Suppression" (11 December 1886, my emphasis).

11 *Natal Advertiser,* 8 December 1886. This was the only such public allegation, which needs to be understood in the context of the "moral panic" about black men and white women that was then taking place in Natal.

12 Two cases from Kimberly, for example, can be found in NAB, I/I/I/15, case 447 of 17 July 1886, and I/I/I/67, indecent assault against Walter Cowen, 24 February 1898.

13 NAB, AGO I/I/31, case 58 of 20 February 1868; NAB, I/I/I/46, case 368 of 16 November 1892.

14 NAB, AGO I/I/101, case 107–111 of 12 September 1885.

15 For the record, the first case of sodomy or male-male indecent assault by an African living in Kimberly did not occur until 1887 (NAB, I/I/I/21, case 498 of 9 September 1887, attempted sodomy by Umpyonga upon Jan Zulu).

16 Dr Percy Stubbs, testifying in the trial of Daniel Apon (NAB, I/I/I/103, 25 May 1921); and Coplan (1994, 68).

17 Transvaal Archives (TAB), Ampt. Pubs. 6/36 UG 44/1913. *Director of Prisons Report for 1912,* 238, my emphasis. See Achmat (1993) for a trenchant critique of van Onselen's (1984) treatment of Nongoloza's testimony. It should also be noted that Nongoloza was not mentioned by any of the witnesses to the 1907 enquiry into "unnatural vice," which could corroborate his protestations of innocence in that regard.

18 Confidential Enquiry into Alleged Prevalence of Unnatural Vice among Natives Employed in Mines on the Witswatersrand [henceforth Leary-Taberer 1907], transcripts of testimony, 18 January, 12, 25 January, 2 and 29 January, 6, TAB, NTS 10203 I/422.

19 Some romantic possibilities do crop up in the criminal court and inquest records that might be worth further pursuit. Of the five or six possible candidates for *Ishe* Socks who appear in the inquests of African men who died at the mines in the Johannesburg area during the period 1902–07, my best guess would be Sokies (LD 814, AC 4123/04). This Sokies died of a fractured spine after falling (allegedly pushed) from a cyanide vat at New Primrose Gold Mine in October 1904. As in most inquests of African men from this period, no other details were given.

20 "Saunyana," interviewed by Nyaradzo Dzobo, Goto village, Hwedza, February 1998; see also "Philip," interviewed by Sibuyi (1993, 58).

21 TAB, SNA 46, 1540/02, Secretary of Native Affairs, 5 August 1902.

22 TAB, SNA 46, 1540/02, 28 July 1902.

23 TAB, SNA 46, 1540/02, 1 August 1902.

24 T.E. Mavrogordate, CID Johannesburg, C17, vol. 5, South Africa Native Affairs Commission (1904–05), 867.

25 Harries (1994, 191, 182). Further declines in real wages continued until 1912, although improvements in sanitation, food, and housing conditions partially compensated for the deterioration in earnings.

26 On these accusations and the subsequent Bucknill enquiry, see TAB (Pretoria), GOV 210, 52/06, min. #147/96; LD 1361 20, AG 5138/06. On the Chinese labour controversy in general, see Richardson (1982).

27 TAB, GOV 210, 52/06, min #147/96, memo from Governor-General Lord Selbourne to Earl of Elgin, Colonial Office, London, 1 October 1906.

28 TAB, NTS 10203 1/422, A.W. Baker (director of the South African Compounds and Interior Mission) to Lord Selbourne.

29 Harries (1990a, 323). In Work, Culture and Identity (1994, 114) he cites a census that puts the ratio of African women to men aged twenty-five to thirty-nine at 1:98.

30 See Ndatshe (1993), Sibuyi (1993), and Coplan (1994).

31 Leary-Taberer (1907), 21 January, 2. See also the interview of Tsonga ex-miner "Philemon" by Sibuyi (1993), who emphasizes the logic of avoiding fights with other African men in the townships.

32 These have been exhaustively studied – see, notably, van Onselen (1982), Pape (1990), McCulloch (2000), and Martens (2001).

33 TAB, GNLB 229, 583/15/145, "Unnatural Vice."

34 See especially the testimony of the Shangaan "Fifteen" (29 January, 2), as well as Sylvester MacKenzie, compound manager at Robinson Mine. MacKenzie had lived in Mozambique in the late 1890s and claimed fluency in "the language" (25 January, 10).

35 TAB, GOV 210, 52/06, circular of 13 September 1906.

36 For example, Mr Bradbury, 25 January, 4–5, and Mr G.A. Turner, 28 January, 3.

37 Compare F. Edmeston's full, radical recommendations (15 February 1916) with the confidential summary (GNLB 229 583/15/D145).

38 Sibuya (1993, 56). See also "P," as recorded in Epprecht (2002), which I discuss together with the Hlohoangwane interview in chapter 7. Admittedly these are contemporary sources, but they are so *not* modern (that is, homophobic) in tone that they suggest attitudes that are rooted far in time and culture.

39 ZNA D3/6/42, case 995 of 22 April 1907.

40 Leary-Taberer (23 January, 9). Note that the usual compensation for thigh sex only was £1 or less.

41 C17, vol. 5, South Africa Native Affairs Commission (1904–05), 867.

42 Johannesburg Central, TAB, GNLB 229 583/15/D145.

43 TAB, NTS 10203 1/422, G. Lagden to Lord Selbourne, 7 February 1907.

44 TAB, NTS 10203 1/422.

45 TAB, NTS 2091, 213/280.

46 Report of a conference between representatives of the Union government, Transvaal Chamber of Mines, Transkeian and Pondoland General councils, Johannesburg, 30 November 1928 (NTS 2091, 213/280). See also Pondoland General Council Session 1930, Resolution No. 33: Prevention of Evil Practices at the Mines (NTS 10203 1/422). This, it should be noted, was at the height of the popularity and power of Mpondo *isitshozi* gangs, renowned, like the mostly Zulu Ninevites, for their homosexual preferences (Breckenridge 1990).

47 Chairman Major H.S. Cooke, director of Native Labour, NTS 2091, 213/280.

48 Laubscher (1937, 283); interviews by N. Dzobo of various men and women in Hwedza and Buhera districts, February/March 1998.

49 "Sekuru J," interviewed by Nyaradzo Dzobo, Rundu village, Sengezi resettlement, February 1998.

CHAPTER THREE

1 See Kocheski et al. among other chapters in Hensley (2002) for analysis of the literature on prison and situational homosexuality.

2 Ivy Ncube, "Former Convict Shylet Tells of Vices and Horrors of Life inside Chikurubi Prison," *Harare Herald,* 7 January 2000. This story also found its way, with photos of the comely Shylet, into the monthly magazine *Parade.* Other depictions of degrading and degraded male prison sex in South Africa can be found in Lanham and Mopeli-Paulus (1953), Kente [1963] (1992), and Moloi (1987).

3 The Hon. Sipho Mzimela, quoted in Achmat (1995, 1).

4 Frank Meki, quoted in Ncube (2000).

5 Koscheki et al. (2002), for example, discusses data on U.S. inmates who had had homosexual experiences prior to their incarceration, or who identified as homosexual and bisexual. Among males, bisexuality averages around 21 per cent of the survey samples, that is, significantly above the rates estimated in the general population. Among females, rates of pre-incarceration homosexual experience were even higher – double, triple, or even quadruple the rates of "girl stuff"/lesbianism that occurs in the general, non-prison population.

6 Farai Mutsaka, "Severe Hunger Stalks Prisons," *Harare Daily News*, 7 August 2003.

7 KAB, GH 1/336 #166, Earl of Kimberly to Henry Barkly, 7 October 1872.

8 KAB, Supreme Court, 1/1/1/29, #7 of November 1881.

9 KAB, AG 1813 14445, 14 February 1908.

10 KAB, AG 1813 14445, 9 March 1908.

11 TAB, LD 1569 AG 399/08, Minister of Native Affairs to Bishop of Pretoria and Superintendent of the Swiss Mission, 5 February 1908.

12 Union of South Africa, *Director of Prisons Report for 1912*, 236. TAB, Ampt. Pubs. 6/36 UG 44/1913, discussed in van Onselen (1984) and Achmat (1993).

13 Ibid.

14 Ibid. and van Onselen (1984).

15 This and all subsequent quotations pertaining to the Apon and Stout case are taken from the same court docket, KAB, 1/1/1/103, 25 May 1921.

16 This and all subsequent quotations pertaining to the Dhlamini case are taken from same file, NAB, JUS 1223 1/94/30.

17 Director of Prisons, Charles I. Pienaar, to Convict Prison-Point, Durban, 11 March 1930. NAB, JUS 1223 1/94/30.

18 Magistrate, Convict Prison-Point, Durban, to the Director of Prisons, 3 April 1930, NAB, JUS 1223 1/94/30.

19 Manalil Gandhi, letter to the editor, *Drum*, February 1954; and A.S. Mopeli-Paulus's memoirs as serialized in *Drum* in 1954–55, discussed in Clowes (2002).

20 Sekuru "G," interviewed by Nyaradzo Dzobo, Goto village, Hwedza, February 1998.

21 Ibid.

22 Sekuru "Saunyana," interviewed by Nyaradzo Dzobo, Goto village, Hwedza, February 1998.

23 NAB, GG 51, 1805/8711, Native High Court of Natal, Rex v. Dhlamini 25 September 1929.

24 "Saunyana," interviewed by Nyaradzo Dzobo, Goto village, Hwedza, February 1998.

25 Chetty (1994, 131). Interestingly, from the one published photograph we have of Williams, she/he was clearly not unattractive by conventional definitions of feminine beauty. This may partially account for her need to perform her masculinity through actual violence rather than simply by attire and demeanour.

26 See, notably, Coplan (1994) and the contrast drawn by Mopeli-Paulus's portrayal of mine hostel/township versus prison sex.

27 Union of South Africa, *Director of Prisons Report for 1912*, 238. TAB, Ampt. Pubs. 6/36 UG 44/1913.

28 Former inmates aged thirty-four and thirty-nine, interviewed by N. Dzobo at Madya village, Buhera, Zimbabwe, February 1998.

CHAPTER FOUR

1 Rotberg (1988, 404, 408, 680). These claims are based, it appears, primarily on Robert Blake's consideration (and dismissal) of undocumented speculation (1977, 36). See also Lane (1995) on the cult of imperial masculinity.

2 Criminal registers of Salisbury and Umtali, ZNA, D4/3/1 and D4/7/1. Please note that the accuracy of these tribal designations must be taken with a large grain

of salt. Moreover, "Matabele" and "MaShona" tended to be more narrowly defined in the period under discussion than at present. In accordance with contemporary practice, I lump together their many constituent "tribes" (Ndebele including Kalanga, "indigenous" Basotho, Venda, Mnyai as well as Matabele proper, and Shona principally including Zezuru, Korekore, Manyika, Karanga, and Ndau). "Zambesi," by contrast, tended to be a rather careless, generic term for anyone from the river valley, including Tonga, Chikunda, Sena, or Shona offshoots like the Goma of Zambia.

3 In addition to the Noble case, which is discussed below, the other cases of European men allegedly assaulting Africans are 1396 of 13 December 1896 (D4/1/2), 794 of 19 July 1907 (D3/5/18), 1221 of 1908 (D3/5/21), 1453 of 19 November 1908 (D3/5/22), 1517 of 29 September 1911 (D3/5/28), 2471 of 4 July 1927 (D3/5/77), 3537 of 1936 (S1679 High Court), no case number, June 1912 (D3/2/6), 319 of 11 August 1922 (D3/39/6), 358 of 14 June 1913 (D3/7/27), 725 of 23 October 1916 (D3/7/35), 5 of 15 January 1909 (D3/15/1), 116 of 7 April 1908 (D3/15/1), 537 of 3 September 1912 (D3/18/2), 798 of 12 November 1912 (D3/18/3 777), 449 of 1 June 1914 (D3/18/5), 240 of 1909 (D3/21/2), 10 March 1910 (D3/21/3), 15 of 29 January 1929 (D3/1/56), 643 of 21 December 1926 (D3/2/26), 436 of 8 May 1929 (D3/18/37), 740 of 18 May 1924 (D3/20/14), 469 of 18 June 1900 (D3/6/17), 147 of 14 February 1902 (D3/6/22), 1109 of 2 September 1910 (D3/6/56), 3696 of 14 November 1923 (D3/6/119).

4 For these singular cases, see respectively, D3/6/79, case 2283 of 13 October 1915, and D3/6/114, case 3187 of 17 October 1922 (Abdul Karim of Bulawayo, described as "Indian"); D3/1/56, case 15 of 29 January 1929, and D3/18/3, case 436 of 8 May 1929 (James McKeand Battersby, a commercial traveller from England), and D3/21/2, case 240 of 1909 and D3/15/1, case 116 of 7 April 1908 (Raphael Gabriel Benatar, a "Turkish Jew").

5 D3/6/161, case 5094 of 2 December 1929, discussed below.

6 See the trial of British South African Police officer Edgar Baker for indecent assault in 1908, for example (D3/5/21, case 1221 of 1908).

7 See appendix 1 for a discussion of court language and the biases it imparts.

8 D3/39/6, case 319 of 11 August 1922. MacNair protested to the court that he did not in fact know the meaning of the word *nkotshana* and that the allegations were a set-up. The magistrate ultimately concurred, principally, it seems, on the evidence that Ranganai's anus "gaped considerably."

9 Harry Weincier, D3/32/34, case 347 of 5 March 1928. The court made certain to qualify Mr Weincier's whiteness, perhaps further to downplay the potential influence. He was, the record insists, a "British Jew."

10 D3/35/1 (Sipolilo Lomagundi district), case 7 of 1921.

11 See, for example, D3/5/21, case 942 of 30 June 1908, and D3/21/2, case 132 of 25 April 1908.

12 D3/5/60, case 3060 of 21 September 1923.

13 D3/5/84, case 2163 of 22 May 1928.

14 D3/1/3, case 47 of 7 July 1899, involving a certain "Villem," described only as "indigenous," in the service of a European shopkeeper.

15 RG 3/BRI 41, Southern Rhodesia, *Annual Report of the British South Africa Police*, 1947–8 and 1949, pp. 35 and 25 respectively.

16 D3/39/6, case 319 of 11 August 1922.

17 D3/6/22, case 147 of 14 February 1902 (Bulawayo). A similar accusation, similarly dismissed for lack of evidence, can be found at D3/5/77, case 2471 of 4 July 1927.

18 D3/18/37, case 436 of 8 May 1929 (Gatooma).

19 D3/21/1, case 36/656 of 5 Janary 1904.

20 D3/5/28, case 1517 of 29 September 1911.

21 D3/7/9, case 696 of 12 January 1903 (Umtali).

22 D3/21/3, 10 March 1910 (Hartley), D3/6/37, 22 February 1906, case 465 of 1906 (Bulawayo).

23 D3/6/55, case 15 of 1910, D3/18/3, case 778 of 14 November 1912, D3/2/15, 30 April 1918.

24 See, for example, the fairly clear-cut case of consensual anal intercourse by Mack upon Majamandi when Mack's wife lived nearby, D3/5/15, case 546 of 1906 (Salisbury), or D3/6/42, case 561 of 1907 (Old Nick Mine, Bulawayo district).

25 D3/21/17 (Hartley, case 383 of 14 September 1916).

26 "Sekuru Tendai," interviewed by Cuthbert Karise, University of Zimbabwe, September 1997.

27 D3/6/85, case 3320 of 12 January 1917.

28 D3/6/42 (testimony of Bisamu, a forty-year old Tonka "boss boy" at Bush Tick Mine, case 995 of 22 April 1907).

29 D3/6/101, case 3433 of 22 December 1919.

30 Ibid.

31 D3/5/93, case 5830 of 30 November 1929. Perhaps not coincidentally, this word derives from chiNyanja.

32 D3/18/3, case 791 of 1912 (Gatooma).

33 D3/6/126, case 4493 of 30 December 1924.

34 "Sekuru D," interviewed by N. Dzobo, Madume village, February 1998.

35 D3/18/6, Rex v. Singane, case 1162 of 1915.

36 D3/37/1, case 34 of 4 February 1910.

37 D3/6/42, case 561 of 12 March 1907.

38 D3/5/22, case 1453 of 19 November 1908.

39 Immorality, Personal, 1917–30, s 1222/1.

40 D3/5/9 case 89 of 19 January 1903.

41 D3/2/7, Rex v. Manswa, 1 April 1913.

42 In D3/27/1, 5 December 1910, for example, Rabvu rejected the normal 5/- "to keep quiet" about thigh sex and attempted to extort first five, then fifteen pounds, from Luizi.

43 See, for example, D3/5/2, case 247 of 9 December 1900 (Salisbury), D3/6/22, case 147 of 14 February 1902 (Bulawayo), D3/7/11, case 349 of 1904 (Umtali), and D3/7/11, case 12 of 16 January 1916 (Sinoia).

44 D3/2/15, case 250 of 12 August 1918. Interestingly, this type of accusation for monetary gain was not restricted to insubordinate youths. A Salisbury magistrate in 1930 found that a Domboshawa woman had falsely accused her employee of homosexually assaulting her son in order to escape paying the man the back wages of 25 pounds that she owed him (D3/5/95, case 248 of 5 May 1930).

45 D3/6/17, case 469 of 18 June 1900.

46 D3/6/25, case 1438 of 30 December 1902 (which refers to an earlier undocumented conviction from Gweru, 8 October 1900), and D3/6/26, case 946 of 26 August 1903.

47 D3/5/60, case 3060 of 21 September 1923 (Salisbury). Simonas was a thirty-five-year-old mattress-maker originally from Northern Rhodesia. The four complainants in this case were all his former employees.

48 D3/5/15 (Salisbury), case 546 of 14 August 1906, D3/7/11 (Umtali), case 349 of 1904; D3/6/63 (Bulawayo), case 731 of 1 April 1912.

49 D3/5/77, case 2522 of 1 September 1927.

50 D3/7/4, case 102 of 27 February 1900.

51 D3/5/6, case 751 of 1901, D3/5/21, case 713 of 1908 – two counts, D3/5/29, cases 394 and 808 of 1912, D3/5/43, case 726 of 1917, and D3/18/9, case 172 of 1917, which also refers to a previous conviction in Umtali in 1913, file destroyed. These cases may, of course, have involved different individuals with coincidentally close names, aliases, and physical descriptions.

52 D3/36/7, case 757 of 11 September 1919.

53 D3/37/8, Rex v. Mashumba, case 311 of 1 November 1923.

54 Ibid.

55 A fuller discussion of this word occurs in chapter 6.

56 D3/5/72, case 1787 of 23 June 1926.

57 Mr Nyabonda, interviewed by N. Dzobo, Goto village, February 1998.

58 "Sekuru D," interviewed by N. Dzobo, Madume village, February 1998. Note that other than a couple of obscure and dubious references to immorality among the Atonga by the profoundly racist Harry Johnston (1897, 408–9), the ethnography from Malawi is silent on this topic. A quick search through criminal

courts files at the national archives in Zomba found them, predictably, also mute on this subject.

59 Scarnecchia (1994, 78, 89); also "Sekuru D," interviewed by N. Dzobo, Madume village, and Mr Nyabonda, Goto village, February 1998.

60 Ranger (1987, 203), citing a report by Charles Bullock.

61 S 138/22, SN Bulawayo to the chief native commissioner, 30 December 1929, and s998, Mangoromera file, 28 June 1933.

62 D3/26/2, case 247, 26 November 1917.

63 D3/15/4, case 353 of 10 October 1918.

64 Testimony of Jonas of Lewanika's of Giant Mine, Hartley (D3/21/1, case 184 of 19 September 1905), and Munalula of Barotseland at Letombo labour camp, Salisbury (D3/5/46, case 2045 of 11 October 1918).

65 D3/31/1, case 155 of 5 September 1923.

66 D3/5/60, case 2015 of 13 June 1923 (Avondale).

67 D3/6/144, 674 of 13 February 1927.

68 D3/7/32, case 409 of 7 June 1915.

69 D3/6/42, case 651 of 20 March 1907.

70 D3/18/3, case 791 of 20 November 1912 (Gatooma).

71 D3/2/7, 1 April 1913.

72 See, for example, D3/37/1, case 164 of 27 October 1911 (Wankie), in which Mzira earned the sympathy of the magistrate. He was "roused to passion" and beat his nursing wife to death because she refused to have sex.

73 D3/37/12, case 42 of 31 January 1926.

74 D3/7/35, case 725 of 23 October 1916.

75 D3/14/5, case 93 of 16 July 1925.

76 D3/24/3, case 224 of 5 July 1921 (Marondellas).

77 D3/18/3, case 777 of 7 November 1912.

78 Tredgold (1904, 71). Even today there remains no clear definition of what precise acts can be considered "sodomy" (Phillips 1999).

79 S 235, response to Circular 65 of 10 December 1934.

80 Ibid.

81 ZNA D3/6/161, case 5094 of 2 December 1929.

82 Bylawayo Chronicle, 8 January 1969, p. 2; Vambe (1949); NAZ RG 3/BRI 41, BSAP Departmental Report of 1972, p. 25.

83 D3/21/10, case 406 of 10 November 1913 (Hartley).

84 D3/18/6, case 1162 of 12 November 1915 (Gatooma).

85 D3/18/19, case 637 of 12 July 1922 (Gatooma).

86 D3/46/10, case 40 of 18 February 1921.

87 D3/14/5, case 93 of 16 July 1925.

88 D3/18/3, case 791 of 20 November 1912 (Gatooma).

89 Hartley Criminal Registers, s546, s1030.

CHAPTER FIVE

1 KAB, 1/1/1/37, case 232 of 23 June 1891.

2 NAB, AGO 1/1/142, case 91 of 3 December 1890.

3 Gay and Lesbian Archives of South Africa, AM 2821, no date; 27 August 1931 and 4 October 1931. Permission to cite these otherwise anonymous letters from the donor, courtesy of Anthony Manion.

4 *Zimbabwean Parliamentary Debates* 22, no. 38 (6 September 1995), 2518. I take this point up again below, but would also like to refer readers to Kendall's eloquent exploration of "what is sex" in a different southern African setting (Kendall 1999).

5 My emphasis, *Zimbabwe Parliamentary Debates* 22, no. 38, 2517.

6 Mbuya Chikwizi, interviewed by Wallace Zimunya, Chipinge district, June 1998, my emphasis. See appendix 2 for the full transcript of this interview.

7 As reportedly used by Public Prosecutor Herbert Ushewokunze Jr, in inciting vigilantism against gays and lesbians in 1996 (Goddard 2003).

8 Jordan (2000, 471). See also Sweet (1996) and Fone (2000). Tellingly, Fone notes how men of colour (presumably African slaves) comprised a significant proportion of those burnt to death for sodomy in Seville (Spain) in the late sixteenth century. Research remains to be done on the Inquisition in Mozambique and on state persecution of same-sex sexuality there in the modern era.

9 ZNA D3/6/143 82, case of 24 January 1927.

10 ZNA D3/5/109, case 4203 of 8 October 1931.

11 von Oppell, circa 1896, "Advice to Parents, Tutors and Young People," *South African Independent.*

12 ZNA D3/6/161 5094, case of 2 December 1929.

13 I am indebted for the following to Achmat (n.d.) and his other research notes for Achmat and Lewis (1999) on file at the Gay and Lesbian Archives of South Africa (GALASA).

14 See, in particular, Terry (1999). A Freudian analysis applied to the South African army in this period can be found in Perk (1948). A dissident, gay-friendly view was first broached in South Africa by Renée Liddicoat in the early 1960s (for example, Liddicoat 1962). Judging from evidence given to the subsequent commission of enquiry into white male homosexuality, this view had made very limited headway among state officials by 1968 (Retief 1994).

15 See, notably, Galgut (1982), Gray (1988), de Waul (1994), Gray (1999), and Dunton (2004). See Jolly (1996) for a discussion of homophobia in South African women's writing.

16 E.T. Campbell, acting mayor of Roodepoort-Maraisburg, 13 August 1906, TAB, GOV 210, 52/06, min. #147/96

17 Major H.S. Cooke, director of Native Labour, TAB, NTS 2091, 213/280, report of a conference between representatives of the Union government, the Transvaal

Chamber of Mines, and the Transkeian and Pondoland General councils, Johannesburg, 30 November 1928.

18 E.T. Campbell, acting mayor of Roodepoort-Maraisburg, 13 August 1906, TAB, GOV 210, 52/06, min. #147/96.

19 Governor to Earl of Elgin, 17 December 1906, TAB, LD 1361 20, AG 5138/06.

20 Immigration Act, chapter 4:02, revised edition, 1996, section 14 (1) (f).

21 ZNA D3/32/34, case 347 of 5 March 1928.

22 Documented through oral interviews conducted by the Aversion Project of GALASA – see www.mask.org.za, and van Zyl et al. (1999).

23 No critical study has yet been done on the construction of "Rhodie" masculinity; however, see GALZ (2002) for dreary memoirs of growing up gay in 1960s Rhodesia, and Godwin (1996) for a rare, self-critical appraisal of heterosexual boyhood in the rural areas. On the period from 1965 to 1980, see Godwin and Hancock (1993) and Shamuyarira's (1966) ruminations on the Rhodesian "cowboy" culture. Bolze and Martin (1978) capture that culture in cartoon form, while Kirkwood (1984) analyzes Rhodesian femininity.

24 Government of Zimbabwe, Immigration Act, chapter 4:02, revised edition, 1996, section 14 (1)(f). As this citation suggests, this clause was not only reiterated in subsequent revisions to the act (1966 and 1979) but was maintained after independence.

25 Roland Hawkins, "They Killed a Man They Didn't Even Know," *Illustrated Life Rhodesia* (week ending 16 May 1973), 6–8.

26 ZNA, RG 3/BRI 41, BSAP, *Departmental Report of 1973*, 17–18.

27 NAB, AGO 1/1/31, case 58 of 20 February 1868.

CHAPTER SIX

1 "A Well Known South African Doctor and University Lecturer" (almost certainly Louis Freed), no date (likely late 1940s or 1950s), "Light on the Sex Life of the Bantu People," unpublished speech or article, Gay and Lesbian Archives of South Africa.

2 Sekuru Chiwoyo, interviewed in Runganga and Aggleton (1998, 74).

3 The case of the man is also highly unusual in that it involved an accusation of attempted fellatio (D3/6/22, case 147 of 14 February 1902).

4 See, for example, Summers (1999), as well as Jeater (1993) and McCulloch (2000), and for an empirical study of the same of black South Africans in the police force, Shear (2003).

5 My translation. Hannan (1983, 332) translates it as "Latrine cleaner. Scavenger." However, given that the chiNyanja root *nyere/nyole* "cannot be used without offence, employed also in swearing" (Scott 1892, 486), this seems unduly delicate.

6 See Schmidt (1992), Barnes (1997, 1999), Barnes and Win (1992), and Jeater (1993) for this process in colonial Zimbabwe, which I also discuss in colonial Lesotho (Epprecht 2000). Sexual tensions and conflicts around gender identity among the respectable Christian middle class are movingly treated in literary form as well. See, notably, Dangarembga (1989), whose title is a direct allusion to the work of Frantz Fanon ("nervous conditions" meaning psychological alienation under colonial rule).

7 Vambe terms them "little better than vermin" (1972, 247). See also Barnes (1999). In Sesotho, to give another example of the close association of urbanization and commodified sex, the expression *o ile campong* (literally, "she has gone to town") meant "she had gone to prostitute herself." Numerous studies from South Africa attest to analogous tensions exacerbating male violence against women. See in particular Campbell (1992) and Mager (1999).

8 NAB, AGO 1/1/312, case 7 of 19 January 1907.

9 TAB, GNLB 374, 110/28/110, including minutes of the TTGC session of 4 May 1928.

10 *Moruti* means teacher or missionary. The authors' ambivalence is further underscored by the way Monare is portrayed as being under the influence of marijuana when these lustful feelings (apparently consummated, p. 141) affected him. His eventual rebirth as a "man among men" happens as a result of his son's love and the "white man's medicine" (144).

11 *Drum*, April 1956. See Chetty's analysis of this and a similar exposé in the *Golden City Post* (Chetty 1994).

12 GALASA, *After Nines!* Collection, AM 2894.

13 Ibid. *After Nines!* is a contemporary theatrical production with both entertainment and didactic goals. While the research was done professionally, we may rightly suspect some nostalgia in its critique of modern homophobia. The central image of the play is certainly provocative: the spirits of dead gays and lesbians from the 1930s–'50s return to help heal families in the present that are riven by homophobia – a modern ailment. The title of the play comes from one of the spirits' songs: "Even when it was a crime / Everyone did it all the time / but only after nine."

14 *Drum*, February 1954, 25, discussed in Clowes (2002, 114). The author of this letter was almost certainly Dr Louis Freed, who published elsewhere under the title "distinguished South African Doctor and University Lecturer" and cultivated a reputation as a Freudianist on African sexuality.

15 Mutongi (2000, 19). See also Dunton (1989) for a pan-African perspective of African nationalist ambivalence toward alternative sexualities.

16 "Slashing Attack on Coloured Coons: Moffies Also Deplored," *Cape Standard*, 9 January 1940, p. 3.

17 *Cape Standard*, 30 January 1940.

18 Schmidt (1992), Barnes (1999), and Jackson (2002) in particular.

19 Sithole (1968, 158). Didymus Mutasa also invokes the penis in the struggle: "The white man's civilization will end when too many blacks want to urinate in the same place as the white man" (1974, 102).

20 "Kuzwishora," *African Weekly* 3, no. 18 (2 October 1946): 2. This reference and translation are courtesy of Guy Thompson.

21 Commission of Enquiry into Native Strike, Report, September 1948 (ZNA, S 482/114/8/48).

22 Sithole (1970, 144–5). See also Joshua Nkomo as remembered by informants in Weinrich (1976, 192, 199).

23 This incident is discussed in Barnes (1999); Scarnecchia (1994, 1996), and Raftopoulus (1995). See also nationalist apologia by Nathan Shamuyarira (1966, 43), Enoch Dumbutshena (1975, 45), and Joshua Nkomo (1984, 70).

24 West (1990, 130) cites a government circular to that effect: "Sexual knowledge, in short, should be kept strictly beyond the reach of Africans," out of fear that they might use it to perverse end.

25 Cited by Kriger (1992, 192).

26 Unpublished memo from the ZANU-PF archives, Harare, cited by Lyons (2002, 315–6).

27 Cited by Bhebe and Ranger (1995, 10).

28 On African-American Afrocentricity, see Asante's (1980, 64–5) explication of how homosexuality among blacks undermines the struggle against racism.

29 Kriger (1992, 193–5), Kesby (1996). See also Veit-Wild (1993), Schmidt (1997), and Alexander et al. (2000) for an entry into the growing body of scholarship and literature that raises questions about the social conflicts generated by the liberation struggle.

30 ZNA, RG 3/BRI 41, British South Africa Police, Departmental Report of 1965 (Salisbury 1966, 25). Rapes in the rural areas associated with the bush war would not, for the most part, appear in the BSAP statistics.

31 See *House of Hunger* (1978) in particular, as well as Ibrahim's analysis (1990).

32 The destabilization of masculinist nationalist myths is the subject of much current scholarship and debate in the popular media. In addition to the works cited in notes 29 and 31 above, see Staunton (1990), Barnes (1995), Hotz (1990), Kanengoni (1987, 1997), Sibanyoni (1995), and Nhongo-Simbanegavi (2000). The theme is also treated cinematically by Sinclair (1996). Two studies from South Africa that make suggestive comparisons about the crisis in African masculinity arising from the anti-apartheid struggle are Xaba (2001) and Niehaus (2000).

33 "Sekuru Manyame," interviewed by author, translated by Suzie Bruce, Odzi, 12 February 1998.

34 *Harare Sunday Mail Magazine*, 29 May 1983.

35 *Harare Sunday Mail*, 13 March 1983.

36 "200 at Gay Wedding," *Harare Herald*, 13 April 1986.

37 The anti-"prostitute" campaign is discussed – and linked to a culture of misogyny – in Zimbabwe Women's Action Group with Rudo Gaidzanwa (1987) and in Jackson (1993).

38 According to the testimony of ex-senior assistant commissioner of the police, John Chadamana, as reported in the *Harare Herald*, 25 February 1997.

39 *Harare Herald*, 16 June 1998.

40 This type of incident has been reported regularly in the daily press and is discussed along with other aspects of male violence against women in Armstrong (1997) and the Zimbabwe Women's Resource Centre and Network (1997). The number of rapes reported nationwide in the first six months of 1997 was 1,770 – that is, approximately four times the rate as at the eve of independence. Anecdotally, as well, the traditional "joking" relationship between a brother-in-law and his unmarried sisters-in-law has become sexualized to a degree that has led to widespread fears of increasing frequency of incest.

41 A parallel development can be seen in the case of Winnie Mandela in South Africa, who garnered enormous popularity among black women during her 1991 trial for assault and kidnapping by characterizing herself as a defender of African motherhood against the homosexualization of African boys (Holmes 1994).

42 As the headline put it, *Harare Daily Gazette*, 24 January 1994. Dabengwa subsequently claimed to GALZ representatives that he had been misquoted (Goddard 2004a).

43 *Harare Herald*, 11 January 1995; *Harare Sunday Mail*, 22 January 1995. The latter, without a scintilla of irony, quoted a European Catholic priest as an expert on African culture.

44 *Bulawayo Chronicle*, 3 February 1995.

45 Lewis Machipisa, "Zimbabwean Homosexuals Observe the UN Human Rights Anniversary," *Interpress Service*, 10 December 1998.

46 *Harare Herald*, 27 February 1997.

47 "Leonard Chaza," "It's a Gay Thing!" *Mahogony* (July/August 1995): 8–9; personal communication.

48 See, for example, Z. Chibanda, "Gays and Lesbians Are Atoms of Chaos Unleashed on Earth," *Harare Sunday Mail*, 4 August 1996, or the weekly homophobic and anti-feminist diatribes of North Carolina-based Ken Mufuka.

49 "Banana Breaks Silence," *Zimbabwe Independent*, 20–26 June 1997. See GALZ's measured response to his subsequent homophobic statements, 25 January 2000. Open letter from GALZ to Rev. Canaan Sodindo Banana.

50 *Harare Herald*, 25 July 1996

51 Basildon Peta, "Mugabe Goes on Gay Bashing Safari," *Star Foreign Service and The Independent* (online), 14 March 2000.

52 Peter Osborne, citing allegations made against Ncube in the *Bulawayo Chronicle*, "British Churchmen Back Mugabe," *Spectator*, 24 May 2003.

53 Basildon Peta, "Mugabe Anti-Gay Policy Brings Down Trusted Ally," Johannesburg *Mail and Guardian*, 4 April 2002. "Under the Cloak of Marriage," statement from the Gays and Lesbians of Zimbabwe (GALZ) regarding the case of chief executive of the ZBC, Alum Mpofu, 4 April 2002.

54 "Zimbabwe Struck by New Reign of Terror," *Guardian*, 28 March 2002

55 Geoff Hill and Peter Conradi, "Savage Beatings for Mugabe Opponents," *Sunday Times*, 30 March 2003.

CHAPTER SEVEN

1 Zimbabwe, *Zimbabwean Parliamentary Debates* 22, no. 2 (28 September 1995), 2781.

2 Union of South Africa (1932, 214), which compares an infection rate of between 25 and 30 per cent of all mine recruits from Basutoland to only 2 per cent among Xhosa men.

3 The following draws principally upon my own earlier research on the history of women and gender in Lesotho (Epprecht 2000), as well as the anthropological work of Ashton (1952), David Coplan (1994, 2001) and the unpublished, remarkably frank interviews of Basotho elders about Sesotho customs conducted in the 1960s (Ellenberger 1994).

4 An Nguni informant, cited in Longmore (1959, 40–1). See also Maloka (1995, 1997) on Basotho women in South Africa.

5 I say virtual because a German anthropologist at the time hinted at male debauchery among adolescent Basotho using the word *buben*, which could, in the German of the period, suggest mutual masturbation (Grützer 1877, 78). No other allusion to such behaviour appears again, however, including where one might expect it in the harshly anti-Sesotho propaganda by Christian missionaries against traditional initiation ceremonies.

6 In 1956, for example, there were eight convictions for "unnatural crimes" (including against animals). To be sure, this was slightly more than the other High Commission Territories but insignificant in a territory counting approximately a million inhabitants (Basutoland 1956). See also Maloka (1995, 305).

7 NAB, AGO 1/1/60, case 3 of 21 February 1878.

8 "M," an openly gay man, interviewed by the author at Motimposo, 16 March 1996. The full reconstruction of this and another "conversation" with another self-identified gay Mosotho can be found in Epprecht (2002). Also of possible relevance is that the Basotho shared with their neighbours both some of the

gender-bending qualities of traditional healers and ideas around or medicinal "cures" for underdeveloped heterosexual appetite or performance ("Ngaka," interviewed by the author at Phuthatidjaba, 5 December 2000). More formal interviews of traditional Basotho doctors on this issue that corroborate the point can be found in the as yet unpublished research by the Sangoma Project at GALASA. Three of the informants are the focus of the film *Everything Must Come to Light* (Njinje and Alberton 2002).

9 ZNA D3/21/2, case 132 of 25 April 1908.

10 ZNA D3/21/2, case 390 of 26 October 1909.

11 Transvaal Archive Depot (TAB), SNA 466 NA 1715/10.

12 TAB, LD 1496 AG 3518/07.

13 TAB, GNLB 229, 583/15/145, PC 34/67, 2 December 1914, S.M. Pritchard to all Native Inspectors.

14 TAB, GNLB 229, 583/15/145, "Unnatural Vice," 15 February 1916.

15 TAB, GNLB 229, 4/15/C, "Izinkotshana," 28 September 1915.

16 TAB, GNLB 229, 583/15/145, "Unnatural Vice," 15 February 1916.

17 "Remarks of Unnatural Vice among the British Basutos" (A2/37, 16 February 1916), TAB, GNLB 583/15/D145.

18 16 February 1916, TAB, GNLB 583/15/D145.

19 TAB, GNLB 229, 583/15/145. See also the letter from Native Affairs Department Inspector of Benoni to the Director of Native Labour (IB 254/19, 10 October 1919). Moodie (1994) also discusses this case. Like me, he seems to have been unable to identify whatever happened to poor Mokete.

20 TAB, SAP 15/17/38, from L.D. Doubell to Secretary for Native Affairs, 28 October 1941. Moodie (1994) also discusses this case, drawing upon a very similar report in NTS 7675, 102/332. Again, neither of our sources indicates the ultimate outcome of the disturbance, although on previous record we may probably assume that the mine managers gave in to the strikers as much as saving face would allow. Coplan's comments on this case are also worth noting. The homoerotic dance by which the Basotho "boss boys" seduced new arrivals was (is) apparently known as *seakhi*, from the verb "which describes the flapping motion of a young boy's penis as he runs carelessly clad about the fields" (Coplan 1994, 140).

21 London, Public Records Office (PRO) DO 35/3/60, "The Situation in Basutoland, June 1946."

22 Basutoland. *Basutoland National Council Debates*, M.S. Mohasi, 16 January, 1961, 10.

23 "M" and "P" interviewed by the author, Motimposo, 16 March 1996.

24 "P" interviewed by the author, Motimposo, 16 March 1996.

25 As a straight man, I have to admit that I was at first somewhat incredulous about this claim. However, similar claims elsewhere both lend it credibility and

support my earlier point stressing the power of African culture of discretion/denial. As graphically described by Linda in Soweto, South Africa, for example, and as confirmed by some of my own informants in Zimbabwe, this aspect of African culture makes it relatively easy for even well-hung queens to cruise (seduce) straight men who do not notice (or who can plausibly deny noticing) that the "women" they have sex with have penises. See, for example, McLean and Ngcobo (1994, 72). Prieur (1998) presents a study of somewhat analogous dynamics among *machos*, *mayates*, *tortillas*, and other trans-gendered men in a poor Mexico City neighbourhood.

26 Zimbabwean men and women who were in South Africa in the 1970s also recalled an abundance of female prostitutes but noted that not only did this not preclude *nkotshane* but it may actually have stimulated it. According to one interview by one of my History majors at the University of Zimbabwe, "although prostitutes were available, they were not enough and were also expensive. They demanded much. This prompted some to make other men 'wives'" (Mrs Hlengani, interviewed by Last Hobwani, Harare, September 1997).

27 Consider, for example, Monare's painful and ultimately humiliating courting efforts in Lanham and Mopeli-Paulus (1953).

28 Ellenberger (1994, 47). The editor speculates in a footnote that this practice had been adopted from the "voluptuous" Bushmen.

29 Please refer to Epprecht (2000) for a fuller discussion of this, based upon interviews with Catholic and Anglican nuns and the private correspondence within the Catholic mission.

30 Gay (1985). Kendall (1999) maintains that the sexual activity within these relationships could in fact be quite a bit more genital-oriented than Gay acknowledges. I hesitate to speculate. However, I can note my conversation with "P," who asked me if there were any lesbians in Zimbabwe. "Not many," I said. "Are there any here?" He replied, as if I were foolish to ask such a question, "PLENTY!"

31 "M" interviewed by the author, Motimposo, 16 March 1996.

CHAPTER EIGHT

1 See, in particular, Isaacs and McKendrick (1992), Gevisser and Cameron (1994), Donham (1998), Murray (1998), Jara (1998), Aarmo (1999), Palmberg (1999), Luirink (2000), Gevisser (2000), Spurlin (2001), and Croucher (2002). The website Behind the Mask (www.mask.org) has up-to-date, continent-wide news and views about gay rights activism. Krouse and Berman (1993), Schiller (1998), Ditsie and Newman (2001), and Duiker (2001) are exemplary pioneers on the literary and cinematic fronts. On the achievements and challenges facing GALZ, see Clark (1995), GALZ (2002), Tsourillis (2001), and Goddard (2004a) as well as issues of the GALZ newsletters *Galzette* and *The Avid Queer Reader*.

2 See, for example, Oliver Tambo's interview in Schiller (1998).

3 See The Aversion Project files at GALASA, as well as Krouse (1994) and Lewis and Phungula (1998) on gay life in the military.

4 Mark Gevisser, "How South Africa's ANC Became Pro-Gay," *Mail and Guardian*, 18 June 2001.

5 NCGLE press statement, 12 February 1999.

6 "Equal Benefits for SA Gays," 17 March 2003.

7 www.geocities.com/kencage/saps.htm.

8 "Winnie to Help Cape Town Massacre Victims' Families," *SAPA*, 28 January 2003.

9 See the GayZim website www.angelfire.com/zine/gayzim.

10 GALZ statement on Canaan Banana's sentence, 20 January 1999.

11 NCGLE press statement, 12 February 1999.

12 "Homosexuality Okay, Just Don't Flaunt It: Museveni," *SAPA*, 15 November 1999; Denis Jjuuko, "Counselors Disregard Inborn Homosexuality," *New Vision* (Kampala), 30 August 2002.

13 "Gays Demand Rights," *Harare Daily News*, 25 October 1999, p. 1.

14 Statement from Gays and Lesbians of Zimbabwe (GALZ) regarding the attempted arrest of President Robert Mugabe in Belgium by Peter Tatchell of *Outrage!*, 7 March 2001.

15 "Historic Victory for Africa: Statement from the AIDS Treatment Action Campaign (ATAC) regarding the TAC South Africa victory against the International Pharmaceutical Companies" (19 April 2001), "No Plans for Anti-AIDS Drugs: Minister" (*SAPA*, 5 June 2001), Chris McGreal, "Activists Who Put the Drug Makers to Flight," *Guardian Weekly* (26 April – 2 May 2001) and Tilley (2001) for a spotlight on TAC founder Zackie Achmat.

16 TAC briefing document on the civil disobedience campaign, March 2003 (www.tac.org.za/). The Cape Town march was estimated at fifteen to twenty thousand people.

17 "Gays Win Right to Give Blood," *SAPA*, 23 March 2000

18 Statement from GALZ regarding the death of Hitler Hunzi, 8 June 2001.

19 "Gay to Fight for Rights," *Harare Daily News*, 13 September 1999.

CONCLUSION

1 ZNA D3/10/2, Mbata, testifying in Rex v. Jenwa, case 149 of 1921.

2 Ibid.

APPENDIX ONE

1 Please refer to my review of some of the most pertinent of this theory in the introductory chapter, but see also Murray (2002) for a provocative engagement with the literature.

2 Corroborating my own experience in this respect with research from a later period and in the Cape Province of South Africa (whence Zimbabwean law originated), Oliver Phillips found that there has never been a case of lesbian indecent assault tried under the Roman-Dutch law in those jurisdictions (1999, 190).

3 *Crimen injuria* charge sheets were nonetheless well worth investigating. Representing insults to modesty by word or glance, they rewarded me with Zimbabwe's first known "queen" (Maggie, 1924), as well as rich commentary on contrasting attitudes (and fantasies) around sexuality and the body. Charges relating to the importation, distribution, and possession of "obscene" material and other charges arising from the censorship laws may be another source for the late colonial and post-colonial period. For the early period, however, no homosexual material of any description, let alone real lesbian erotica, ever came to the consideration of the courts. Negative evidence, of course, is still important evidence.

4 ZNA D3/35/1, case 7 of 1921 (Sipolilo, Lomagundi district). The same observation applied to the other predominantly "native" jurisdictions in the region that I checked – Nyasaland (Malawi) and Basutoland (Lesotho). People familiar with Mozambican records tell me that this applies there as well, perhaps even more so given that consensual male-male sexual relations were not a criminal offence under Portuguese law.

5 As Phillips has convincingly shown from his examination of the sodomy cases that made it to the High or Supreme courts in the thirty-year period of 1965–95, twenty-two out of twenty-five of those cases involved white men as defendants (1999, 201). This is almost precisely the inverse of the proportion of cases of homosexual crime that I found in my survey of the lower courts in an earlier period.

6 ZNA D3/35/1, case 7 of 1921.

7 See, for example, Geiger (1990), Personal Narratives Group (1989), Gluck and Patai (1991), Geiger (1992), and Wolf (1996). Feminist oral history methods in southern Africa are exemplified in Nthunya (1996) and Ndambuki and Robertson (2000), for example, and considered in rural Zimbabwean settings in Goebel (1998).

8 The Lesotho conversations are reproduced in Epprecht (2002), with some reflection on my own and my Africanist colleagues' masculinism as researchers.

9 GALZ, "Outreach Programme," unpublished document, July 1997.

10 Francis, *Galzette* 1, no. 3 (September 1997): 2.

11 This is discussed in fuller detail, *sans* sober final assessment, in Epprecht (1999), but see also Goddard (2004a) for an insider perspective upon the social tensions besetting GALZ at the time.

Bibliography

UNPUBLISHED ARCHIVAL SOURCES

CAPE TOWN, KAP ARGEIF BEREPLEK (KAB)
1/KIM 1/1/1/1–91 Kimberly Criminal Court Dockets.
1/2/1/2–339 Cape Circuit Court.
CSC 1/1/1/1–339 Cape Supreme Court.
GH 23/31.
GH 1/336.
AG 1813 14445.

PRETORIA, TRANSVAAL ARGEIF BEREPLEK (TAB)
GOV 210, 52/06, "Unnatural Vice" among the Chinese.
LD 1361 20.
AG 5138/06.
SAP 15/17/38, Disturbances among the Basotho.
LD 1496 AG 3518/07.
SNA 466 NA 1715/10.
SNA 46, 1540/02, Crime of Sodomy Practiced by Natives on Mines.
GNLB 229, 583/15/145, "Unnatural Vice."
South African Native Affairs Commission (1904–05), C17, vol. 5.
NTS 10203 1/422.
NTS 2091, 213/280, Transkeian Authorities.
GNLB 374, 110/28/110.
JUS 1223 1/94/30, Enquiry into Alleged Practice of Sodomy in Prisons.
GG 51 1805/8711.

GAY AND LESBIAN ARCHIVES, UNIVERSITY OF WITWATERSRAND, JOHANNESBURG

Apostles of Civilised Vice files (AM 2909).

von Oppell. Ca. 1896. "Advice to Parents, Tutors and Young People." *South African Independent.*

"A Well Known South African Doctor and University Lecturer." No date. "Light on the Sex Life of the Bantu People." Unpublished speech or article.

Renée Liddicoat Collection, ca. 1942 to 1962 (AM 2800).

Alma-Moira Letters (AM 2821).

After Nines collection (AM 2894).

PIETERMARITZBURG, NATAL ARGEIF BEREPLEK (NAB)

AGO 1/1/60.

CNC 207 1915/664, Public Health: Sodomy amongst Natives on Rand.

1/BLR 8 P64/1887.

AGO 1/2/1 Criminal register 1851–.

AGO 1/2/25.

AGO 1/1/57, 1635 of 29 March 1877.

AGO 1/1/60, 3 of 21 February 1878.

AGO 1/1/70.

AGO 1/1/101, 107–111.

AGO 1/1/142.

AGO 1/1/312.

HARARE, ZIMBABWE NATIONAL ARCHIVES (ZNA)

D3/1–49 Criminal court dockets.

D4/1/2 Criminal Register, Bulawayo.

D4/3/1 Criminal Register, Umtali.

D4/7/1 Criminal Register, Salisbury.

RG 3/BRI 41 British South Africa Police.

S1252.

S1679.

S1880.

S1222/1, Immorality, Personal, 1917–30.

S1227, Immorality file.

S1542/S12.

S235.

AOH 3, 39, 40 (oral history).

SWAZILAND NATIONAL ARCHIVES

Swaziland Vol. 1. "Notes on Selected Criminal Cases, 1907–32."

LONDON PUBLIC RECORDS OFFICE (*PRO*)
DO 35/3/60, The Situation in Basutoland, June 1946.

BOOKS, ARTICLES, FILMS, WEB ARTICLES,
AND UNPUBLISHED PAPERS

Aarmo, Margrete. 1999. "How Homosexuality Became 'Un-African': The Case of Zimbabwe." In Evelyn Blackwood and Saskia Wieringa, eds., *Same-Sex Relations and Female Desires: Transgender Practices across Cultures*. New York: Columbia University Press, 255–80.

Abelove, Henry. 1992. "Some Speculations on the History of 'Sexual Intercourse' during the 'Long Eighteenth Century' in England." In Andrew Parker, Mary Russo, Doris Sommer, and Patricia Yaeger, eds., *Nationalisms and Sexualities*. New York: Routledge, 335–42

Achmat, Zackie, 1993. "'Apostles Of Civilised Vice': 'Immoral Practices' and 'Unnatural Vice' in South African Prisons and Compounds, 1890–1920." *Social Dynamics* 19, no. 2: 92–110.

– 1995. "Sex in Prisons." *Exit* 72: 1–3.

– n.d. "A Cape Coloured, a Botha, As Well As a Lesbian: Carl Buckle, Louis Freed, and the Psychiatrization of Male Homosexuality." Draft, Masters dissertation, GALASA.

Achmat, Zackie, and Jack Lewis (director/producer). 1999. *Apostles of Civilised Vice*. Muizenberg, South Africa: Idol Pictures.

Afrika, Tatamkhulu. 1996. *Tightrope*. Cape Town: Majibuye Books.

Agency for Industrial Mission (AIM). 1976a *Another Blanket: Report of an Investigation into the Migrant Situation*. Roodepoort: Agency for Industrial Mission.

– 1976b. *South Africa Today: A Good Host Country for Migrant Workers?* International Consultation on the Role of the Church among Migrant Mine-Workers. Report on the Johannesburg conference, 18–19 June 1976.

Aina, Tade Akin. 1991. "Patterns of Bisexuality in Sub-Saharan Africa." In Rob Tielman, Manuel Carball, and Aaft Hendriks, eds., *Bisexuality and HIV/AIDS: A Global Perspective*. Buffalo, N.Y.: Prometheus, 81–90.

Alberton, Paulo, and Graeme Reid (director/producer). 2000. *Dark and Lovely, Soft and Free*. Brazil: Franmi Produções and Gay and Lesbian Archives of South Africa.

Alexander, Jocelyn, JoAnn McGregor, and Terence Ranger. 2000. *Violence and Memory: One Hundred Years in the "Dark Forests" of Matabele-land*. Oxford: James Currey; Harare: Weaver; Cape Town: David Philip; Portsmouth, N.H.: Heinemann.

Altman, Dennis. 2001. *Global Sex*. Chicago and London: University of Chicago Press.

Amadiume, Ifi. 1987. *Male Daughters and Female Husbands: Gender and Sex in an African Society*. London: Zed Press.

Amory, Deborah P. 1997. "'Homosexuality' in Africa: Issues and Debates." *Issue 25*, no. 1: 5–10.

– 1998. "*Mashoga, Mabasha*, and *Magai*: 'Homosexuality' on the East African Coast." In Murray and Roscoe, eds., *Boy-Wives*, 67–91.

Annan, Noel. 1990. "The Cult of Homosexuality in England, 1850–1950." *Biography* 13, no. 3: 189–202.

Antonio, Edward P. 1997. "Homosexuality and African Culture." In Paul Germond and Steve de Gruchy, eds., *Aliens in the Household Of God: Homosexuality and Christian Faith in South Africa*. Cape Town: David Philip, 295–315.

Armstrong, Alice. 1997. "Sexual Violence: Preliminary Research Results." Unpublished paper, Zimbabwe Women's Resource Centre and Network, Harare.

Asante, Molefi. 1980. *Afrocentricity: The Theory of Social Change*. Buffalo: Amulefi.

Aschwanden, Herbert. 1982. *Symbols of Life: An Analysis of the Consciousness of the Karanga*. Gweru: Mambo Press.

– 1989. *Karanga Mythology*. Gweru: Mambo Press.

Ashe, R.P. 1890. *Two Kings of Uganda*. London: n.p.

Ashton, Hugh. 1952. *The Basuto*. Oxford: Oxford University Press.

Banana, Canaan. 1980. *The Woman of My Imagination*. Gweru: Mambo Press.

Barnes, Theresa A. 1993. "'We Women Worked So Hard': Gender, Labour and Social Reproduction in Colonial Harare, Zimbabwe, 1930–1956." Doctoral dissertation, University of Zimbabwe.

– 1995. "The Heroes Struggle: Life after the Liberation War for Four Ex-Combatants in Zimbabwe." In N. Bhebe and T. Ranger, eds., *Soldiers in Zimbabwe's Liberation War*. Harare: University of Zimbabwe Press, 118–138.

– 1997. "'Am I a Man?': Gender and the Pass Laws in Urban Colonial Zimbabwe." *African Studies Review* 40, no. 1 (April): 59–81.

– 1999. "*We Women Worked So Hard*": *Gender, Labour and Social Reproduction in Colonial Harare, Zimbabwe, 1930–1956*. Portsmouth, N.H.: Heinemann.

Barnes, T., and Everjoice Win. 1992. *To Live a Better Life*. Harare: Baobab.

Basutoland, The Bechuanaland Protectorate and Swaziland. 1956. *Judicial Annual Report for the Year 1956*.

Baum, Robert M. 1995. "Homosexuality in the Traditional Religions of the Americas and Africa." In Arlene Swindler, ed., *Homosexuality and World Religions*. Valley Forge, P.A.: Trinity Press, 1–46.

Beach, David. 1980. *The Shona and Zimbabwe, 900–1850*. New York: Africana.

– 1994. *The Shona and Their Neighbours*. Oxford: Blackwell.

– 1998. "Cognitive Archaeology and Imaginary History at Great Zimbabwe." *Current Anthropology* 39, no. 1: 47–72.

Bederman, Gail. 1995. *Manliness and Civilization: A Cultural History of Gender and Race in the United States, 1880–1917*. Chicago: University of Chicago Press.

Bent, J.T. 1892. *The Ruined Cities of Mashonaland*. London: Longman's.

Bereng, Patrick Mohlalefi. 1982. *I Am a Mosotho*. Roma: National University of Lesotho.

Berglund, Axel-Ivar. 1970. "Transition from Traditional to a Westernized Outlook on Life." In *Migrant Labour and Church Involvement*. Umpumulo: Missiological Institute.

Bérubé, Alan. 1990. *Coming Out under Fire: The History of Gay Men and Women in World War II*. New York: Free Press.

Beyala, Calixthe. 1996. *Your Name Shall Be Tanga*. Portsmouth, N.H.: Heinemann.

Bhebe, Ngwabi, and Terence Ranger. 1995. Volume introduction. In Bhebe and Ranger, eds., *Society in Zimbabwe's Liberation War*. Vol. 2. Harare: University of Zimbabwe Publications, 6–34.

Blackmore, Josiah, and Gregory S. Hutcheson, eds. 1999, *Queer Iberia: Sexualities, Cultures and Crossings from the Middle Ages to the Renaissance*. Durham, N.C.: Duke University Press.

Blackwood, Evelyn, and Saskia Wieringa, eds. 1999. *Same-Sex Relations and Female Desires: Transgender Practices across Cultures*. New York: Columbia University Press.

Blair, Arthur, and John Gay. 1980. "Growing up in Lesotho (A Basotho Interpretation)." Unpublished paper, Department of Education, National University of Lesotho.

Blake, Robert. 1977. *A History of Rhodesia*. London: Eyre Methuen.

Bleys, Rudi C. 1995. *The Geography of Perversion: Male-Male Sexual Behaviour outside the West and the Ethnographic Imagination*. New York: New York University Press.

Blumenfeld, Warren J., ed. 1992. *Homophobia: How We All Pay the Price*. Boston: Beacon Press.

Bolze, Louis, and Rose Martin. 1978. *The Whenwes of Rhodesia*. Bulawayo: Books of Rhodesia.

Bond-Smith, Sylvia. 1977. "Salisbury's Gay Club Is Alive and Flourishing."
    Illustrated Life Rhodesia (week ending 20 January): 8–9.

Boswell, John D. 1980. *Christianity, Social Tolerance, and Homosexuality:
    Gay People in Western Europe from the Beginning of the Christian Era
    to the Fourteenth Century.* Chicago and London: University of Chicago
    Press.

Botha, Kevin, and Edwin Cameron. 1997. "South Africa." In Donald West
    and Richard Green, eds., *Socio-Legal Control of Homosexuality: A
    Multi-Nation Comparison.* New York: Plenum, 43–56.

Bourdillon, M.F.C. 1976. *The Shona Peoples: An Ethnography of Contem-
    porary Shona with Special Reference to Their Religion.* Gwelo: Mambo
    Press.

– 1995. *Where Are the Ancestors? Changing Culture in Zimbabwe.* Harare:
    University of Zimbabwe Publications.

Bozongwana, Wallace. 1983. *Ndebele Religion and Customs.* Gweru:
    Mambo Press.

Bradford, Helen. 1991. "Herbs, Knives, and Plastic: 150 Years of Abortion
    in South Africa." In Teresa Meade and Mark Walker, eds., *Science,
    Medicine and Cultural Imperialism.* New York: St Martin's Press, 120–47.

Breckenridge, Keith. 1990. "Migrancy, Crime, and Faction-Fighting: The
    Role of the *Isitshozi* in the Development of Ethnic Organizations in the
    Compounds." *Journal of Southern African Studies* 16, no. 1, 55–78.

Brooks, Philip, and Lawrent Bocahut (director/producer). 1998. *Woubi
    Cheri.* Abidjan.

Brooks, Shirley. 2001. "Changing Nature: A Critical Historical Geography
    of the Unfolozi and Hluhluwe Game Reserves, Zululand, 1887–1947."
    Doctoral dissertation, Queen's University, Kingston, Ont.

Brouwer, Johan. 1990. "'n Moffie Chaff' n Kaffer." In Hennie Aucamp,
    ed., *Wisselstroom: Homoerotiek in die Afrikaanse Verhaalkuns.* Cape
    Town: Human and Rousseau, 114–17.

Brown, Lester R. 2000. "HIV Epidemic Restructuring Africa's Population."
    Washington: Worldwatch Institute.

Bryant, Alfred T. 1929. *Olden Times in Zululand and Natal.* Cape Town:
    C. Struik.

Bryk, Felix. 1964. *Voodoo-EROS: Ethnological Studies in the Sex-Life of
    the African Aborigines.* Translated Mayne F. Sexton. New York: United
    Book Guild.

Bucher, Hubert. 1980. *Spirits and Power: An Analysis of Shona Cosmol-
    ogy.* Oxford: Oxford University Press.

Bullock, Charles. 1912. *Mashona Laws and Customs.* Cape Town: Juta.

– 1950. *The Mashona and the Matabele.* Cape Town: Juta.

Buntman, Fran. 2003. *Robben Island and Prisoner Resistance to Apartheid*. Cambridge: Cambridge University Press.

Burke, Timothy. 1996. *Lifebuoy Men, Lux Women: Commodification, Consumption and Cleanliness in Modern Zimbabwe*. Durham, N.C.: Duke University Press.

Burshatin, Israel. 1999. "Written on the Body: Slave or Hermaphrodite in Sixteenth-Century Spain." In Blackmore and Hutcheson, eds., *Queer Iberia*, 420–56.

Burton, Richard. 1885. *A Plain and Literal Translation of the Arabian Nights' Entertainments, Now Entitled: The Book of the Thousand Nights and a Night. With Introduction, Explanatory Notes on the Manners and Customs of Moslem Men and a Terminal Essay upon the History of the Nights*. Vol. 10. London: Burton Club.

Butler, Judith. 1990. *Gender Trouble: Feminism and the Subversion of Identity*. New York and London: Routledge.

Cage, Ken. 2003a. *Gayle: The Language of Kinks and Queens*. Johannesburg: Jacana Press.

– 2003. "From *Moffietaal* to *Gayle* – The Evolution of a South African Gay Argot." Paper presented to the Sex and Secrecy Conference, Johannesburg.

Caldwell, John C., Pat Caldwell, and Pat Quiggin. 1989. "The Social Context of AIDS in Sub-Saharan Africa." *Population and Development Review* 15, no. 2: 185–233.

Camara, Mohammed (director). 1997. *Dakan*. Conakry: ArtMattan.

Cameron, Edwin. 1994. "Unapprehended Felons: Gays and Lesbians and the Law in South Africa." In Gevisser and Cameron, eds., *Defiant Desire*, 89–98.

Campbell, Catherine. 1992. "Learning to Kill? Masculinity, the Family and Violence in Natal." *Journal of Southern African Studies* 18, no. 3: 614–28.

– 2003. *"Letting Them Die": How HIV/AIDS Prevention Programmes Often Fail*. Oxford: James Currey.

Campbell, Horace. 2003. *Reclaiming Zimbabwe: The Exhaustion of the Patriarchal Model of Liberation*. Cape Town: David Philip.

Cape Colony. 1873. *Report and Evidence of the Commission on Native Laws and Customs of the Basutos*. Cape Town: n.p.

– 1883. *Report and Proceedings with Appendices on the Government Commission on Native Laws and Customs*. Cape Town: Richards and Sons.

Carrier, Joseph. 1995. *De Los Otros: Intimacy and Homosexuality among Mexican Men*. New York: Columbia University Press.

Carrier, Joseph M., and Stephen O. Murray. 1998. "Woman-Woman Marriage in Africa." In Murray and Roscoe, eds., *Boy-Wives and Female Husbands*, 255–66.

Castilhon, J.L. [1769] 1993. *Zingha, reine d'Angola, histoire africaine.* Edited by Patrick Graille and Laurent Quilerie. Bourges: Ganymede.

Chauncey, George. 1994. *Gay New York: Gender, Urban Culture and the Making of the Gay Male World, 1890–1940.* New York: Basic Books.

Chaza, Leonard. 1995. "It's a Gay Thing!" *Mahogony* (July/August): 8–9.

Chetty, Dhiannaraj. 1994. "A Drag at Madame Costello's" and "Lesbian Gangster: The Gertie Williams Story." In Gevisser and Cameron, eds., *Defiant Desire,* 115–33.

Chévrier, Odilon. n.d. *Croyances et coutumes chez les Basotho.* Mimeograph. Morija Museum and Archives, Lesotho.

Chigweshe, Rudo. 1996. "Homosexuality: A Zimbabwean Religious Perspective." Honours dissertation, University of Zimbabwe.

Chinodya, Shimmer. 1990. *Harvest of Thorns.* Portsmouth, N.H.: Heinemann Educational Books.

Clark, Bev. 1995. "Zimbabwe." In Rachel Rosenblum, ed., *Unspoken Rules: Sexual Orientation and Women's Human Rights.* San Francisco: International Gay and Lesbian Human Rights Commission, 237–42.

Clowes, Lindsay. 2002. "A Modernized Man? Changing Constructions of Masculinity in *Drum* Magazine, 1951–1984." Doctoral dissertation, University of Cape Town.

Cobbing, Julian. 1974. "The Evolution of Ndebele Amabutho." *Journal of African History* 15, no. 4: 607–31.

Colman, Robert (director) 1998. *After Nines!* Unpublished play transcript and oral history research. GALASA, AM 2894.

Colson, Elizabeth. 1958. *Marriage and the Family among the Plateau Tonga of Northern Rhodesia.* Manchester: Manchester University Press.

Coplan, David. 1994. *In the Time of Cannibals: The Word Music of South Africa's Basotho Migrants.* Chicago: University of Chicago Press.

– 2001. "You Have Left Me Wandering About: Basotho Women and the Culture of Mobility." In D. Hodgson and S. McCurdy, eds., *Wicked Women and the Reconfiguration of Gender in Africa.* Portsmouth N.H.: Heinemann; Oxford: James Currey; and Cape Town: David Philip, 188–211.

Coutinho, Mike. 1993. "Black Gay Life in Zimbabwe." In A. Hendriks, R. Tielman, and E. van der Veen, eds., *The Third Pink Book: A Global View of Lesbian and Gay Liberation and Oppression.* Buffalo, N.Y.: Prometheus Press, 62–5.

Croucher, Sheila. 2002. "South Africa's Democratisation and the Politics of Gay Liberation." *Journal of Southern African Studies* 28, no. 2: 315–30.

Cruz-Malavé, Arnaldo, and Martin F. Manalansan IV, eds. 2002. *Queer Globalizations: Citizenship and the Afterlife of Colonialism.* New York: New York University Press.

Cureau, A.L. 1915. *Savage Man in Central Africa*. Translated by E. Andrews. London: T. Fisher Unwin.

Dangarembga, Tsitsi. 1989. *Nervous Conditions*. Seattle: Seal Press.

Dashwood, Hevina. 2000. *Zimbabwe: The Political Economy of Transformation*. Toronto: University of Toronto Press.

Davies, C. 1931. "Chikwambo and Chitsina." *NADA* 9: 41–3.

Davison, Jean. 1997. *Gender, Lineage, and Ethnicity in Southern Africa*. Boulder, Colo.: Westview.

Davison, Michael. [1970]. 1988. *Some Boys*. Swaffham, U.K.: Gay Men's Press.

De Waal, Shawn. 1994. "A Thousand Forms of Love: Representations of Homosexuality in South African Literature." In Gevisser and Cameron, eds., *Defiant Desire*, 232–45.

Delius, Peter, and Clive Glaser. 2002. "Sexual Socialisation in South Africa: A Historical Perspective." *African Studies* 61, no. 1: 27–54.

D'Emilio, John. 1989. "The Homosexual Menace: The Politics of Sexuality in Cold War America." In Kathy Peiss and Christina Simmons, with Robert A. Padgug, eds., *Passion and Power: Sexuality in History*. Philadelphia: Temple University Press.

Dent, G.R., and C.L.S. Nyembezi. 1969. *A Scholar's Zulu Dictionary*. Pietermaritzburg: Schuter and Shooter.

Desai, Gaurav. 2001. "Out in Africa." In John C. Hawley, ed., *Post-Colonial Queer: Theoretical Intersections*. Albany: SUNY Press, 139–64.

Ditsie, Beverley Palesa, and Nicky Newman (directors). 2001. *Simon and I*. Cape Town/Johannesburg: See Thru Media/Steps for the Future.

Dlamini, Moses. 1984. *Hell Hole, Robben Island: Reminiscences of a Political Prisoner in South Africa*. Trenton, N.J.: Africa World Press.

Donham, Donald L. 1998. "Freeing South Africa: The 'Modernization' of Male-Male Sexuality in Soweto." *Cultural Anthropology* 13, no. 1: 3–21.

Dube, Dumisane M. 2000. "(Un) African? History Tells All." Behind the Mask, www.mask.org.

Duiker, Sello. 2001. *The Quiet Violence of Dreams*. Cape Town: Kwela Books.

Dumbutshena, Enoch. 1975. *Zimbabwe Tragedy*. Nairobi: East African Publishing House.

Dunton, Chris. 1989. "'Wheyting Be Dat?' The Treatment of Homosexuality in African Literature." *Research in African Literatures* 20, no. 3: 422–48.

Dunton, Chris. 2004. "Tatamkhula Afrika: The Testing of Masculinity." *Research in African Literatures* 35, no. 1: 148–61.

Dunton, Chris, and Mai Palmberg. 1996. *Human Rights and Homosexuality in Southern Africa*. Uppsala: Nordiska Afrikainstituet.

Du Plessis, Andries. 1997. "Searching in an 'Empty Closet'? A History of Homosexuality in South Africa." *Historia* 42, no. 1: 116–29.

Edkins, Don (director). 1992. *The Color of Gold*. New York: Icarus Films.

Eichler, Margrit. 1991. *Nonsexist Research Methods: A Practical Guide*. New York and London: Routledge.

Elbl, Ivana. 1996. "'Men without Wives': Sexual Arrangements in the Early Portuguese Expansion in West Africa." In Jacqueline Murray and Konrad Eisenbichler, eds., *Desire and Discipline: Sex and Sexuality in the Premodern West*. Toronto: University of Toronto Press, 215–28.

Elder, Glen S. 2003. *Hostels, Sexuality, and the Apartheid Legacy: Malevolent Geographies*. Athens, Ohio: Ohio University Press.

– 1995. "Of Moffies, Kaffirs, and Perverts: Male Homosexuality and the Discourse of Moral Order in the Apartheid State." In David Bell and Gill Valentine, eds., *Mapping Desire*. New York: Routledge, 56–65.

Ellenberger, François. 1994. "Mœurs et coutumes traditionelles des Basotho." Unpublished thesis. Morija Museum and Archives, Lesotho.

Elphick, Richard, and Robert Shell. 1979. "Intergroup Relations: Khoikhoi, Settlers, Slaves and Free Blacks, 1652–1795." In R. Elphick and H. Giliomee, eds., *The Shaping of South African Society, 1652–1840*. Cape Town: Maskew Miller Longman, 184–242.

Epprecht, Marc. 1998a. "'Good God Almighty, What's This!': Homosexual 'Crime' in Early Colonial Zimbabwe." In Stephen O. Murray and Will Roscoe, eds., *Boy Wives and Female Husbands*, 197–220.

– 1998b. "The 'Unsaying' of Homosexuality among Indigenous Black Zimbabweans: Mapping a Blindspot in an African Masculinity." *Journal of Southern African Studies* 24, no. 4 (December): 631–51.

– 1999. "The Gay Oral History Project: Black Empowerment, Human Rights, and the Research Process." *History in Africa: A Journal of Method* 26: 25–41.

– 2000. *"This Matter of Women Is Getting Very Bad": Gender, Development and Politics in Colonial Lesotho, 1870–1965*. Pietermaritzburg: University of Natal Press.

– 2001a. "'What an Abomination, a Rottenness of Culture': Reflections upon the Gay Rights Movement in Southern Africa." *Canadian Journal of Development Studies* 22: 1089–107.

– 2001b. "'Unnatural Vice' in South Africa: The 1907 Commission of Enquiry." *International Journal of African Historical Studies* 34, no. 1: 121–40.

– 2002. "Male-Male Sexuality in Lesotho: Two Conversations." *Journal of Men's Studies* 10, no. 3: 373–89.

– Forthcoming. "Black Skin, 'Cowboy' Masculinity: A Genealogy of Homophobia in the African Nationalist Movement in Zimbabwe to 1983." *Culture, Health and Sexuality.*

Erlich, Susan. 1995. Critical Linguistics As Feminist Methodology." In S. Burt and L. Code, eds., *Changing Methods.* Peterborough, Ont.: Broadview.

Evans-Pritchard, E.E. 1970. "Sexual Inversion among the Azande." *American Anthropologist* 72: 1428–34.

Falk, Kurt. [1926] 1998. "Homosexuality among the Natives of Southwest Africa." Translated from 1926 German publication by B. Rose and W. Roscoe. In Murray and Roscoe, *Boy-Wives,* 187–96.

Fanon, Frantz. 1967. *Black Skin, White Masks.* New York: Grove Press.

Fone, Byrne. 2000. *Homophobia: A History.* New York: Metropolitan Books.

Fortune, G., and A.C. Hodza. 1974. "Shona Praise Poetry." *Bulletin of the School of Oriental and African Studies* 37: 65–75.

Foucault, Michel. 1978. *A History of Sexuality.* New York: Random House.

Galgut, Damon. 1982. *A Sinless Season.* Cape Town: Jonathan Ball.

GALZ [Gays and Lesbians of Zimbabwe]. No date. "Homosexuality" (pamphlet).

– 26 November 1998. Statement on the Conviction of Rev. Canaan Banana.

– 20 January 1999. Statement on the Sentence of Rev. Canaan Banana.

– 25 January 2000. Open Letter from GALZ to Rev. Canaan Sodindo Banana.

– March 2000. Statement from Gays and Lesbians of Zimbabwe (GALZ) Regarding the Attempted Arrest of President Robert Mugabe in Belgium by Peter Tatchell of *Outrage!*

– 2000. An Open Letter to Morgan Tsvangirai. Unpublished paper, GALZ Centre, Harare.

– April 2001. Open letter to Mr Elliot Magunje, leader within Zimbabwe National Network of People Living with HIV and AIDS Regarding his Anti-Gay Activities at the Recent ZNNP+ Congress.

– 5 April 2001. Letter to the *Harare Daily News.*

– 9 April 2001. Statement from the AIDS Treatment Action Campaign (ATAC) Regarding the TAC South Africa Victory against the International Pharmaceutical Companies.

– 14 May 2001. Obituary notice for Tsitsi Tiripano

– 8 June 2001. Statement from GALZ Regarding the Death of Hitler Hunzi.

– 2002. *Sahwira: Being Gay and Lesbian in Zimbabwe.* Harare: Gays and Lesbians of Zimbabwe. 2nd ed.

– 2004. "Homosexualities and History, Zimbabwe, Africa." Unpublished paper, GALZ Centre, Harare.

Garlake, Peter. 1995. *The Hunter's Vision.* London: British Museum.

Gay, Judith. 1985. "'Mummies and Babies' and Friends and Lovers in Lesotho." *Journal of Homosexuality* 11, no. 3–4: 93–116.

Gear, Sasha, and Kindiza Ngubeni. 2002. *"Daai Ding": Sex, Sexual Violence, and Coercion in Men's Prisons.* Braamfontein: Centre for the Study of Violence and Reconciliation.

Geiger, Susan. 1990. "What's So Feminist about Doing Women's Oral History?" *Journal of Women's History* 2, no. 1: 305–18.

Gelfand, Michael. 1964. *Witch Doctor: Traditional Medicine Man of Rhodesia.* New York and Washington: Praeger.

– 1965. "The Normal Man: A New Concept of Shona Philosophy." NADA 9, no. 2: 78–93.

– 1979. "The Infrequency of Homosexuality in Traditional Shona Society." *Central African Journal of Medicine* 25, no. 9: 201–2.

– 1985. "Apparent Absence of Homosexuality and Lesbianism in Traditional Zimbabweans." *Central African Journal of Medicine* 31, no. 7: 137–8.

Germond, Paul, and Steve de Gruchy, eds. 1997. *Aliens in the Household of God: Homosexuality and Christian Faith in South Africa.* Cape Town: David Philip.

Gevisser, Mark. 2000. "Mandela's Stepchildren: Homosexual Identity in Post-Apartheid South Africa." In Peter Drucker, ed., *Different Rainbows.* London: Gay Men's Press, 111–36.

Gevisser, Mark, and Edwin Cameron, eds. 1994. *Defiant Desire: Gay and Lesbian Lives in South Africa.* Johannesburg: Ravan.

Gibbon, Edward. [1781] 1925. *The Decline and Fall of the Roman Empire.* Vol. 4. London: Methuen.

Gibson-Graham, J.K. 1996–97. "Querying Globalization." *Rethinking Marxism* 9, no. 1: 1–27.

Gluck, Sherna Berger, and Daphne Patai, eds. 1991. *Women's Words: The Feminist Practice of Oral History.* New York and London: Routledge.

Gluckman, Max. 1974. "The Individual in a Social Framework: The Rise of King Shaka of Zululand." *Journal of African Studies* 1, no. 2: 113–44.

Goddard, Keith. 2004a. "A Fair Representation: GALZ and the History of the Gay Movement in Zimbabwe." *Journal of Gay and Lesbian Social Services Issues in Practice, Policy and Research* (special issue on

Community Organizing against Homophobia and Heterosexism: The World through Rainbow-Colored Glasses) 16, no. 1: 75–98.

– 2004b. "Towards an All-Africa Rights Initiative." Unpublished report, Harare.

Godwin, Peter. 1996. *Mukiwa: A White Boy in Africa*. London: Macmillan.

Godwin, Peter, and Ian Hancock. 1993. *Rhodesians Never Die: The Impact of War and Political Change on White Rhodesia*. Oxford: Oxford University Press.

Goebel, Allison. 1998. "Process, Perception and Power: Notes from 'Participatory' Research in a Zimbabwean Resettlement Area." *Development and Change* 29, no. 2: 277–305.

– 2002. "'Men These Days, They Are a Problem': Husband-Taming Herbs and Gender Wars in Rural Zimbabwe." *Canadian Journal of African Studies* 36, no. 3: 460–89.

– Forthcoming. *"Here It Is Our Land, the Two of Us": Gendering Zimbabwe's Land Reform Process*. Unpublished manuscript. Institute of Women's Studies, Queen's University, Kingston, Ont.

Golan, Daphne. 1990. "The Life Story of King Shaka and Gender Tensions in the Zulu State." *History in Africa* 17: 95–111.

– 1994. *Inventing Shaka: Using History in the Construction of Zulu Nationalism*. Boulder, Colo.: Westview Press.

Gordimer, Nadine. 1980. *Burger's Daughter*. Harmondsworth: Penguin.

Grace, H.J., and W.E.B. Edge. 1973. "A White Hermaphrodite in South Africa." *South African Journal of Medicine* 19: 1553–4.

Gray, Robert W. 1999. "Black Mirrors and Young Boy Friends: Colonization, Sublimation, and Sadomasochism in Stephen Gray's 'Time of Our Darkness.'" ARIEL: *A Review of International English Literature* 3012 (April): 77–98.

Gray, Stephen. 1988. *Time of Our Darkness*. London: Frederick Muller.

Grützer, H. 1877. "Die Gebräuche der Basuto." *Verhandelungen der Berliner Gesellschaft für Anthropologie, Ethnologie und Urgeschichte*.

Guy, Jeff. 1990. "Gender Oppression in Pre-Colonial Southern Africa." In Cherryl Walker, ed., *Women and Gender in Southern Africa to 1945*. Cape Town: David Philip, 33–47.

Guy, Jeff, and Motlatsi Thabane. 1988. "Technology, Ethnicity and Ideology: Basotho Miners and Shaft-Sinking on the South African Gold Mines." *Journal of Southern African Studies* 14, no. 2: 257–78.

Hamel, L. 1965. *English-Southern SeSotho Dictionary*. Mazenod: The Catholic Centre.

Hamilton, Carolyn, ed. 1995. *The Mfecane Aftermath: Reconstructive Debates in Southern African History.* Johannesburg: Witwatersrand University Press.

Hannan, M. 1983. *Standard Shona Dictionary.* Harare: College Press.

Harries, Patrick. 1990a. "La symbolique du sexe: L'identité culturelle au début d'exploitation des mines d'or du Witwatersrand." *Cahiers d'Etudes Africaines* 120: 451–74.

– 1990b. "Symbols and Sexuality: Culture and Identity on the Early Witwatersrand Gold Mines." *Gender and History* 11, no. 3: 318–36.

– 1994. *Work, Culture and Identity: Migrant Laborers in Mozambique and South Africa, c. 1860–1910.* Portsmouth, N.H.: Heinemann.

Hatendi, R.P. 1973. "Shona Marriage and Christian Churches." In A.J. Dachs, ed., *Christianity South of the Sahara.* Gwelo: Mambo Press, 135–49.

Hawkins, Roland. 1973. "They Killed a Man They Didn't Even Know." *Illustrated Life Rhodesia* (week ending 16 May): 6–8.

Hawley, John C., ed. 2001. *Post-Colonial, Queer: Theoretical Intersections.* Albany: State University of New York.

Hayes, Jarrod. 2000. *Queer Nations: Marginal Sexualities in the Maghreb.* Chicago: University of Chicago Press.

Haysom, N. 1981. *Towards an Understanding of Prison Gangs.* Cape Town: Institute of Criminology, University of Cape Town.

Head, Bessie. 1974. *A Question of Power.* London: Heinemann.

Hennessy, Rosemary. 1995. "Incorporating Queer Theory on the Left." In Antonio Callari, Stephen Cullenberg, and Carole Biewener, eds., *Marxism in the Postmodern Age: Confronting the New World Order.* New York: Guilford Press, 266–75.

Hensley, Christopher, ed. 2002. *Prison Sex: Practice and Policy.* Boulder, Colo., and London: Lynne Reinner Press.

Herskovits, Melville J. [1938] 1967. *Dahomey: An Ancient West African Kingdom.* Evanston: Northwestern University Press.

Heyns, Michiel. 1998. "A Man's World: White South African Gay Writing and the State of Emergency." In Derek Attridge and Rosemary Jolly, eds., *Writing South Africa: Literature, Apartheid and Democracy, 1970–1995.* New York: Cambridge University Press, 108–22.

Hoad, Neville. 1999. "Between the White Man's Burden and the White Man's Disease." *Journal of Lesbian and Gay Studies* 5, no. 4: 559–84.

– 2000. "Arrested Development or the Queerness of Savages." *Postcolonial Studies* 3, no. 2.

Hole, H. Marshall. 1928. *Old Rhodesian Days.* London: Macmillan.

Holleman, J.F. 1969. *Shona Customary Law: With Reference to Kinship, Marriage, the Family and the Estate*. Manchester: Manchester University Press.

Holmes, Rachel, 1994. "White Rapists Make Coloureds (and Homosexuals): The Winnie Mandela Trial and the Politics of Race and Sexuality." In Gevisser and Cameron, *Defiant Desire*, 284–94.

Hotz, Paul. 1990. *Muzukuru*. Johannesburg: Ravan.

Howes, Robert. 2000. "Portugal." In George E. Haggerty, ed., *Gay Histories and Cultures: An Encyclopedia*. New York and London: Garland.

Huffman, Thomas N. 1996. *Snakes and Crocodiles: Power and Symbolism in Ancient Zimbabwe*. Johannesburg: Witwatersrand University Press.

Human Rights Watch and International Gay and Lesbian Human Rights Commission (HRW). 2003. *More Than a Name: State-Sponsored Homophobia and Its Consequences in Southern Africa*. New York: Human Rights Watch and International Gay and Lesbian Human Rights Commission.

Ibrahim, Huma. 1990. "The Violated Universe: Neo-Colonial Sexual and Political Consciousness in Dambudzo Marechera." *Research in African Literature* 21, no. 2: 79–90.

Isaacman, Allen F. 1975. *Mozambique: The Africanization of a European Institution, the Zambesi Prazos, 1750–1902*. Madison: University of Wisconsin Press.

Isaacs, Gordon, and Brian McKendrick. 1992. *Male Homosexuality in South Africa: Identity Formation, Culture and Crisis*. Cape Town: Oxford University Press.

Jackson, Lynnette. 2002. "'When in the White Man's Town': Zimbabwean Women Remember *Chibeura*." In Jean Allman, Susan Geiger, and Nyakanyiki Musisi, eds., *Women in African Colonial Histories*. Bloomington: Indiana University Press, 191–215.

– 1993. "Friday the 13th University of Zimbabwe Mini-Skirt Saga." *Southern Africa Political Economy Monthly* (December/January): 25–6.

Jackson, Paul. 2002. "Courting Homosexuals in the Military: The Management of Homosexuality in the Canadian Military, 1939–1945." Doctoral dissertation, Queen's University, Kingston, Ont.

Jara, Mazibuko. 1998. "Gay and Lesbian Rights: Forcing Change in S.A." *Southern Africa Report* 13, no. 3: 31–3.

Jeater, Diana. 1993. *Marriage, Perversion and Power: The Construction of Moral Discourse in Southern Rhodesia, 1890–1920*. Oxford: Clarendon Press.

– 1995. "'The Way You Tell Them': Language, Ideology and Development Policy in Southern Rhodesia." *African Studies* 54, no. 2: 1–15.

Johnson, Cary Alan. 2001. "Hearing Voices: Unearthing Evidence of Homosexuality in Precolonial Africa." In Delroy Constantine-Simms, ed., *The Greatest Taboo: Homosexuality in Black Communities*. Alyson Press, 132–48.

Johnston, H.H. 1897. *British Central Africa*. London: Methuen.

Jolly, Rosemary. 1996. "'Intersecting Marginalities': The Problem of Homophobia in South African Women's Writing." In John C. Hawley, ed., *Cross-Addressing: Resistance Literature in Cultural Borders*. Albany: SUNY Press, 107–20.

Jordan, Mark D. 2000. "Inquisition: Spain." In George E. Haggerty, ed., *Gay Histories and Cultures: An Encyclopedia*. New York and London: Garland, 470–1.

Junod, Henri. 1911. *Zidji: Étude de mœurs sud-africaines*. St Blaise: Foyer Solidariste.

– [1916] 1962. "Unnatural Vice in the Johannesburg Compounds." In *The Life of a South African Tribe*. Vol. 1. New York: University Books.

Kaarsholm, Preben. 1991. "From Decadence to Authenticity and Beyond: Fantasies and Mythologies of War in Rhodesia and Zimbabwe, 1965–1985." In P. Kaarsholm, ed., *Cultural Struggle and Development in Southern Africa*. Harare: Baobab Books, 33–60.

Kala, Violet. 1994. *Waste Not Your Tears*. Harare: Baobab.

Kaler, Amy. 2003. *Running after Pills: Gender, Politics and Contraception in Colonial Rhodesia*. Portsmouth, N.H.: Heinemann.

Kanengoni, Alexander. 1987. *When the Rainbird Cries*. Harare: Longman.
– 1997. *Echoing Silences*. Harare: Baobab.

Kendall, K. Limakatso. 1999. "Women in Lesotho and the (Western) Construction of Homophobia." In Evelyn Blackwood and Saskia Wieringa, eds., *Same-Sex Relations and Female Desires: Transgender Practices across Cultures*. New York: Columbia University Press, 157–78.

Kente, Gilbert. [1963] 1992. "Too Late." In Robert Mshengu Kavanagh, ed., *South African People's Plays*. Johannesburg: Heinemann.

Kesby, Mike. 1996. "Arenas for Control, Terrains of Gender Contestation: Guerrilla Struggle and Counter-Insurgency Warfare in Zimbabwe, 1972–1980." *Journal of Southern African Studies* 22, no. 4: 561–84.

– 1999. "Locating and Dislocating Gender in Rural Zimbabwe: The Making of Space and the Texturing of Bodies." *Gender, Place and Culture* 6, no. 1: 27–47.

Kethusile, Bookie M., Alice Kwaramba, and Barbara Lopi, comps. 2000. *Beyond Inequalities: Women in Southern Africa*. Harare: Southern African Research and Documentation Centre.

Kirby, Percival R. 1942. "A Secret Musical Instrument: The *Ekola* of the Ovakuanyama of Ovamboland." *South African Journal of Science* 28 (January): 345–51.

Kirkwood, Deborah. 1984. "Settler Wives in Southern Rhodesia: A Case Study." In Hilary Callan and Shirley Ardener, eds., *The Incorporated Wife*. London: Croom Helm, 143–164.

Kolb, Peter. [1719] 1968. *The Present State of the Cape of Good Hope*. New York: Johnson Reprint Corp.

Koscheski, Mary, C. Hensley, J. Wright, and R. Tewksbury. 2002. "Consensual Sexual Behaviour." In C. Hensley, ed., *Prison Sex: Practice and Policy*. Boulder, Colo., and London: Lynne Reinner Press, 111–32.

Kraak, Gerald, ed. 1998. "The Right to Be: Sexuality and Sexual Rights in Southern Africa." *Development Update* 2, no. 2.

Krige, Eileen Jensen. 1974. "Woman-Marriage, with Special Reference to the Lovedu." *Africa* 44: 11–36.

Kriger, Norma. 1992. *Zimbabwe's Guerrilla War: Peasant Voices*. Cambridge: Cambridge University Press.

Krouse, Matthew. 1994. "The Arista Sisters – September 1984: An Account of Army Drag." In Gevisser and Cameron, eds. *Defiant Desire*, 209–18.

Krouse, Matthew, and Kim Berman, eds., 1993. *The Invisible Ghetto: Lesbian and Gay Writing from South Africa*. Johannesburg: COSAW.

Kuper, Hilda. 1947. *An African Aristocracy: Rank among the Swazi*. Oxford: Oxford University Press.

Kynoch, Gary. 2000. "Marashea on the Mines: Economic, Social and Criminal Networks on the South African Gold Fields, 1947–1999." *Journal of Southern African Studies* 26, no. 1: 79–103.

– 2001. "'A Man Among Men': Gender, Identity and Power in South Africa's Marashea Gangs." *Gender and History 13*, no. 2: 249–72.

Lan, David. 1985. *Guns and Rain: Guerrillas and Spirit Mediums in Zimbabwe*. Berkeley: University of California Press.

Landes, Ruth. 1940. "A Cult Matriarchate and Male Homosexuality." *Journal of Abnormal and Social Psychology* 35: pp 386–97.

Landry, Donna, and Gerald MacLean. 1993. *Materialist Feminisms*. Cambridge Mass.: Blackwell.

Lane, Christopher. 1995. *Ruling Passion: British Colonial Allegory and the Paradox of Homosexual Desire*. Durham, N.C.: Duke University Press.

Lanham, Peter, and A.S. Mopeli-Paulus. 1953. *Blanket Boy's Moon*. London: Collins.

Latham, C.J.K. 1972. "Munhumutapa: Oral Traditions." NADA 10, no. 4: 77–82.

Laubscher, B.J.F. 1937. *Sex, Custom and Psychopathology: A Study of South African Pagan Natives*. London: George Routledge.

Leap, William L. 2002. "'Strangers on a Train': Sexual Citizenship and the Politics of Public Transportation in Apartheid Cape Town." In Arnaldo-Cruz and Manalansan, eds., *Queer Globalizations*, 219–35.

Leary, Glenn, and Henry Taberer. 1907. "Confidential Enquiry into Alleged Prevalence of Unnatural Vice amongst Natives in Mine Compounds on the Witwatersrand." Unpublished report to the Attorney General of Transvaal, TAB, NTS 10203, 1/422.

Lee, Richard B. 1979. *!Kung San: Men, Women and Work in a Foraging Society*. Cambridge: Cambridge University Press.

Lewis, Ethelreda. [1933] 1984. *Wild Deer*. Cape Town: David Philip.

Lewis, Jack, and Thulanie Phungula (directors). 1998. *Sando to Samantha: AKA The Art of Dikvel*. Muizenberg, South Africa: Idol Pictures.

Liddicoat, Renée. 1962. "Homosexuality." *South African Journal of Science* (May): 145–9.

Lindgren, Bjorn. 2001. "Men Rule but Blood Speaks: Gender, Identity, and Kinship at the Installation of a Female Chief in Matabeleland, Zimbabwe." In R. Morrell, ed., *Changing Men*, 177–94.

– 2002. "The Politics of Ndebele Ethnicity: Origins, Nationality and Gender in Southern Zimbabwe." Doctoral dissertation. Uppsala University.

Livingstone, David, and Charles Livingstone. 1865. *Narrative of the Expedition to the Zambezi*. London: John Murray.

Longmore, Laura. 1959. *The Dispossessed: A Study of the Sex-Life of Bantu Women in Urban Areas in and around Johannesburg*. London: Jonathan Cape.

Louw, Ronald. 1998. "Gay and Lesbian Sexualities in South Africa: From Outlawed to Constitutionally Protected." In L.J. Moran et al., eds., *Legal Queeries: Lesbian, Gay and Transgender Legal Studies*. London: Cassell, 139–54.

– 2001. "Mkhumbane and New Traditions of (Un)African Same-Sex Weddings." In Morrell, ed., *Changing Men in Southern Africa*, 287–96.

Luirink, Bart. 2000. *Moffies: Gay Life in Southern Africa*. Cape Town: Ink Inc.

Lumsden, Ian. 1996. *Machos, Maricones, and Gays: Cuba and Homosexuality*. Philadelphia: Temple University Press.

Lyons, Tanya. 2002. "Guerrilla Girls and Women in the Zimbabwean National Liberation Struggle." In Jean Allman et al., eds., *Women in African Colonial Histories*. Bloomington: Indiana University Press, 305–26.

McClintock, Ann. 1995. *Imperial Leather: Race, Gender, and Sexuality in the Colonial Context*. New York and London: Routledge.

McCulloch, Jock. 2000. *Black Peril, White Virtue: Sexual Crime in Southern Rhodesia, 1902–1935*. Bloomington: Indiana University Press.

McFadden, Patricia. 1992. "Sex, Sexuality, and the Problem of AIDS in Africa." In Ruth Meena, ed., *Gender in Southern Africa*. Harare: SAPES, 157–95.

– 2000. "Preface." SAFERE: *Southern African Feminist Review* 4, no. 1: i-iv.

Machida, Tina. 1996. "Sisters of Mercy." In Monica Reinfelder, ed., *Amazon to Zuni: Towards a Global Lesbian Feminism*. London: Cassell, 118–30.

– No date. "My Coming Out Story." Unpublished paper. GALZ Centre, Harare.

McLaren, J. 1923. *A Concise English-Kaffir Dictionary*. London and New York: Longmans.

McLean, Hugh, and Linda Ngcobo. 1994. "*Abangibhamayo bathi ngimnandi* (Those Who Fuck Me Say I'm Tasty): Gay Sexuality in Reef Township." In Gevisser and Cameron, eds., *Defiant Desire*, 158–85.

MacLean, Col. John. 1906. *Compendium of Kafir Laws and Customs*. Grahamstown: J. Slater.

Mager, Ann Kelk. 1999. *Gender and the Making of a South African Bantustan: A Social History of the Ciskei, 1945–59*. Portsmouth, N.H.: Heinemann; Oxford: James Currey; Cape Town: David Philip.

Magubane, Zine. 2002. "Mines, Minstrels and Masculinity: Race, Class, Gender, and the Formation of the South African Working Class, 1870–1900." *Journal of Men's Studies* 10, no. 3: 271–89.

Mahamba, Barbara. 1996. "Women in the History of the Ndebele State." M.Phil. dissertation. University of Zimbabwe.

Maloka, Edward Tshidiso. 1995. "Basotho and the Mines: Towards a History of Labour Migrancy." Doctoral dissertation, University of Cape Town.

– 1997. "*Khomo lia oela*: Canteens, Brothels, and Labour Migrancy in Colonial Lesotho, 1900–1940." *Journal of African History* 38, no. 1: 101–22.

Mandaza, Ibbo. 1997. *Race, Colour and Class in Southern Africa: A Study of the Coloured Question in the Context of an Analysis of the Colonial and White Settler Racial Ideology, and African Nationalism in Twentieth Century Zimbabwe, Zambia, and Malawi*. Harare: SAPES Books.

Mandivenda, Ephraim. 1989. "The History and 'Reconversion' of the Varemba of Zimbabwe." *Journal of Religion in Africa* 19, no. 2: 98–124.

Marechera, Dambudzo. 1978. *House of Hunger: Short Stories*. London: Heinemann.

– 1984. *Mindblast*. Harare: College Press.

Martens, Jeremy. 2001. "'Repugnant to the Laws of England': Settler Domesticity, 'Race' and the Regulation of African Behaviour in Colonial Natal, 1843–1893." Doctoral dissertation, Queen's University, Kingston, Ont.

Martin, Denis-Constant. 1999. *Coon-Carnival: New Year in Cape Town, Past and Present*. Cape Town: David Philip.

Martin, Maurice. 1913. *Au Cœur de l'Afrique équitoriale*. Paris: Libraire Chapelot.

Mathabane, Mark. 1986. *Kaffir Boy: The True Story of a Black Man's Coming of Age in Apartheid South Africa*. New York: Macmillan.

Matory, J. Lorand. 1992. "Government by Seduction: History and the Tropes of 'Mounting' in Oyo-Yoruba Religion." In Jean Comaroff and John Comaroff, eds., *Modernity and Its Malcontents: Ritual and Power in Postcolonial Africa*. Chicago: University of Chicago Press, 58–85.

Maxwell, David. 1999. *Christianity and Chiefs in Zimbabwe: A Social History*. Edinburgh: Edinburgh University Press.

Mazrui, Ali. 1975. "The Resurrection of the Warrior Tradition in African Political Culture." *Journal of Modern African Studies* 13, no. 1: 67–84.

Mburu, John. 2000. "Awakenings: Dreams and Delusions of an Incipient Lesbian and Gay Movement in Kenya." In P. Drucker, ed., *Different Rainbows*. London: Gay Men's Press, 179–91.

Meena, Ruth, ed. 1992. *Gender in Southern Africa: Conceptual and Theoretical Issues*. Harare: SAPES.

Miescher, Stephan F., and Lisa A. Lindsay, eds. 2003. *Men and Masculinities in Modern Africa*. Portsmouth, N.H.: Heinemann.

Mkhize, Victor. 2001. "A Gay Zulu Language." Behind the Mask, www.mask.org.

Mohapeloa, J.M. 1971. *Government by Proxy: Ten Years of Cape Colonial Rule in Lesotho, 1871–81*. Morija: Sesuto Book Depot.

– 2002. *Tentative British Imperialism in Lesotho, 1884–1910*. Morija: Morija Museum and Archives.

Mokhoane, Mpapa. 1995. *Teba*. Manzini: Macmillan Boleswa.

Moloi, Godrey. 1987. *My Life*. Vol. 1. Johannesburg: Ravan Press.

Monro, Surya. 2002. "Beyond Male and Female: Transgender, Gender Studies, and Social Change." Paper presented to the Worlds of Women conference, Kampala (July).

Moodie, T. Dunbar. 2001. "Black Migrant Mine Labourers and the Vicissitudes of Male Desire." In Morrell, ed., *Changing Men in Southern Africa*, 297–316.

– 1994. With Vivienne Ndatshe. *Going for Gold: Men's Lives on the Mines*. Berkeley: University of California Press.

– 1988. With Vivienne Ndatshe and British Sibuyi. "Migrancy and Male Sexuality on the South African Gold Mines." *Journal of Southern African Studies* 14, no. 2: 229–45.

Mooney, Katie. 1998. "'Ducktails, Flick-Knives and Pugnacity': Subcultural and Hegemonic Masculinities in South Africa, 1948–1960." *Journal of Southern African Studies* 24, no. 4: 753–74.

Morrell, Robert. 1996. "Forging a Ruling Race: Rugby and White Masculinity in Colonial Natal, c. 1870–1910." In John Nauright and Timothy J.L. Chandler, eds., *Making Men: Rugby and Masculine Identity*. London: Frank Cass, 91–120.

– 1998. "Of Boys and Men: Masculinity and Gender in Southern African Studies." *Journal of Southern African Studies* 24, no. 4: 605–30.

Morrell, Robert, ed. 2001a. *Changing Men in Southern Africa*. Pietermaritzburg: University of Natal Press; London: Zed Press.

– 2001b. *From Boys to Gentlemen: Settler Masculinity in Colonial Natal, 1880–1920*. Pretoria: University of South Africa Press.

Mott, Luiz. 1988. "Love's Labors Lost: Five Letters from a Seventeenth Century Portuguese Sodomite." *Journal of Homosexuality* 16, no. 1, 2: 91–101.

– 2000. "Inquisition: Portugal." In George E. Haggerty, ed., *Gay Histories and Cultures: An Encyclopedia*. New York and London: Garland, 471–2.

Mungoshi, Charles. 1996. "A Marriage of Convenience." *Horizon* (August).

– 1997. "Of Lovers and Wives." In *Walking Still*. Harare: Baobab.

Murage, Mbogo. 2000. "Kenya." In George E. Haggerty, ed., *Gay Histories and Cultures*. New York and London: Garland, 512–14.

Murray, Colin. 1975, "Sex, Smoking and the Shades." In M.G. Whisson and M. West, eds., *Religion and Social Change in Southern Africa*. Cape Town: David Philip; London: Rex Collings, 58–77.

Murray, Stephen O. 1998. "Sexual Politics in Contemporary Southern Africa." In Murray and Roscoe, eds., *Boy Wives and Female Husbands*, 243–54.

– 2000. *Homosexualities*. Chicago and London: University of Chicago Press.

Murray, Stephen O., and William Roscoe, eds. 1998. *Boy Wives and Female Husbands: Studies in African Homosexualities*. New York: St Martin's Press.

– 1997. *Islamic Homosexualities: Culture, History and Literature*. New York: New York University Press.

Musisi, Nakanyike B. 1991. "Women, 'Elite Polygyny' and Buganda State Formation." *Signs* 16, no. 4: 757–86.

Mutasa, Didymus. 1974. *Rhodesian Black behind Bars*. London and Oxford: Mowbray's.

Mutongi, Kenda. 2000. "Dear Dolly's Advice: Representations of Youth, Courtship, and Sexualities in Africa, 1960–1980." *International Journal of African Historical Studies* 33, no. 1: 1–23.

Nanda, Serena. 1990. *Neither Man nor Woman: The Hijras of India*. Belmont, Calif.: Wadsworth.

Nare, Paulos Matjaka. 1995. "Education and the War." In Bhebe and Ranger, eds., *Society in Zimbabwe's Liberation War*, 130–8.

Ncube, Ivy. 2000. "Former Convict Shylet Tells of Vices and Horrors of Life inside Chikurubi Prison." *Harare Herald*, 7 January.

Ndambuki, Berida, and Claire Robertson. 2000. *We Only Come Here to Struggle: Stories from Berida's Life*. Bloomington: Indiana University Press.

Ndatshe, Vivienne. 1993. "Love on the Mines." In Krouse and Matthews, eds., *The Invisible Ghetto*, 45–51.

Newton-King, Susie. 2002. "For the Love of Adam: Two Sodomy Trials at the Cape of Good Hope." *Kronos* 28: 21–42.

Nfah-Abbenyi, Juliana. 1997. *Gender in African Women's Writing: Identity, Sexuality, and Difference*. Bloomington: Indiana University Press.

Ngubane, Harriet. 1977. *Body and Mind in Zulu Medicine*. London: Academic Press.

Nhongo-Simbanegavi, Josephine. 2000. *For Better or Worse? Women and ZANLA in Zimbabwe's Liberation Struggle*. Harare: Weaver Press.

Niehaus, Isak. 2000. "Towards a Dubious Liberation: Masculinity, Sexuality, and Power in South African Lowveld Schools, 1953–1999." *Journal of Southern African Studies* 26, no. 3: 387–407.

– 2002a. "Renegotiating Masculinity in the South African Lowveld: Narratives of Male-Male Sex in Labour Compounds and in Prisons." *African Studies* 61, no. 1: 77–97.

– 2002b. "Perversion of Power: Witchcraft and the Sexuality of Evil in the South African Lowveld." *Journal of Religion in Africa* 32, no. 3: 269–99.

Njinje, Mpumi, and Paolo Alberton (directors). 2002. *Everything Must Come to Light*. Johannesburg: Out of Africa Films.

Nkoli, Simon. 1994. "Wardrobes: Coming Out As a Black Gay Activist in South Africa." In Gevisser and Cameron, eds., *Defiant Desire*, 249–57.

Nkomo, Joshua. 1984. *The Story of My Life*. London: Methuen.

Ntabeni, Maria Nombulelo. 1996. "War and Society in Colonial Lesotho, 1939–1945." Doctoral dissertation, Queen's University, Kingston, Ont.

Nthunya, Mpho 'M'atsepo. 1996. "When a Woman Loves a Woman." In *Singing Away the Hunger: Stories of a Life in Lesotho.* Pietermaritzburg: University of Natal Press, 69–72.

Nyagumbo, Maurice. 1980. *With the People: An Autobiography from the Zimbabwe Struggle.* London: Allison and Busby.

Olivier, Gerrit. 1994. "From Ada to Zelda: Notes on Gays and Language in South Africa." In Gevisser and Cameron, eds., *Defiant Desire*, 219–24.

Oosterhoff, Jan. 1988. "Sodomy at Sea and at the Cape of Good Hope during the 18th Century." *Journal of Homosexuality* 16, no. 2: 229–35.

Oppong, Joseph R., and Ezekiel Kalipeni. 1996. "A Cross-Cultural Perspective on AIDS in Africa: A Response to Rushing." *African Rural and Urban Studies* 3, no. 2: 91–112.

Owen, Michelle. 2000. "'Not the Same Story': Conducting Interviews with Queer Community Activists." *Resources for Feminist Research* 28, no. 1–2: 49–60.

Ouzgane, Lahoucine. 2002. "Guest Editorial: An Introduction." *Journal of Men's Studies* (special issue on African Masculinities) 10, no. 3: 243–5.

Oyéwùmí, Oyèrónké. 1997. *The Invention of Women: Making an African Sense of Western Gender Discourses.* Minneapolis: University of Minnesota Press.

Palmberg, Mai. 1999. "Emerging Visibility of Gays and Lesbians in Southern Africa: Contrasting Contexts." in B.D. Adam, Jan Willem Duyvendak, and A. Krouwel, eds., *The Global Emergence of Gay and Lesbian Politics: National Imprints of a Worldwide Movement.* Philadelphia: Temple University Press, 266–92.

Pape, John. 1990. "Black and White: The 'Perils of Sex' in Colonial Zimbabwe." *Journal of Southern African Studies* 16, no. 4: 699–720.

Parker, Richard G. 1999. *Beneath the Equator: Cultures of Desire, Male Homosexuality, and Emerging Gay Communities in Brazil.* New York: Routledge.

Perk, David. 1948. "Homosexuality in the Army." *South African Medical Journal* 22, no. 16: 513–4.

Personal Narratives Group, ed. 1989. *Interpreting Women's Lives: Feminist Theory and Personal Narratives.* Bloomington: Indiana University Press.

Phillips, Oliver. 1999. "Sexual Offences in Zimbabwe: Fetishisms of Procreation, Perversion, and Individual Autonomy." Doctoral dissertation, University of Cambridge.

- 1997a. "Zimbabwean Law and the Production of a White Man's Disease." In L. Moran, ed., *Social and Legal Studies* 6, no. 4: 471–92.
- 1997b. "Zimbabwe." In Donald West and Richard Green, eds., *Socio-Legal Control of Homosexuality: A Multi-Nation Comparison*. New York: Plenum, 43–56.
- (2004) "The Invisible Presence of Homosexuality: Implications for HIV/AIDS and Rights in Southern Africa." In E. Kalipeni, S. Craddock, J. Oppong, and J. Ghosh, eds., *HIV/AIDS in Africa: Beyond Epidemiology*. Oxford: Blackwell, 155–66.
- Phimister, Ian. 1988. *An Economic and Social History of Zimbabwe: Capital Accumulation and Class Struggle, 1890–1948*. London: Longman.
- 1997. "From Ian Phimister." *Zimbabwean Review* 3, no. 4: 31.
- Phimister, Ian and Charles van Onselen. 1997. "The Labour Movement in Zimbabwe: 1900–1945." In Brian Raftopoulos and Ian Phimister, eds., *Keep on Knocking: A History of the Labour Movement in Zimbabwe, 1900–97*. Harare: Baobab, 15–16.
- Porter, Mary A. 1995. "Talking at the Margins: Kenyan Discourses on Homosexuality." In William L. Leap, ed., *Beyond the Lavender Lexicon: Authenticity, Imagination and Appropriation in Lesbian and Gay Languages*. Amsterdam: Gordon and Breach, 133–53.
- Posselt, F.W.T. 1935. *Fact and Fiction: A Short Account of the Natives of Southern Rhodesia*. Bulawayo: Rhodesian Printing and Publishing.
- Prieur, Annick. 1998. *Mema's House, Mexico City: On Transvestites, Queens, and Machos*. Chicago: University of Chicago Press.
- Purchas, Samuel. 1625. *Purchas, His Pilgrimes*. Vol. 2. London: William Standby.
- Raftopoulus, Brian. 1995. "Gender, Nationalist Politics, and the Struggle for the City: Harare, 1940–1950s." *Southern African Feminist Review* 1, no. 2: 30–45.
- Ranger, Terence. 1987. "Pugilism and Pathology: African Boxing and the Black Urban Experience in Southern Rhodesia." In William J. Baker and James A. Mangan, eds., *Sport in Africa: Essays in Social History*. New York and London: Africana, 196–216.
- 1993. "Tales of the Wild West: Gold-Diggers and Rustlers in South West Zimbabwe, 1898–1949; an Essay in the Use of Criminal Court Records for Social History." *South African Historical Journal* 28.
- 1994. "Murder, Rape and Witchcraft: Criminal Court Data for Gender Relations in Colonial Matabeleland." Unpublished paper, St Anthony's College, Oxford.

– 1995. *Are We Not Also Men? The Samkange Family and African Politics in Zimbabwe, 1920–64*. Portsmouth, N.H.: Heinemann.

Ray, Sunanda, Nyasha Gumbo, and Michael Mbizvo. 1996. "Local Voices: What Some Harare Men Say about Preparation for Sex." *Reproductive Health Matters* 7 (May): 63–73.

Reddy, Vasu. 2001. "Institutionalizing Sexuality: Theorizing Queer in Post-Apartheid South Africa." In Delroy Constantine-Simms, ed., *The Greatest Taboo: Homosexuality in Black Communities*. Alyson Press, 163–84.

Reddy, Vasu, and Ronald Louw. 2002. "Black and Gay: Perceptions and Interventions around HIV in Durban." *Agenda* 53: 89–95.

Reid, Graeme. 2002. "'The History of the Past Is the Trust of the Future': Preservation and Excavation in the Gay and Lesbian Archives of South Africa." In Carolyn Hamilton, Verne Harris, Jane Taylor, Michele Pickover, Graeme Reid, and Razia Saleh, eds., *Refiguring the Archive*. Cape Town: David Philip, 193–207.

– 1998. "Going Back to God, Just As We Are: Contesting Identities in the Hope and Unity Metropolitan Community Church." *Development Update* 2, no. 2: 57–65.

Reid, Graeme, and Theresa Dirsuweit. 2001. "Understanding Systemic Violence: Homomphobic Attacks in Johannesburg and Its Surrounds." *Urban Forum* 13, no. 3: 99–124.

Reid, Richard. 1999. "Images of an African Ruler: *Kabaka* Mutesa of Buganda, ca. 1857–1884." *History in Africa* 26: 269–98.

Retief, Glen. 1994. "Keeping Sodom out of the Laager." In Gevisser and Cameron, eds., *Defiant Desire*, 99–111.

Richardson, Peter. 1982. *Chinese Mine Labour in the Transvaal*. London: Macmillan.

Ritchie, John F. 1943. *The African As Suckling and As Adult: A Psychological Study*. Livingstone: Rhodes-Livingstone Institute.

Ritter, E.A. 1955. *Shaka Zulu*. London: Longmans.

Ross, Robert. 1979. "Oppression, Sexuality and Slavery at the Cape of Good Hope." *Historical Reflections* 6: 421–3.

Rotberg, Robert I. 1988. *The Founder: Cecil Rhodes and the Pursuit of Power*. New York and Oxford: Oxford University Press.

Runganga, Agnes, and P. Aggleton. 1998. "Migration, the Family and the Transformation of a Sexual Culture." *Sexualities* 1, no. 1: 63–81.

Runganga, Agnes, Marian Pitts, and John McMaster. 1992. "The Use of Herbal and Other Agents to Enhance Sexual Experience." *Social Science and Medicine* 35, no. 8: 1037–42.

Sachs, Wulf. 1937. *Black Hamlet: The Mind of the Black Negro Revealed by Psychoanalysis*. London: Geoffrey Bles.

Sam, Tanya Chan. 1994. "Five Women: Black Lesbian Life on the Reef As Told to Tanya Chan Sam." In Gevisser and Cameron, eds., *Defiant Desire*, 186–97.

Sandoval, Chela. 2002. "Dissident Globalizations, Emancipatory Methods, Social-erotics." In Arnaldo-Cruz and Manalansan, eds., *Queer Globalizations*, 20–32.

Scarnecchia, Timothy. 1994. "The Politics of Gender and Class in the Creation of African Communities, Salisbury, Rhodesia, 1937–1957." Doctoral dissertation, University of Michigan.

– 1996. "Poor Women and Nationalist Politics: Alliances and Fissures in the Formation of a Nationalist Political Movement in Salisbury, Rhodesia, 1950–56." *Journal of African History* 37, no. 2: 283–310.

Schapera, Isaac. 1963. *The Khoisan Peoples of South Africa: Bushmen and Hottentots*. London: Routledge and Kegan Paul.

Schiller, Greta (director). 1998. *The Man Who Drove with Mandela*. London: Jezebel Productions.

Schmidt, Elizabeth. 1992. *Peasants, Traders, and Wives: Shona Women in the History of Zimbabwe, 1870–1939*. Portsmouth, N.H.: Heinemann.

Schmidt, Heike. 1997. "Healing the Wounds of War: Memories of Violence and the Making of History in Zimbabwe's Most Recent Past." *Journal of Southern African Studies* 23, no. 2: 301–10.

Schreiner, Barbara. 1992. *A Snake with Ice Water: Prison Writings by South African Women*. Johannesburg: Congress of South African Writers.

Scott, David. 1892. *A Cyclopaedic Dictionary of the Mang'anja Language*. Edinburgh: Church of Scotland.

Scully, William. 1912. *Daniel Vananda*. Cape Town: Juta.

– 1923. *The Ridge of the White Waters*. Cape Town: Juta.

Sedgwick, Eve Kosofsky. 1990. *Epistemology of the Closet*. Berkeley: University of California Press.

Shamuyarira, Nathan. 1966. *Crisis in Rhodesia*. New York: Transatlantic Arts.

Shear, Keith. 2003. "'Taken As Boys': The Politics of Black Police Employment and Experience in Early Twentieth-Century South Africa." In Lisa A. Lindsay and Stephan F. Miescher, eds., *Men and Masculinities in Modern Africa*. Portsmouth, N.H.: Heinemann, 109–27.

Shell, Robert C.-H. 1994. "The Tower of Babel: The Slave Trade and Creolization at the Cape, 1652–1834." In E. Eldredge and F. Morton, eds., *Slavery in South Africa*. Boulder, Colo., Westview Press, 11–39.

Shepherd, Robert. 1996. "Sexual Rumours in English Politics: The Cases of Elizabeth I and James I." In J. Murray and K. Eisenbichler, eds., *Desire and Discipline: Sex and Sexuality in the Premodern West*. Toronto: University of Toronto Press, 101–22.

Shire, Chenjerai. 1994. "Men Don't Go to the Moon': Language, Space and Masculinities in Zimbabwe." In Andrea Cornwall and Nancy Lindisfarne, eds., *Dislocating Masculinities: Comparative Ethnographies*. London: Routledge, 147–58.

Shostak, Marjorie. 1981. *Nisa: The Life and Words of a !Kung Woman*. Cambridge, Mass.: Harvard University Press.

Sibanda, Melusi. 1998. "Attitudes towards Homosexuality among Christian Zimbabweans." Honours dissertation, University of Zimbabwe.

Sibanyoni, Mxolisi R. 1995. "'The Fading Songs of the Chimurenga': Chenjerai Hove and the Subversion of Nationalist Politics in Zimbabwean Literature." *African Studies* 54, no. 2: 52–72.

Sibuyi, Mpande wa. 1993. "*Tinconcana etimayinini*: The Wives of the Mine." In Krouse and Matthews, ed., *The Invisible Ghetto*, 52–64.

Sinclair, Ingrid (director). 1996. *Flame*. Harare: Bright Productions.

Sithole, Ndabaningi. 1968. *African Nationalism*. London: Oxford University Press.

– 1970. *Obed Mutezo: The Mudzimu Christian Nationalist*. London: Oxford University Press.

Southey, Nicholas. 1997a. "Uncovering Homosexuality in Colonial South Africa: The Case of Bishop Twells." *South African Historical Journal* 36 (May): 48–67.

– 1997b. "Confessions of a Gay Ordinand: A Personal History." In Paul Germond and Steve de Gruchy, eds., *Aliens in the Household of God*, 39–56.

Spurlin, William J. 2001. "Broadening Postcolonial Studies/Decolonizing Queer Studies: Emerging 'Queer' Identities and Cultures in Southern Africa." In John C. Hawley, ed., *Post-Colonial Queer: Theoretical Intersections*. Albany: SUNY Press, 185–205.

Staunton, Irene, ed. *Mothers of the Revolution*. Harare: Baobab.

Stockinger, J. 1978. "Homotextuality: A Proposal." In Louie Crew, ed., *The Gay Academic*. Palm Springs, Calif.: ETC Publications, 135–51.

Stoler, Ann Laura. 1995. *Race and the Education of Desire*. Durham, N.C.: Duke University Press.

– 2002. *Carnal Knowledge and Imperial Power: Race and the Intimate in Colonial Rule*. Berkeley: University of California Press.

Strongman, Roberto. 2002. "Syncretic Religion and Dissident Sexualities." In Arnaldo-Cruz and Manalansan, eds., *Queer Globalizations*, 176–92.

Stuart, Deanne. 1997. "Homosexual Christian Communities in Gauteng." In Germond and De Gruchy, eds., *Aliens in the Household of God*, 78–100.

Stychin, Carl Franklin. 1996. "Constituting Sexuality: The Struggle for Sexual Orientation in the South African Bill of Rights." *Journal of Law and Society* 23, no. 4: 455–83.

– 1998. *A Nation by Rights: National Cultures, Sexual Identity Politics, and the Discourse of Rights*. Philadelphia: Temple University Press.

Summers, Carol. 1994. *From Civilization to Segregation: Social Ideas and Social Control in Southern Rhodesia, 1890–1934*. Athens, Ohio: Ohio University Press.

– 1999. "Mission Boys, Civilized Men, and Marriage: Educated African Men in the Missions of Southern Rhodesia, 1920–1945." *Journal of Religious History* 23, no. 1: 75–91.

Swart, Sandra. 1998. "'A Boer and His Gun and His Wife Are Three Things Always Together': Republican Masculinity and the 1914 Rebellion." *Journal of Southern African Studies* 24, no. 4 (December): 737–52.

Sweet, James. 1996. "Male Homosexuality and Spiritism in the African Diaspora: The Legacies of a Link." *Journal of the History of Sexuality* 7, no. 2: 184–202.

Sweetman, David. 1993. *Mary Renault: A Biography*. London: Chatto and Windus.

Symington, P.B. 1972. "Sexual Behaviour of Rhodesian Africans." *Journal of Biosocial Science* 4: 263–75.

Terry, Jennifer. 1999. *An American Obsession: Science, Medicine, and Homosexuality in Modern Society*. Chicago: University of Chicago Press.

"Thanks to the Efforts of a Group of Norwegian Researchers ..." n.d. Behind the Mask, www.mask.org.

Theal, G.M. 1895–1903. *Records of South-Eastern Africa*. London: Clowes.

Thornton, John. 1991. "Legitimacy and Political Power: Queen Njinga, 1624–1663." *Journal of African History* 32: 25-40.

Tilley, Brian (director). 2001. *It's My Life*. Cape Town: Steps for the Future/ Dominant 7/Big World Cinema.

Treatment Action Campaign. 19 April 2001. "Victory for Activists, People with HIV/AIDS and Poor People Everywhere! Pharmaceutical Companies Beaten!" www.tac.org.za/.

Trexler, Richard. 1995. *Sex and Conquest: Gendered Violence, Political Order, and the European Conquest of the Americas*. Cambridge: Polity Press.

Tsourillis, Evan. 2001. "Gay Life in Harare in the Eighties: A Prelude to the Formation of GALZ." Unpublished paper, GALZ archives, Harare.

Tutu, Desmond. 1996. Foreword, In M.B. Alexander and James Preston, eds., *We Were Baptized Too: Claiming God's Grace for Lesbians and Gays*. Louisville, Ky. and Westminster: John Knox Press.

Union of South Africa. 1913. *Annual Report for the Calendar Year 1912*. Department of Justice.

– 1932. *Report of the Native Economic Commission*. Pretoria.

Vambe, Lawrence. 1949. "Shameful Practices at Industrial Sites and Power Station Compound." *African Weekly* (May 18).

– 1972. *An Ill-Fated People*. Pittsburg: University of Pittsburg Press.

– 1976. *From Rhodesia to Zimbabwe*. Pittsburg: University of Pittsburg Press.

Van der Meer, Theo. 1997. "Sodom's Seed in the Netherlands: The Emergence of Homosexuality in the Early Modern Period." *Journal of Homosexuality* 34, no. 1: 1–16.

Van Onselen, Charles. 1976. *Chibaro: African Mine Labour in Southern Rhodesia, 1900–33*. London: Pluto Press.

– 1982. *Studies in the Social and Economic History of the Witswatersrand, 1886–1914*. Burnt Hill, U.K.: Longman.

– 1984. *The Small Matter of a Horse: The Life of 'Nongoloza' Mathebula, 1867–1948*. Johannesburg: Ravan.

Van Zyl, Mikki, et al. 1999. *The aVersion Project: Human Rights Abuses of Gays and Lesbians in the SADF by Health Workers during the Apartheid Era*. GALASA.

Veit-Wild, Flora. 1993. *Teachers, Preachers, Non-Believers: A Social History of Zimbabwean Literature*. Harare: Baobab Books.

Vignal, Daniel. 1983. "L'homophilie dans le roman négro-africain d'expression anglaise et française." *Peuples Noirs, Peuples Africains* 33: 63–81.

Wallis, J.P.R. 1945. *The Matabele Journals of Robert Moffat*. London: Chatto and Windus.

Webb, C. de B. and J.B. Wright, eds. and trans. 1982, 1986, 2001. *The James Stuart Archives*. Vols. 3, 4 and 5. Pietermaritzburg: University of Natal Press.

Weinrich, A.K.H. 1976. *Mucheke: Race, Status, and Politics in a Rhodesian Community*. Paris: UNESCO.

Weinstock, Carolyn B. 1996. "An Exploration of Meanings Ascribed to Homophobic Statements in the Printed Media by Gays and Lesbians in Harare." Unpublished paper, GALZ Centre, Harare.

Wells, Robin E. 1994. *An Introduction to the Music of the Basotho*. Morija: Morija Museum and Archives.

West, Michael. 2002. *The Rise of an African Middle-Class*. Bloomington: Indiana University Press.

– 1997. "Liquor and Libido: 'Joint Drinking' and the Politics of Sexual Control in Colonial Zimbabwe." *Journal of Social History* (spring): 645–67.

– 1990. "African Middle-Class Formation in Colonial Zimbabwe, 1890–1965." Doctoral dissertation, Harvard University.

"Whose Culture Is It?" 1996. *WomanPlus* 1, no. 2 (May-August): 17.

Wolf, Diane L., ed. 1996. *Feminist Dilemmas in Fieldwork*. Boulder, Colo.: Westview.

Wrathall, John D. 1992. "Provenance As Text: Reading the Silences around Sexuality in Manuscript Collections." *Journal of American History*. 79, no. 1 (June).

Xaba, Thokozani. 2001. "Masculinity and 'Post-Struggle Masculinity' 1990–1997." In Morrell, ed., *Changing Men in Southern Africa*, 105–24.

Zeleza, Paul Tiyambe. 1997. *Manufacturing African Studies and Crises*. Dakar: CODESRIA.

Zimbabwe Women's Action Group, with Rudo Gaidzanwa. 1987. "Operation Clean-up." In Miranda Davies, comp. *Third World, Second Sex*. London: Zed Books, 225–8.

Zimbabwe Women's Resource Centre and Network. 1997. *WomanPlus: Women and Rape* 2, no. 2 (December).

Zinanga, Evelyn. 1996. "Sexuality and the Heterosexual Form: The Case of Zimbabwe." *Southern African Feminist Review* 2, no. 1: 3–6.

Index

abortion, 31, 46, 158, 233
abstinence, 33, 46, 47
Achmat, Zackie, 10, 20, 66, 84, 218
Ackerman, Judge L., 6
adultery, 29, 33, 36, 45, 46, 48, 56, 187, 203, 248, 254–5n12
African Christian Democratic Party, 213
African National Congress. *See* ANC
African nationalism, 4–5, 155, 162–75, 180–3, 194, 208–9, 212, 226–8
Afrika, Tatamkulu, 167
Afrikaners. *See* Boers
Afrocentrism, 173, 270n28
After Nines!, 164, 168
AIDS. *See* HIV/AIDS
AIDS Law Project, 218
AIDS Township Project, 218
Airforce (gang), 97. *See also* gangs
All-Africa Rights Initiative, 219
Alma letters, 131–2
amachicken. See mummy-baby relationship
Amani Trust, 182
American aboriginals: viewed by Spanish, 53
American Psychiatric Association, 139–40, 150

anal sex, 65, 73–5, 97–8, 102, 118, 120, 124, 128. *See also* sodomy laws
ANC, 14, 167, 208, 212–4. *See also* Mbeki, Thabo; Mandela, Nelson; Mandela, Winnie
androcentrism, 21, 230
Anglican church, 134, 142–3, 199
Angola, 26, 41–2
Apon, Daniel, 89–90
Arabs, 8, 43–4, 53, 69, 137
Asians, 53, 105–6, 231. *See* Arabs, Chinese
aversion therapy, 147
Azande, 257n39

Baker, Albert, 64, 71, 78, 127
Banana, Canaan, 4, 172–3, 177, 180, 216
Bande, 76, 77
Bande, Rodgers, 236–7
Barkly, Sir Henry, 55
Barnes, Andrew, 219
BaSili. *See* Bushmen
Battersby, James, 112
Bederman, Gail, 137
Behind the Mask, 216, 238
Beka, Gamat, 90